PUBLISHER — DAMIAN A. WASSEL

EDITOR-IN-CHIEF — ADRIAN F. WASSEL

ART DIRECTOR — NATHAN C. GOODEN

BRANDING & DESIGN — TIM DANIEL

MANAGING EDITOR — REBECCA TAYLOR

MARKETING DIRECTOR — DAVID DISSANAYAKE

PRODUCTION MANAGER — IAN BALDESSARI

PRINCIPAL — DAMIAN A. WASSEL SR.

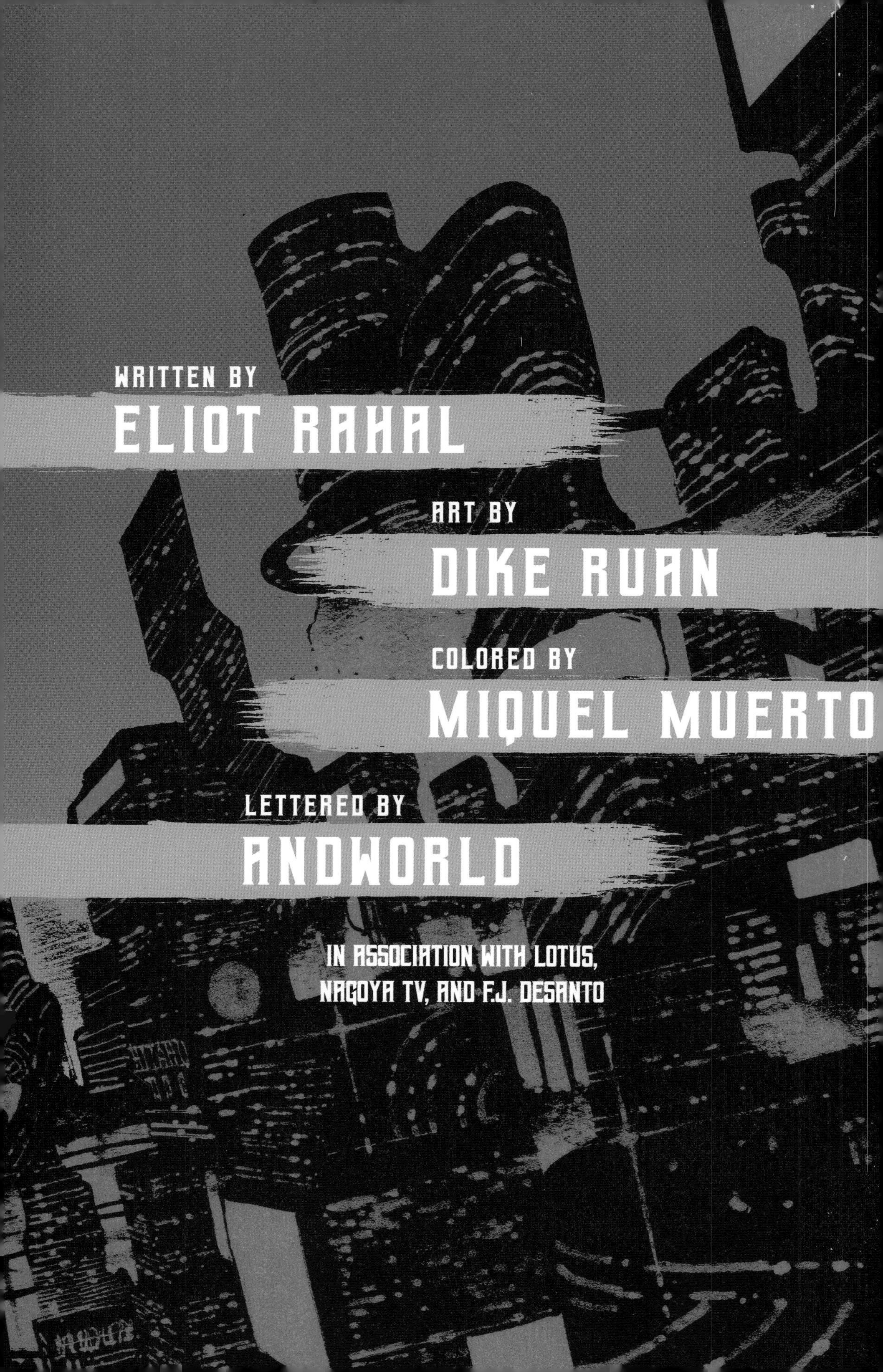

WRITTEN BY
ELIOT RAHAL

ART BY
DIKE RUAN

COLORED BY
MIQUEL MUERTO

LETTERED BY
ANDWORLD

IN ASSOCIATION WITH LOTUS,
NAGOYA TV, AND F.J. DESANTO

VAULT COMICS
PRESENTS

A NINJA VAMPIRE TALE

BLEED

THEM DRY

CREATED BY HIROSHI KOIZUMI

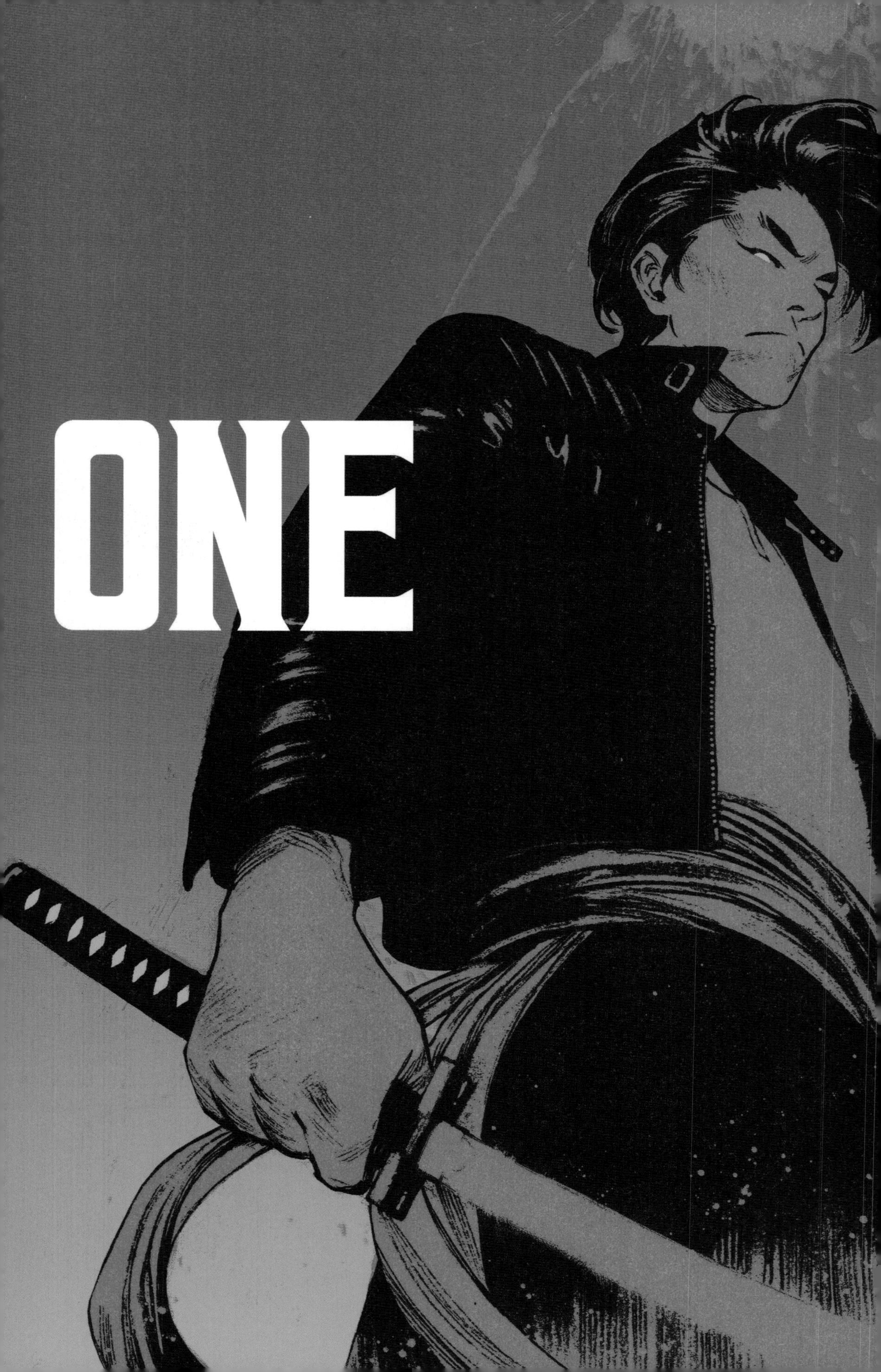
ONE

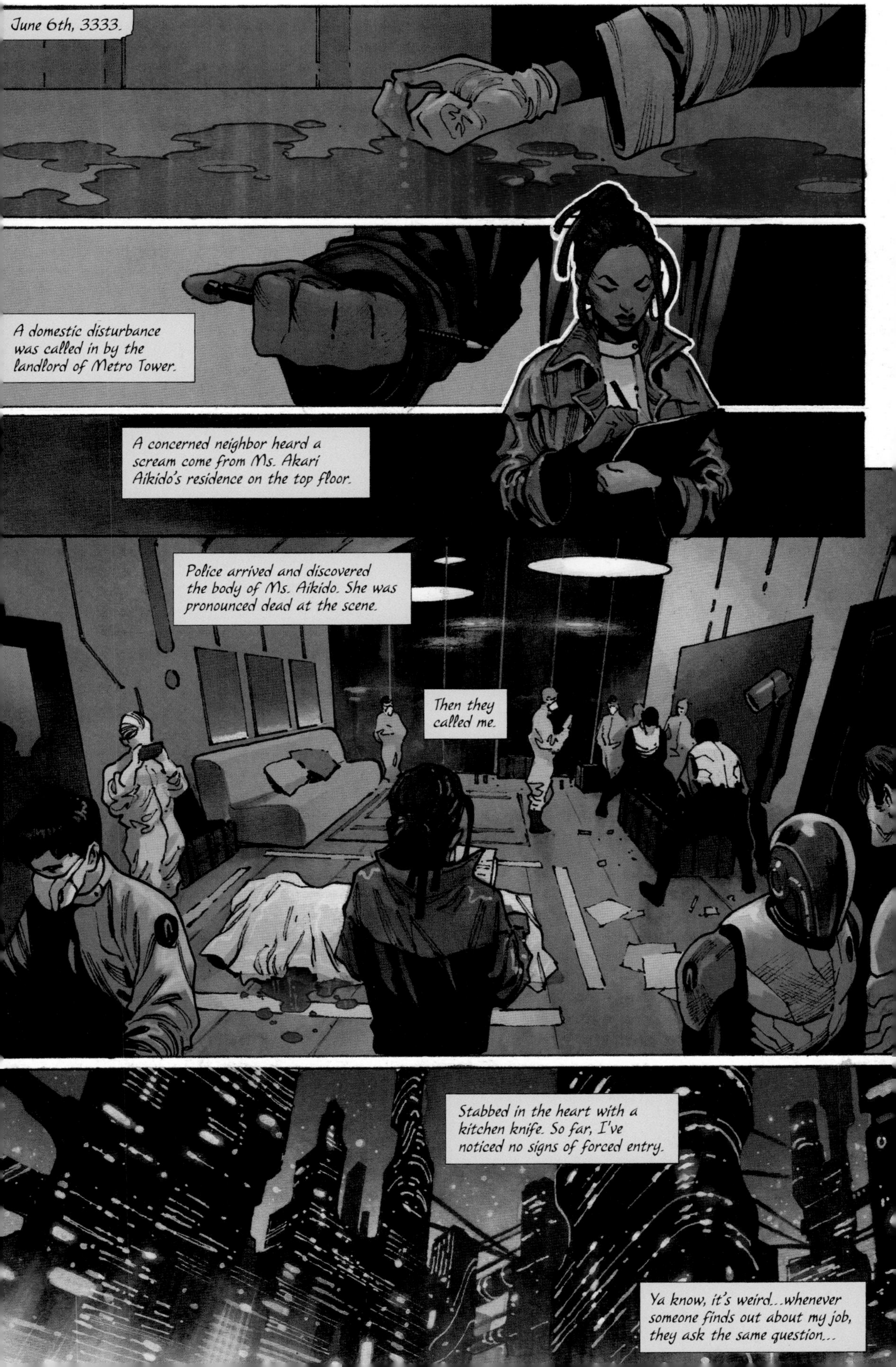
June 6th, 3333.
A domestic disturbance was called in by the landlord of Metro Tower.
A concerned neighbor heard a scream come from Ms. Akari Aikido's residence on the top floor.
Police arrived and discovered the body of Ms. Aikido. She was pronounced dead at the scene.
Then they called me.
Stabbed in the heart with a kitchen knife. So far, I've noticed no signs of forced entry.
Ya know, it's weird...whenever someone finds out about my job, they ask the same question...

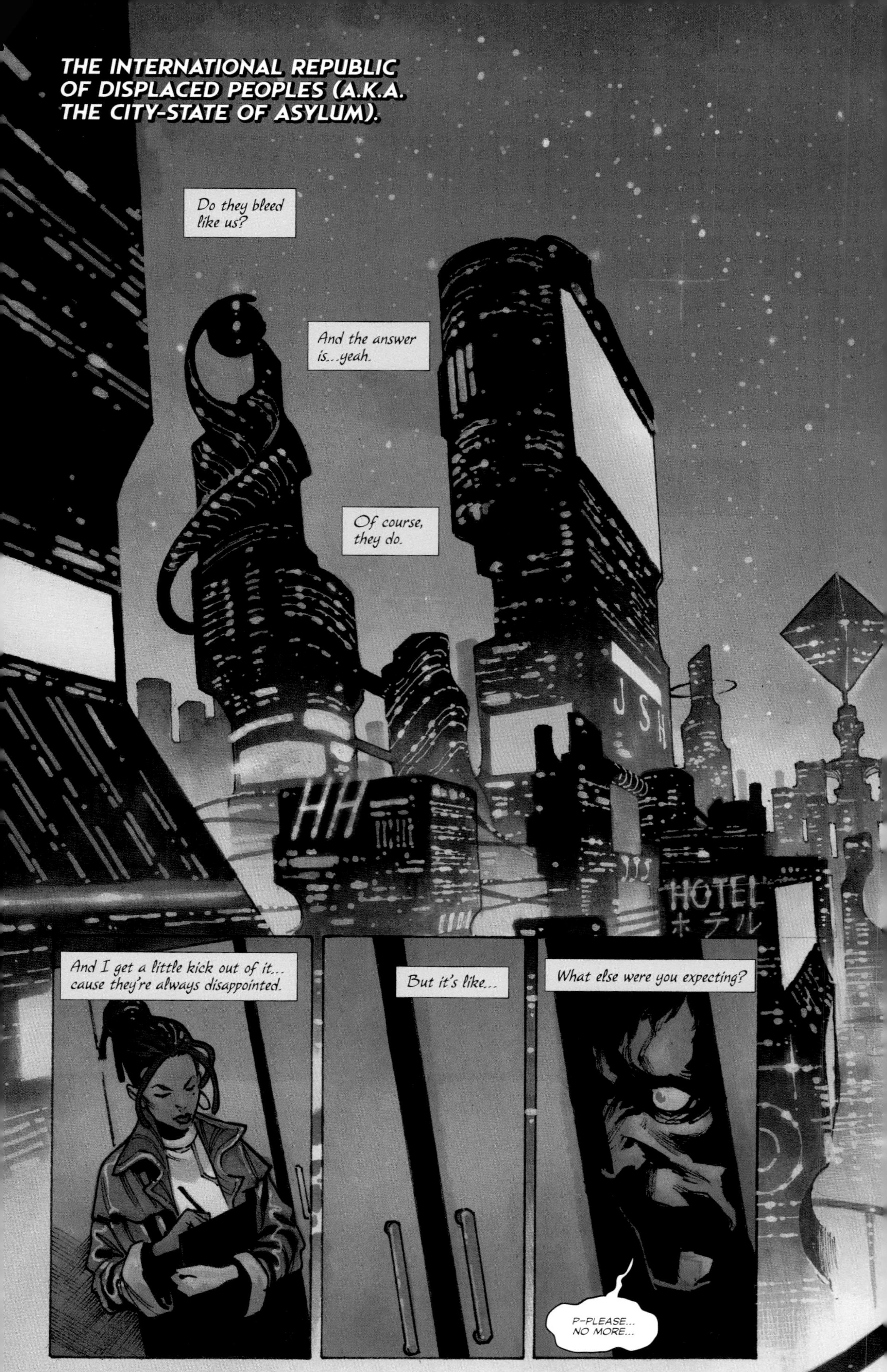

THE INTERNATIONAL REPUBLIC OF DISPLACED PEOPLES (A.K.A. THE CITY-STATE OF ASYLUM).
Do they bleed like us?
And the answer is...yeah.
Of course, they do.
JSH
HH
HOTEL
ホテル
And I get a little kick out of it... cause they're always disappointed.
But it's like...
What else were you expecting?
P-PLEASE... NO MORE...

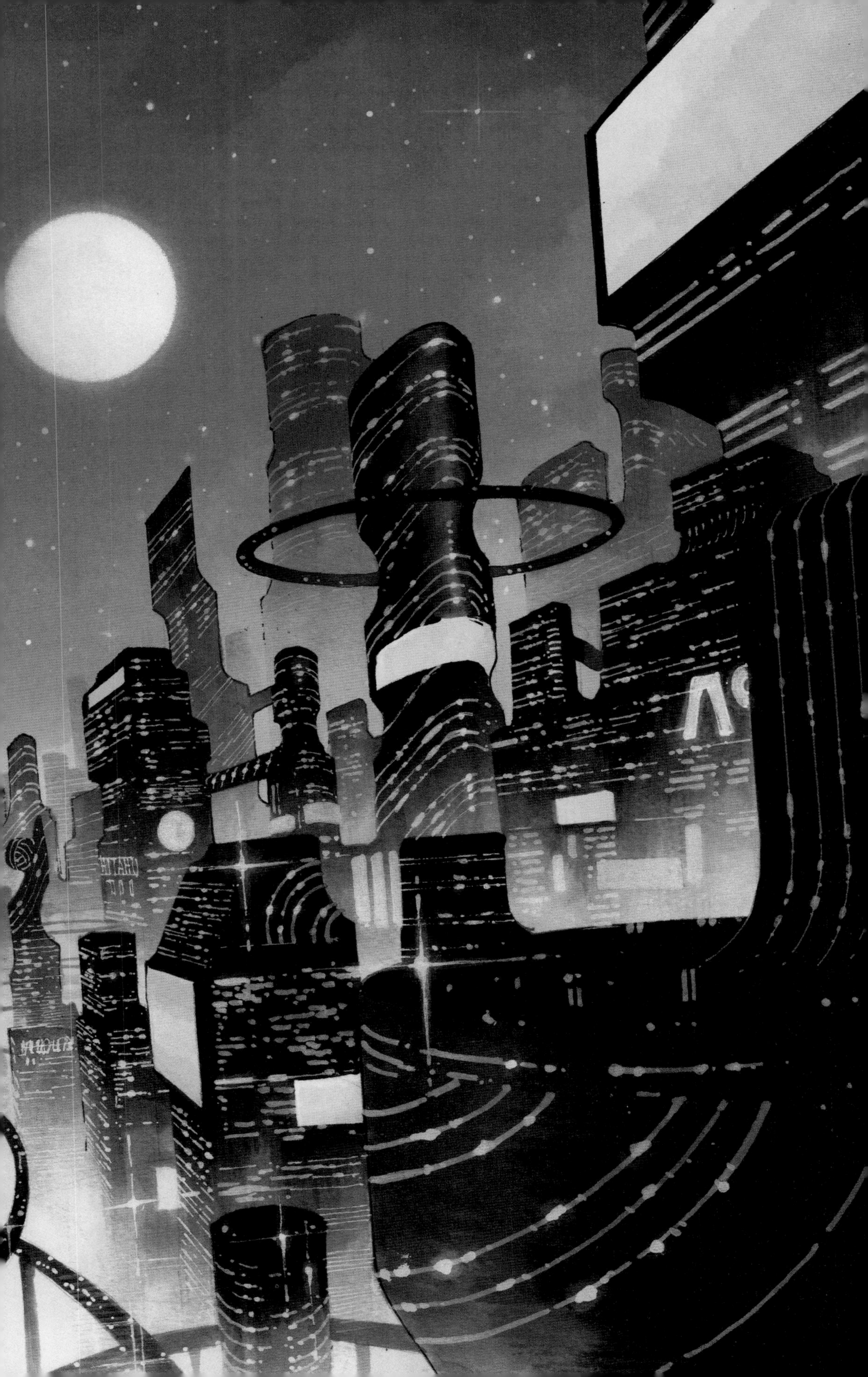

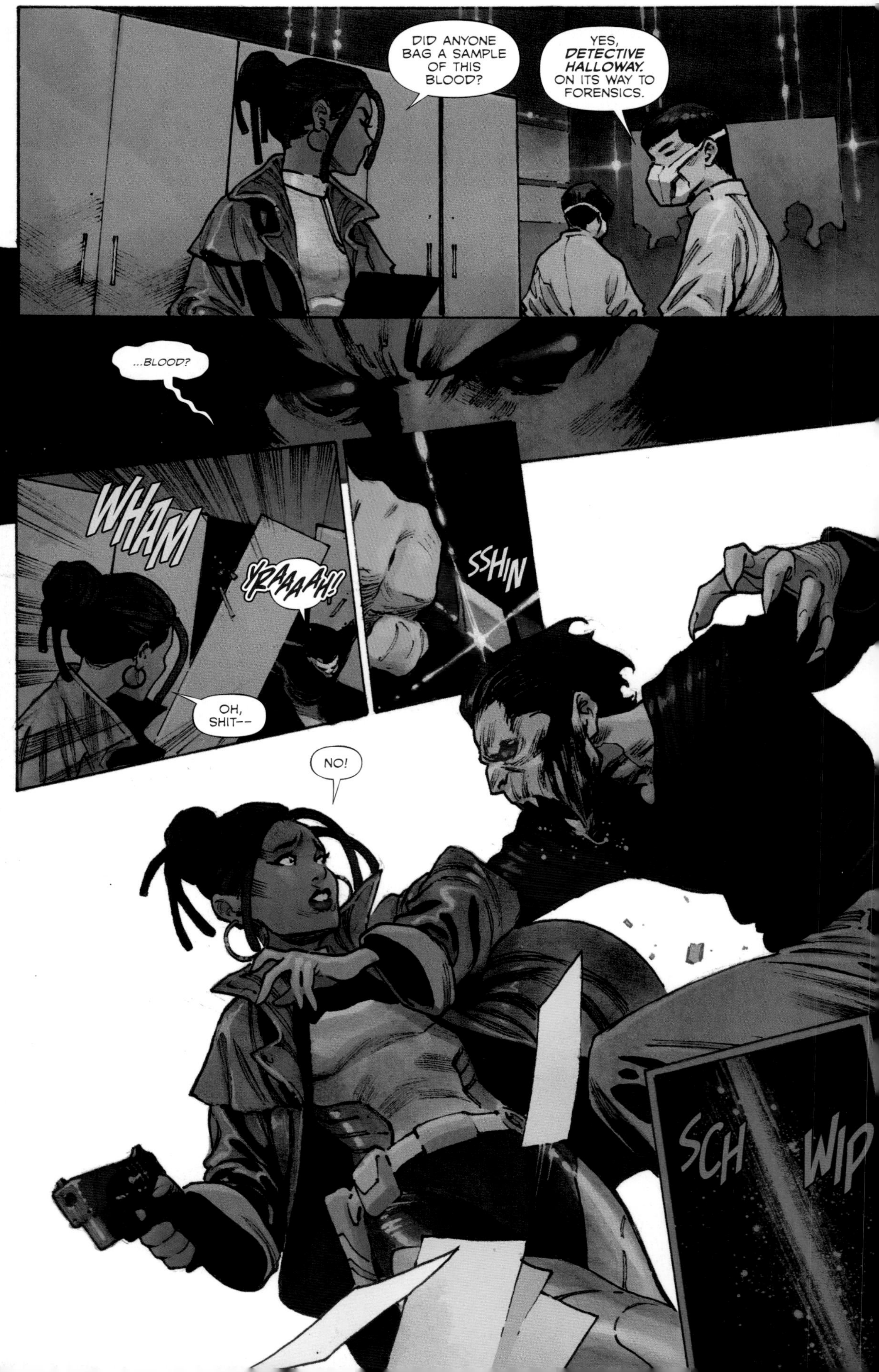
DID ANYONE BAG A SAMPLE OF THIS BLOOD?
YES, DETECTIVE HALLOWAY. ON ITS WAY TO FORENSICS.
...BLOOD?
WHAM
YRAAAAH!
OH, SHIT--
SSHIN
NO!
SCH
WIP

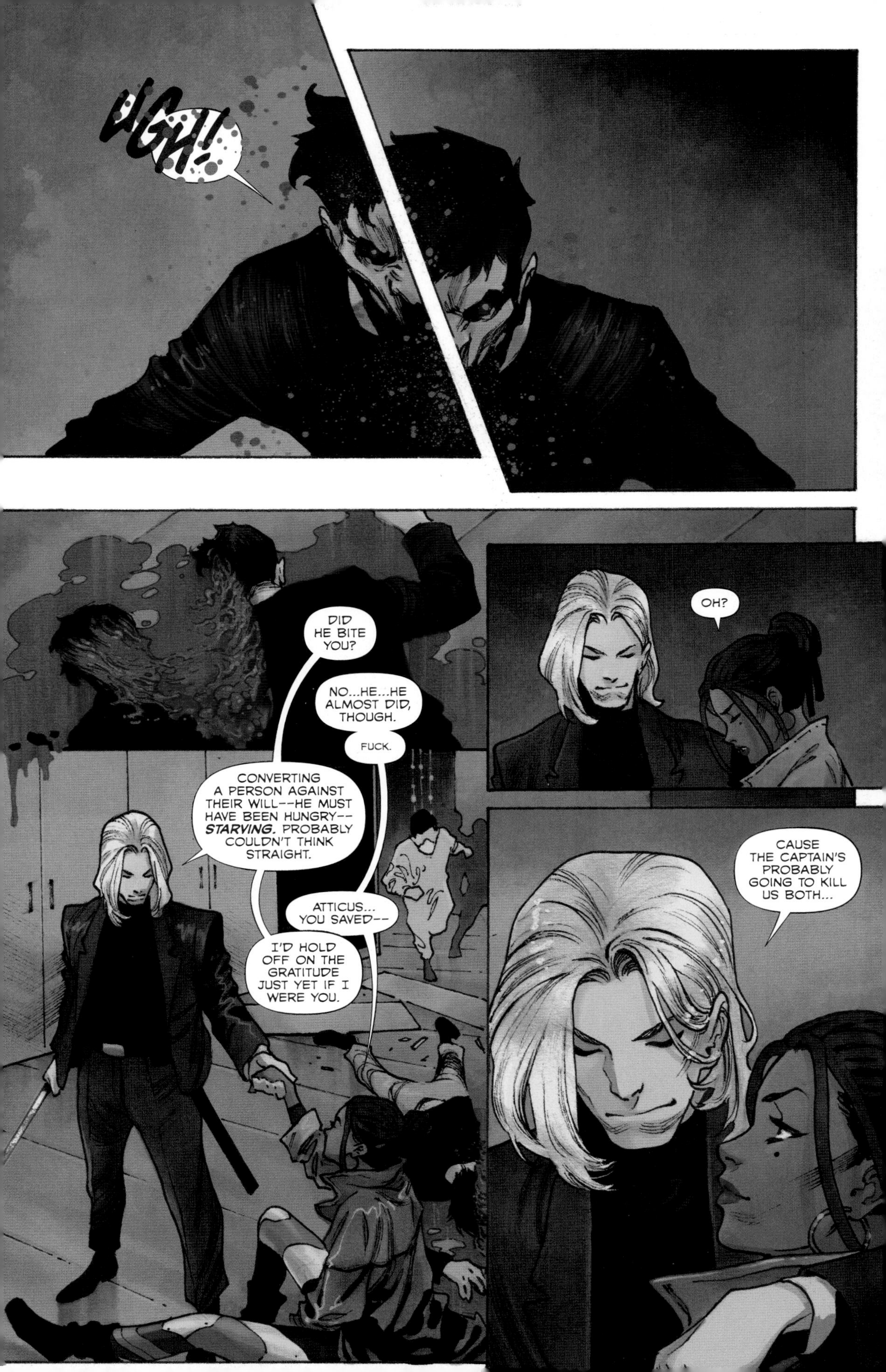
UGH!
DID HE BITE YOU?
NO...HE...HE ALMOST DID, THOUGH.
FUCK.
CONVERTING A PERSON AGAINST THEIR WILL--HE MUST HAVE BEEN HUNGRY--STARVING. PROBABLY COULDN'T THINK STRAIGHT.
ATTICUS... YOU SAVED--
I'D HOLD OFF ON THE GRATITUDE JUST YET IF I WERE YOU.
OH?
CAUSE THE CAPTAIN'S PROBABLY GOING TO KILL US BOTH...

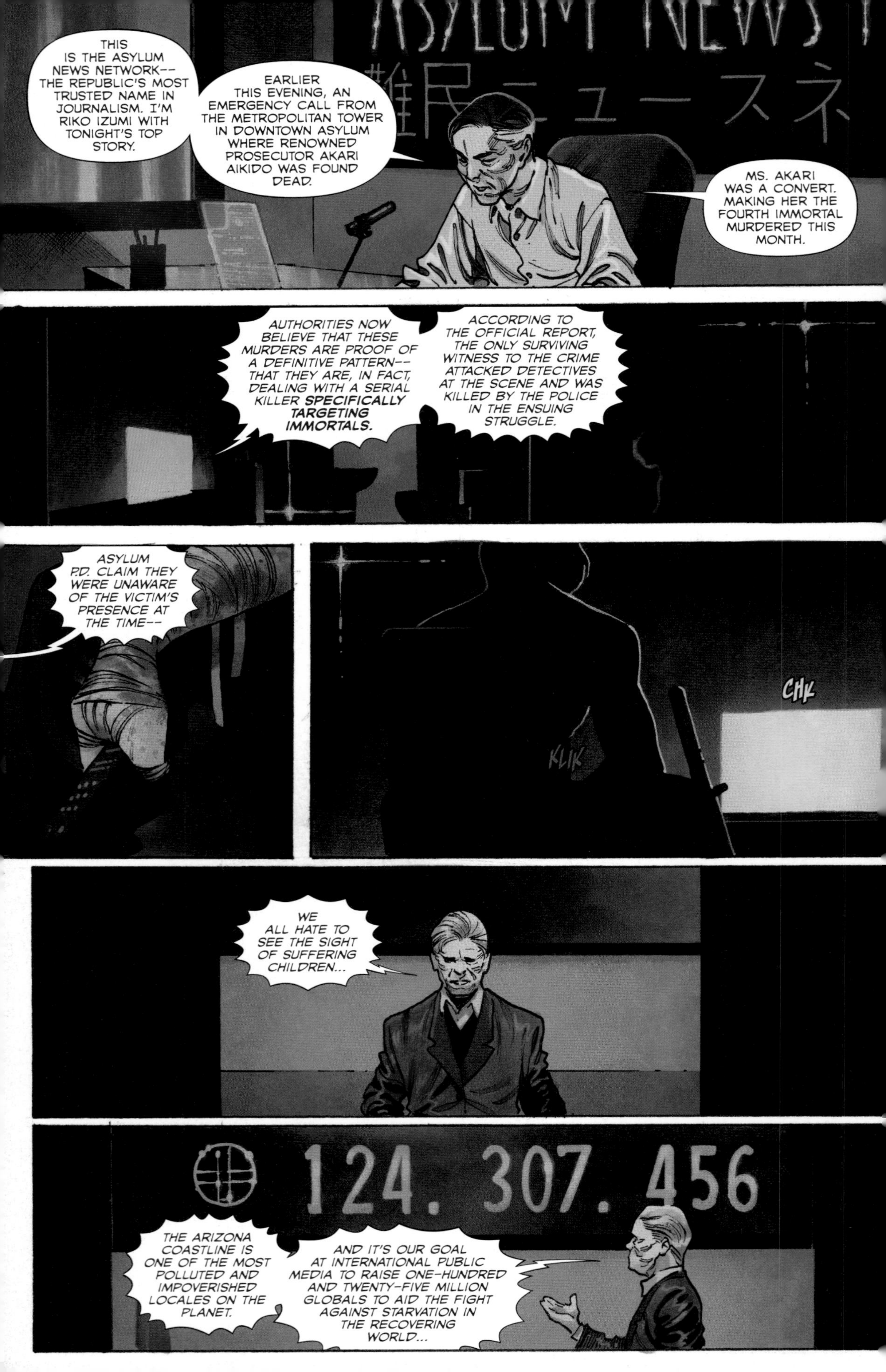
ASYLUM NEWS
THIS IS THE ASYLUM NEWS NETWORK-- THE REPUBLIC'S MOST TRUSTED NAME IN JOURNALISM. I'M RIKO IZUMI WITH TONIGHT'S TOP STORY.
EARLIER THIS EVENING, AN EMERGENCY CALL FROM THE METROPOLITAN TOWER IN DOWNTOWN ASYLUM WHERE RENOWNED PROSECUTOR AKARI AIKIDO WAS FOUND DEAD.
MS. AKARI WAS A CONVERT. MAKING HER THE FOURTH IMMORTAL MURDERED THIS MONTH.
AUTHORITIES NOW BELIEVE THAT THESE MURDERS ARE PROOF OF A DEFINITIVE PATTERN-- THAT THEY ARE, IN FACT, DEALING WITH A SERIAL KILLER **SPECIFICALLY TARGETING IMMORTALS.**
ACCORDING TO THE OFFICIAL REPORT, THE ONLY SURVIVING **WITNESS** TO THE CRIME ATTACKED DETECTIVES AT THE SCENE AND WAS KILLED BY THE POLICE IN THE ENSUING STRUGGLE.
ASYLUM P.D. CLAIM THEY WERE UNAWARE OF THE VICTIM'S PRESENCE AT THE TIME--
CHK
KLIK
WE ALL HATE TO SEE THE SIGHT OF SUFFERING CHILDREN...
124. 307. 456
THE ARIZONA COASTLINE IS ONE OF THE MOST POLLUTED AND IMPOVERISHED LOCALES ON THE PLANET.
AND IT'S OUR GOAL AT INTERNATIONAL PUBLIC MEDIA TO RAISE ONE-HUNDRED AND TWENTY-FIVE MILLION GLOBALS TO AID THE FIGHT AGAINST STARVATION IN THE RECOVERING WORLD...

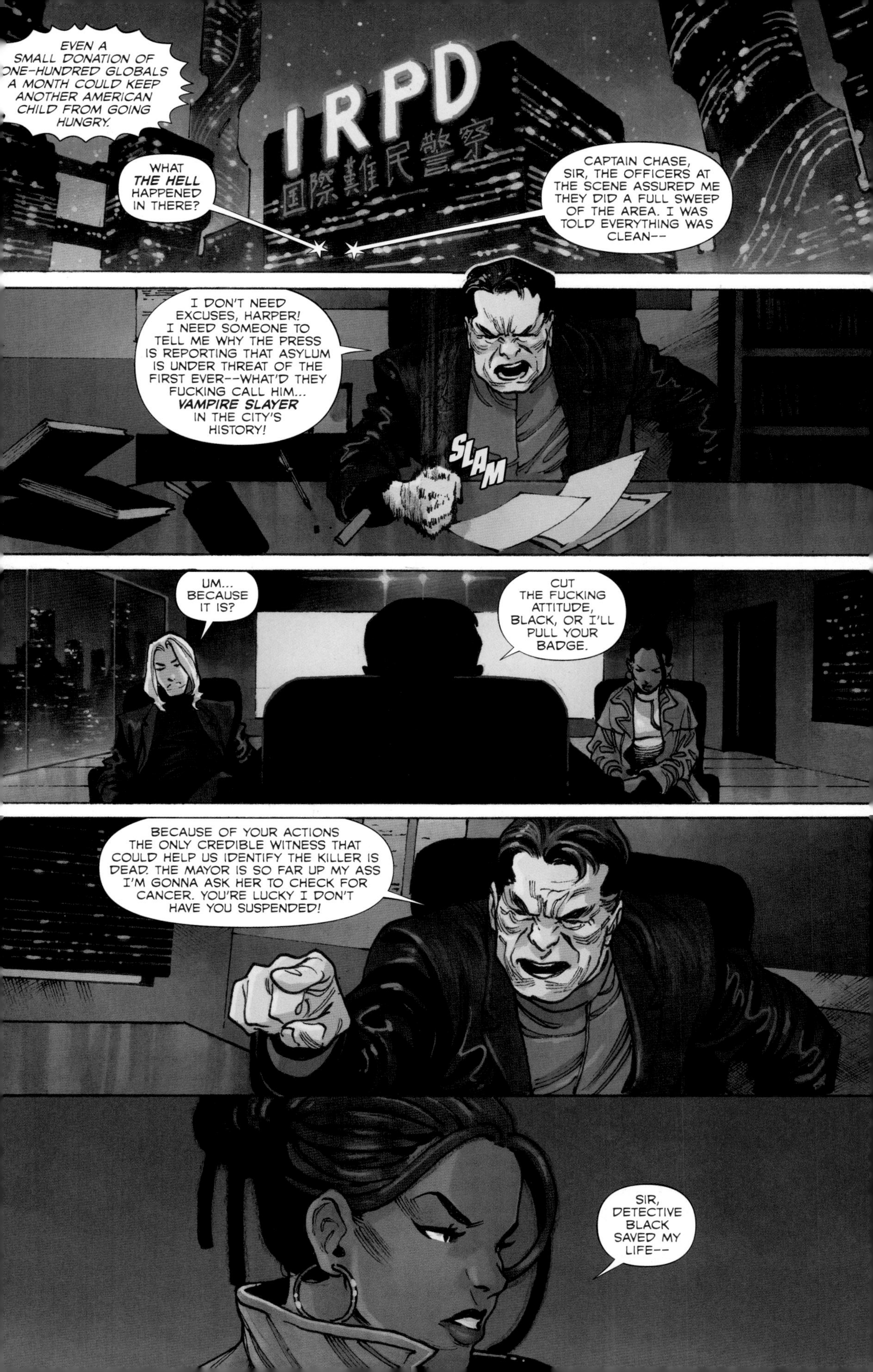

EVEN A SMALL DONATION OF ONE-HUNDRED GLOBALS A MONTH COULD KEEP ANOTHER AMERICAN CHILD FROM GOING HUNGRY.
IRPD
国際難民警察
WHAT *THE HELL* HAPPENED IN THERE?
CAPTAIN CHASE, SIR, THE OFFICERS AT THE SCENE ASSURED ME THEY DID A FULL SWEEP OF THE AREA. I WAS TOLD EVERYTHING WAS CLEAN--
I DON'T NEED EXCUSES, HARPER! I NEED SOMEONE TO TELL ME WHY THE PRESS IS REPORTING THAT ASYLUM IS UNDER THREAT OF THE FIRST EVER--WHAT'D THEY FUCKING CALL HIM... *VAMPIRE SLAYER* IN THE CITY'S HISTORY!
SLAM
UM... BECAUSE IT IS?
CUT THE FUCKING ATTITUDE, BLACK, OR I'LL PULL YOUR BADGE.
BECAUSE OF YOUR ACTIONS THE ONLY CREDIBLE WITNESS THAT COULD HELP US IDENTIFY THE KILLER IS DEAD. THE MAYOR IS SO FAR UP MY ASS I'M GONNA ASK HER TO CHECK FOR CANCER. YOU'RE LUCKY I DON'T HAVE YOU SUSPENDED!
SIR, DETECTIVE BLACK SAVED MY LIFE--

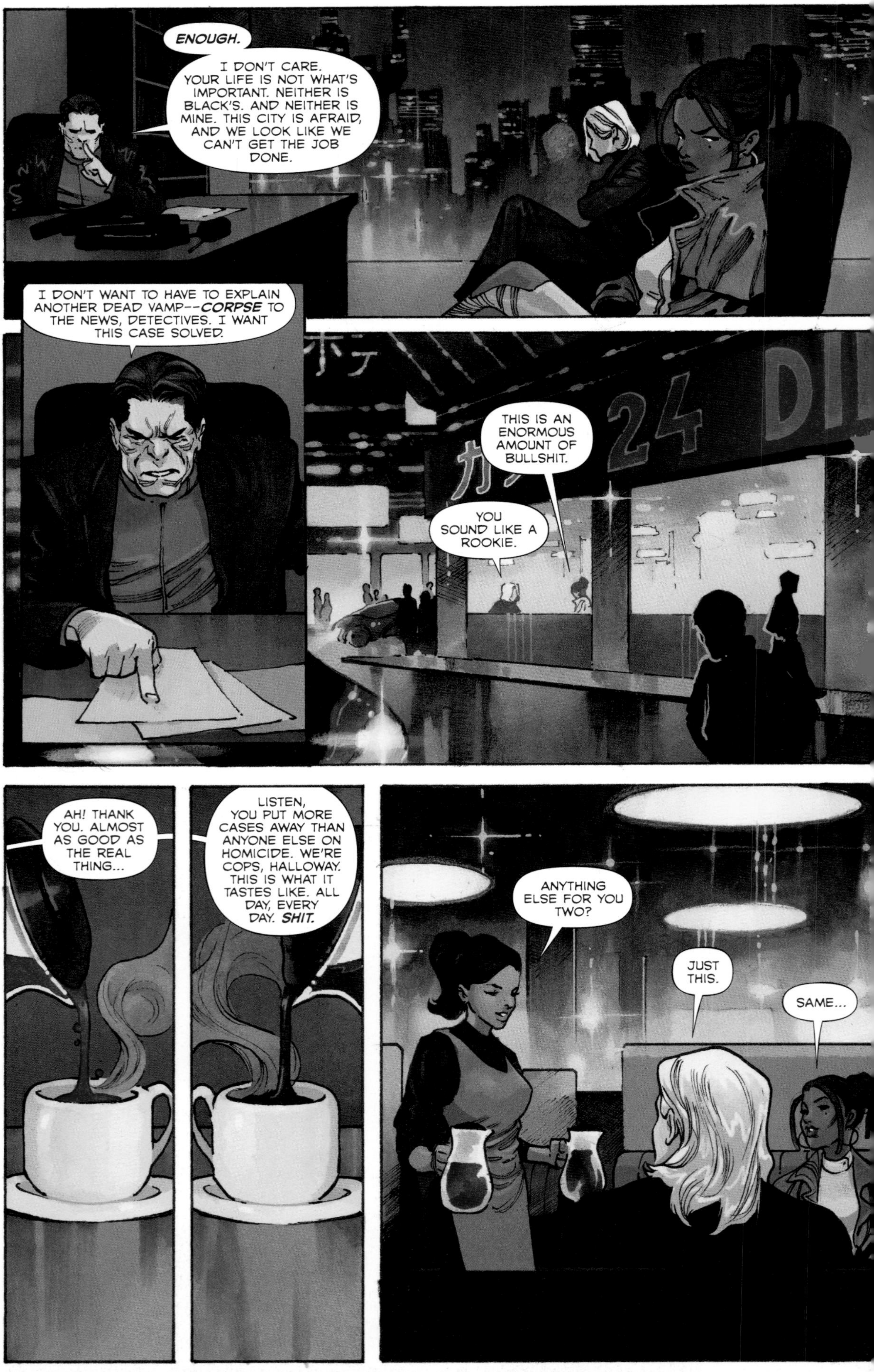
ENOUGH.
I DON'T CARE. YOUR LIFE IS NOT WHAT'S IMPORTANT. NEITHER IS BLACK'S. AND NEITHER IS MINE. THIS CITY IS AFRAID, AND WE LOOK LIKE WE CAN'T GET THE JOB DONE.
I DON'T WANT TO HAVE TO EXPLAIN ANOTHER DEAD VAMP--CORPSE TO THE NEWS, DETECTIVES. I WANT THIS CASE SOLVED.
24 DI
THIS IS AN ENORMOUS AMOUNT OF BULLSHIT.
YOU SOUND LIKE A ROOKIE.
AH! THANK YOU. ALMOST AS GOOD AS THE REAL THING...
LISTEN, YOU PUT MORE CASES AWAY THAN ANYONE ELSE ON HOMICIDE. WE'RE COPS, HALLOWAY. THIS IS WHAT IT TASTES LIKE. ALL DAY, EVERY DAY. SHIT.
ANYTHING ELSE FOR YOU TWO?
JUST THIS.
SAME...

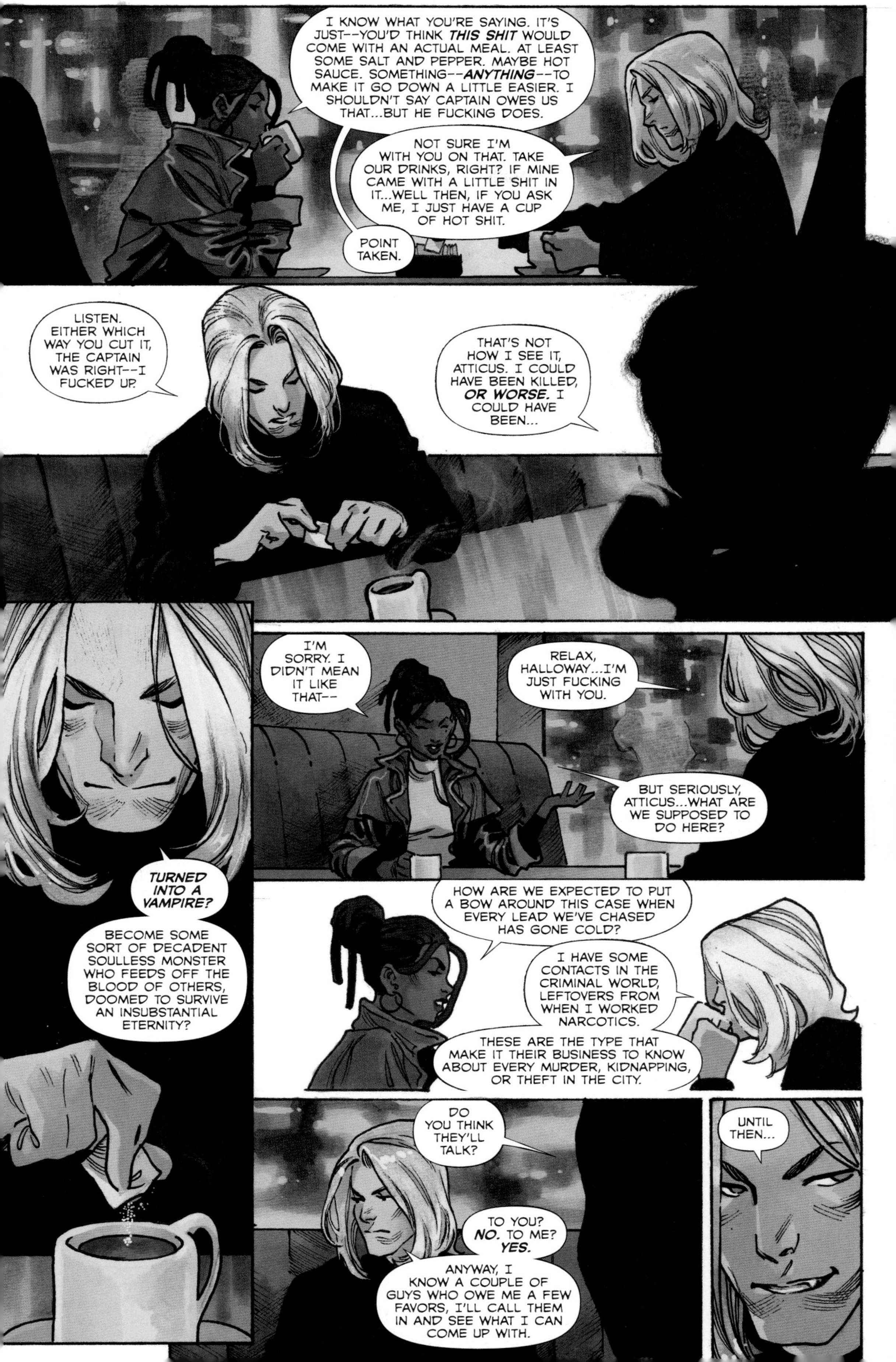
I KNOW WHAT YOU'RE SAYING. IT'S JUST--YOU'D THINK **THIS SHIT** WOULD COME WITH AN ACTUAL MEAL. AT LEAST SOME SALT AND PEPPER. MAYBE HOT SAUCE. SOMETHING--**ANYTHING**--TO MAKE IT GO DOWN A LITTLE EASIER. I SHOULDN'T SAY CAPTAIN OWES US THAT...BUT HE FUCKING DOES.
NOT SURE I'M WITH YOU ON THAT. TAKE OUR DRINKS, RIGHT? IF MINE CAME WITH A LITTLE SHIT IN IT...WELL THEN, IF YOU ASK ME, I JUST HAVE A CUP OF HOT SHIT.
POINT TAKEN.
LISTEN. EITHER WHICH WAY YOU CUT IT, THE CAPTAIN WAS RIGHT--I FUCKED UP.
THAT'S NOT HOW I SEE IT, ATTICUS. I COULD HAVE BEEN KILLED, **OR WORSE.** I COULD HAVE BEEN...
TURNED INTO A VAMPIRE?
BECOME SOME SORT OF DECADENT SOULLESS MONSTER WHO FEEDS OFF THE BLOOD OF OTHERS, DOOMED TO SURVIVE AN INSUBSTANTIAL ETERNITY?
I'M SORRY. I DIDN'T MEAN IT LIKE THAT--
RELAX, HALLOWAY...I'M JUST FUCKING WITH YOU.
BUT SERIOUSLY, ATTICUS...WHAT ARE WE SUPPOSED TO DO HERE?
HOW ARE WE EXPECTED TO PUT A BOW AROUND THIS CASE WHEN EVERY LEAD WE'VE CHASED HAS GONE COLD?
I HAVE SOME CONTACTS IN THE CRIMINAL WORLD, LEFTOVERS FROM WHEN I WORKED NARCOTICS.
THESE ARE THE TYPE THAT MAKE IT THEIR BUSINESS TO KNOW ABOUT EVERY MURDER, KIDNAPPING, OR THEFT IN THE CITY.
DO YOU THINK THEY'LL TALK?
TO YOU? **NO.** TO ME? **YES.**
ANYWAY, I KNOW A COUPLE OF GUYS WHO OWE ME A FEW FAVORS, I'LL CALL THEM IN AND SEE WHAT I CAN COME UP WITH.
UNTIL THEN...

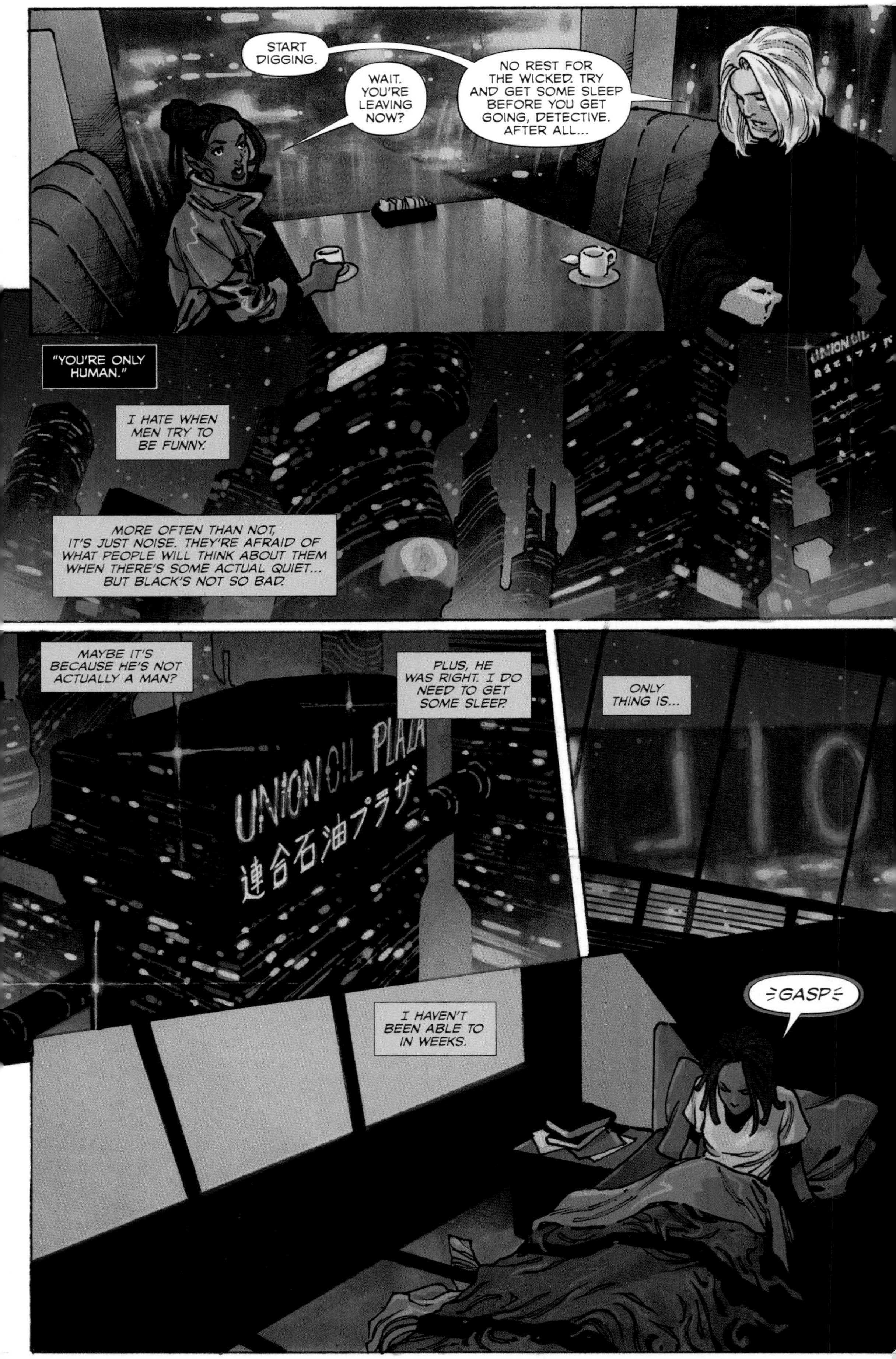
START DIGGING.
WAIT. YOU'RE LEAVING NOW?
NO REST FOR THE WICKED. TRY AND GET SOME SLEEP BEFORE YOU GET GOING, DETECTIVE. AFTER ALL...
"YOU'RE ONLY HUMAN."
I HATE WHEN MEN TRY TO BE FUNNY.
MORE OFTEN THAN NOT, IT'S JUST NOISE. THEY'RE AFRAID OF WHAT PEOPLE WILL THINK ABOUT THEM WHEN THERE'S SOME ACTUAL QUIET... BUT BLACK'S NOT SO BAD.
MAYBE IT'S BECAUSE HE'S NOT ACTUALLY A MAN?
PLUS, HE WAS RIGHT. I DO NEED TO GET SOME SLEEP.
UNION OIL PLAZA
連合石油プラザ
ONLY THING IS...
I HAVEN'T BEEN ABLE TO IN WEEKS.
GASP

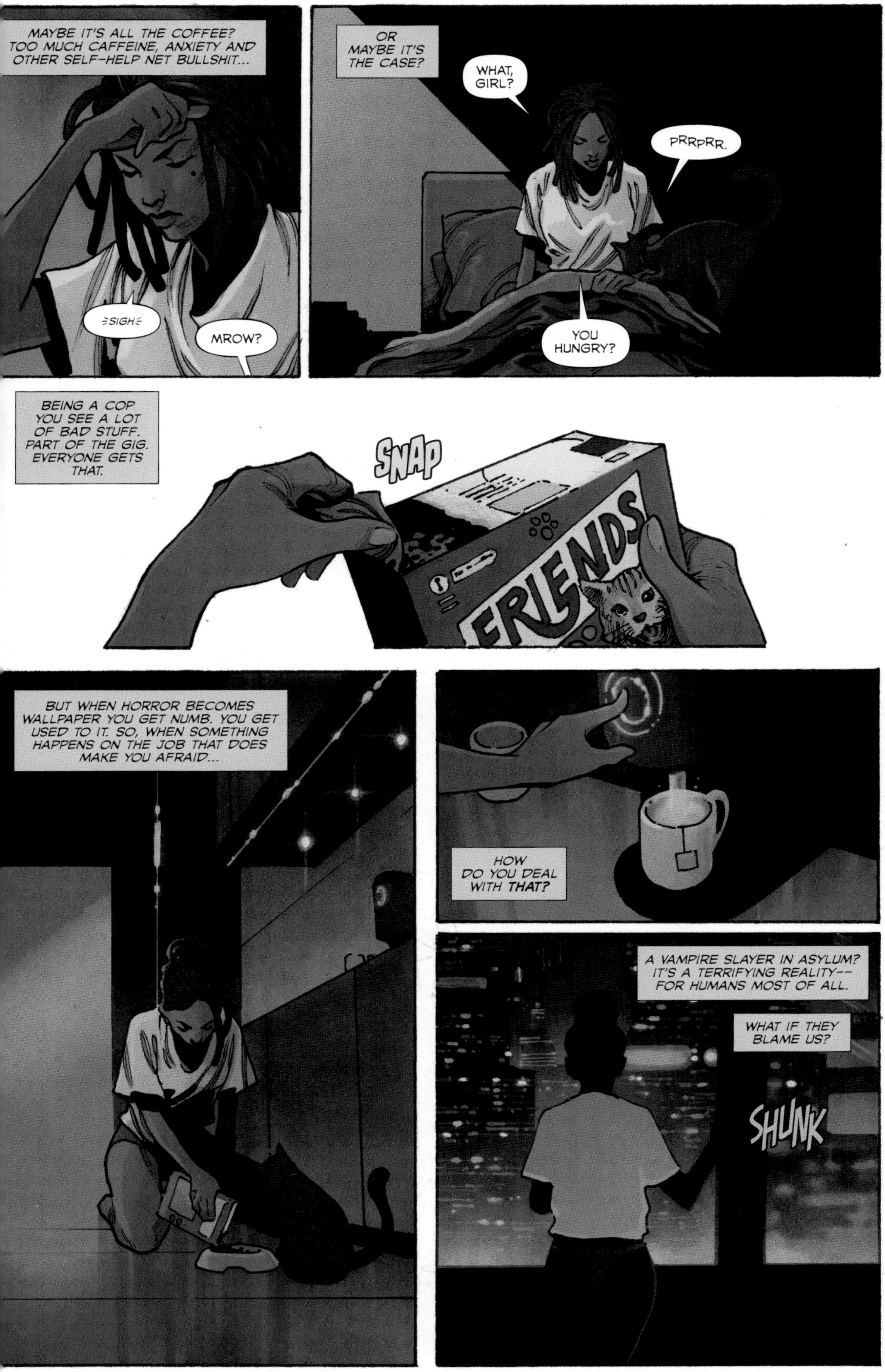
MAYBE IT'S ALL THE COFFEE? TOO MUCH CAFFEINE, ANXIETY AND OTHER SELF-HELP NET BULLSHIT...
≈SIGH≈
MROW?
OR MAYBE IT'S THE CASE?
WHAT, GIRL?
PRRPRR.
YOU HUNGRY?
BEING A COP YOU SEE A LOT OF BAD STUFF. PART OF THE GIG. EVERYONE GETS THAT.
SNAP
FRIENDS
BUT WHEN HORROR BECOMES WALLPAPER YOU GET NUMB. YOU GET USED TO IT. SO, WHEN SOMETHING HAPPENS ON THE JOB THAT DOES MAKE YOU AFRAID...
HOW DO YOU DEAL WITH THAT?
A VAMPIRE SLAYER IN ASYLUM? IT'S A TERRIFYING REALITY-- FOR HUMANS MOST OF ALL.
WHAT IF THEY BLAME US?
SHUNK

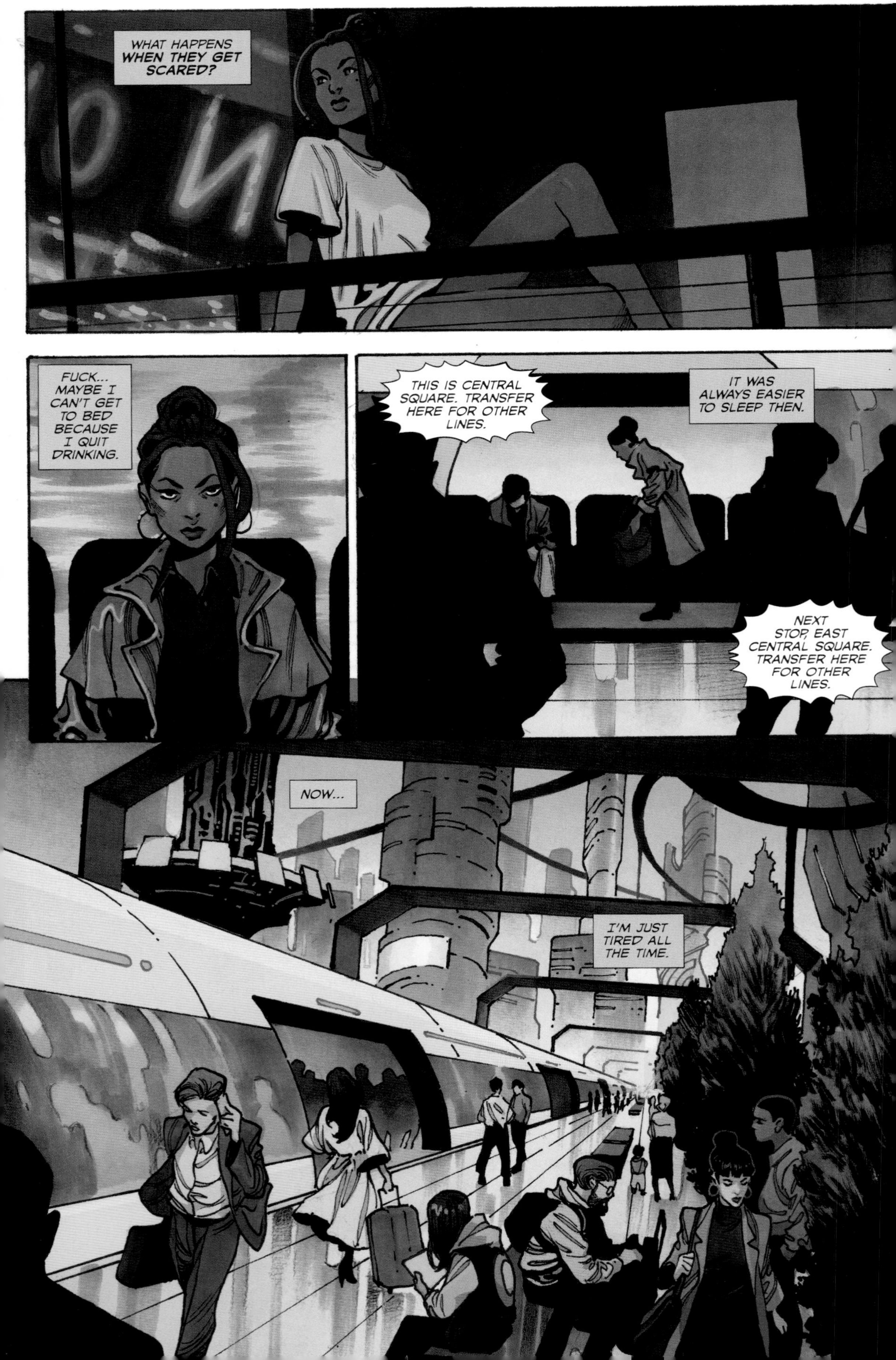
WHAT HAPPENS WHEN THEY GET SCARED?
FUCK... MAYBE I CAN'T GET TO BED BECAUSE I QUIT DRINKING.
THIS IS CENTRAL SQUARE. TRANSFER HERE FOR OTHER LINES.
IT WAS ALWAYS EASIER TO SLEEP THEN.
NEXT STOP, EAST CENTRAL SQUARE. TRANSFER HERE FOR OTHER LINES.
NOW...
I'M JUST TIRED ALL THE TIME.

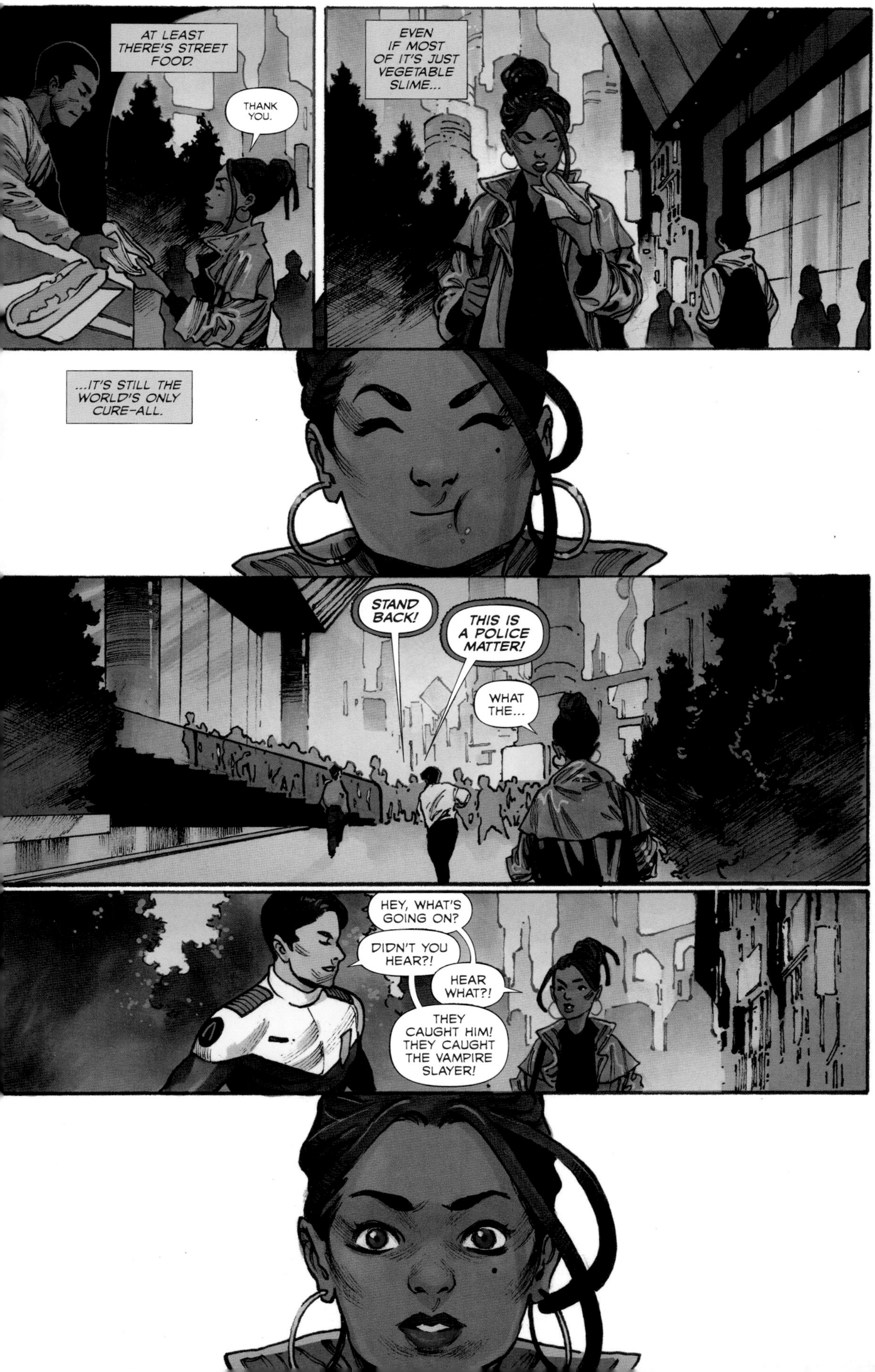
AT LEAST THERE'S STREET FOOD.
THANK YOU.
EVEN IF MOST OF IT'S JUST VEGETABLE SLIME...
...IT'S STILL THE WORLD'S ONLY CURE-ALL.
STAND BACK!
THIS IS A POLICE MATTER!
WHAT THE...
HEY, WHAT'S GOING ON?
DIDN'T YOU HEAR?!
HEAR WHAT?!
THEY CAUGHT HIM! THEY CAUGHT THE VAMPIRE SLAYER!

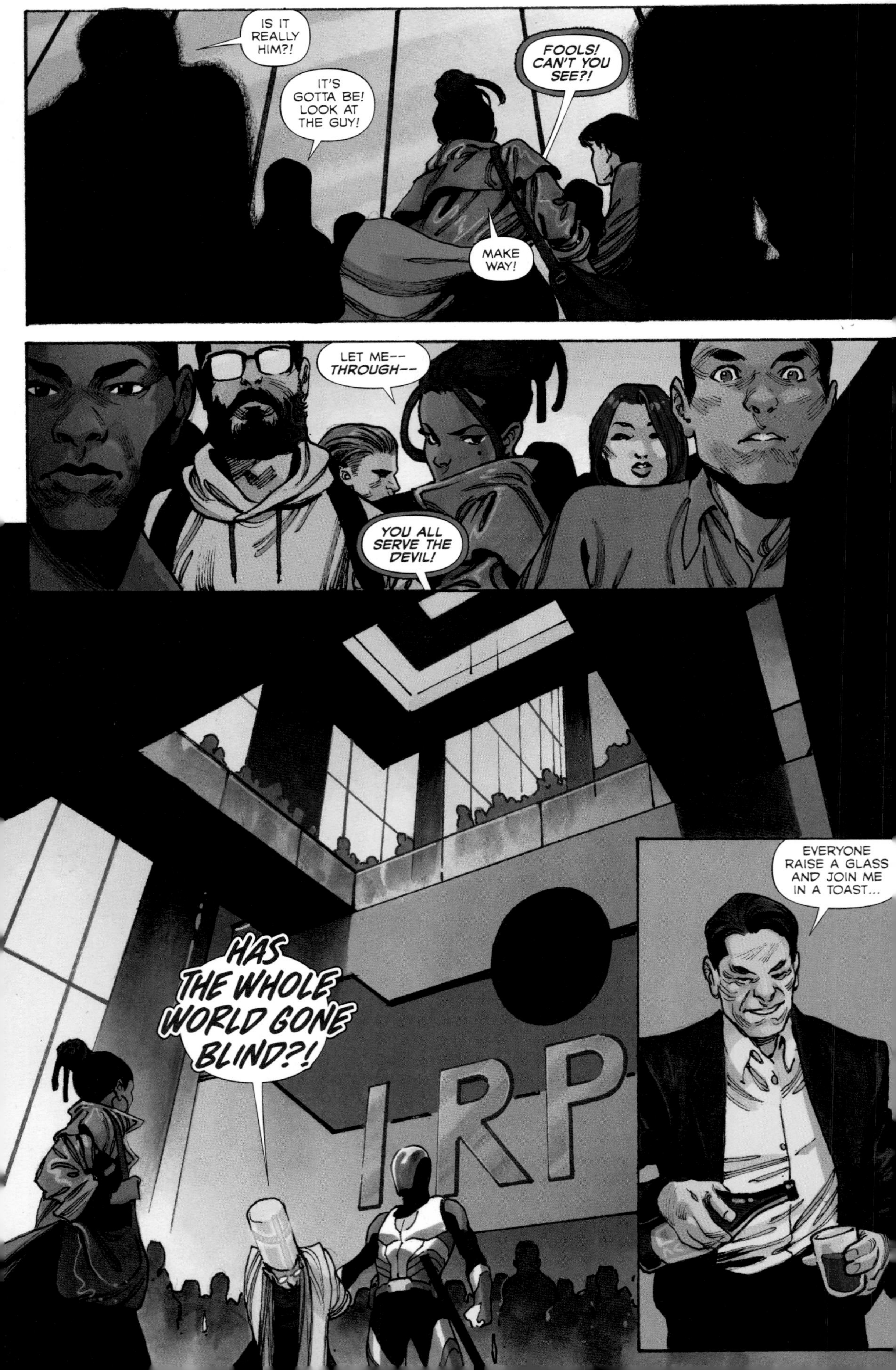
IS IT REALLY HIM?!
IT'S GOTTA BE! LOOK AT THE GUY!
FOOLS! CAN'T YOU SEE?!
MAKE WAY!
LET ME-- *THROUGH--*
YOU ALL SERVE THE DEVIL!
HAS THE WHOLE WORLD GONE BLIND?!
IRP
EVERYONE RAISE A GLASS AND JOIN ME IN A TOAST...

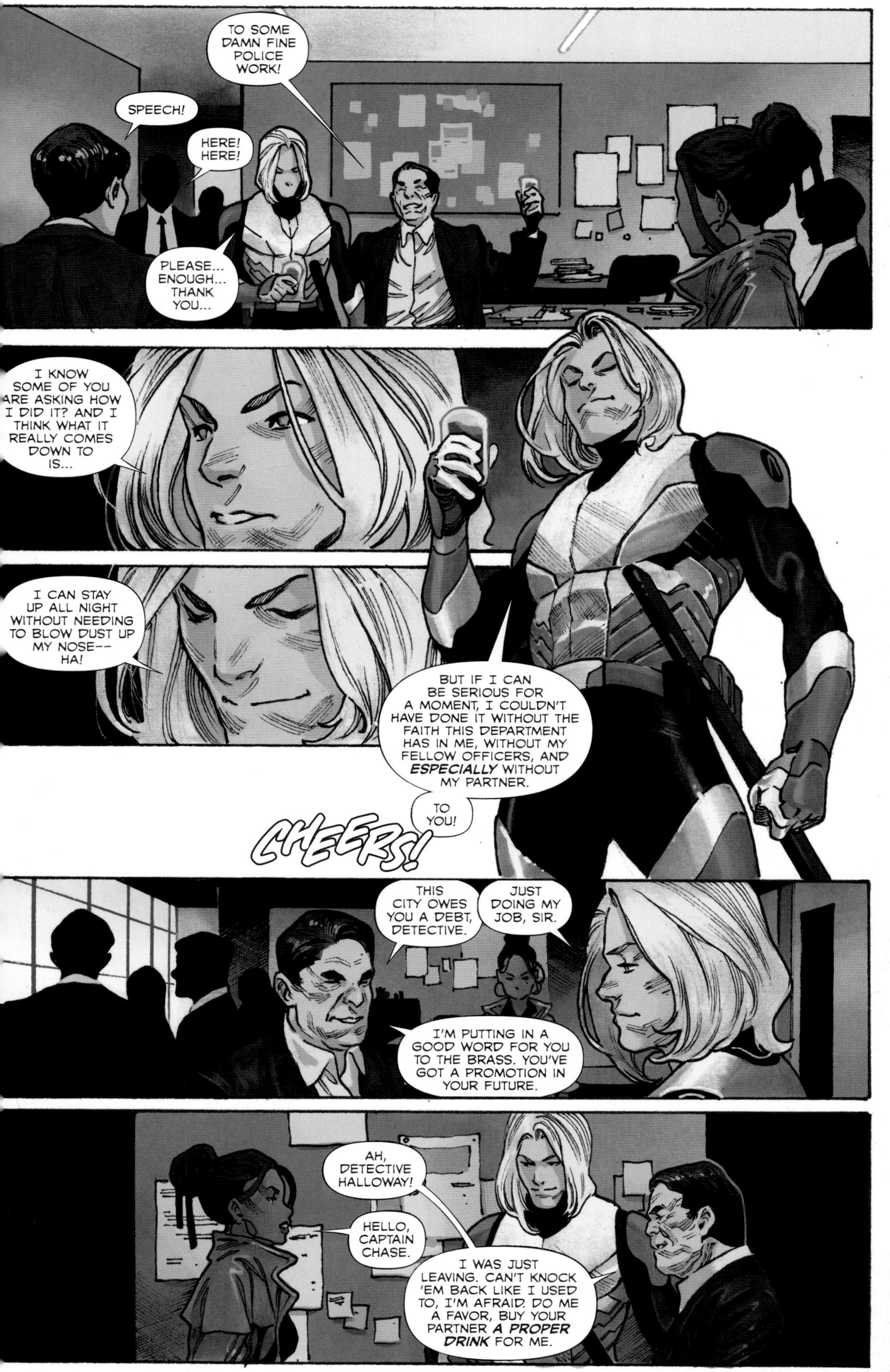
TO SOME DAMN FINE POLICE WORK!
SPEECH!
HERE! HERE!
PLEASE... ENOUGH... THANK YOU...
I KNOW SOME OF YOU ARE ASKING HOW I DID IT? AND I THINK WHAT IT REALLY COMES DOWN TO IS...
I CAN STAY UP ALL NIGHT WITHOUT NEEDING TO BLOW DUST UP MY NOSE-- HA!
BUT IF I CAN BE SERIOUS FOR A MOMENT, I COULDN'T HAVE DONE IT WITHOUT THE FAITH THIS DEPARTMENT HAS IN ME, WITHOUT MY FELLOW OFFICERS, AND ESPECIALLY WITHOUT MY PARTNER.
TO YOU!
CHEERS!
THIS CITY OWES YOU A DEBT, DETECTIVE.
JUST DOING MY JOB, SIR.
I'M PUTTING IN A GOOD WORD FOR YOU TO THE BRASS. YOU'VE GOT A PROMOTION IN YOUR FUTURE.
AH, DETECTIVE HALLOWAY!
HELLO, CAPTAIN CHASE.
I WAS JUST LEAVING. CAN'T KNOCK 'EM BACK LIKE I USED TO, I'M AFRAID. DO ME A FAVOR, BUY YOUR PARTNER A PROPER DRINK FOR ME.

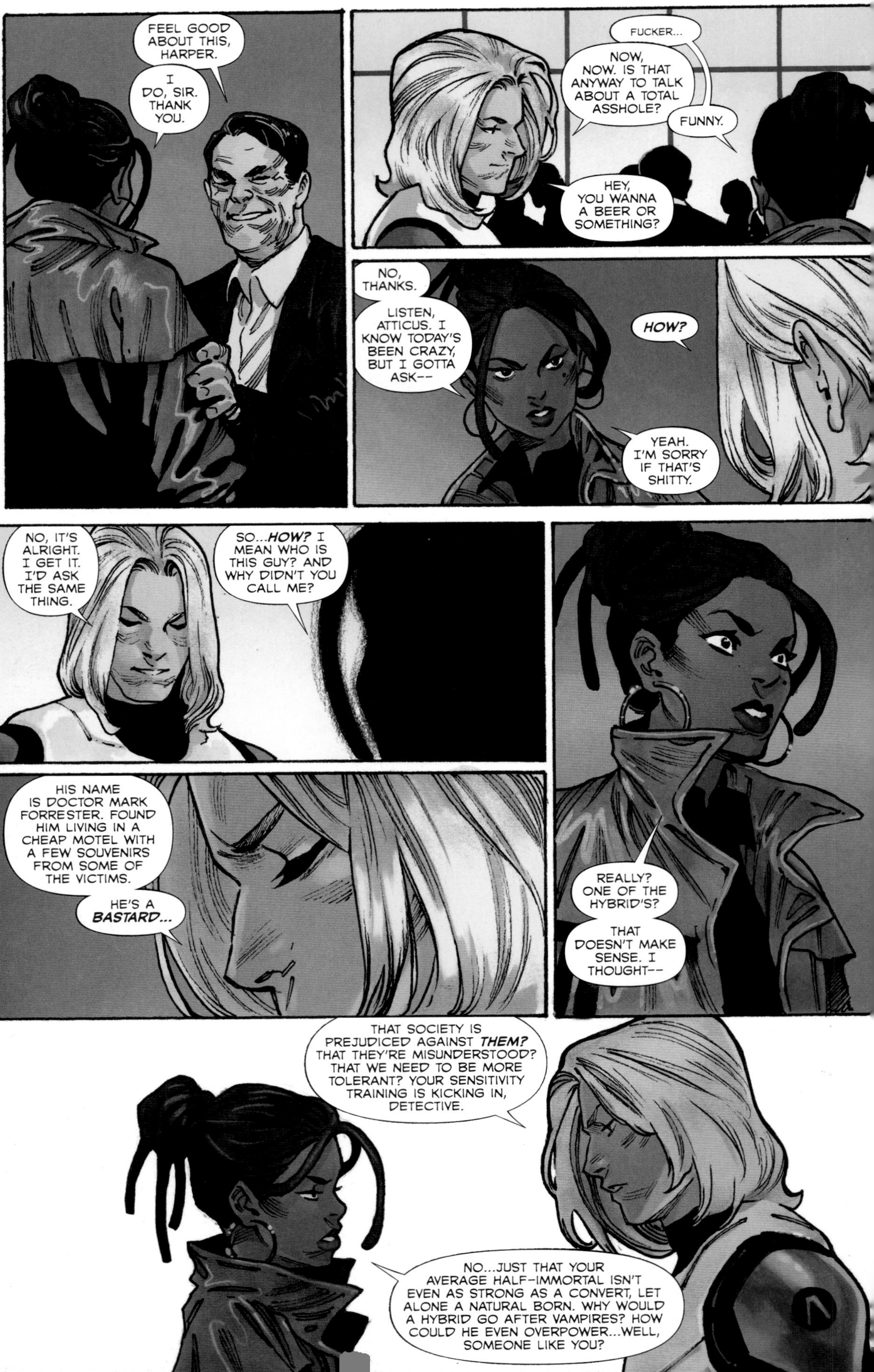
FEEL GOOD ABOUT THIS, HARPER.
I DO, SIR. THANK YOU.
FUCKER...
NOW, NOW. IS THAT ANYWAY TO TALK ABOUT A TOTAL ASSHOLE?
FUNNY.
HEY, YOU WANNA A BEER OR SOMETHING?
NO, THANKS.
LISTEN, ATTICUS. I KNOW TODAY'S BEEN CRAZY, BUT I GOTTA ASK--
HOW?
YEAH. I'M SORRY IF THAT'S SHITTY.
NO, IT'S ALRIGHT. I GET IT. I'D ASK THE SAME THING.
SO...HOW? I MEAN WHO IS THIS GUY? AND WHY DIDN'T YOU CALL ME?
HIS NAME IS DOCTOR MARK FORRESTER. FOUND HIM LIVING IN A CHEAP MOTEL WITH A FEW SOUVENIRS FROM SOME OF THE VICTIMS.
HE'S A BASTARD...
REALLY? ONE OF THE HYBRID'S?
THAT DOESN'T MAKE SENSE. I THOUGHT--
THAT SOCIETY IS PREJUDICED AGAINST THEM? THAT THEY'RE MISUNDERSTOOD? THAT WE NEED TO BE MORE TOLERANT? YOUR SENSITIVITY TRAINING IS KICKING IN, DETECTIVE.
NO...JUST THAT YOUR AVERAGE HALF-IMMORTAL ISN'T EVEN AS STRONG AS A CONVERT, LET ALONE A NATURAL BORN. WHY WOULD A HYBRID GO AFTER VAMPIRES? HOW COULD HE EVEN OVERPOWER...WELL, SOMEONE LIKE YOU?

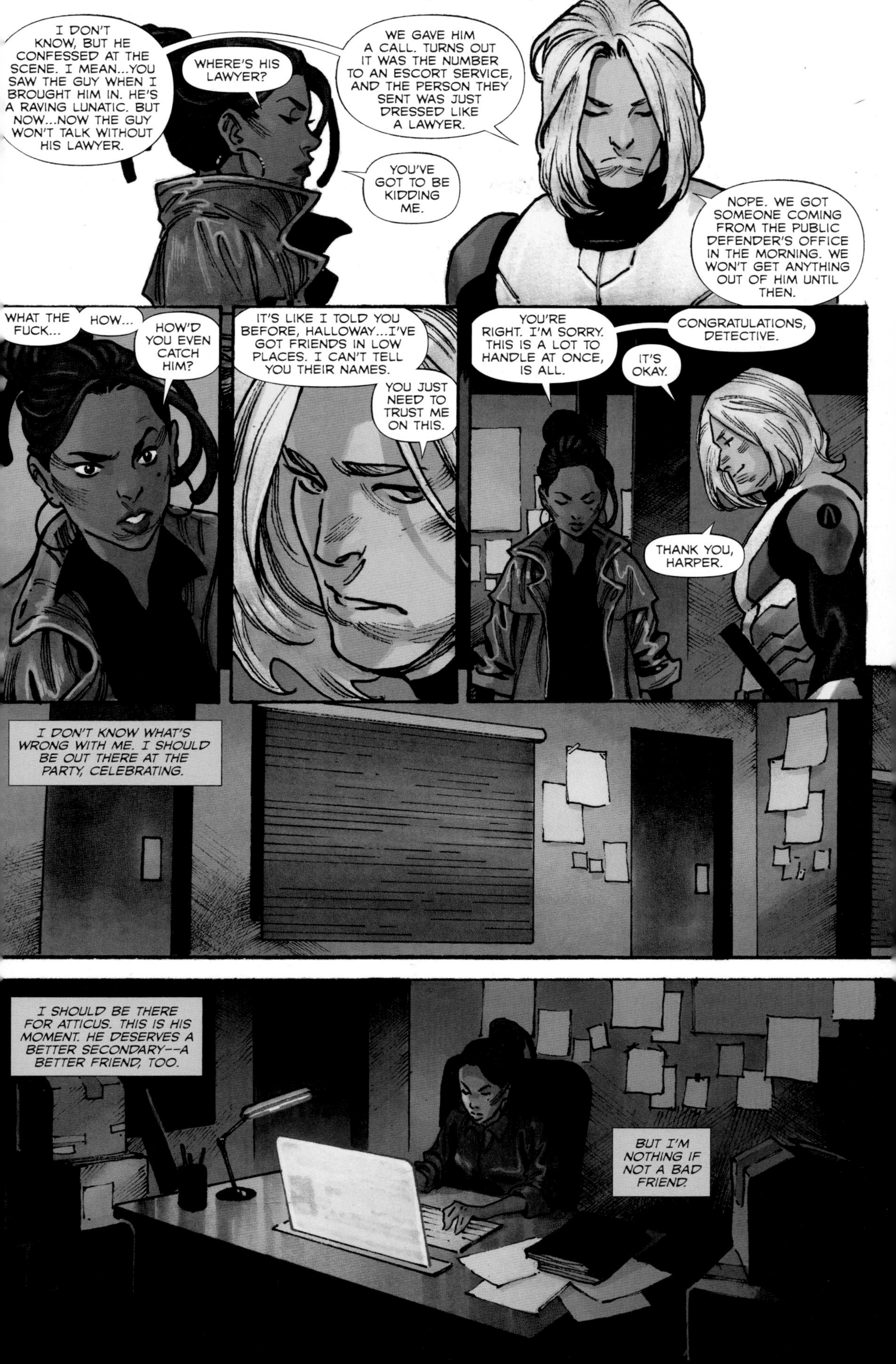
I DON'T KNOW, BUT HE CONFESSED AT THE SCENE. I MEAN...YOU SAW THE GUY WHEN I BROUGHT HIM IN. HE'S A RAVING LUNATIC. BUT NOW...NOW THE GUY WON'T TALK WITHOUT HIS LAWYER.
WHERE'S HIS LAWYER?
WE GAVE HIM A CALL. TURNS OUT IT WAS THE NUMBER TO AN ESCORT SERVICE, AND THE PERSON THEY SENT WAS JUST DRESSED LIKE A LAWYER.
YOU'VE GOT TO BE KIDDING ME.
NOPE. WE GOT SOMEONE COMING FROM THE PUBLIC DEFENDER'S OFFICE IN THE MORNING. WE WON'T GET ANYTHING OUT OF HIM UNTIL THEN.
WHAT THE FUCK...
HOW...
HOW'D YOU EVEN CATCH HIM?
IT'S LIKE I TOLD YOU BEFORE, HALLOWAY...I'VE GOT FRIENDS IN LOW PLACES. I CAN'T TELL YOU THEIR NAMES.
YOU JUST NEED TO TRUST ME ON THIS.
YOU'RE RIGHT. I'M SORRY. THIS IS A LOT TO HANDLE AT ONCE, IS ALL.
CONGRATULATIONS, DETECTIVE.
IT'S OKAY.
THANK YOU, HARPER.
I DON'T KNOW WHAT'S WRONG WITH ME. I SHOULD BE OUT THERE AT THE PARTY, CELEBRATING.
I SHOULD BE THERE FOR ATTICUS. THIS IS HIS MOMENT. HE DESERVES A BETTER SECONDARY--A BETTER FRIEND, TOO.
BUT I'M NOTHING IF NOT A BAD FRIEND.

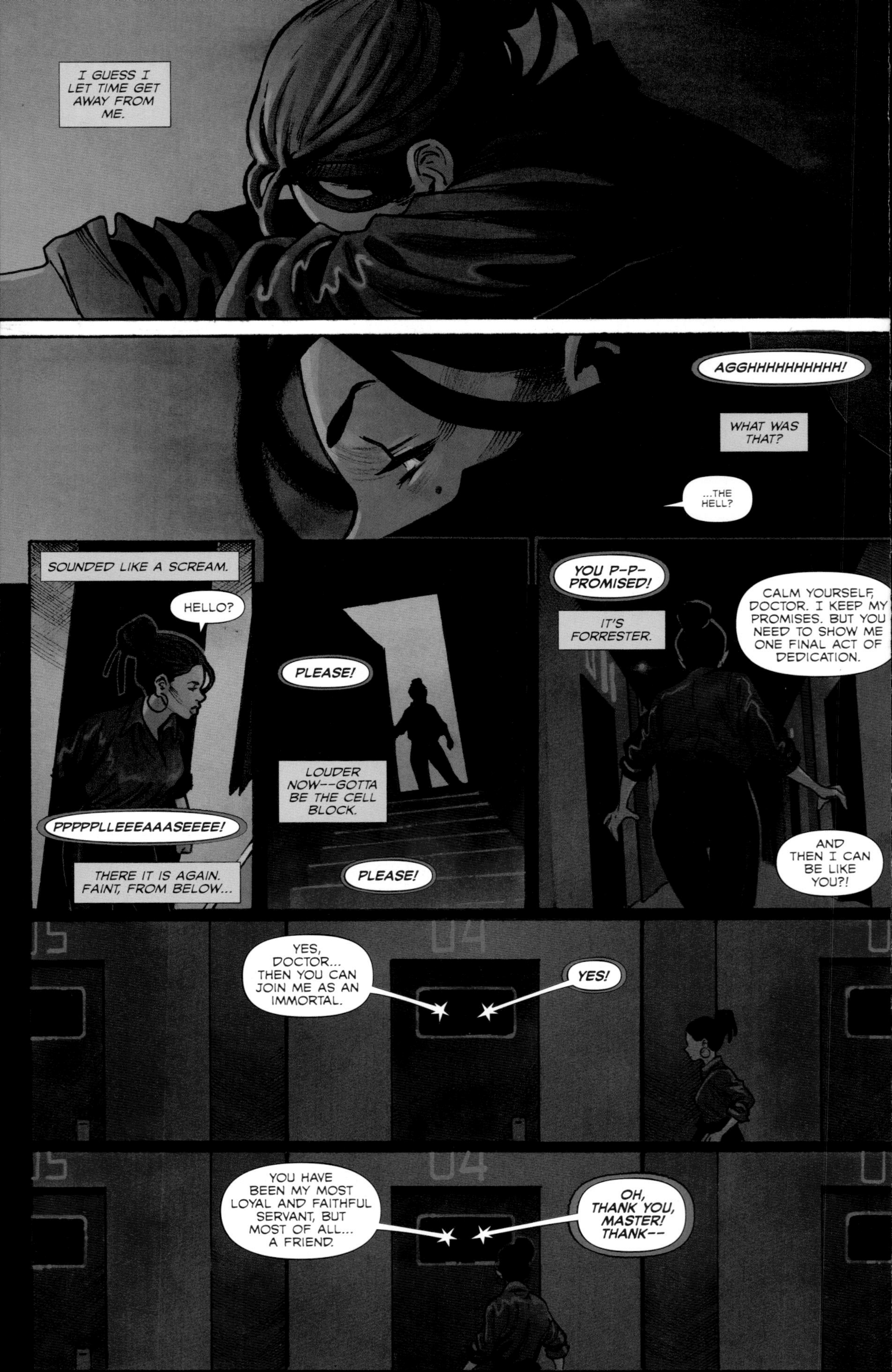
I GUESS I LET TIME GET AWAY FROM ME.
AGGHHHHHHHHHH!
WHAT WAS THAT?
...THE HELL?
SOUNDED LIKE A SCREAM.
HELLO?
PPPPPLLEEEAAASEEEE!
THERE IT IS AGAIN. FAINT, FROM BELOW...
PLEASE!
LOUDER NOW--GOTTA BE THE CELL BLOCK.
PLEASE!
YOU P-P-PROMISED!
IT'S FORRESTER.
CALM YOURSELF, DOCTOR. I KEEP MY PROMISES. BUT YOU NEED TO SHOW ME ONE FINAL ACT OF DEDICATION.
AND THEN I CAN BE LIKE YOU?!
YES, DOCTOR... THEN YOU CAN JOIN ME AS AN IMMORTAL.
YES!
YOU HAVE BEEN MY MOST LOYAL AND FAITHFUL SERVANT, BUT MOST OF ALL... A FRIEND.
OH, THANK YOU, MASTER! THANK--

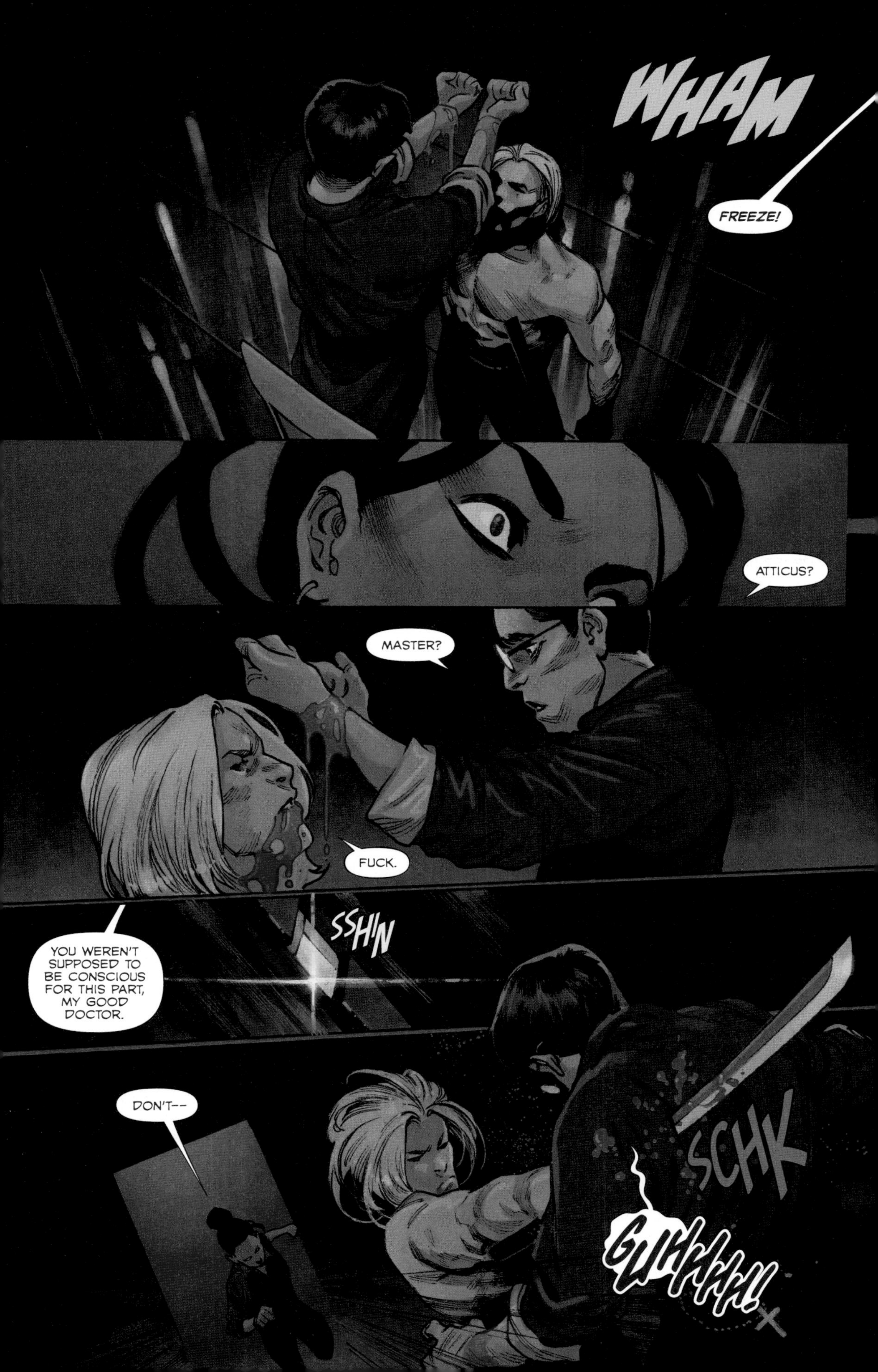
WHAM
FREEZE!
ATTICUS?
MASTER?
FUCK.
YOU WEREN'T SUPPOSED TO BE CONSCIOUS FOR THIS PART, MY GOOD DOCTOR.
SSHIN
DON'T--
SCHK
GUHHHH!

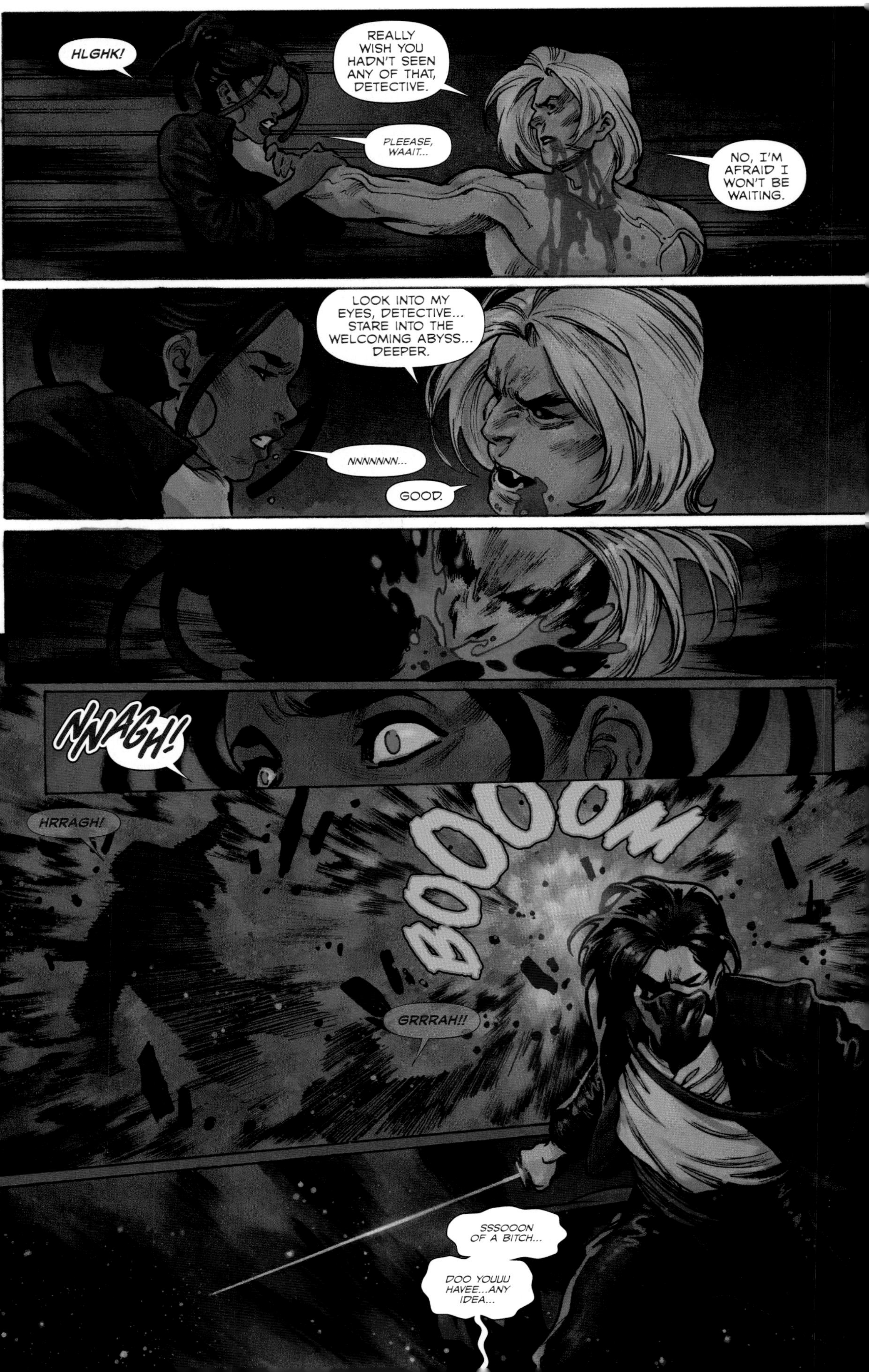
HLGHK!
REALLY WISH YOU HADN'T SEEN ANY OF THAT, DETECTIVE.
PLEEASE, WAAIT...
NO, I'M AFRAID I WON'T BE WAITING.
LOOK INTO MY EYES, DETECTIVE... STARE INTO THE WELCOMING ABYSS... DEEPER.
NNNNNNN...
GOOD.
NNAGH!
HRRAGH!
BOOOOOM
GRRRAH!!
SSSOOON OF A BITCH...
DOO YOUUU HAVEE...ANY IDEA...

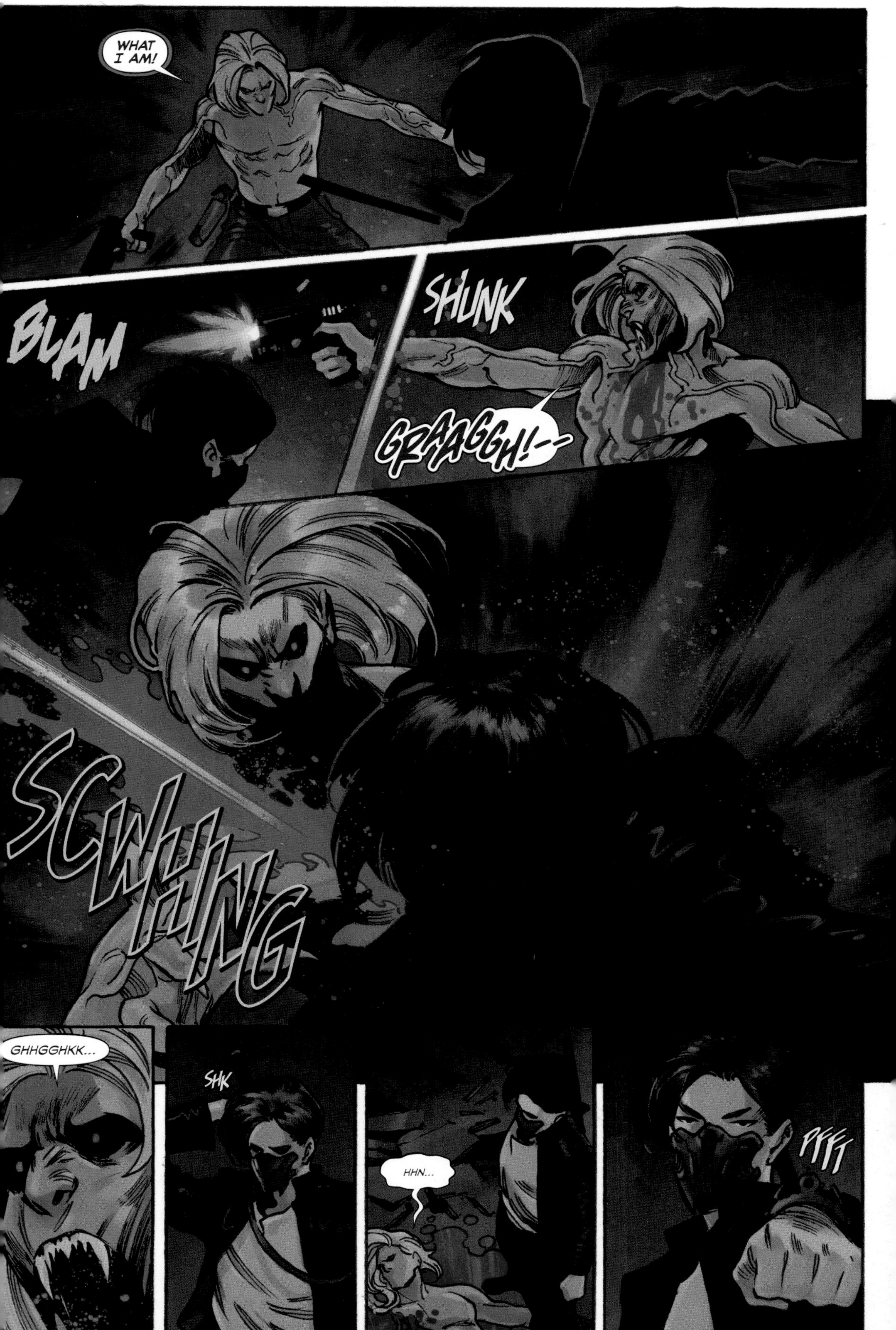
WHAT I AM!
BLAM
SHUNK
GRAAGGH!--
SCWHING
GHHGGHKK...
SHK
HHN...
PFFT

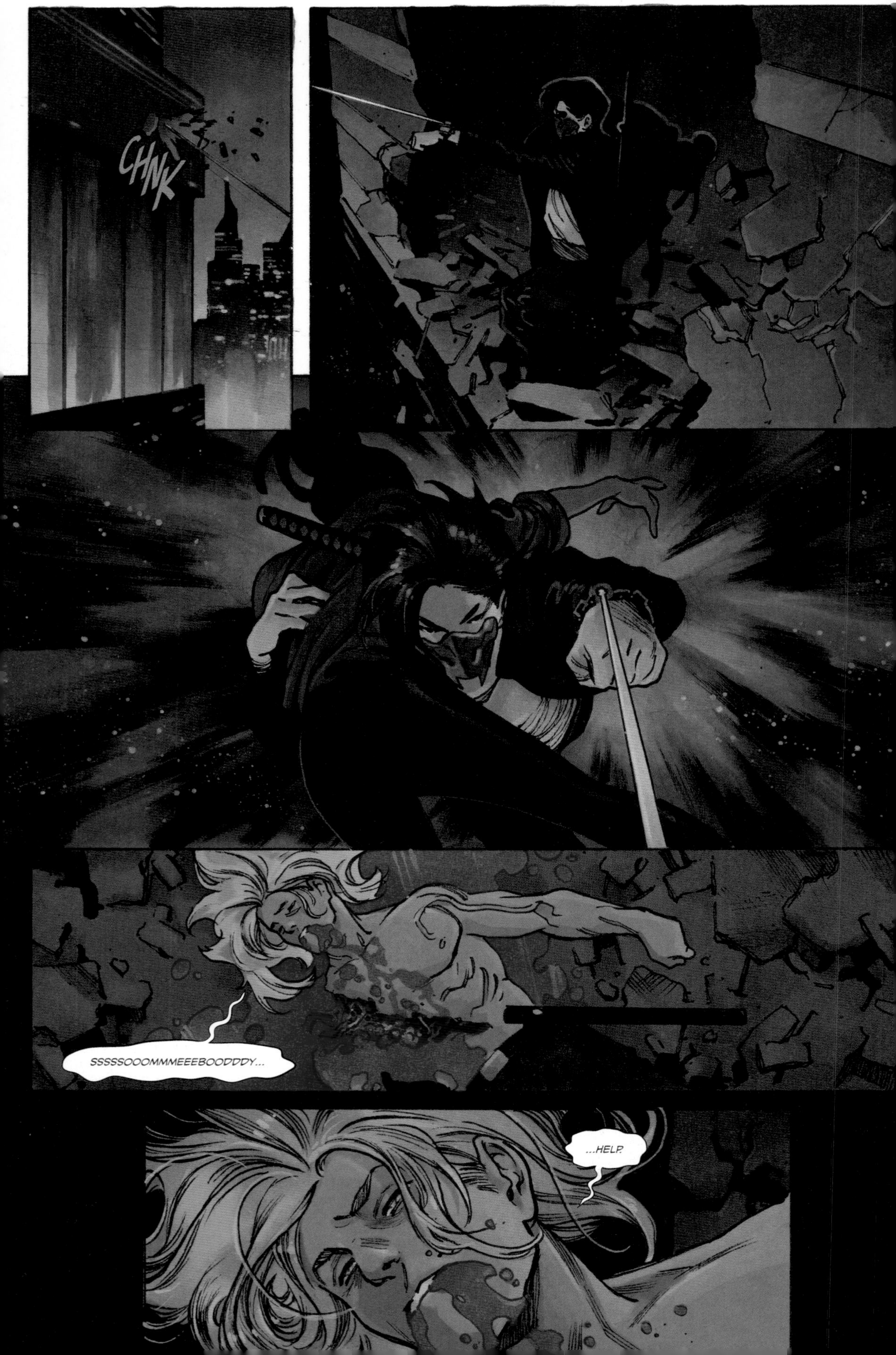
CHNK
SSSSSOOOMMMEEEBOODDDY...
...HELP.

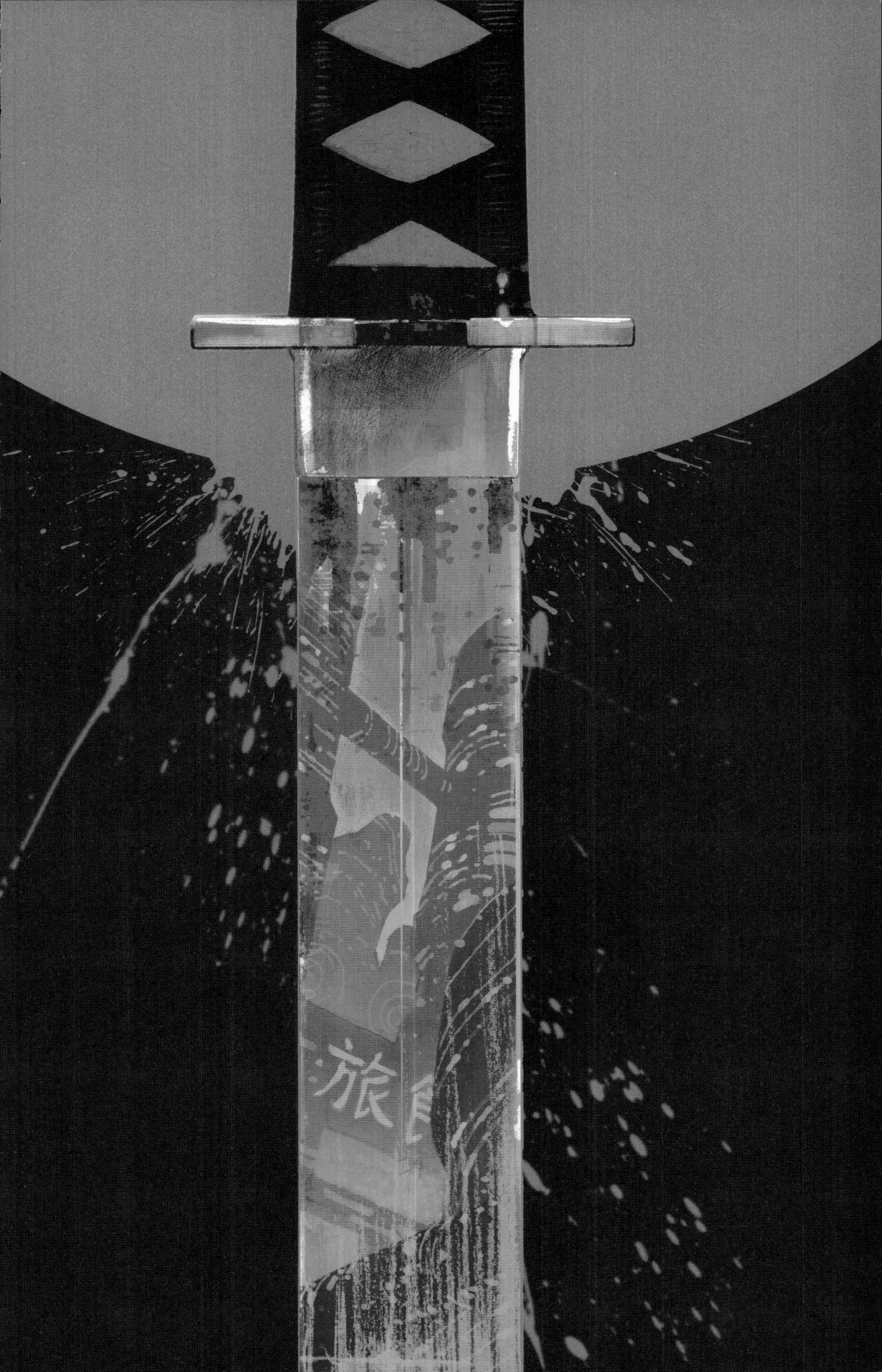
旅

TWO

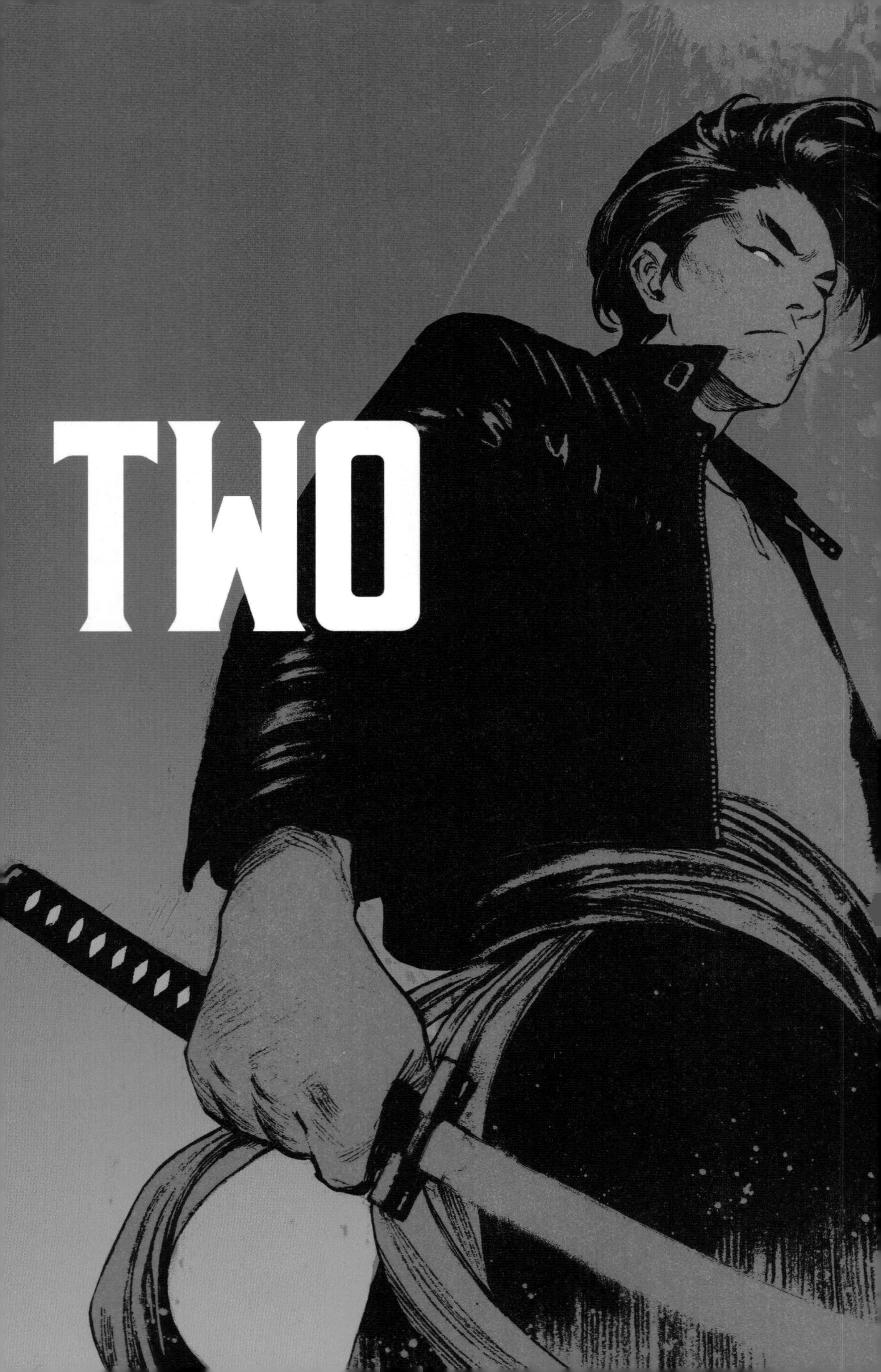

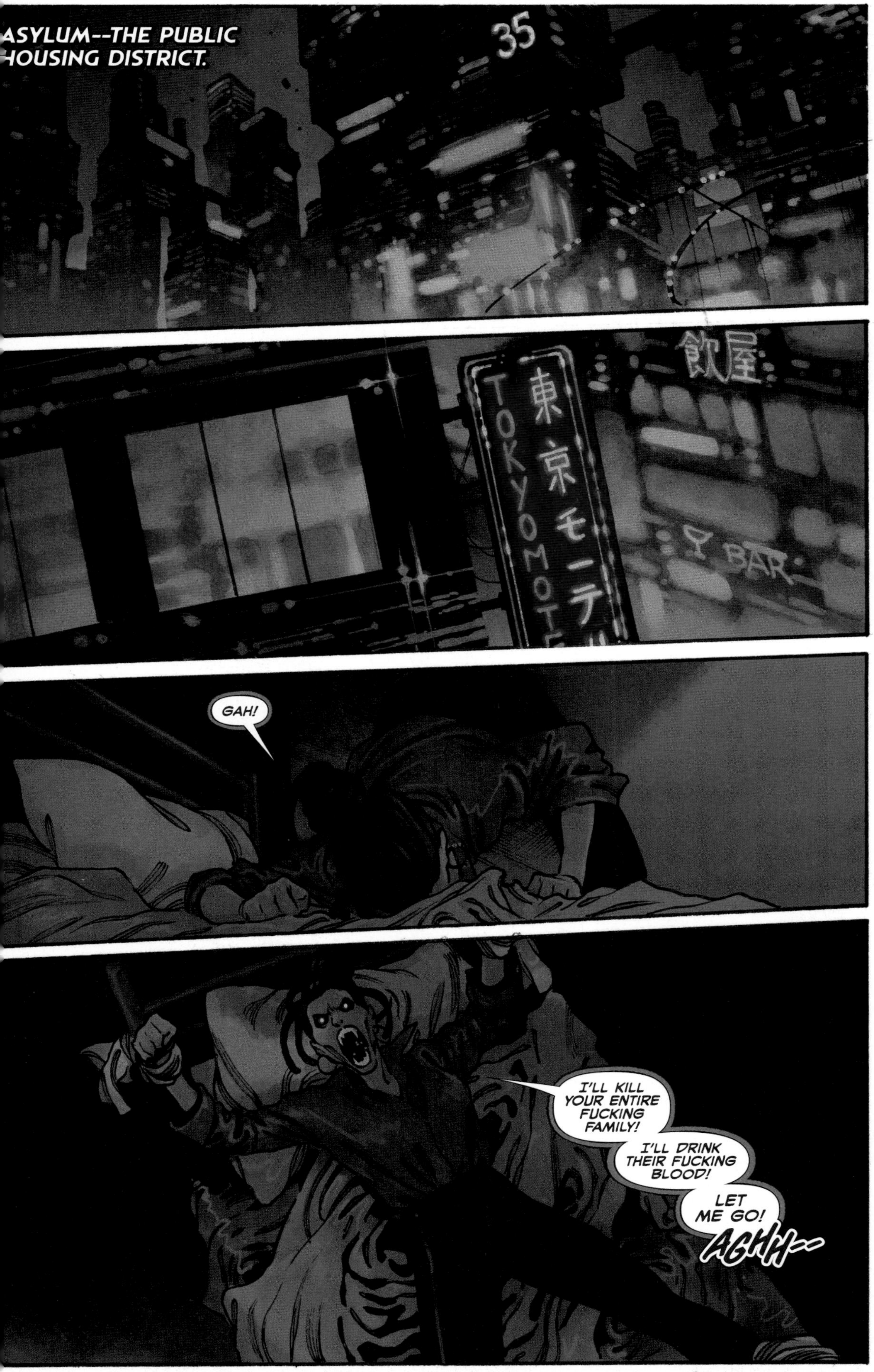
ASYLUM--THE PUBLIC
HOUSING DISTRICT.
35
飲屋
BAR
GAH!
I'LL KILL YOUR ENTIRE FUCKING FAMILY!
I'LL DRINK THEIR FUCKING BLOOD!
LET ME GO!
AGHH--

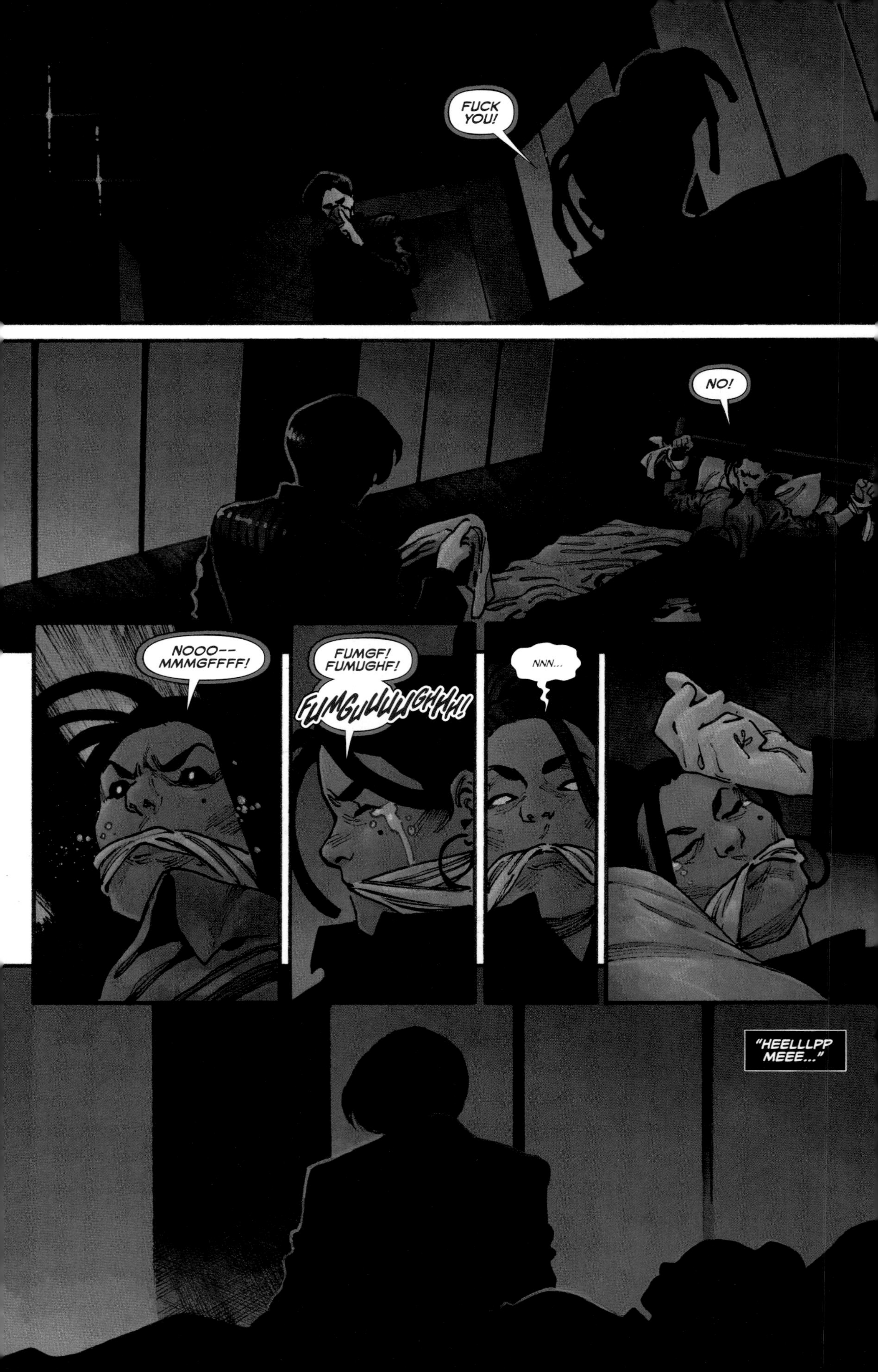
FUCK YOU!
NO!
NOOO--MMMGFFFF!
FUMGF! FUMUGHF!
FUMGULLLLGHHH!
NNN...
"HEELLLPP MEEE..."

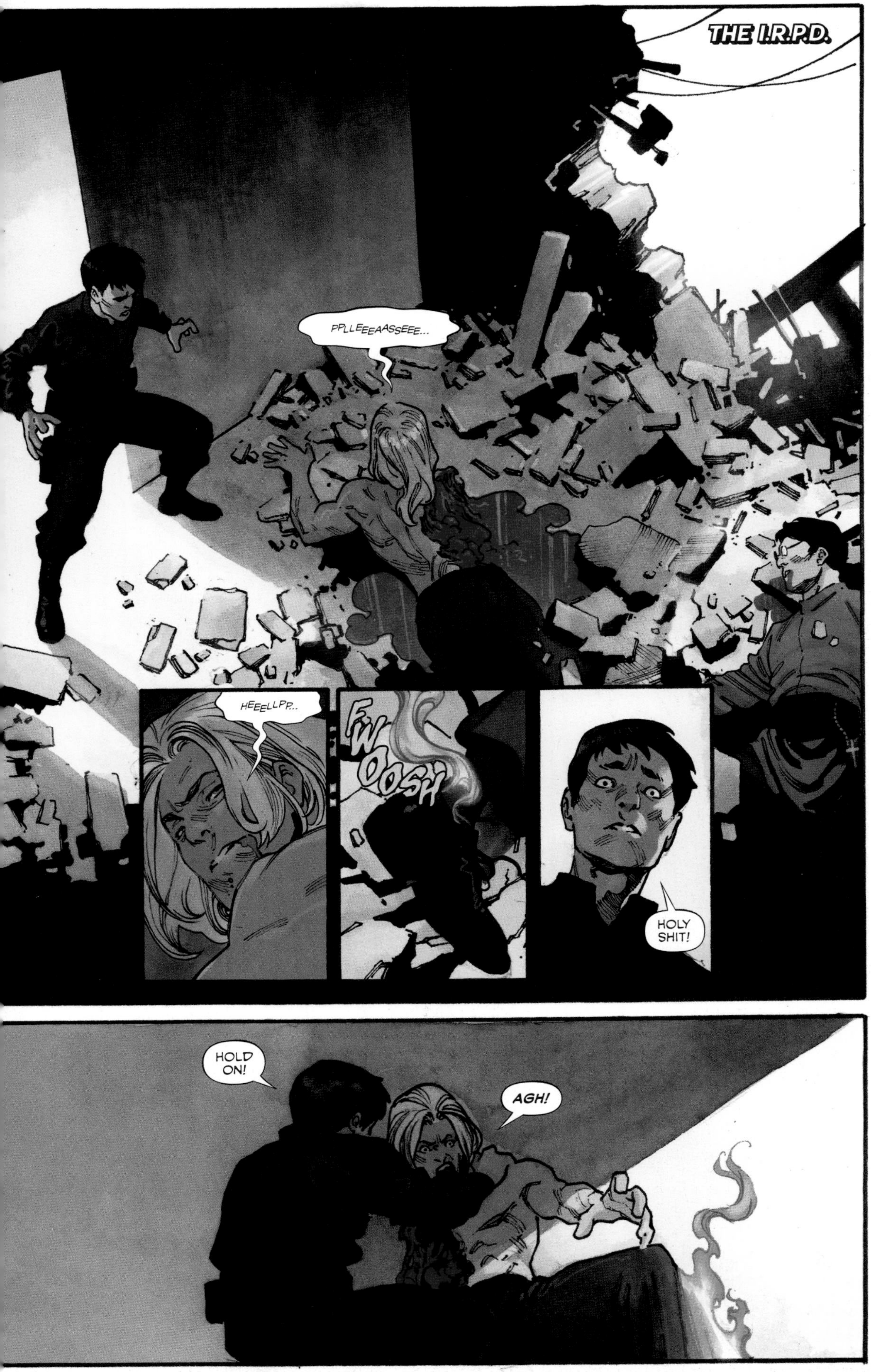
THE I.R.P.D.
PPLLEEEAASSEEE...
HEEELLPP..
FWOOSH
HOLY SHIT!
HOLD ON!
AGH!

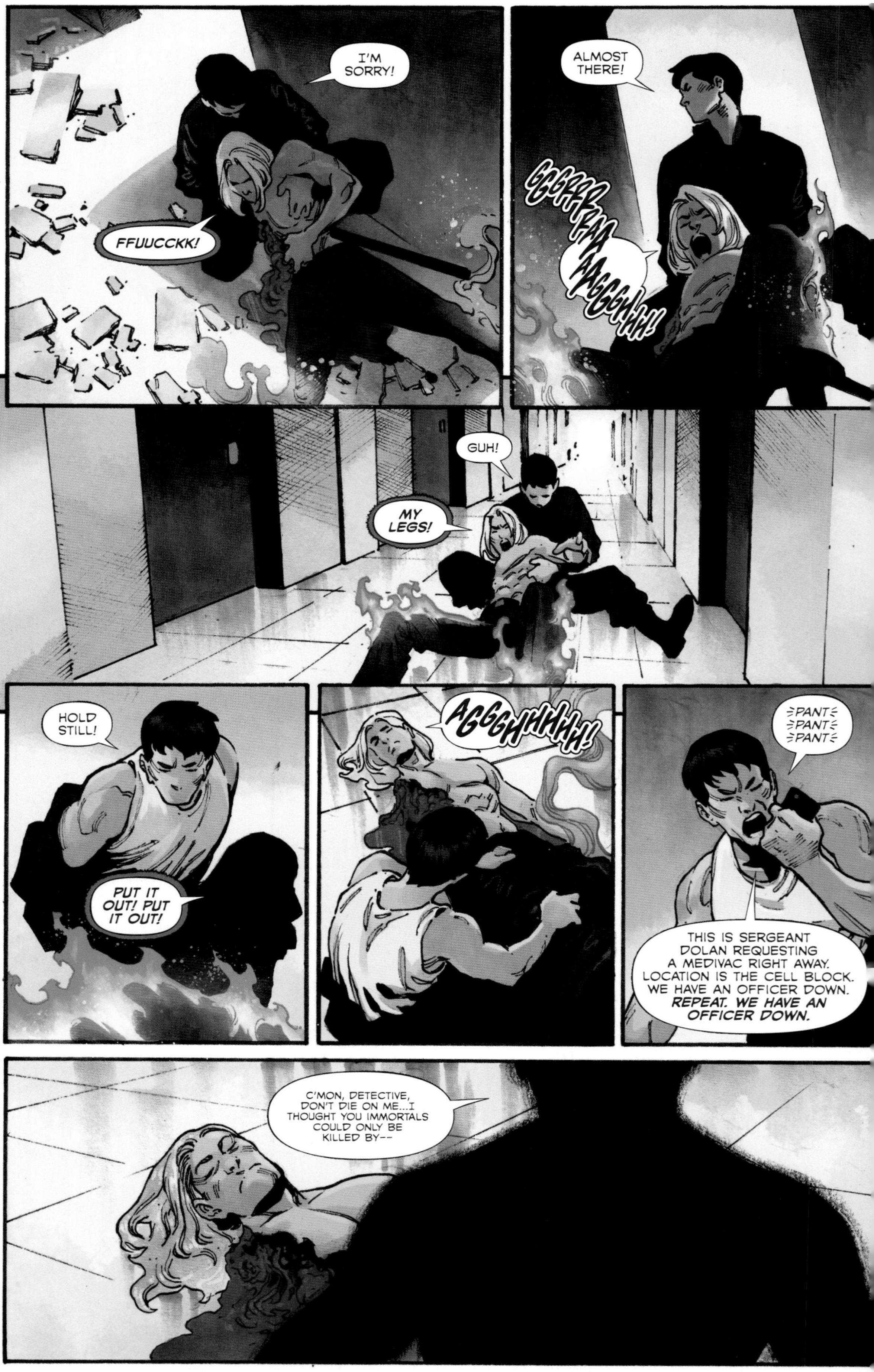

I'M SORRY!
FFUUCCKK!
ALMOST THERE!
GGGRRAAAAGGHHHH!
GUH!
MY LEGS!
HOLD STILL!
PUT IT OUT! PUT IT OUT!
AGGGHHHHHH!
PANT PANT PANT
THIS IS SERGEANT DOLAN REQUESTING A MEDIVAC RIGHT AWAY. LOCATION IS THE CELL BLOCK. WE HAVE AN OFFICER DOWN. ***REPEAT. WE HAVE AN OFFICER DOWN.***
C'MON, DETECTIVE, DON'T DIE ON ME...I THOUGHT YOU IMMORTALS COULD ONLY BE KILLED BY--

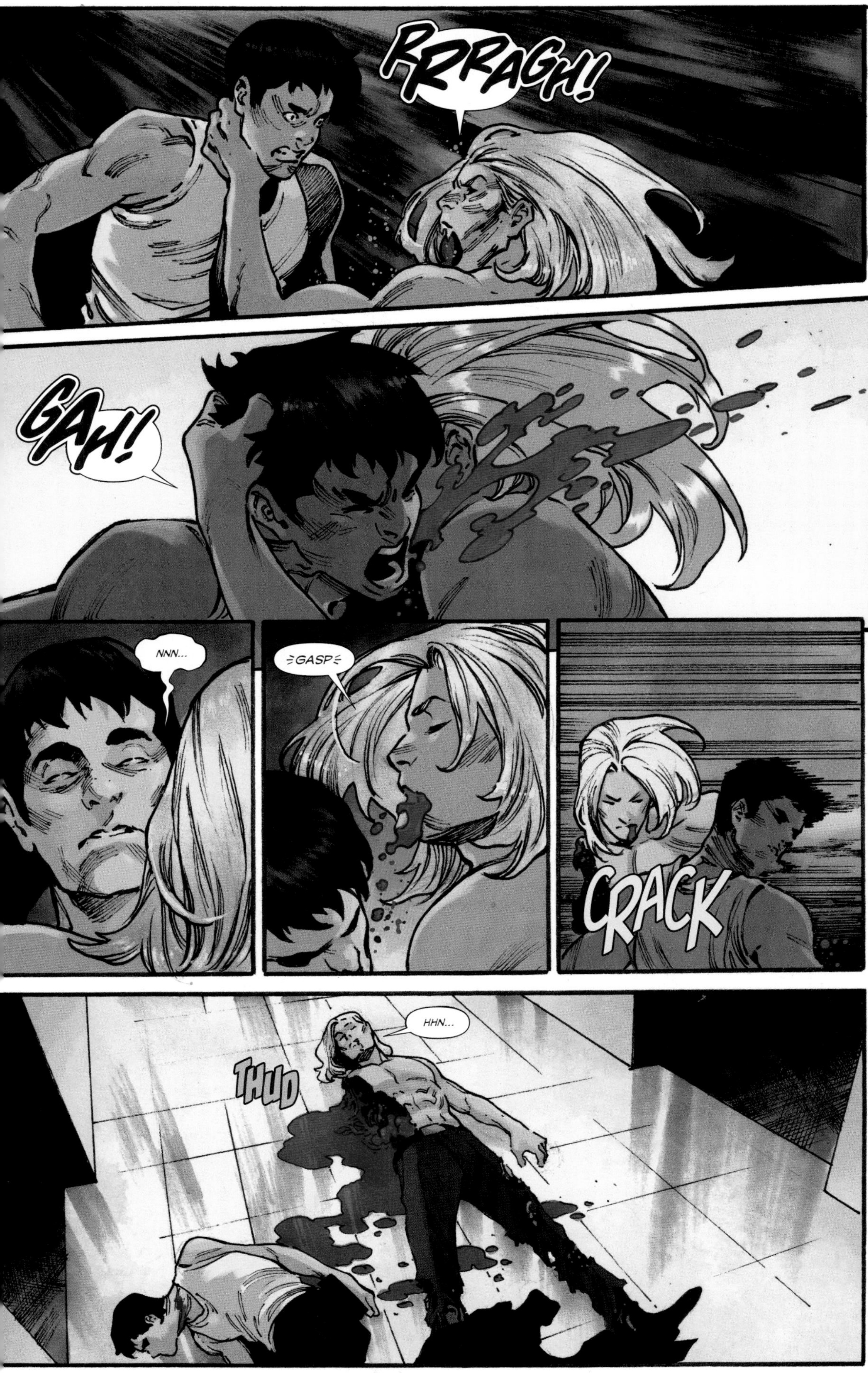
RRRAGH!
GAH!
NNN...
GASP
CRACK
HHN...
THUD

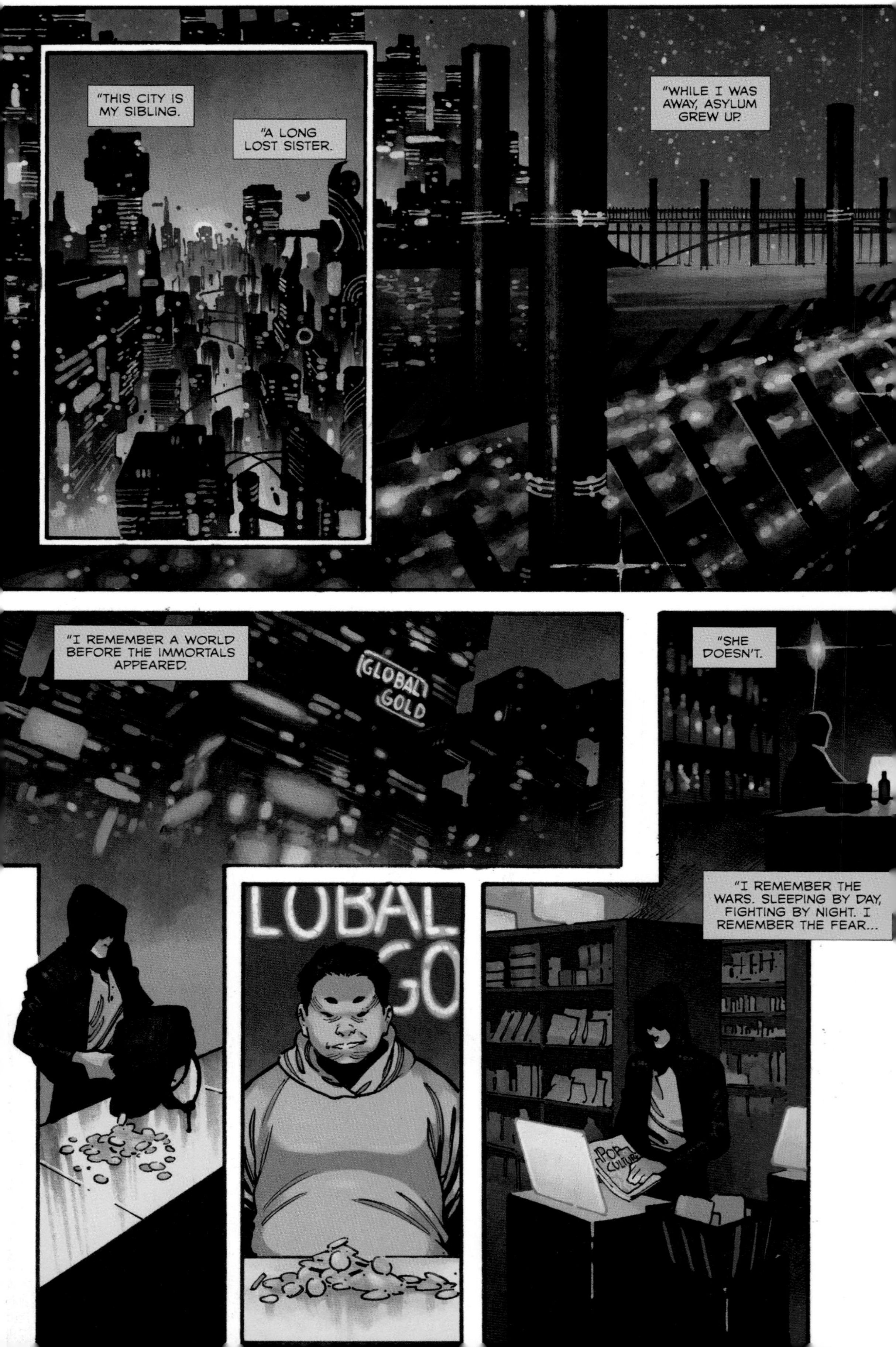
"THIS CITY IS MY SIBLING.
"A LONG LOST SISTER.
"WHILE I WAS AWAY, ASYLUM GREW UP.
"I REMEMBER A WORLD BEFORE THE IMMORTALS APPEARED.
GLOBAL GOLD
"SHE DOESN'T.
LOBAL
GO
"I REMEMBER THE WARS. SLEEPING BY DAY, FIGHTING BY NIGHT. I REMEMBER THE FEAR...
POP CULTURE

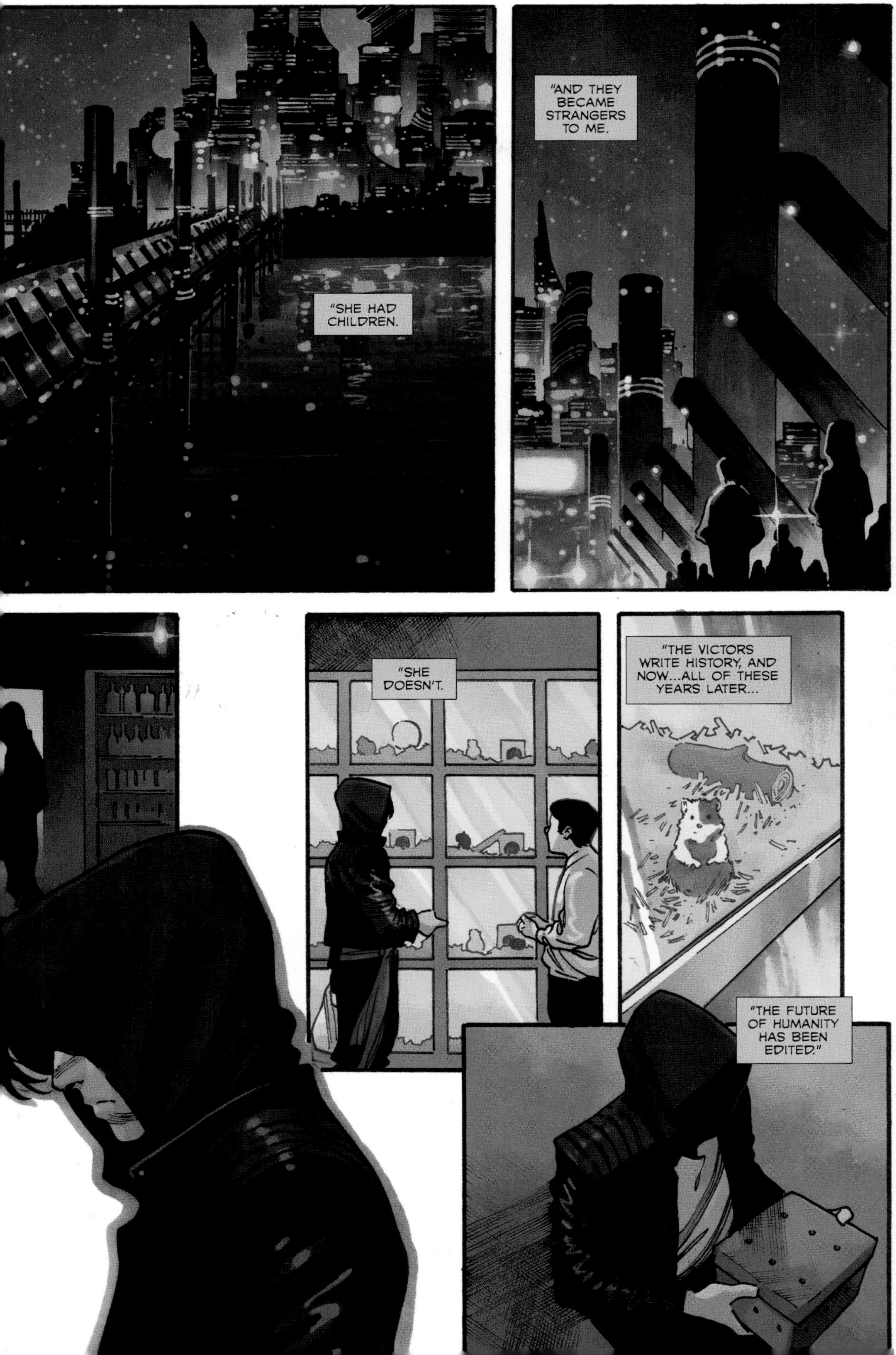
"SHE HAD CHILDREN.
"AND THEY BECAME STRANGERS TO ME.
"SHE DOESN'T.
"THE VICTORS WRITE HISTORY, AND NOW...ALL OF THESE YEARS LATER...
"THE FUTURE OF HUMANITY HAS BEEN EDITED."

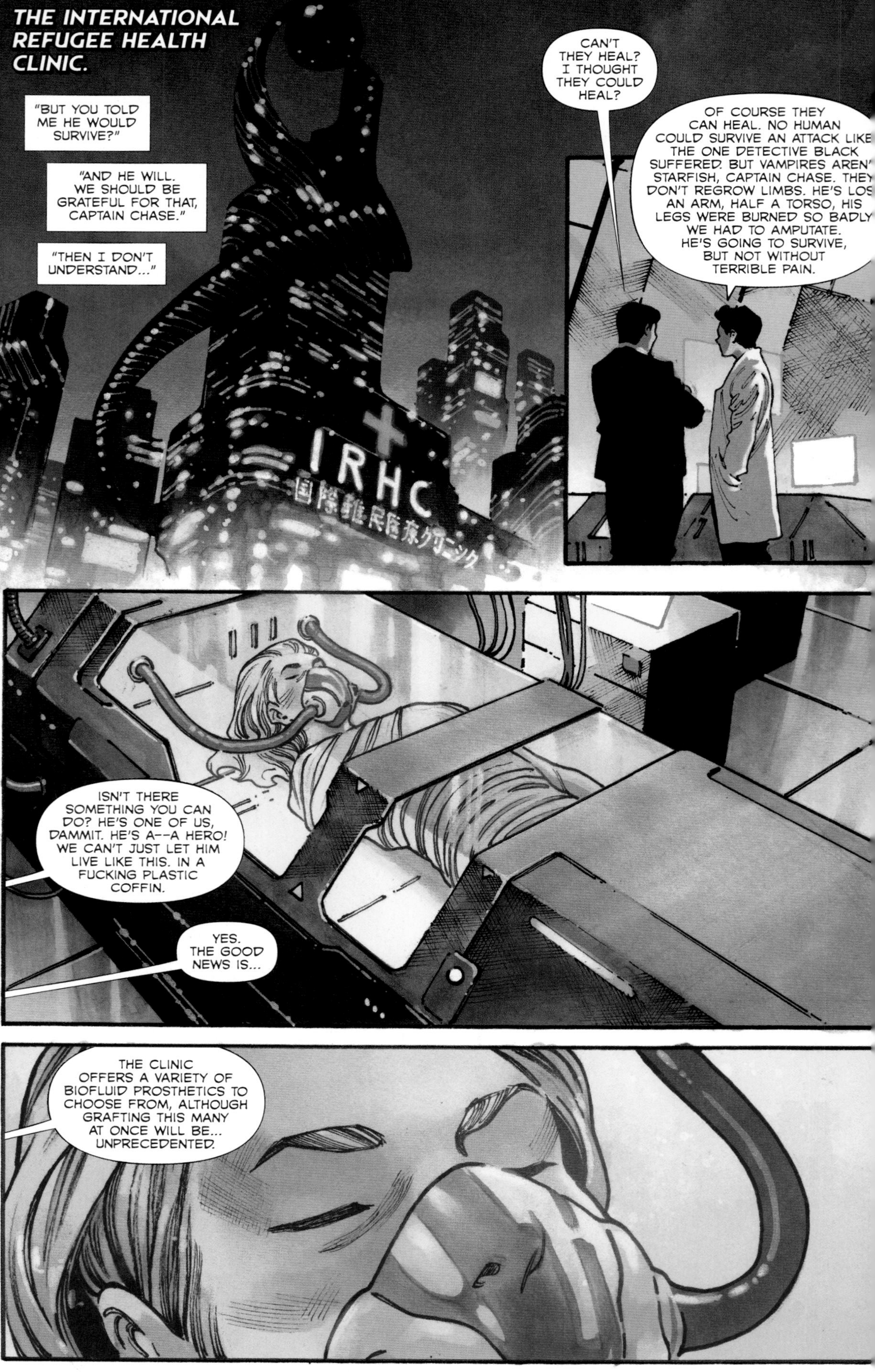
THE INTERNATIONAL REFUGEE HEALTH CLINIC.
"BUT YOU TOLD ME HE WOULD SURVIVE?"
"AND HE WILL. WE SHOULD BE GRATEFUL FOR THAT, CAPTAIN CHASE."
"THEN I DON'T UNDERSTAND..."
IRHC
国際難民医療クリニック
CAN'T THEY HEAL? I THOUGHT THEY COULD HEAL?
OF COURSE THEY CAN HEAL. NO HUMAN COULD SURVIVE AN ATTACK LIKE THE ONE DETECTIVE BLACK SUFFERED. BUT VAMPIRES AREN' STARFISH, CAPTAIN CHASE. THEY DON'T REGROW LIMBS. HE'S LOS AN ARM, HALF A TORSO, HIS LEGS WERE BURNED SO BADLY WE HAD TO AMPUTATE. HE'S GOING TO SURVIVE, BUT NOT WITHOUT TERRIBLE PAIN.
ISN'T THERE SOMETHING YOU CAN DO? HE'S ONE OF US, DAMMIT. HE'S A--A HERO! WE CAN'T JUST LET HIM LIVE LIKE THIS. IN A FUCKING PLASTIC COFFIN.
YES. THE GOOD NEWS IS...
THE CLINIC OFFERS A VARIETY OF BIOFLUID PROSTHETICS TO CHOOSE FROM, ALTHOUGH GRAFTING THIS MANY AT ONCE WILL BE... UNPRECEDENTED.

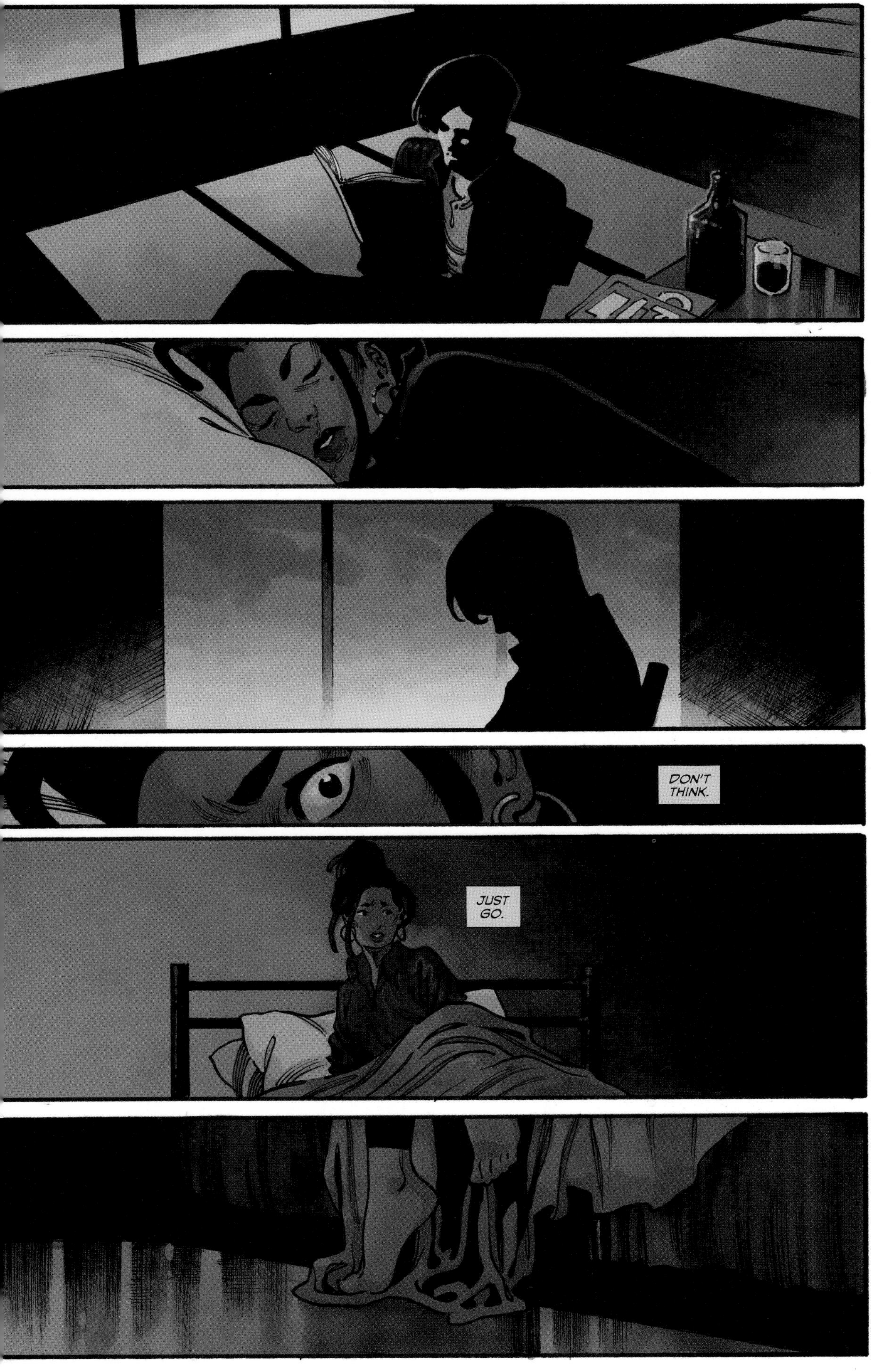
DON'T THINK.
JUST GO.

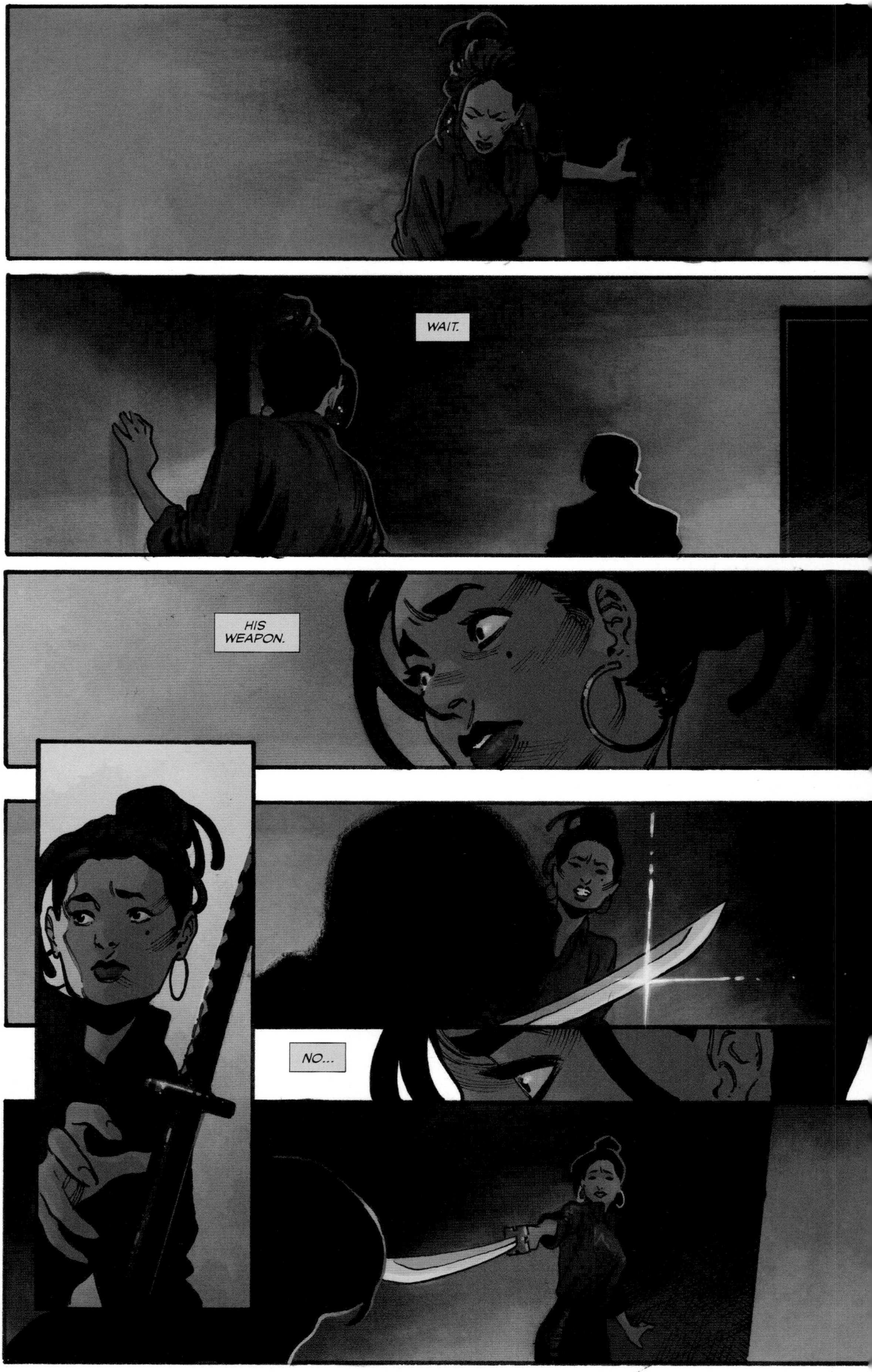
WAIT.
HIS WEAPON.
NO...

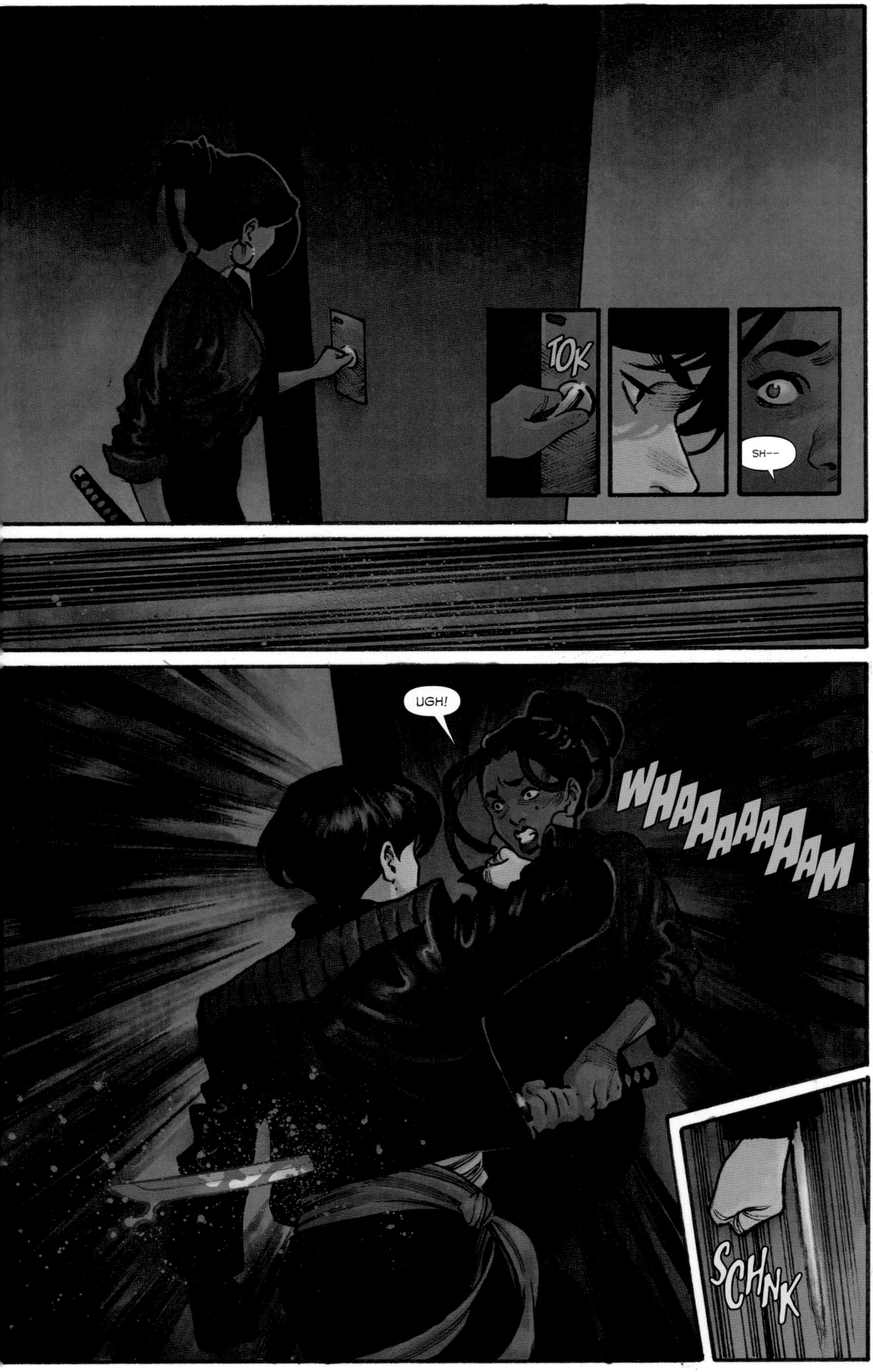
TOK
SH--
UGH!
WHAAAAAAAAM
SCHNK

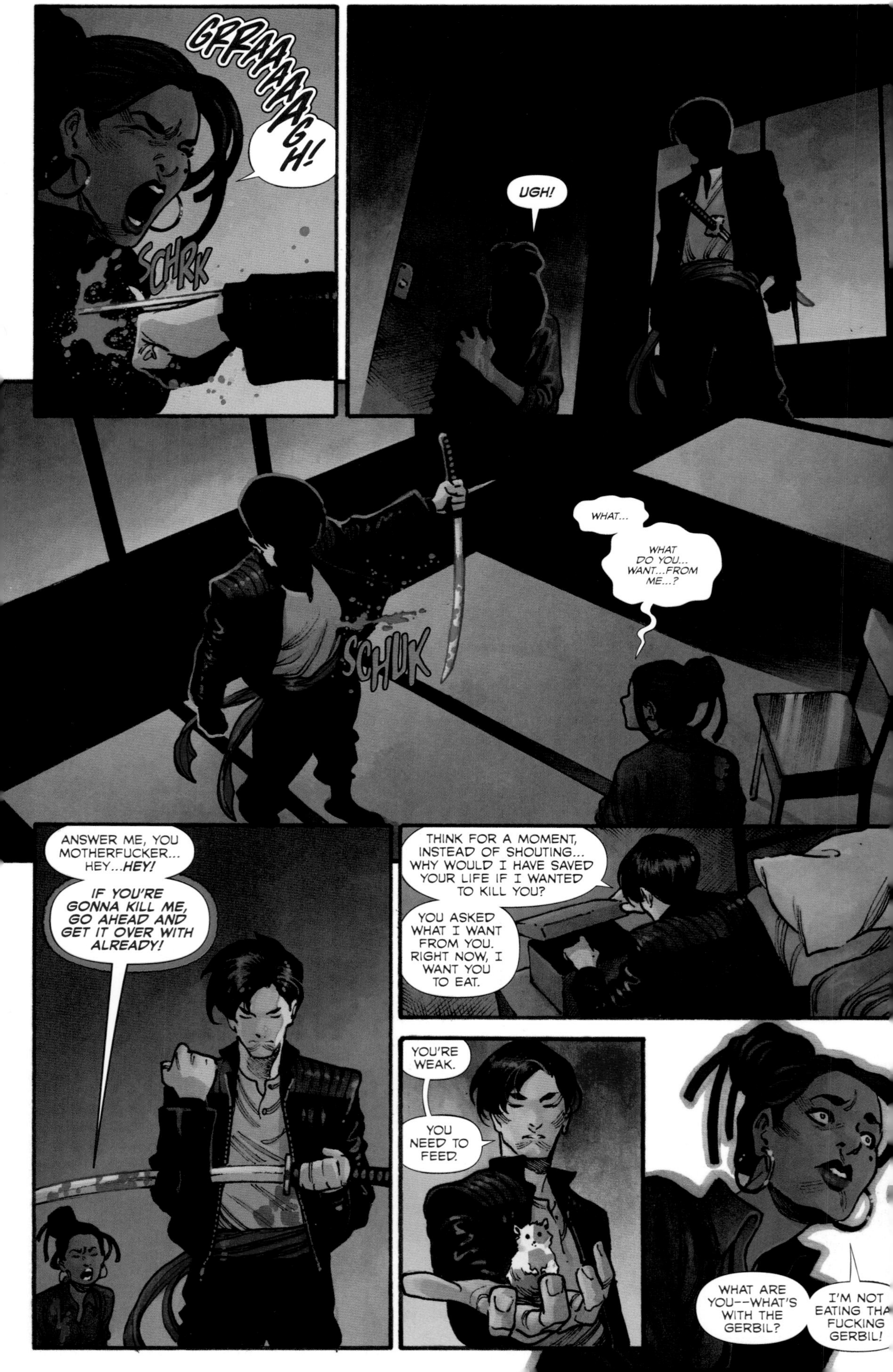
GRRAAAAAAAGH!
SCHRK
UGH!
WHAT...
WHAT DO YOU... WANT...FROM ME...?
SCHUK
ANSWER ME, YOU MOTHERFUCKER... HEY...HEY!
IF YOU'RE GONNA KILL ME, GO AHEAD AND GET IT OVER WITH ALREADY!
THINK FOR A MOMENT, INSTEAD OF SHOUTING... WHY WOULD I HAVE SAVED YOUR LIFE IF I WANTED TO KILL YOU?
YOU ASKED WHAT I WANT FROM YOU. RIGHT NOW, I WANT YOU TO EAT.
YOU'RE WEAK.
YOU NEED TO FEED.
WHAT ARE YOU--WHAT'S WITH THE GERBIL?
I'M NOT EATING THA FUCKING GERBIL!

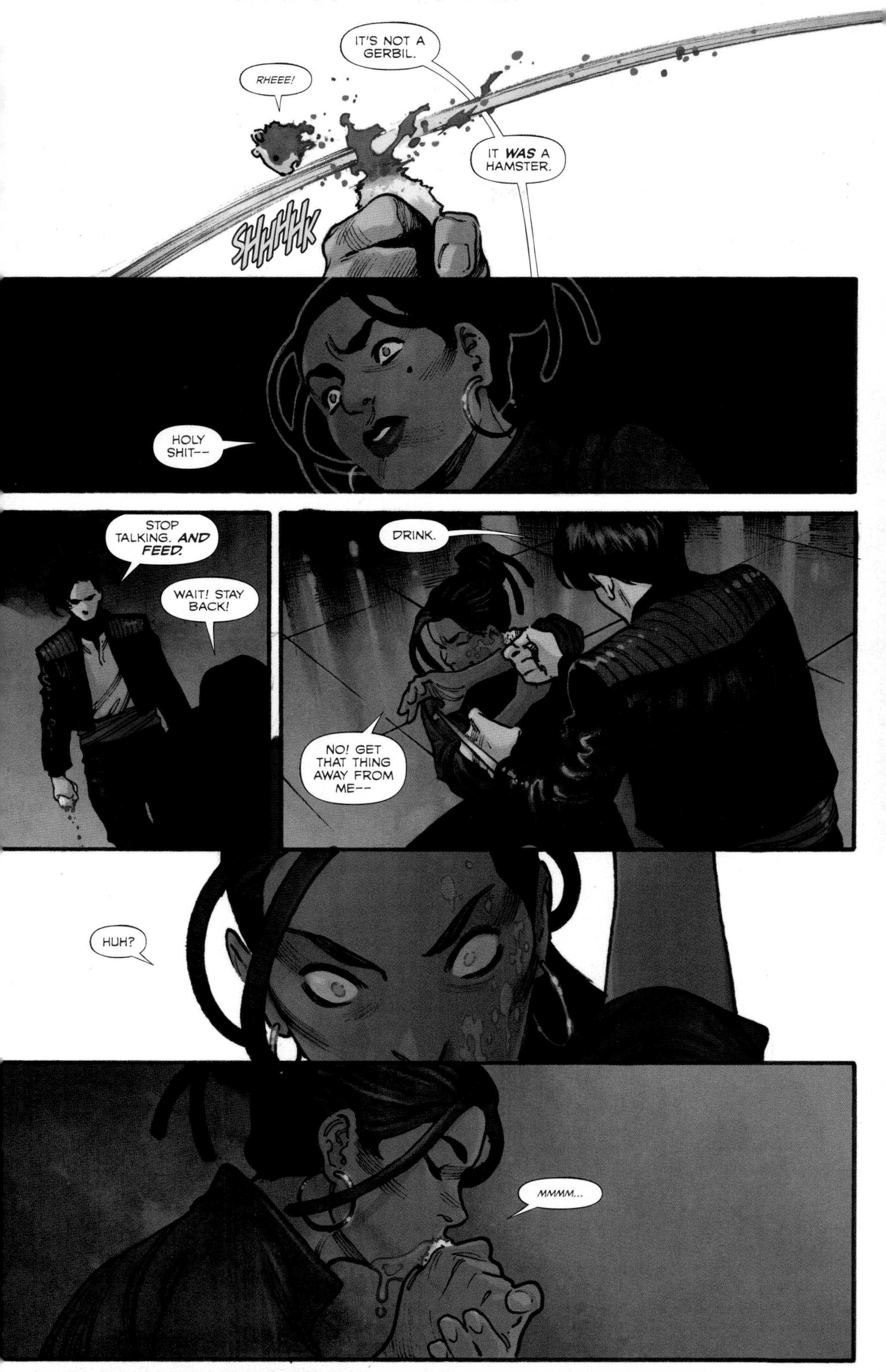
RHEEE!
IT'S NOT A GERBIL.
IT WAS A HAMSTER.
SHHHHK
HOLY SHIT--
STOP TALKING. AND FEED.
WAIT! STAY BACK!
DRINK.
NO! GET THAT THING AWAY FROM ME--
HUH?
MMMM...

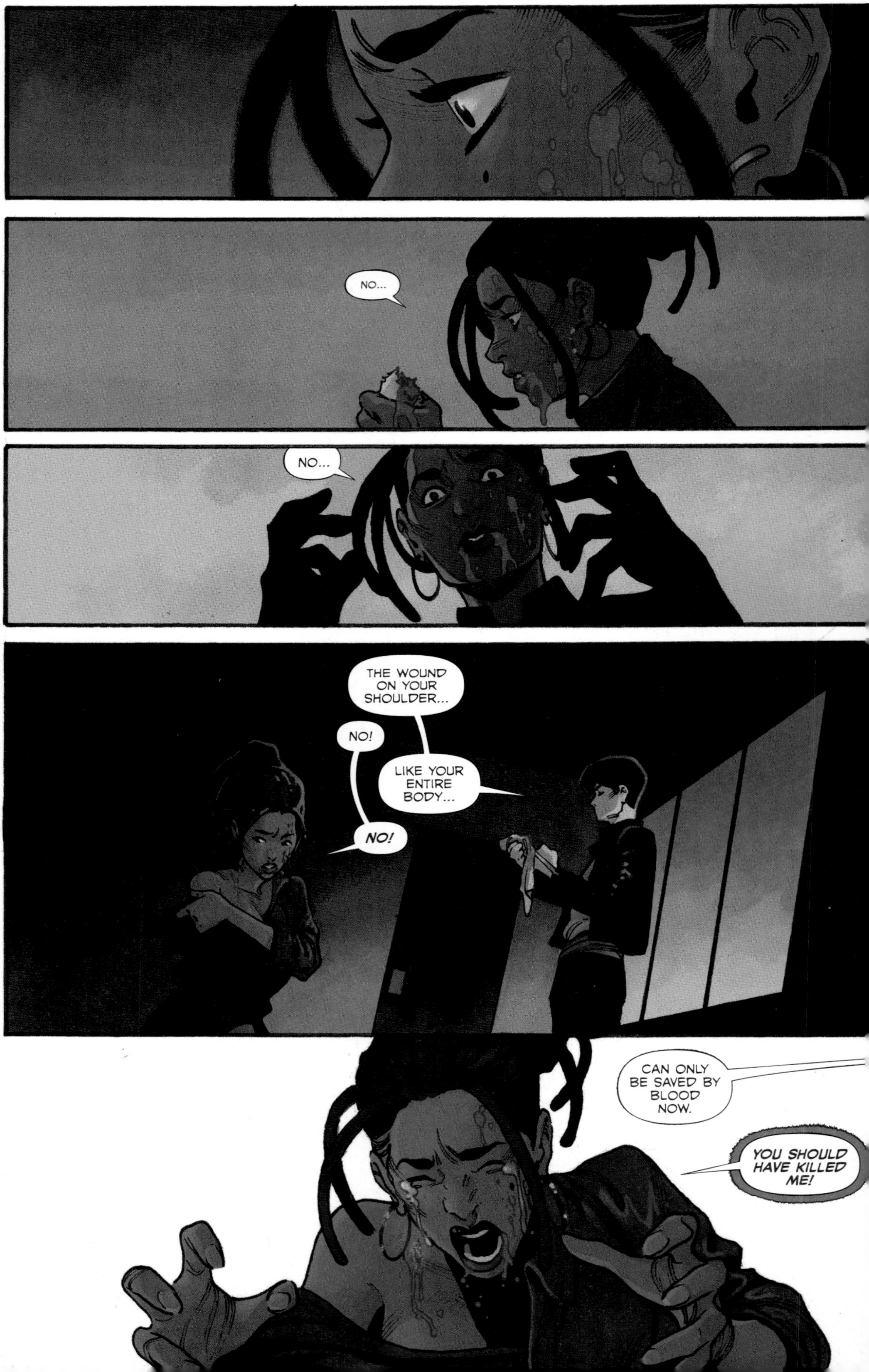
NO...
NO...
THE WOUND ON YOUR SHOULDER...
NO!
LIKE YOUR ENTIRE BODY...
NO!
CAN ONLY BE SAVED BY BLOOD NOW.
YOU SHOULD HAVE KILLED ME!

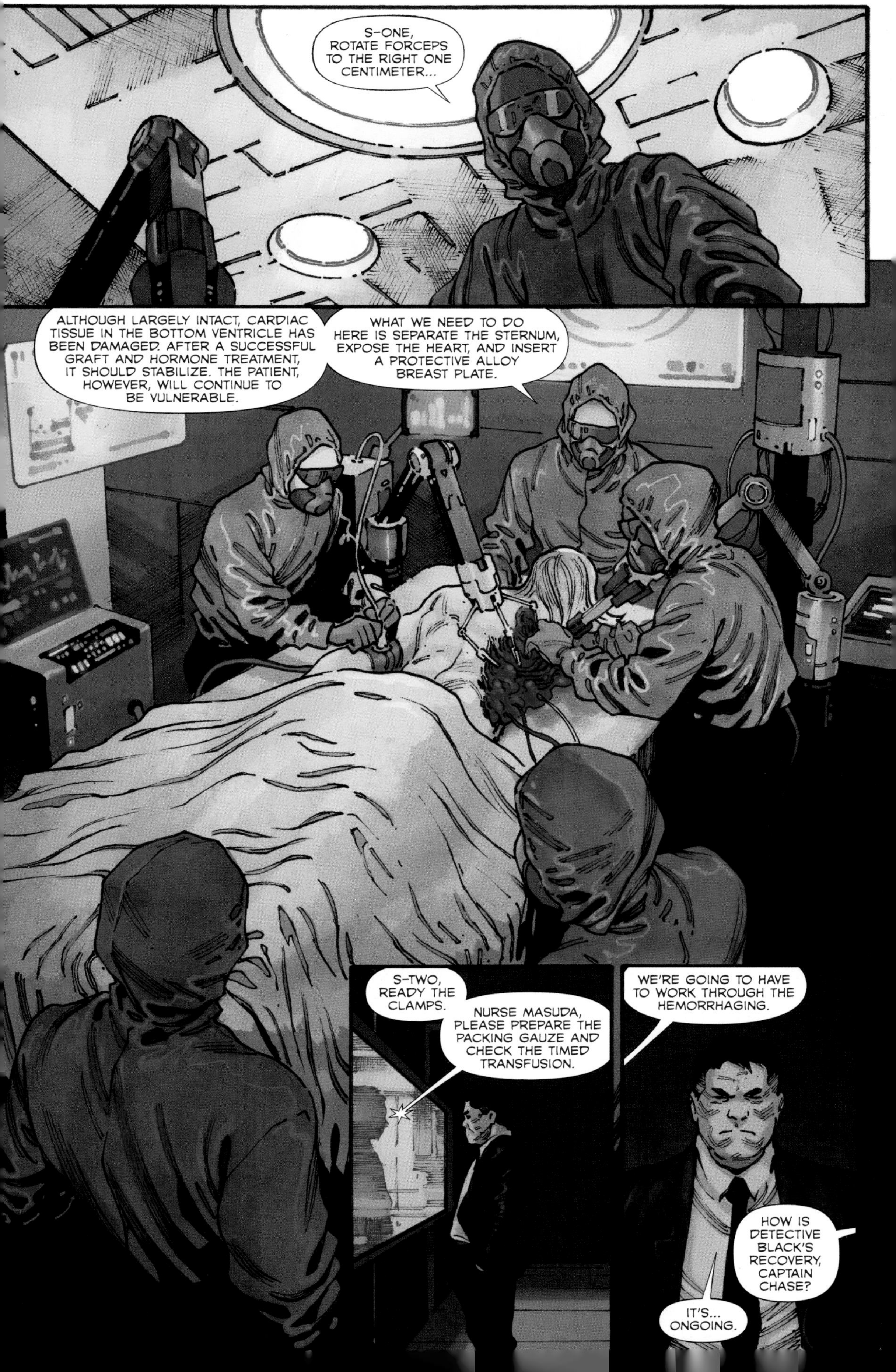
S-ONE, ROTATE FORCEPS TO THE RIGHT ONE CENTIMETER...
ALTHOUGH LARGELY INTACT, CARDIAC TISSUE IN THE BOTTOM VENTRICLE HAS BEEN DAMAGED. AFTER A SUCCESSFUL GRAFT AND HORMONE TREATMENT, IT SHOULD STABILIZE. THE PATIENT, HOWEVER, WILL CONTINUE TO BE VULNERABLE.
WHAT WE NEED TO DO HERE IS SEPARATE THE STERNUM, EXPOSE THE HEART, AND INSERT A PROTECTIVE ALLOY BREAST PLATE.
S-TWO, READY THE CLAMPS.
NURSE MASUDA, PLEASE PREPARE THE PACKING GAUZE AND CHECK THE TIMED TRANSFUSION.
WE'RE GOING TO HAVE TO WORK THROUGH THE HEMORRHAGING.
HOW IS DETECTIVE BLACK'S RECOVERY, CAPTAIN CHASE?
IT'S... ONGOING.

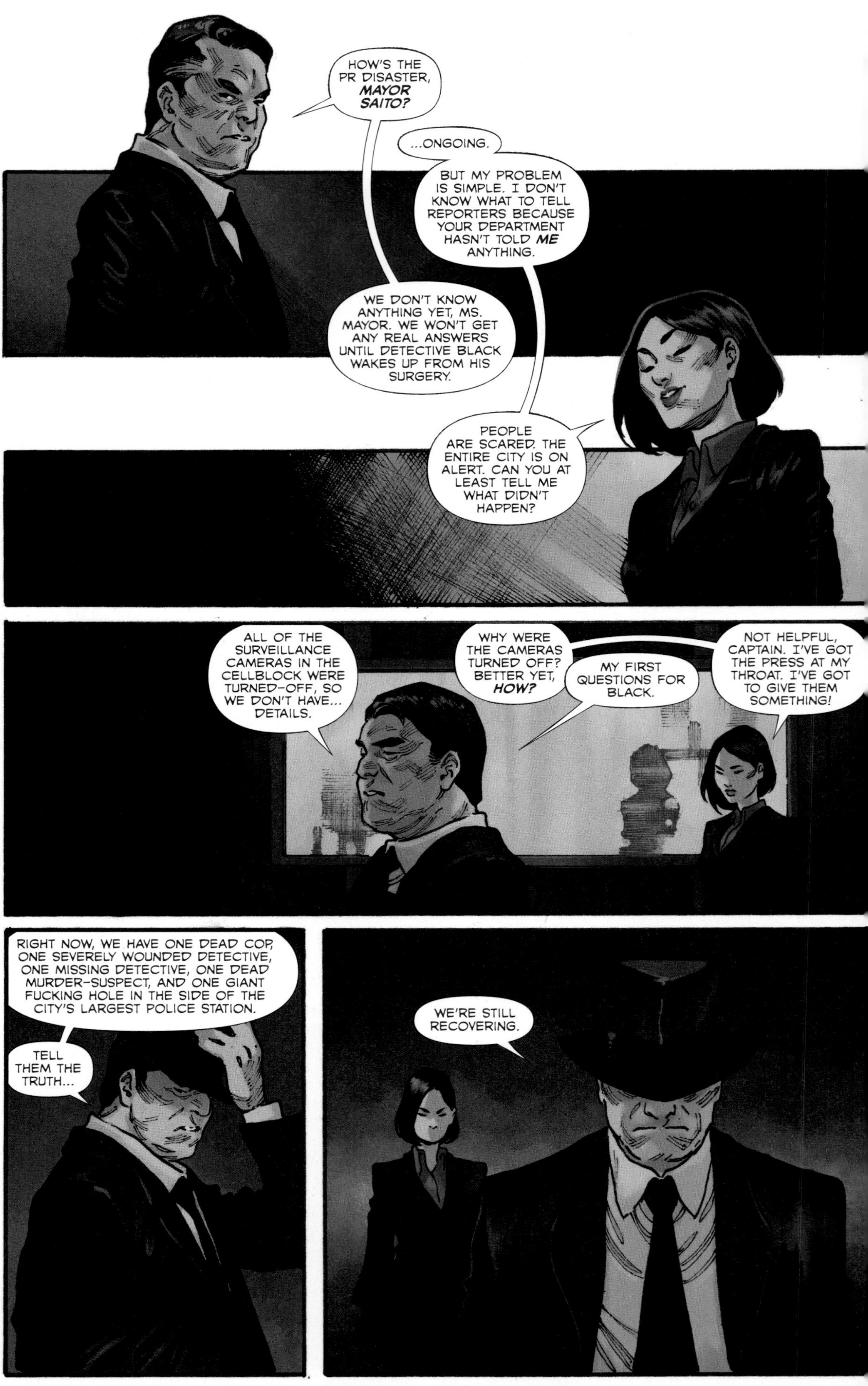
HOW'S THE PR DISASTER, **MAYOR SAITO?**
...ONGOING.
BUT MY PROBLEM IS SIMPLE. I DON'T KNOW WHAT TO TELL REPORTERS BECAUSE YOUR DEPARTMENT HASN'T TOLD **ME** ANYTHING.
WE DON'T KNOW ANYTHING YET, MS. MAYOR. WE WON'T GET ANY REAL ANSWERS UNTIL DETECTIVE BLACK WAKES UP FROM HIS SURGERY.
PEOPLE ARE SCARED. THE ENTIRE CITY IS ON ALERT. CAN YOU AT LEAST TELL ME WHAT DIDN'T HAPPEN?
ALL OF THE SURVEILLANCE CAMERAS IN THE CELLBLOCK WERE TURNED-OFF, SO WE DON'T HAVE... DETAILS.
WHY WERE THE CAMERAS TURNED OFF? BETTER YET, **HOW?**
MY FIRST QUESTIONS FOR BLACK.
NOT HELPFUL, CAPTAIN. I'VE GOT THE PRESS AT MY THROAT. I'VE GOT TO GIVE THEM SOMETHING!
RIGHT NOW, WE HAVE ONE DEAD COP, ONE SEVERELY WOUNDED DETECTIVE, ONE MISSING DETECTIVE, ONE DEAD MURDER-SUSPECT, AND ONE GIANT FUCKING HOLE IN THE SIDE OF THE CITY'S LARGEST POLICE STATION.
TELL THEM THE TRUTH...
WE'RE STILL RECOVERING.

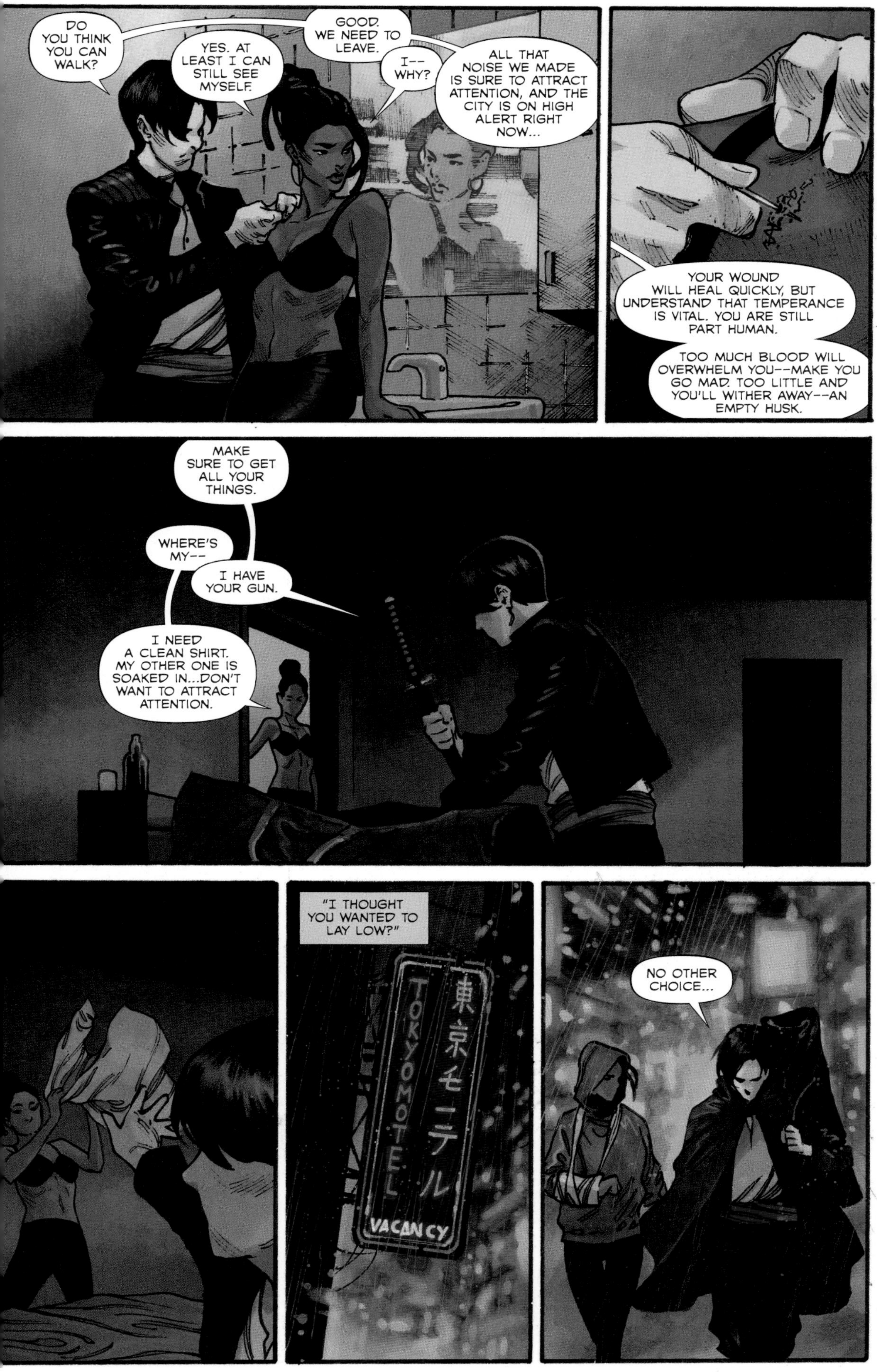
DO YOU THINK YOU CAN WALK?
YES. AT LEAST I CAN STILL SEE MYSELF.
GOOD. WE NEED TO LEAVE.
I-- WHY?
ALL THAT NOISE WE MADE IS SURE TO ATTRACT ATTENTION, AND THE CITY IS ON HIGH ALERT RIGHT NOW...
YOUR WOUND WILL HEAL QUICKLY, BUT UNDERSTAND THAT TEMPERANCE IS VITAL. YOU ARE STILL PART HUMAN.
TOO MUCH BLOOD WILL OVERWHELM YOU--MAKE YOU GO MAD. TOO LITTLE AND YOU'LL WITHER AWAY--AN EMPTY HUSK.
MAKE SURE TO GET ALL YOUR THINGS.
WHERE'S MY--
I HAVE YOUR GUN.
I NEED A CLEAN SHIRT. MY OTHER ONE IS SOAKED IN...DON'T WANT TO ATTRACT ATTENTION.
"I THOUGHT YOU WANTED TO LAY LOW?"
TOKYO MOTEL
東京モーテル
VACANCY
NO OTHER CHOICE...

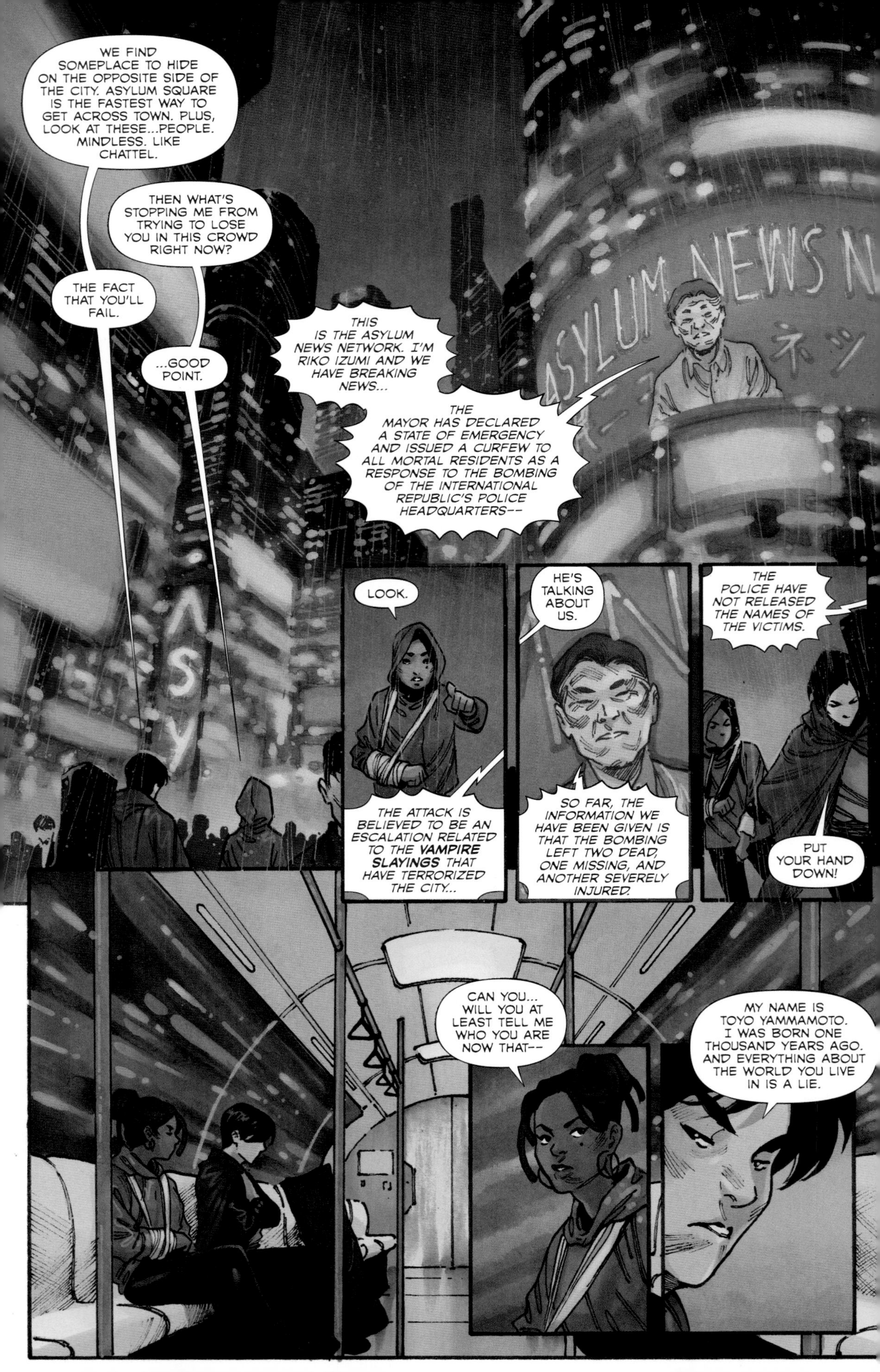

WE FIND SOMEPLACE TO HIDE ON THE OPPOSITE SIDE OF THE CITY. ASYLUM SQUARE IS THE FASTEST WAY TO GET ACROSS TOWN. PLUS, LOOK AT THESE...PEOPLE. MINDLESS. LIKE CHATTEL.
THEN WHAT'S STOPPING ME FROM TRYING TO LOSE YOU IN THIS CROWD RIGHT NOW?
THE FACT THAT YOU'LL FAIL.
...GOOD POINT.
ASYLUM NEWS N
THIS IS THE ASYLUM NEWS NETWORK. I'M RIKO IZUMI AND WE HAVE BREAKING NEWS...
THE MAYOR HAS DECLARED A STATE OF EMERGENCY AND ISSUED A CURFEW TO ALL MORTAL RESIDENTS AS A RESPONSE TO THE BOMBING OF THE INTERNATIONAL REPUBLIC'S POLICE HEADQUARTERS--
ASY
LOOK.
THE ATTACK IS BELIEVED TO BE AN ESCALATION RELATED TO THE **VAMPIRE SLAYINGS** THAT HAVE TERRORIZED THE CITY...
HE'S TALKING ABOUT US.
SO FAR, THE INFORMATION WE HAVE BEEN GIVEN IS THAT THE BOMBING LEFT TWO DEAD, ONE MISSING, AND ANOTHER SEVERELY INJURED.
THE POLICE HAVE NOT RELEASED THE NAMES OF THE VICTIMS.
PUT YOUR HAND DOWN!
CAN YOU... WILL YOU AT LEAST TELL ME WHO YOU ARE NOW THAT--
MY NAME IS TOYO YAMMAMOTO. I WAS BORN ONE THOUSAND YEARS AGO. AND EVERYTHING ABOUT THE WORLD YOU LIVE IN IS A LIE.

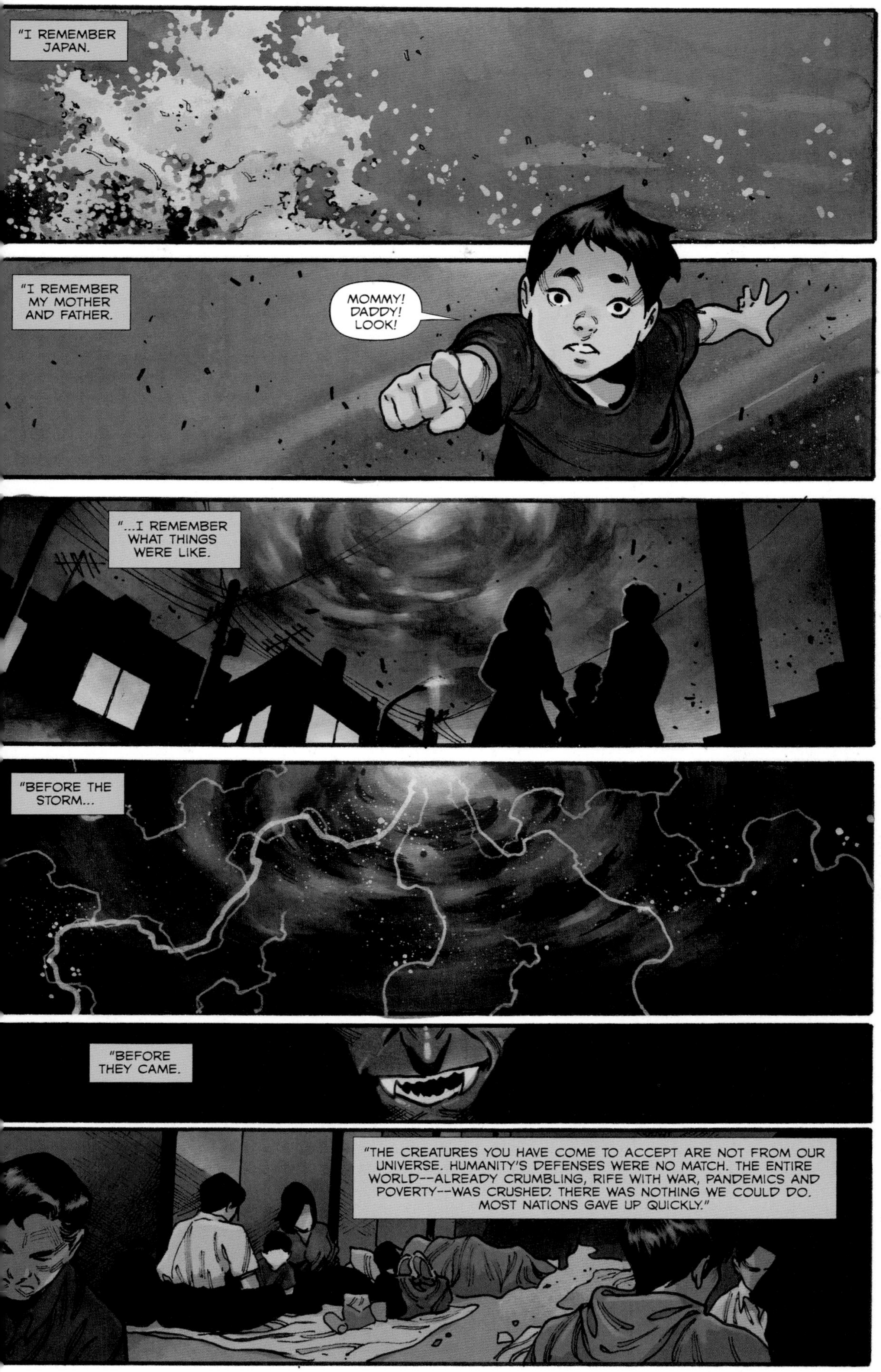
"I REMEMBER JAPAN.
"I REMEMBER MY MOTHER AND FATHER.
MOMMY! DADDY! LOOK!
"...I REMEMBER WHAT THINGS WERE LIKE.
"BEFORE THE STORM...
"BEFORE THEY CAME.
"THE CREATURES YOU HAVE COME TO ACCEPT ARE NOT FROM OUR UNIVERSE. HUMANITY'S DEFENSES WERE NO MATCH. THE ENTIRE WORLD--ALREADY CRUMBLING, RIFE WITH WAR, PANDEMICS AND POVERTY--WAS CRUSHED. THERE WAS NOTHING WE COULD DO. MOST NATIONS GAVE UP QUICKLY."

"OUR NEW IMMORTAL OVERLORDS FORCED THE SURVIVING HUMANS TO BUILD ASYLUM. THEY SAID IT WOULD BE A REFUGE AGAINST THE WORSENING CLIMATE, THE ENDLESS WILDFIRES, THE CEASELESS EPIDEMICS AND HOMELESSNESS. BUT WE ALL KNEW WHAT IT REALLY WAS...

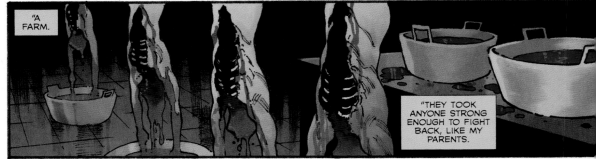

"A FARM.

"THEY TOOK ANYONE STRONG ENOUGH TO FIGHT BACK, LIKE MY PARENTS.

"THEY USED THE WEAK AND YOUNG FOR LABOR.

"NEW EMPIRE'S TAKE A LOT OF CONSTRUCTION.

UGH!

HERE. LET ME HELP YOU.

"THAT'S HOW I MET MY SALVATION, MASAMITSU TSAKUSA—ONE OF THE LAST REMAINING LEADERS OF THE YAKUZA. CONVENTIONAL ARMIES ALL AROUND THE WORLD WERE DESTROYED...

"THE ONLY FORCES THAT WERE ORGANIZED ENOUGH TO FIGHT BACK WERE...UNDERGROUND. GANGS, CRIMINAL SYNDICATES—EVEN TERRORIST CELLS. IT SEEMS THE ONLY THING TERRIFYING ENOUGH TO FACE DOWN A MONSTER IS ANOTHER MONSTER..."

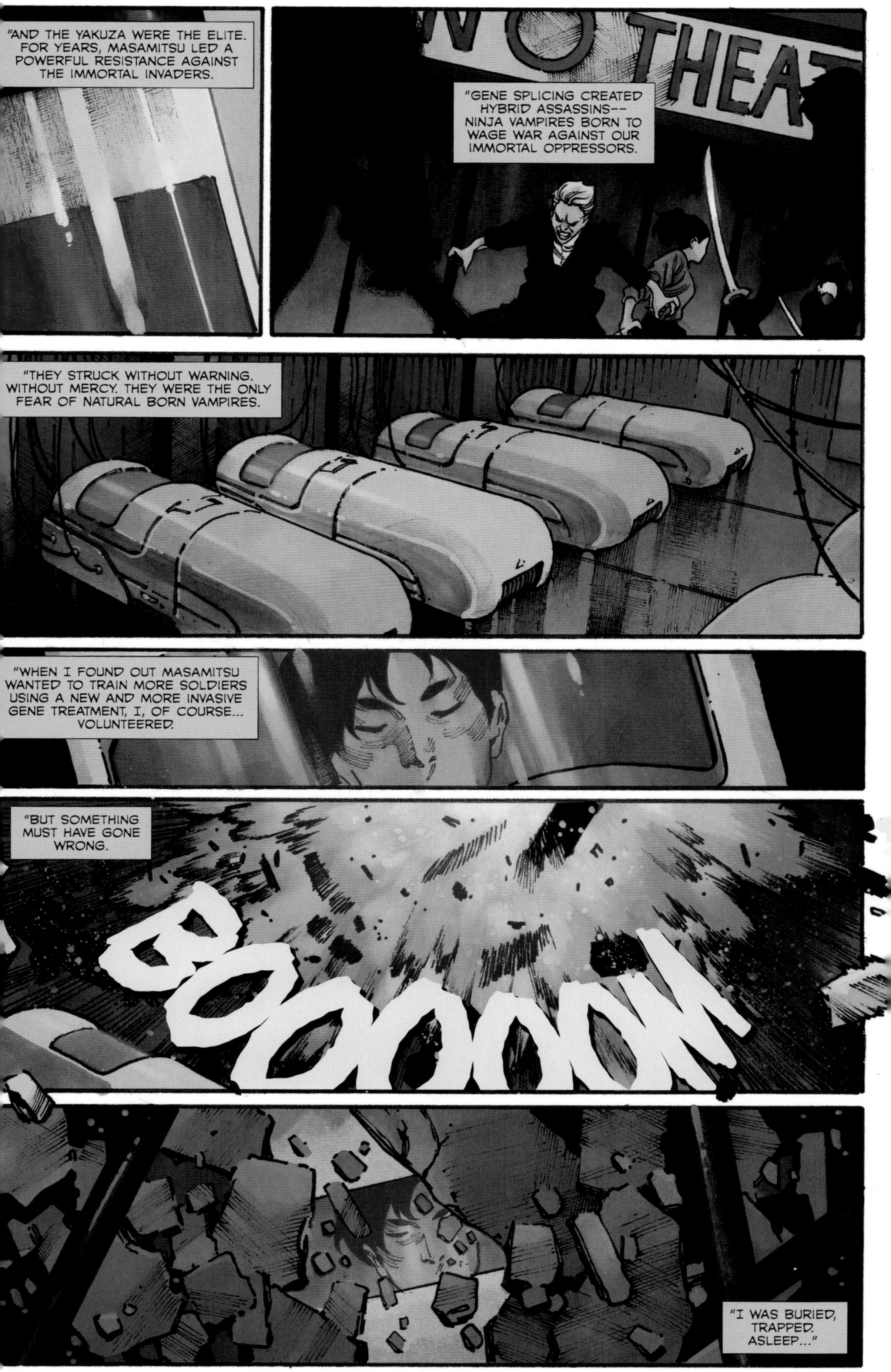
"AND THE YAKUZA WERE THE ELITE. FOR YEARS, MASAMITSU LED A POWERFUL RESISTANCE AGAINST THE IMMORTAL INVADERS.
"GENE SPLICING CREATED HYBRID ASSASSINS--NINJA VAMPIRES BORN TO WAGE WAR AGAINST OUR IMMORTAL OPPRESSORS.
"THEY STRUCK WITHOUT WARNING. WITHOUT MERCY. THEY WERE THE ONLY FEAR OF NATURAL BORN VAMPIRES.
"WHEN I FOUND OUT MASAMITSU WANTED TO TRAIN MORE SOLDIERS USING A NEW AND MORE INVASIVE GENE TREATMENT, I, OF COURSE... VOLUNTEERED.
"BUT SOMETHING MUST HAVE GONE WRONG.
BOOOOOM
"I WAS BURIED, TRAPPED. ASLEEP..."

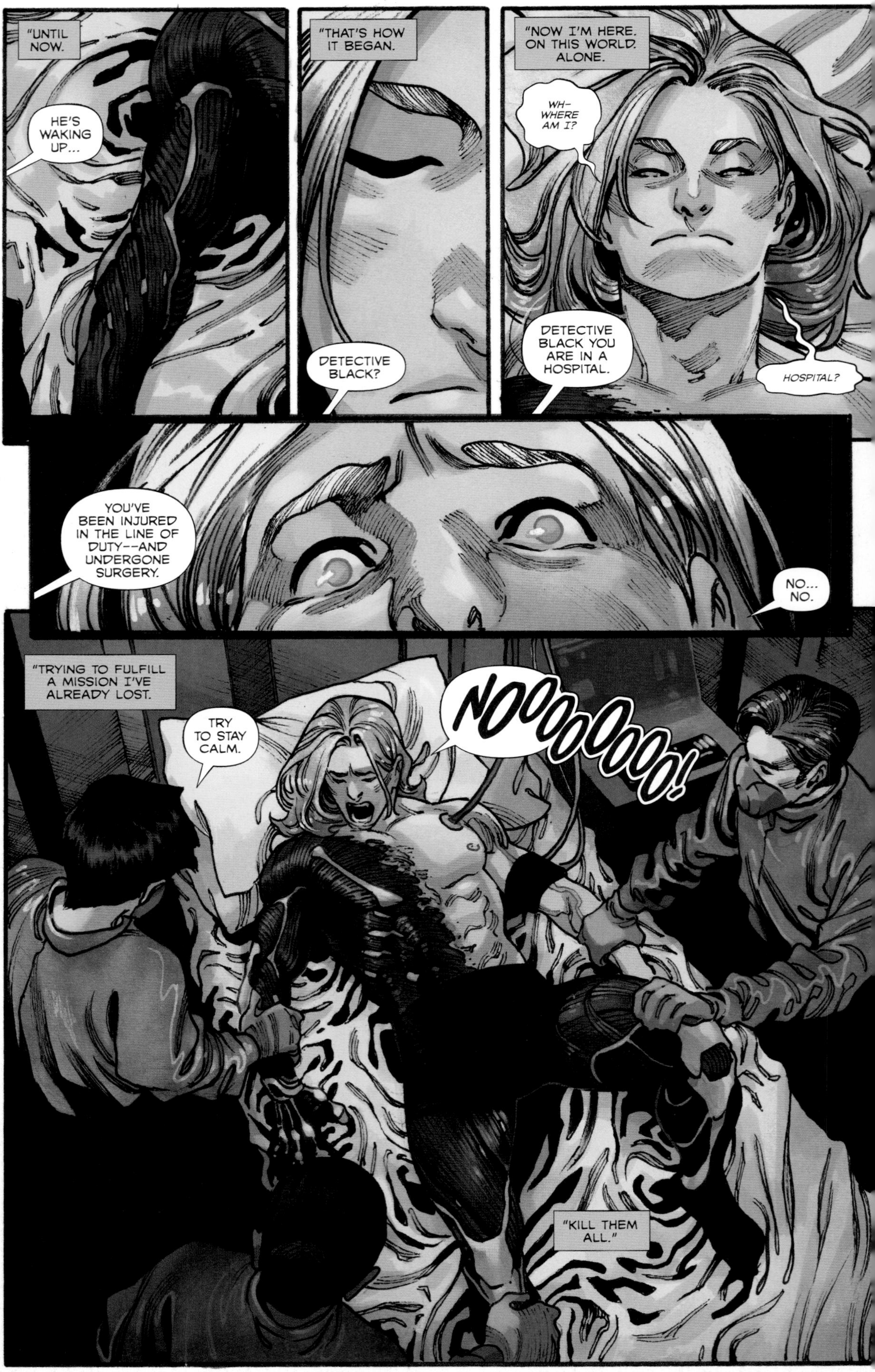
"UNTIL NOW.
HE'S WAKING UP...
"THAT'S HOW IT BEGAN.
DETECTIVE BLACK?
"NOW I'M HERE. ON THIS WORLD. ALONE.
WH- WHERE AM I?
DETECTIVE BLACK YOU ARE IN A HOSPITAL.
HOSPITAL?
YOU'VE BEEN INJURED IN THE LINE OF DUTY--AND UNDERGONE SURGERY.
NO... NO.
"TRYING TO FULFILL A MISSION I'VE ALREADY LOST.
TRY TO STAY CALM.
NOOOOOOOOO!
"KILL THEM ALL."

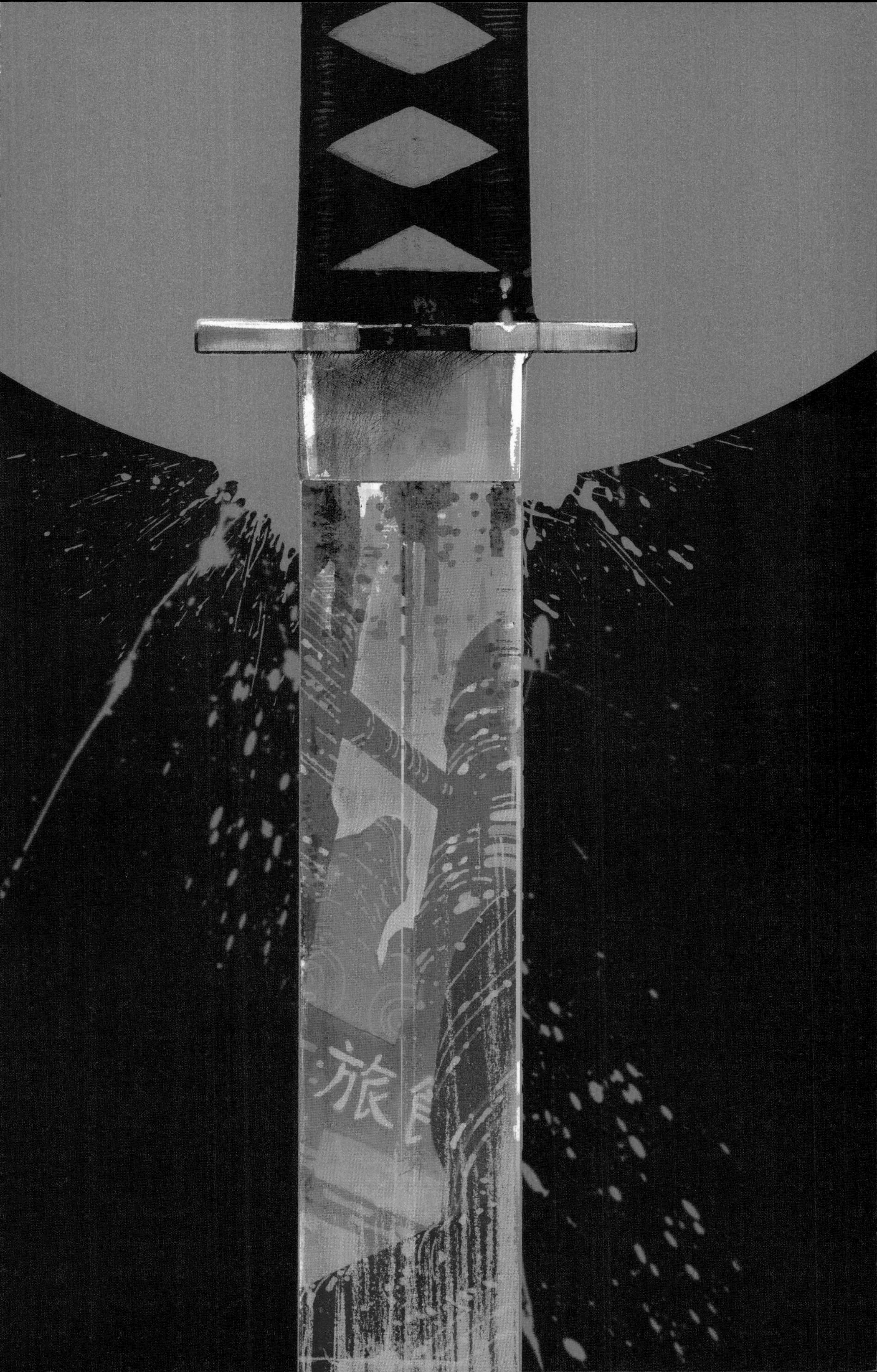
旅

THREE

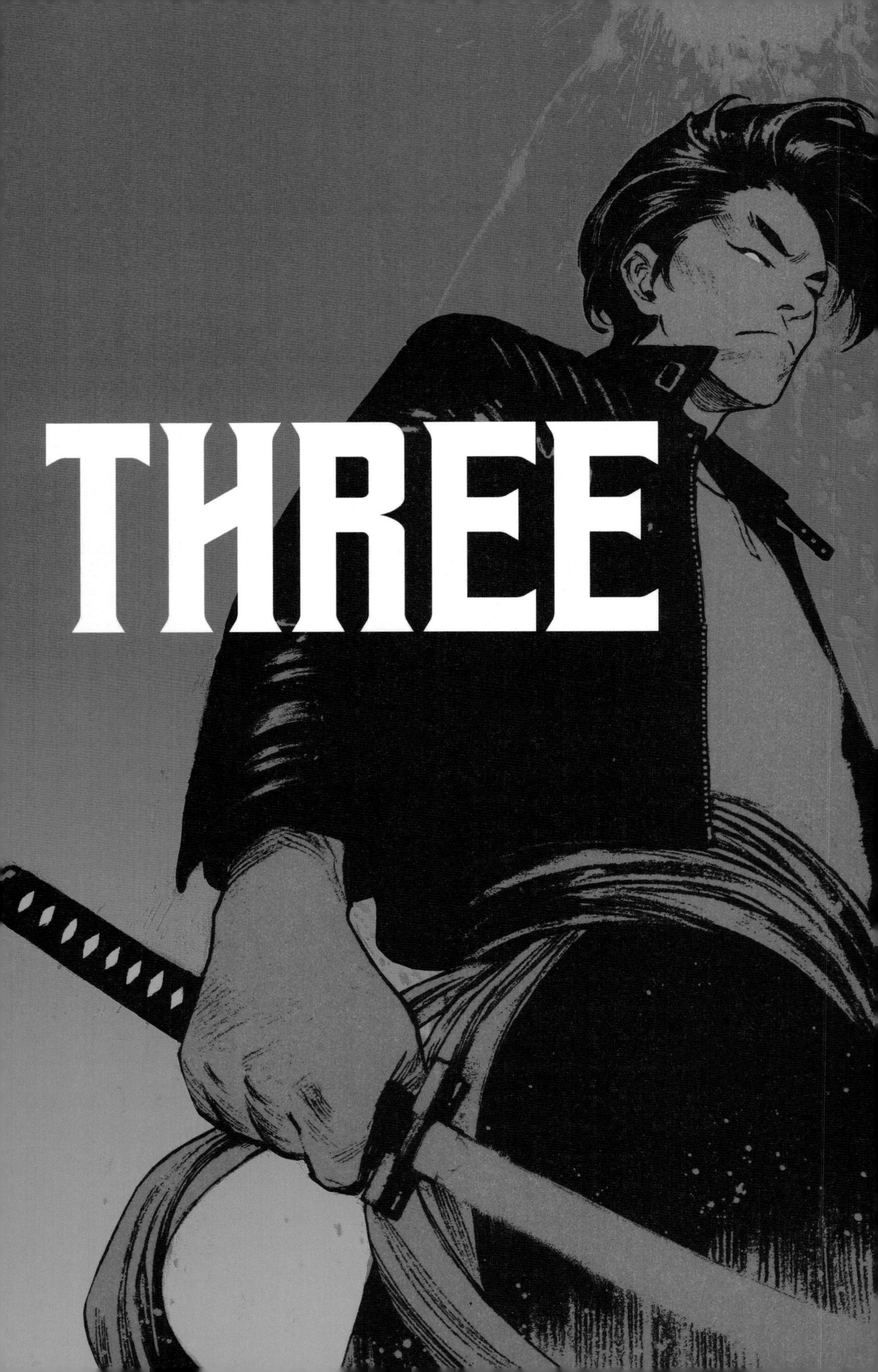

ASYLUM (A.K.A. THE INTERNATIONAL REPUBLIC OF DISPLACED PEOPLES).

THREE MONTHS LATER.

I AM A HOSTAGE.

AND THERE ARE THINGS THAT YOU DO IN A SITUATION LIKE THIS...

WHATEVER YOUR CAPTOR SAYS, ESPECIALLY IF IT HELPS PUT YOU AT LESS RISK. ESTABLISH AND EMPHASIZE TO YOUR CAPTOR THAT YOU ARE A PERSON...

WHICH, RIGHT NOW--FOR ME... NOT EXACTLY TRUE.

LOOKS LIKE OUR BOY REALLY ISN'T AFRAID OF YOU.

EVEN IF YOUR CAPTOR IS FIGHTING A MADE-UP HOLY WAR AGAINST HIS OWN KIND.

EVERYTHING IS LOOKING GOOD. NO MOVEMENT OUTSIDE THE OFFICE. NO CHATTER ON ANY OF THE OTHER LINES. NO COPS.

DO YOU COPY THAT?

I COPY YOU, HARPER...

THERE ARE OTHER THINGS, TOO...DON'T BLAME YOURSELF. AND DON'T ALLOW YOURSELF TO GET BLAMED.

HAVE YOU FOUND A WAY TO DISABLE THEIR VEHICLE'S SECURITY SYSTEM YET?

WORKING ON IT...

I'M A COP. NOT A HACKER.

BE... NON-HOSTILE.

PWOOM

BUT I'LL GET IT. JUST GIVE ME SOME TIME.

COPY THAT. MOVING INTO POSITION.

AND WHEN YOU CAN...

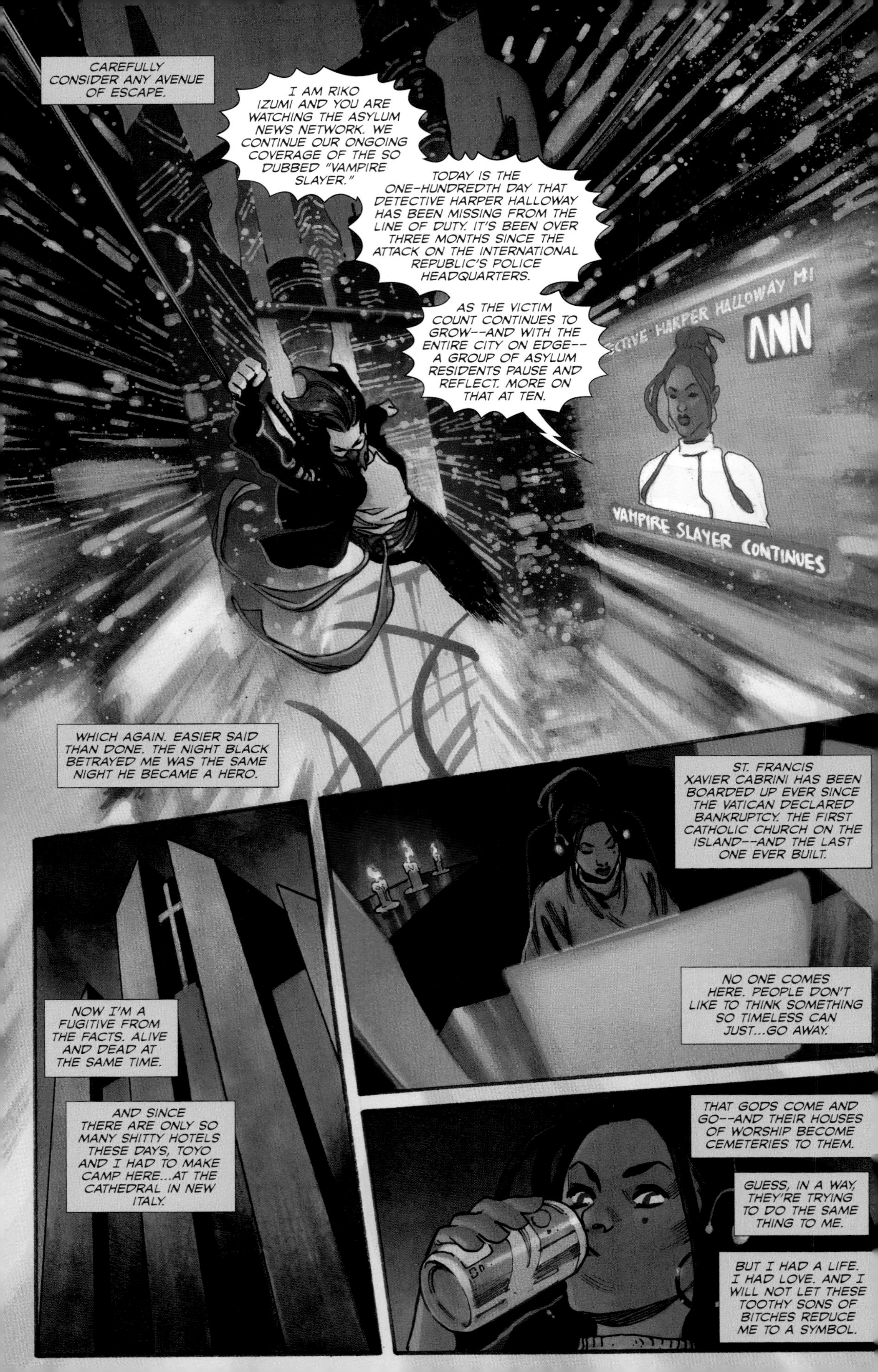
CAREFULLY CONSIDER ANY AVENUE OF ESCAPE.
I AM RIKO IZUMI AND YOU ARE WATCHING THE ASYLUM NEWS NETWORK. WE CONTINUE OUR ONGOING COVERAGE OF THE SO DUBBED "VAMPIRE SLAYER."
TODAY IS THE ONE-HUNDREDTH DAY THAT DETECTIVE HARPER HALLOWAY HAS BEEN MISSING FROM THE LINE OF DUTY. IT'S BEEN OVER THREE MONTHS SINCE THE ATTACK ON THE INTERNATIONAL REPUBLIC'S POLICE HEADQUARTERS.
AS THE VICTIM COUNT CONTINUES TO GROW--AND WITH THE ENTIRE CITY ON EDGE--A GROUP OF ASYLUM RESIDENTS PAUSE AND REFLECT. MORE ON THAT AT TEN.
ECTIVE HARPER HALLOWAY MI
ANN
VAMPIRE SLAYER CONTINUES
WHICH AGAIN. EASIER SAID THAN DONE. THE NIGHT BLACK BETRAYED ME WAS THE SAME NIGHT HE BECAME A HERO.
NOW I'M A FUGITIVE FROM THE FACTS. ALIVE AND DEAD AT THE SAME TIME.
AND SINCE THERE ARE ONLY SO MANY SHITTY HOTELS THESE DAYS, TOYO AND I HAD TO MAKE CAMP HERE...AT THE CATHEDRAL IN NEW ITALY.
ST. FRANCIS XAVIER CABRINI HAS BEEN BOARDED UP EVER SINCE THE VATICAN DECLARED BANKRUPTCY. THE FIRST CATHOLIC CHURCH ON THE ISLAND--AND THE LAST ONE EVER BUILT.
NO ONE COMES HERE. PEOPLE DON'T LIKE TO THINK SOMETHING SO TIMELESS CAN JUST...GO AWAY.
THAT GODS COME AND GO--AND THEIR HOUSES OF WORSHIP BECOME CEMETERIES TO THEM.
GUESS, IN A WAY, THEY'RE TRYING TO DO THE SAME THING TO ME.
BUT I HAD A LIFE. I HAD LOVE. AND I WILL NOT LET THESE TOOTHY SONS OF BITCHES REDUCE ME TO A SYMBOL.

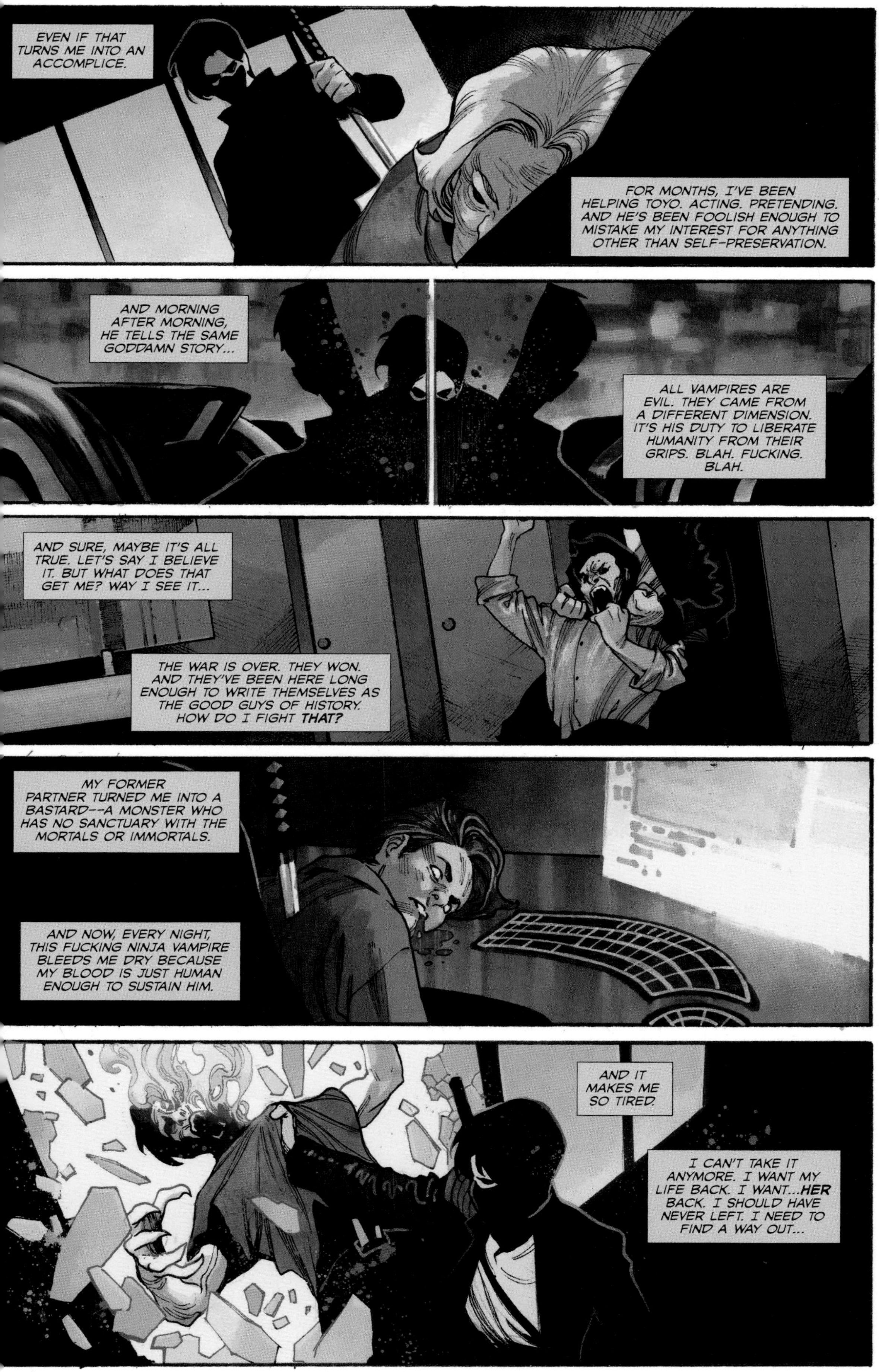
EVEN IF THAT TURNS ME INTO AN ACCOMPLICE.
FOR MONTHS, I'VE BEEN HELPING TOYO. ACTING. PRETENDING. AND HE'S BEEN FOOLISH ENOUGH TO MISTAKE MY INTEREST FOR ANYTHING OTHER THAN SELF-PRESERVATION.
AND MORNING AFTER MORNING, HE TELLS THE SAME GODDAMN STORY...
ALL VAMPIRES ARE EVIL. THEY CAME FROM A DIFFERENT DIMENSION. IT'S HIS DUTY TO LIBERATE HUMANITY FROM THEIR GRIPS. BLAH. FUCKING. BLAH.
AND SURE, MAYBE IT'S ALL TRUE. LET'S SAY I BELIEVE IT. BUT WHAT DOES THAT GET ME? WAY I SEE IT...
THE WAR IS OVER. THEY WON. AND THEY'VE BEEN HERE LONG ENOUGH TO WRITE THEMSELVES AS THE GOOD GUYS OF HISTORY. HOW DO I FIGHT **THAT?**
MY FORMER PARTNER TURNED ME INTO A BASTARD--A MONSTER WHO HAS NO SANCTUARY WITH THE MORTALS OR IMMORTALS.
AND NOW, EVERY NIGHT, THIS FUCKING NINJA VAMPIRE BLEEDS ME DRY BECAUSE MY BLOOD IS JUST HUMAN ENOUGH TO SUSTAIN HIM.
AND IT MAKES ME SO TIRED.
I CAN'T TAKE IT ANYMORE. I WANT MY LIFE BACK. I WANT...**HER** BACK. I SHOULD HAVE NEVER LEFT. I NEED TO FIND A WAY OUT...

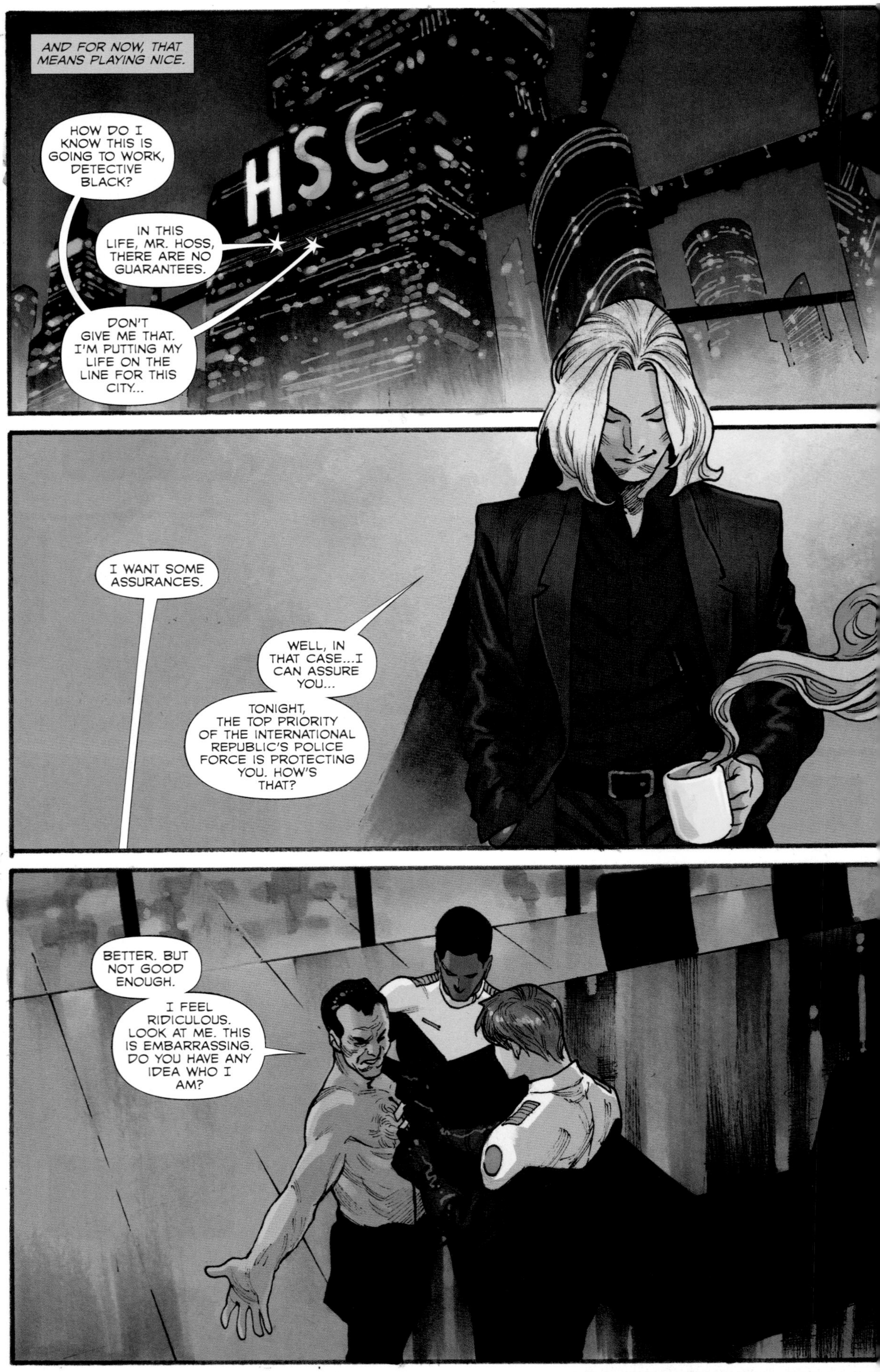
AND FOR NOW, THAT MEANS PLAYING NICE.
HOW DO I KNOW THIS IS GOING TO WORK, DETECTIVE BLACK?
IN THIS LIFE, MR. HOSS, THERE ARE NO GUARANTEES.
DON'T GIVE ME THAT. I'M PUTTING MY LIFE ON THE LINE FOR THIS CITY...
HSC
I WANT SOME ASSURANCES.
WELL, IN THAT CASE...I CAN ASSURE YOU...
TONIGHT, THE TOP PRIORITY OF THE INTERNATIONAL REPUBLIC'S POLICE FORCE IS PROTECTING YOU. HOW'S THAT?
BETTER. BUT NOT GOOD ENOUGH.
I FEEL RIDICULOUS. LOOK AT ME. THIS IS EMBARRASSING. DO YOU HAVE ANY IDEA WHO I AM?

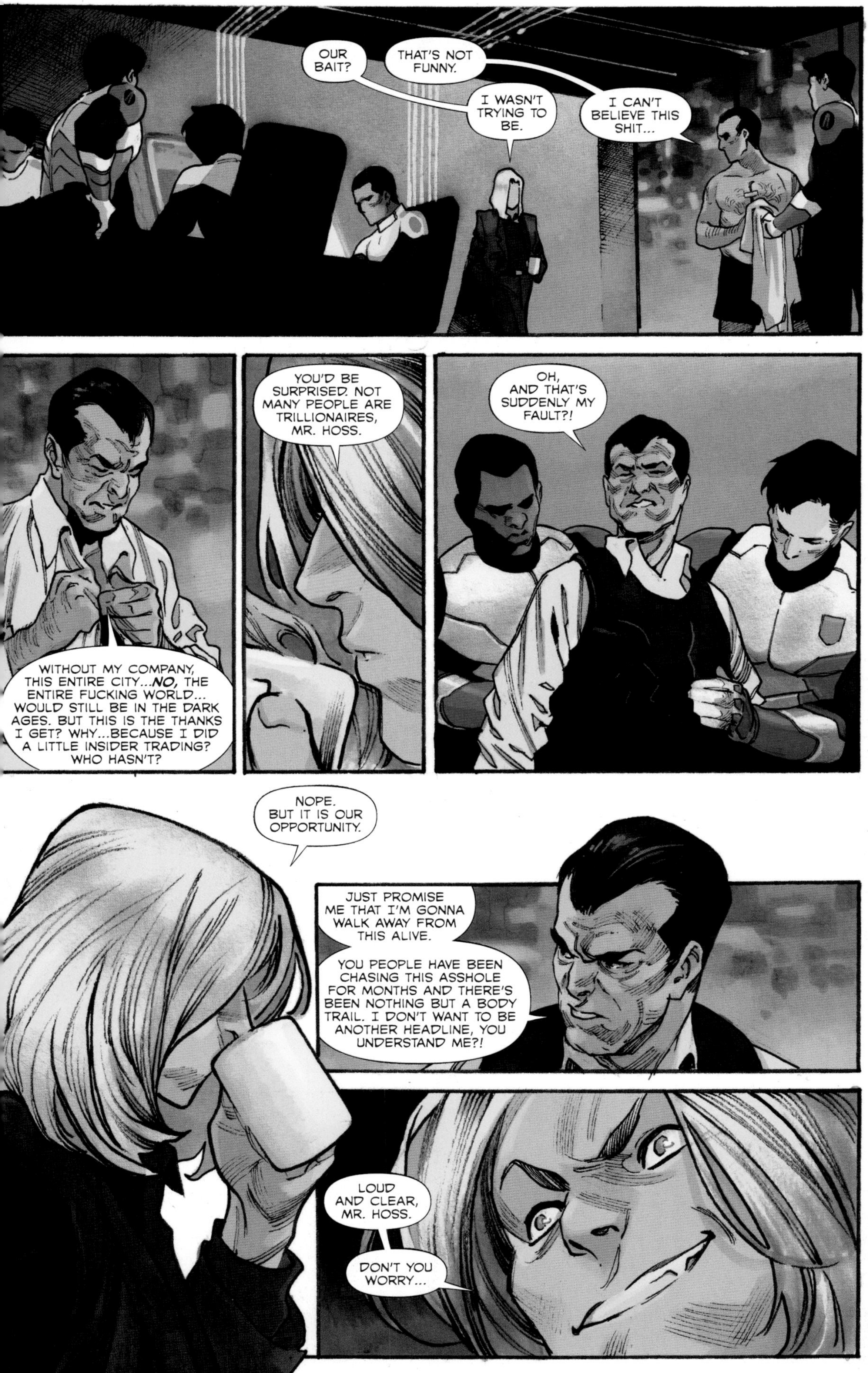
OUR BAIT?
THAT'S NOT FUNNY.
I WASN'T TRYING TO BE.
I CAN'T BELIEVE THIS SHIT...
WITHOUT MY COMPANY, THIS ENTIRE CITY...NO, THE ENTIRE FUCKING WORLD... WOULD STILL BE IN THE DARK AGES. BUT THIS IS THE THANKS I GET? WHY...BECAUSE I DID A LITTLE INSIDER TRADING? WHO HASN'T?
YOU'D BE SURPRISED. NOT MANY PEOPLE ARE TRILLIONAIRES, MR. HOSS.
OH, AND THAT'S SUDDENLY MY FAULT?!
NOPE. BUT IT IS OUR OPPORTUNITY.
JUST PROMISE ME THAT I'M GONNA WALK AWAY FROM THIS ALIVE.
YOU PEOPLE HAVE BEEN CHASING THIS ASSHOLE FOR MONTHS AND THERE'S BEEN NOTHING BUT A BODY TRAIL. I DON'T WANT TO BE ANOTHER HEADLINE, YOU UNDERSTAND ME?!
LOUD AND CLEAR, MR. HOSS.
DON'T YOU WORRY...

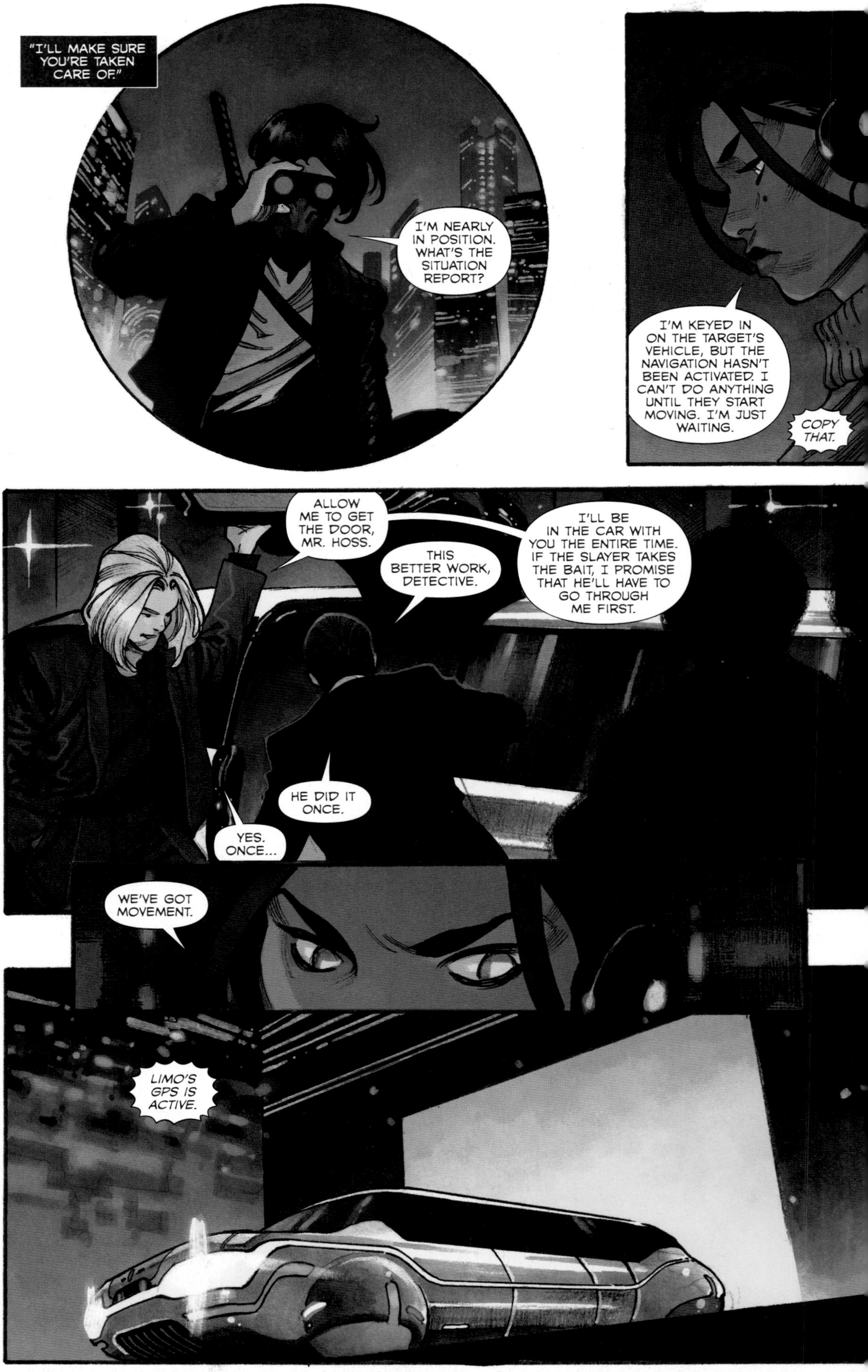
"I'LL MAKE SURE YOU'RE TAKEN CARE OF."
I'M NEARLY IN POSITION. WHAT'S THE SITUATION REPORT?
I'M KEYED IN ON THE TARGET'S VEHICLE, BUT THE NAVIGATION HASN'T BEEN ACTIVATED. I CAN'T DO ANYTHING UNTIL THEY START MOVING. I'M JUST WAITING.
COPY THAT.
ALLOW ME TO GET THE DOOR, MR. HOSS.
THIS BETTER WORK, DETECTIVE.
I'LL BE IN THE CAR WITH YOU THE ENTIRE TIME. IF THE SLAYER TAKES THE BAIT, I PROMISE THAT HE'LL HAVE TO GO THROUGH ME FIRST.
HE DID IT ONCE.
YES. ONCE...
WE'VE GOT MOVEMENT.
LIMO'S GPS IS ACTIVE.

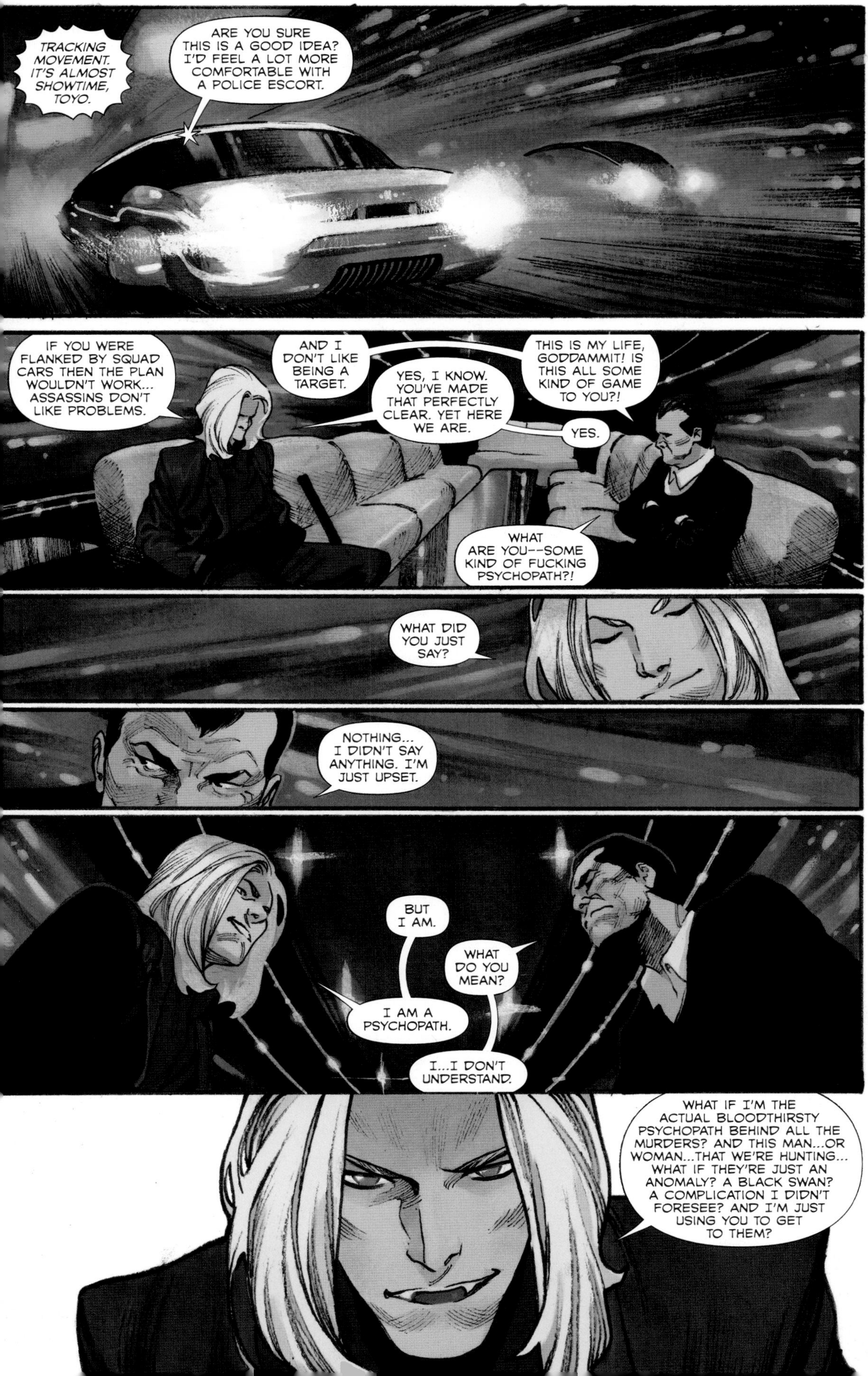
TRACKING MOVEMENT. IT'S ALMOST SHOWTIME, TOYO.
ARE YOU SURE THIS IS A GOOD IDEA? I'D FEEL A LOT MORE COMFORTABLE WITH A POLICE ESCORT.
IF YOU WERE FLANKED BY SQUAD CARS THEN THE PLAN WOULDN'T WORK... ASSASSINS DON'T LIKE PROBLEMS.
AND I DON'T LIKE BEING A TARGET.
YES, I KNOW. YOU'VE MADE THAT PERFECTLY CLEAR. YET HERE WE ARE.
THIS IS MY LIFE, GODDAMMIT! IS THIS ALL SOME KIND OF GAME TO YOU?!
YES.
WHAT ARE YOU--SOME KIND OF FUCKING PSYCHOPATH?!
WHAT DID YOU JUST SAY?
NOTHING... I DIDN'T SAY ANYTHING. I'M JUST UPSET.
BUT I AM.
WHAT DO YOU MEAN?
I AM A PSYCHOPATH.
I...I DON'T UNDERSTAND.
WHAT IF I'M THE ACTUAL BLOODTHIRSTY PSYCHOPATH BEHIND ALL THE MURDERS? AND THIS MAN...OR WOMAN...THAT WE'RE HUNTING... WHAT IF THEY'RE JUST AN ANOMALY? A BLACK SWAN? A COMPLICATION I DIDN'T FORESEE? AND I'M JUST USING YOU TO GET TO THEM?

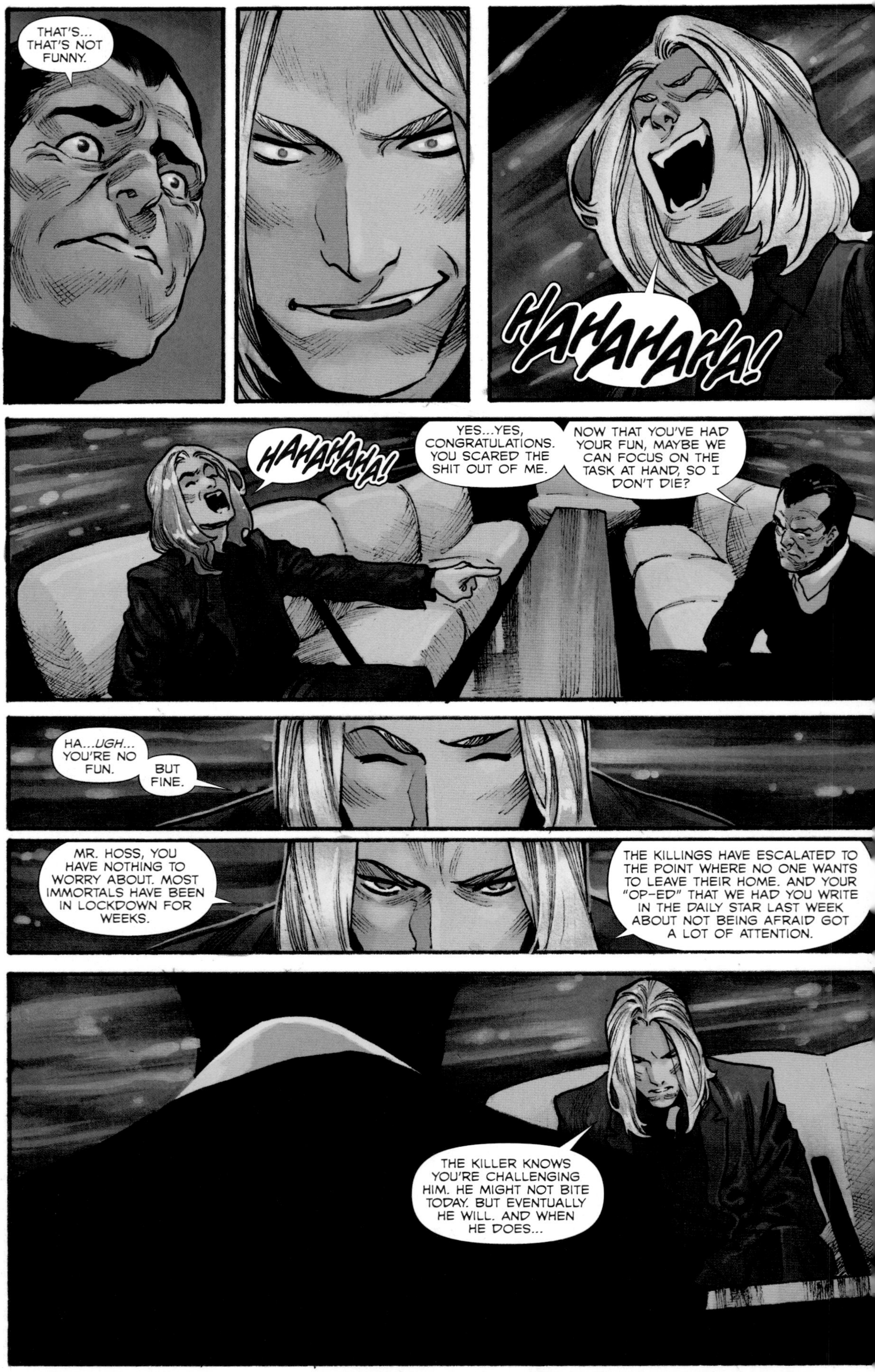
THAT'S... THAT'S NOT FUNNY.
HAHAHAHAHA!
HAHAHAHA!
YES...YES, CONGRATULATIONS. YOU SCARED THE SHIT OUT OF ME.
NOW THAT YOU'VE HAD YOUR FUN, MAYBE WE CAN FOCUS ON THE TASK AT HAND, SO I DON'T DIE?
HA...*UGH*... YOU'RE NO FUN.
BUT FINE.
MR. HOSS, YOU HAVE NOTHING TO WORRY ABOUT. MOST IMMORTALS HAVE BEEN IN LOCKDOWN FOR WEEKS.
THE KILLINGS HAVE ESCALATED TO THE POINT WHERE NO ONE WANTS TO LEAVE THEIR HOME. AND YOUR "OP-ED" THAT WE HAD YOU WRITE IN THE DAILY STAR LAST WEEK ABOUT NOT BEING AFRAID GOT A LOT OF ATTENTION.
THE KILLER KNOWS YOU'RE CHALLENGING HIM. HE MIGHT NOT BITE TODAY. BUT EVENTUALLY HE WILL. AND WHEN HE DOES...

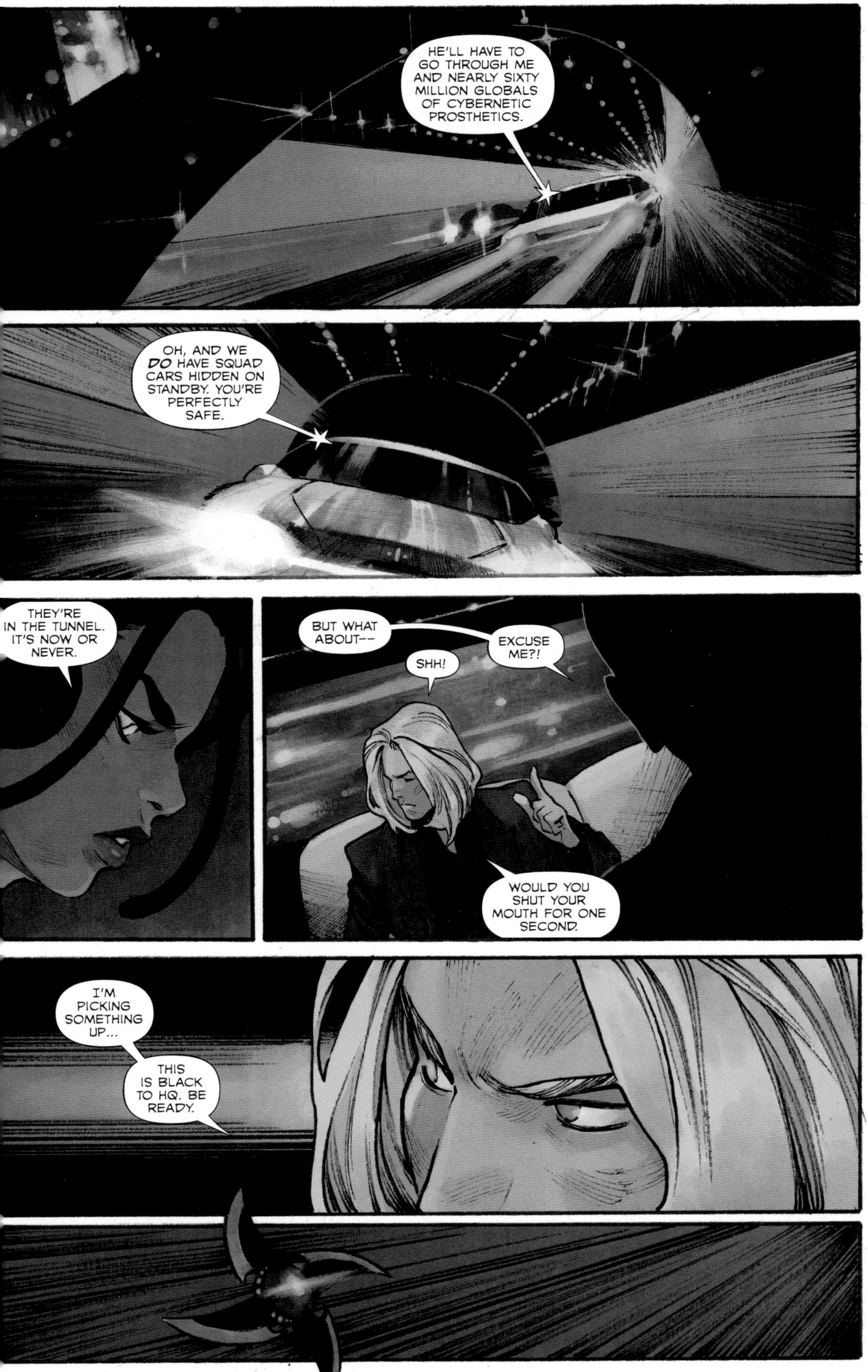
HE'LL HAVE TO GO THROUGH ME AND NEARLY SIXTY MILLION GLOBALS OF CYBERNETIC PROSTHETICS.
OH, AND WE DO HAVE SQUAD CARS HIDDEN ON STANDBY. YOU'RE PERFECTLY SAFE.
THEY'RE IN THE TUNNEL. IT'S NOW OR NEVER.
BUT WHAT ABOUT--
EXCUSE ME?!
SHH!
WOULD YOU SHUT YOUR MOUTH FOR ONE SECOND.
I'M PICKING SOMETHING UP...
THIS IS BLACK TO HQ. BE READY.

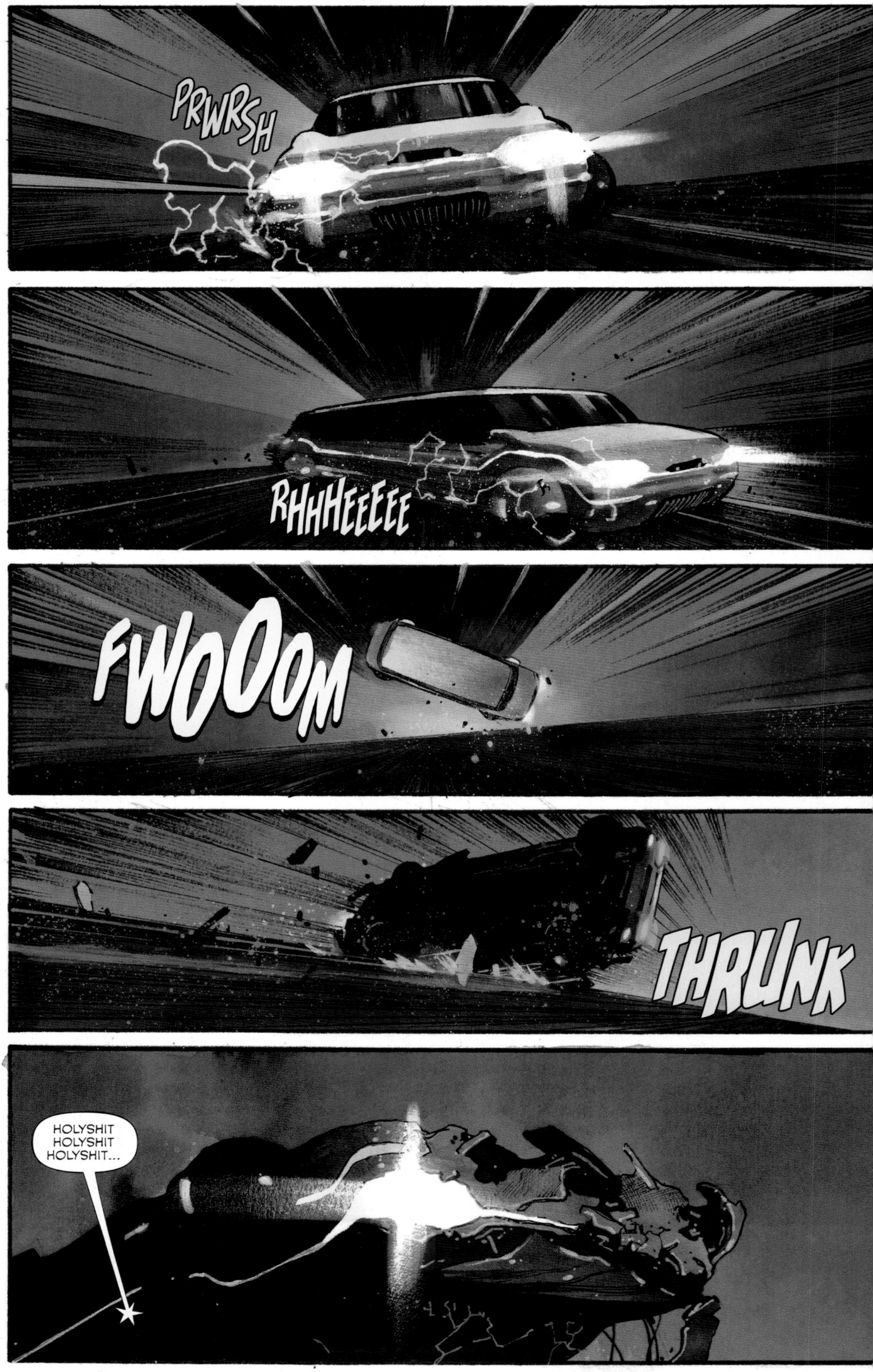
PRWRSH
RHHHEEEEE
FWOOOM
THRUNK
HOLYSHIT
HOLYSHIT
HOLYSHIT...

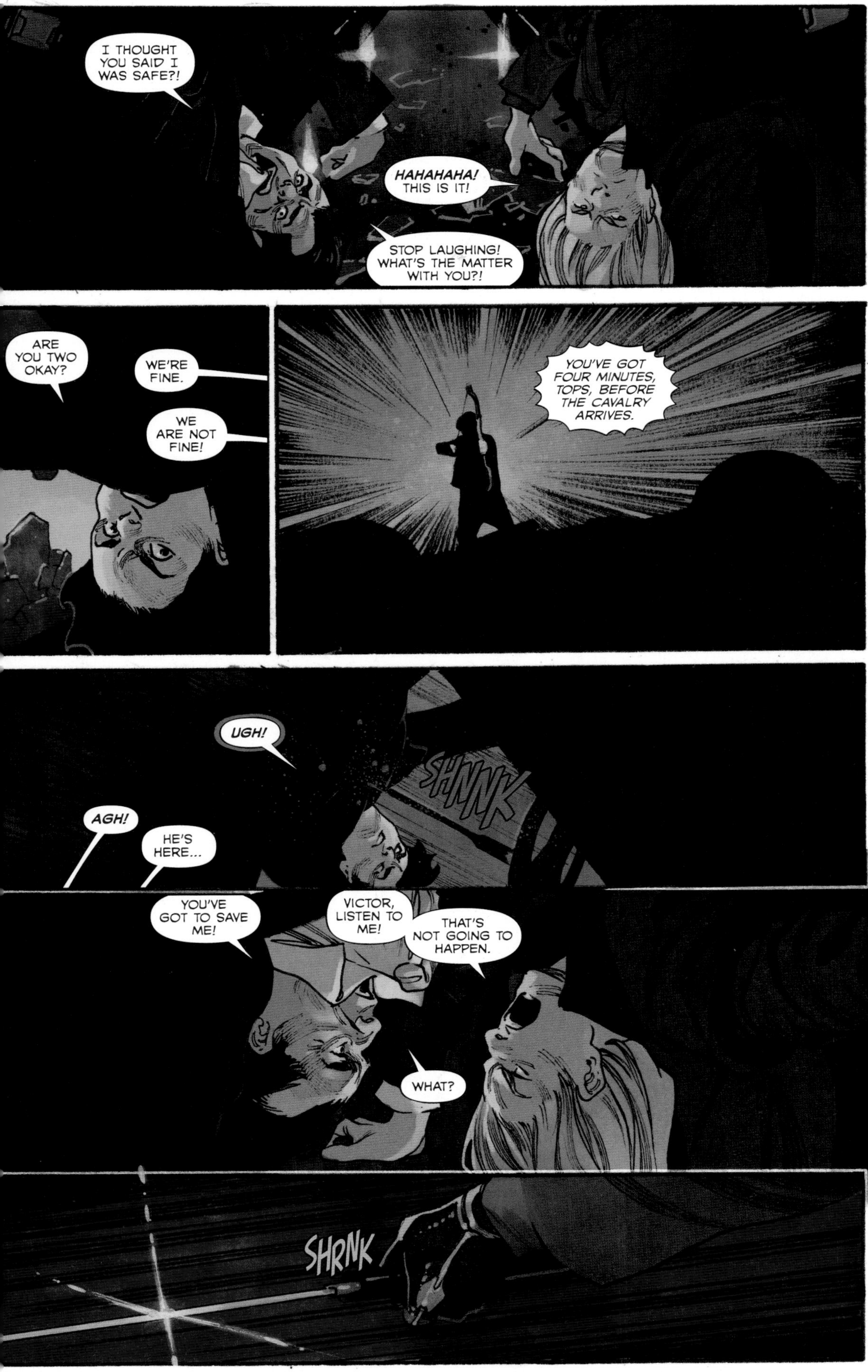
I THOUGHT YOU SAID I WAS SAFE?!
HAHAHAHA! THIS IS IT!
STOP LAUGHING! WHAT'S THE MATTER WITH YOU?!
ARE YOU TWO OKAY?
WE'RE FINE.
WE ARE NOT FINE!
YOU'VE GOT FOUR MINUTES, TOPS, BEFORE THE CAVALRY ARRIVES.
UGH!
SHNNK
AGH!
HE'S HERE...
YOU'VE GOT TO SAVE ME!
VICTOR, LISTEN TO ME!
THAT'S NOT GOING TO HAPPEN.
WHAT?
SHRNK

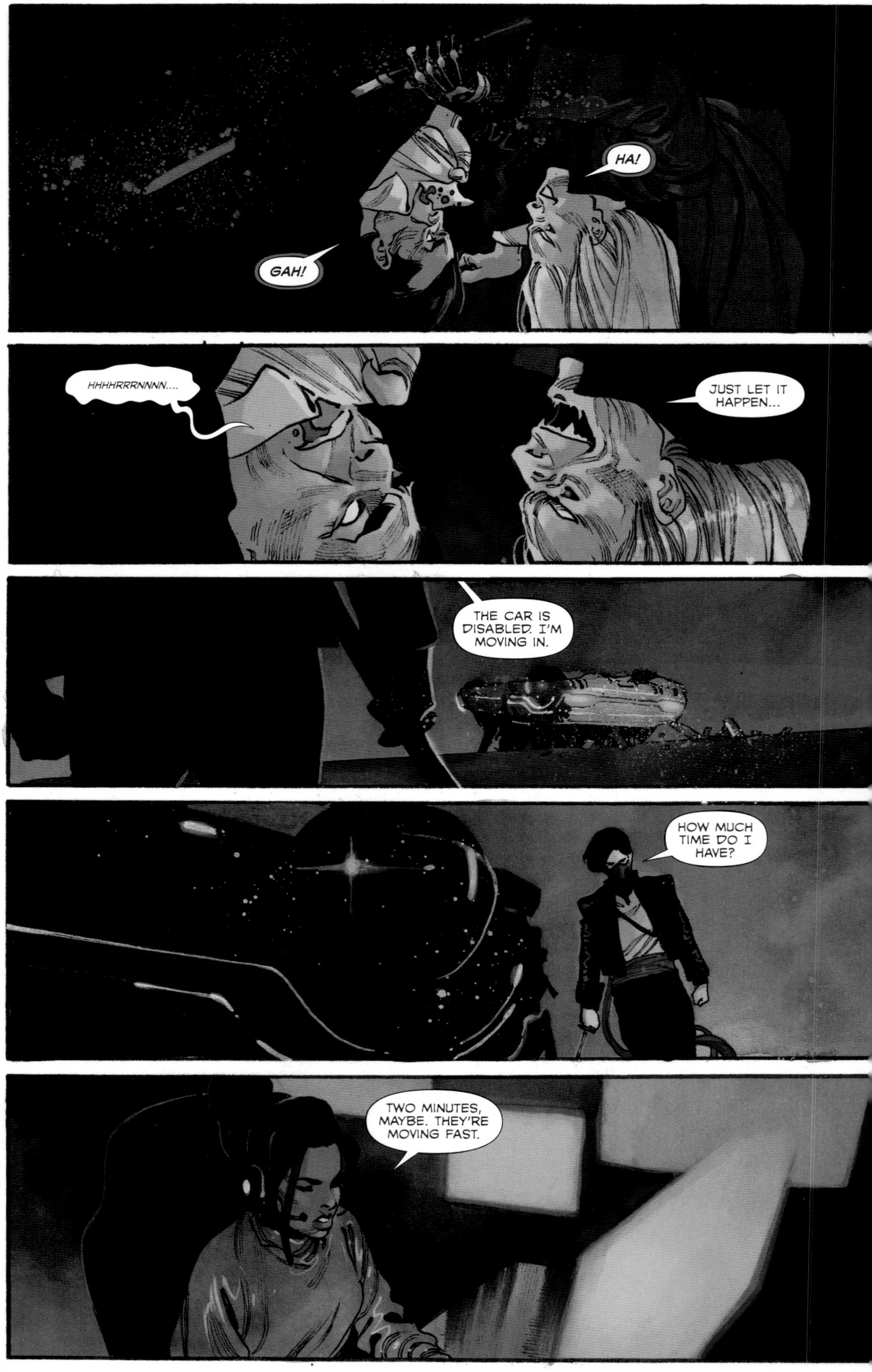
GAH!
HA!
HHHHRRRNNNN....
JUST LET IT HAPPEN...
THE CAR IS DISABLED. I'M MOVING IN.
HOW MUCH TIME DO I HAVE?
TWO MINUTES, MAYBE. THEY'RE MOVING FAST.

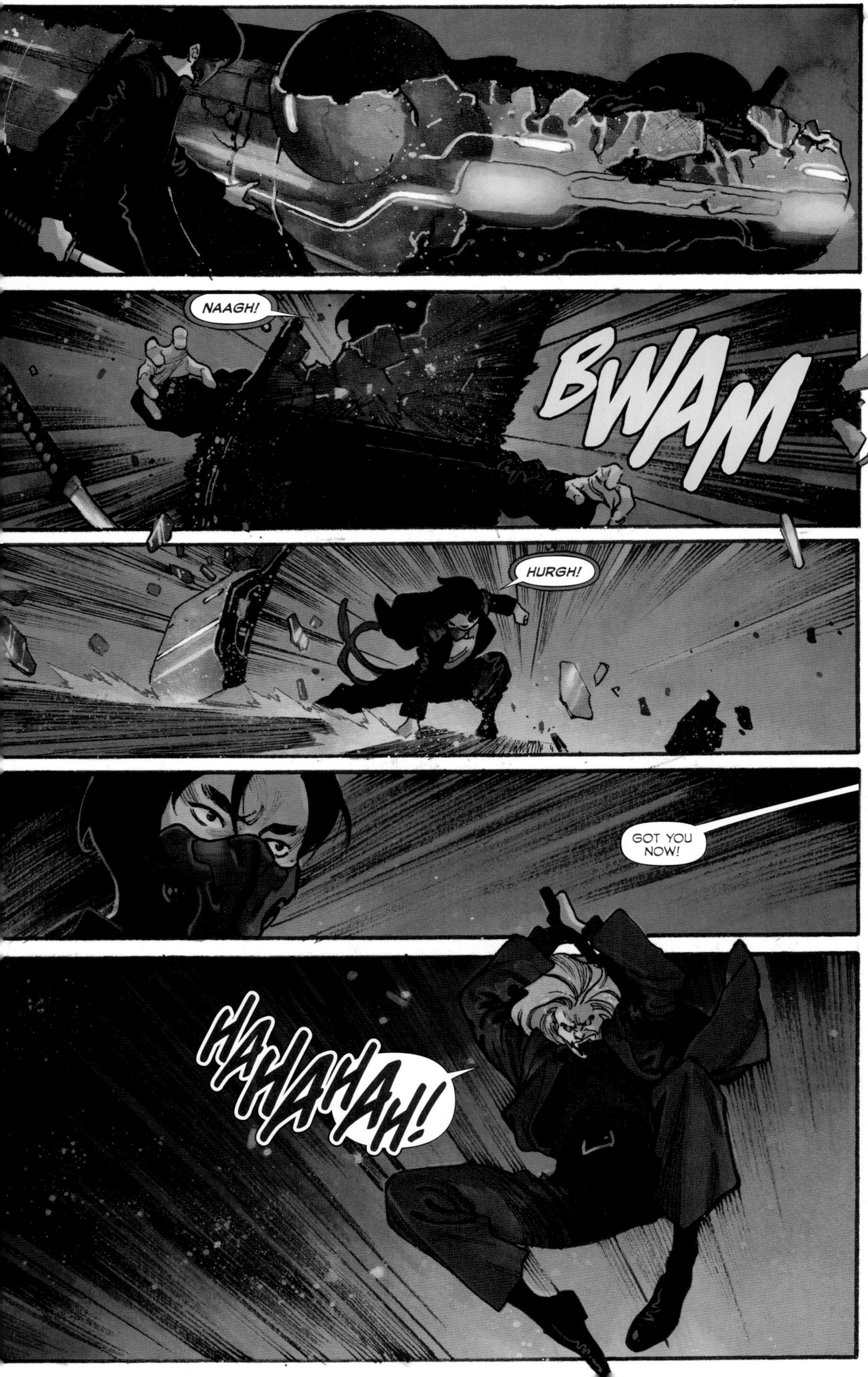
NAAGH!
BWAM
HURGH!
GOT YOU NOW!
HAHAHAH!

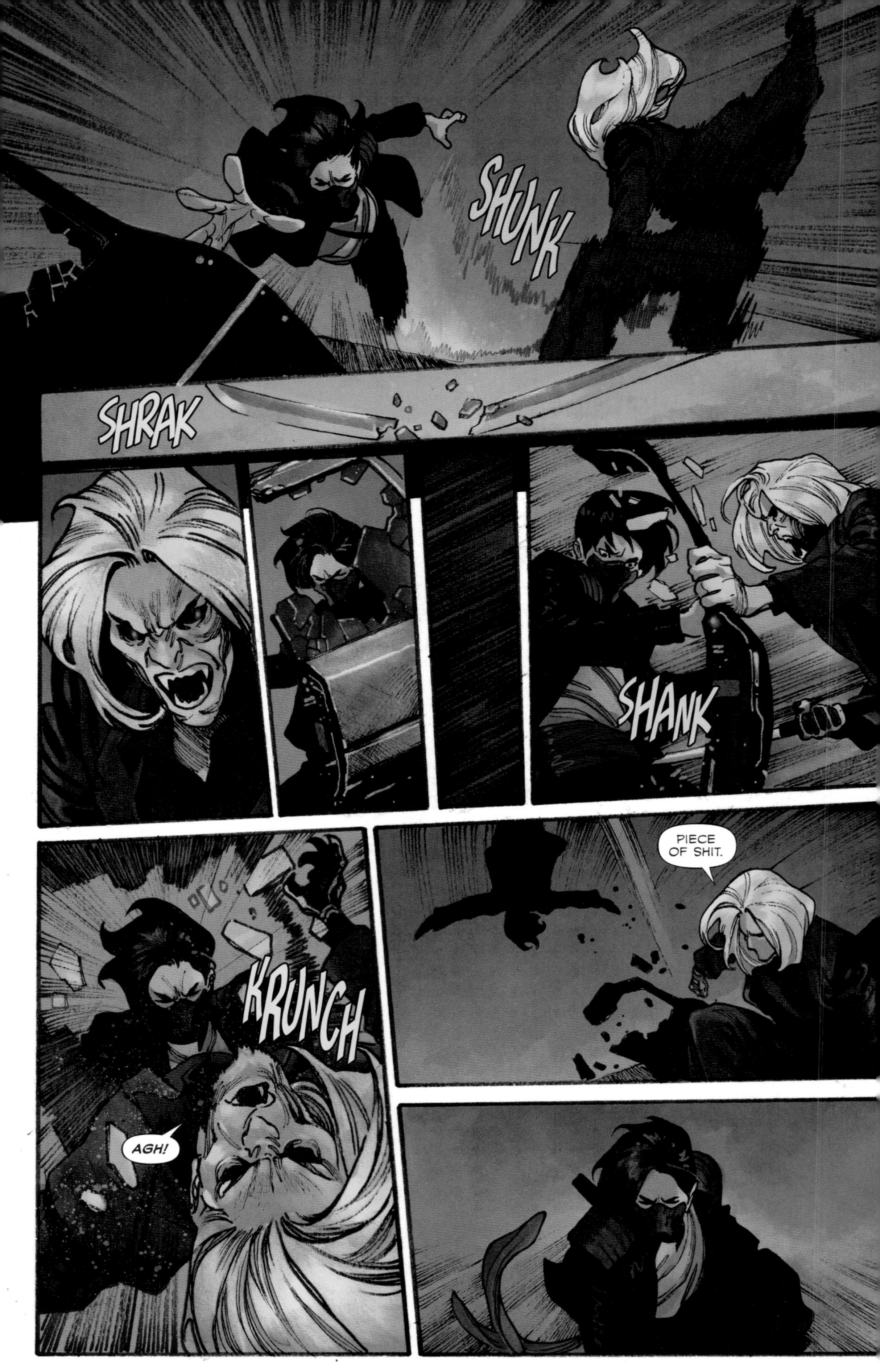
SHUNK
SHRAK
SHANK
KRUNCH
AGH!
PIECE OF SHIT.

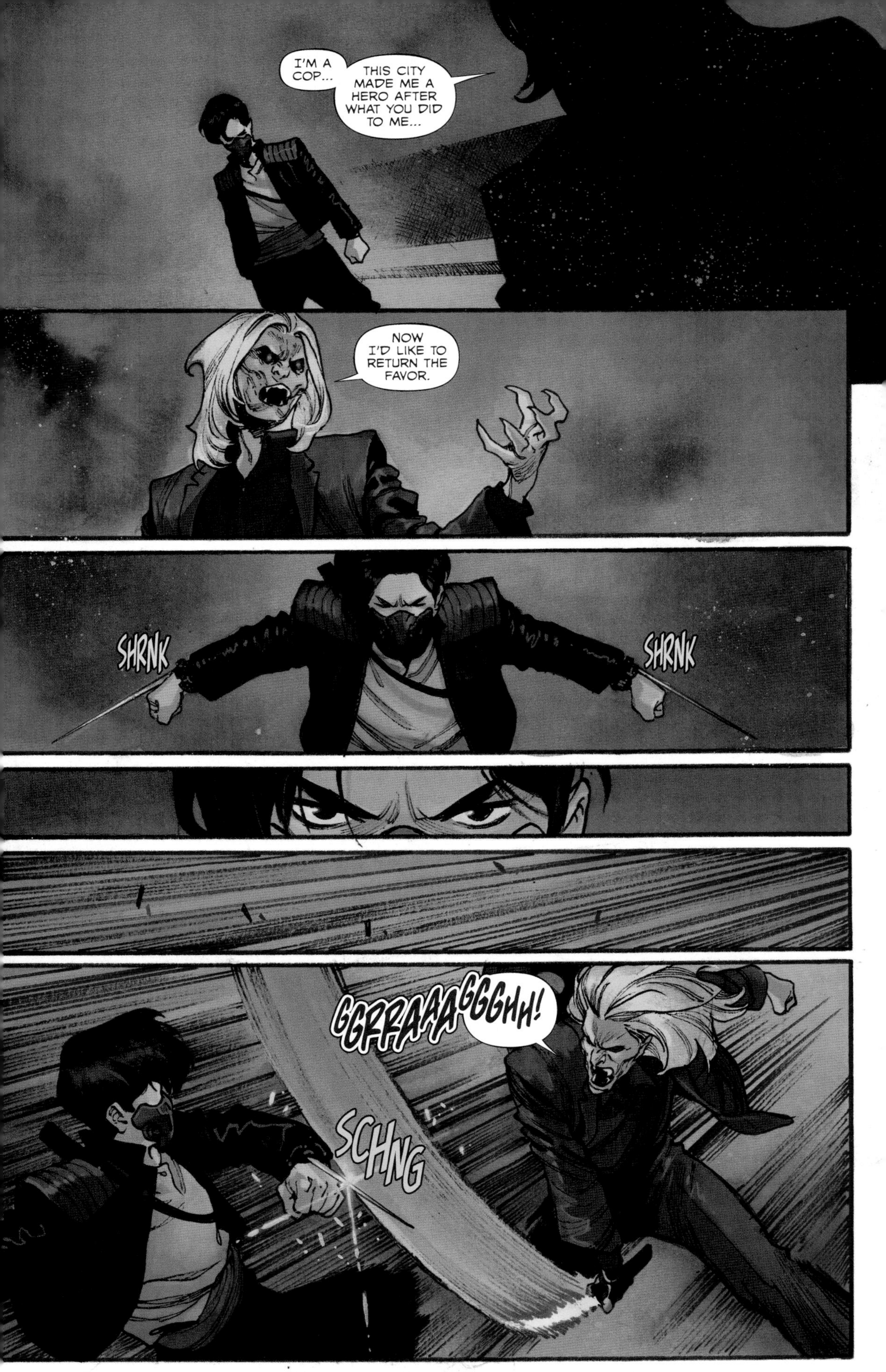
I'M A COP...
THIS CITY MADE ME A HERO AFTER WHAT YOU DID TO ME...
NOW I'D LIKE TO RETURN THE FAVOR.
SHRNK
SHRNK
GGRRAAAGGGHH!
SCHNG

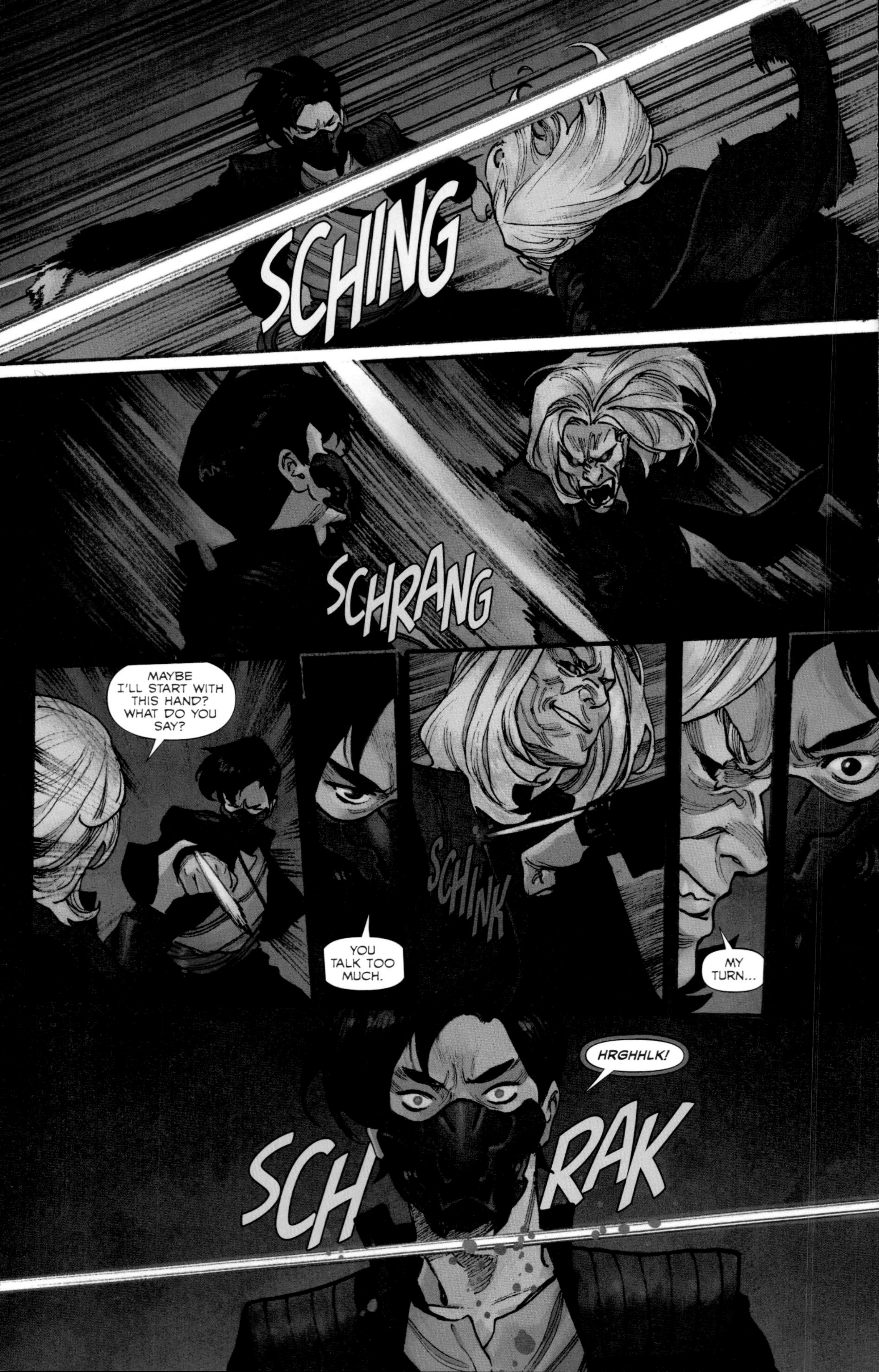
SCHING
SCHRANG
MAYBE I'LL START WITH THIS HAND? WHAT DO YOU SAY?
SCHINK
YOU TALK TOO MUCH.
MY TURN...
HRGHHLK!
SCH RAK

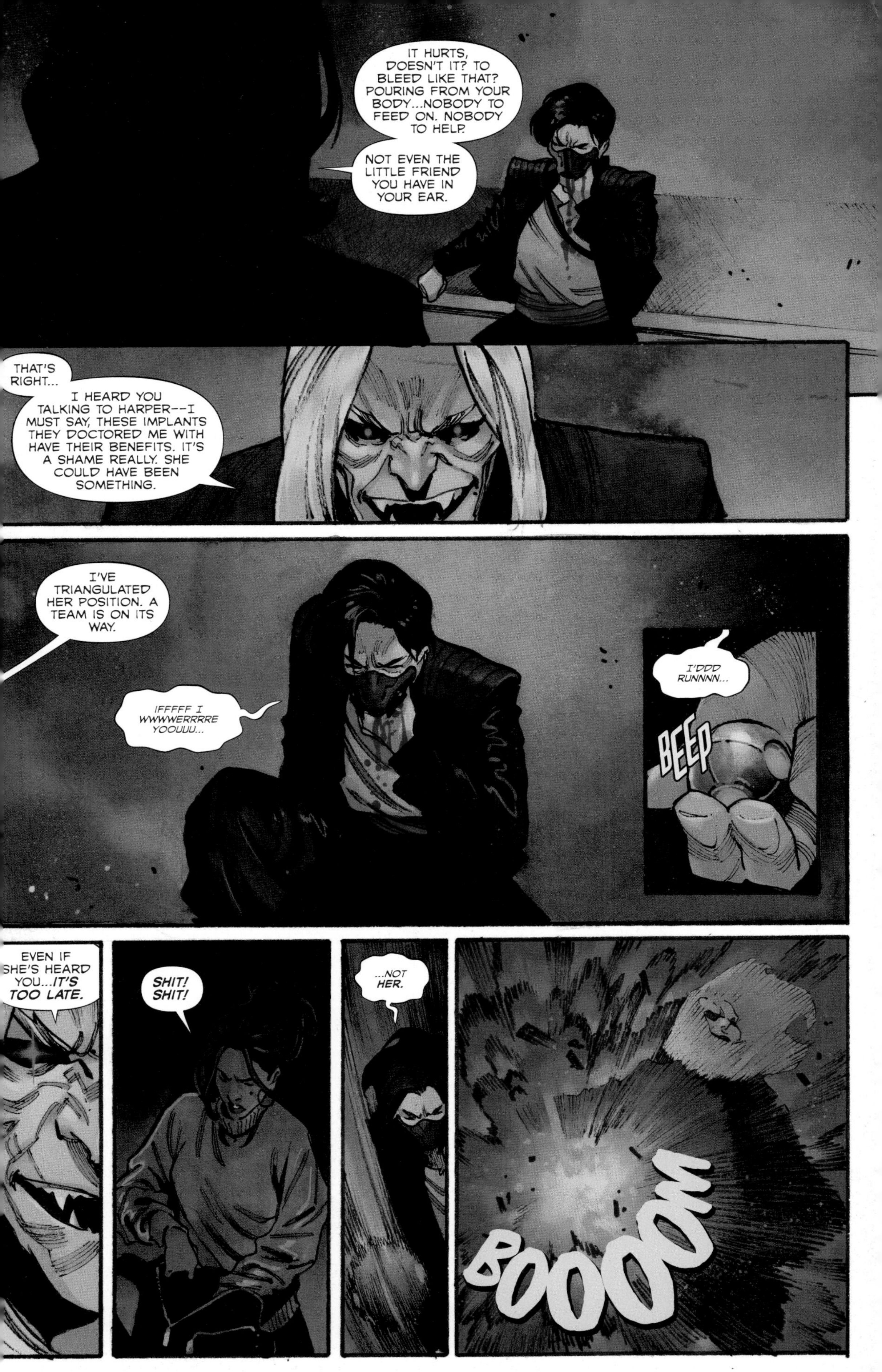
IT HURTS, DOESN'T IT? TO BLEED LIKE THAT? POURING FROM YOUR BODY...NOBODY TO FEED ON. NOBODY TO HELP.
NOT EVEN THE LITTLE FRIEND YOU HAVE IN YOUR EAR.
THAT'S RIGHT...
I HEARD YOU TALKING TO HARPER--I MUST SAY, THESE IMPLANTS THEY DOCTORED ME WITH HAVE THEIR BENEFITS. IT'S A SHAME REALLY. SHE COULD HAVE BEEN SOMETHING.
I'VE TRIANGULATED HER POSITION. A TEAM IS ON ITS WAY.
IFFFFF I WWWWERRRRE YOOUUU...
I'DDD RUNNNN...
BEEP
EVEN IF SHE'S HEARD YOU...*IT'S TOO LATE.*
SHIT! SHIT!
...NOT *HER.*
BOOOOM

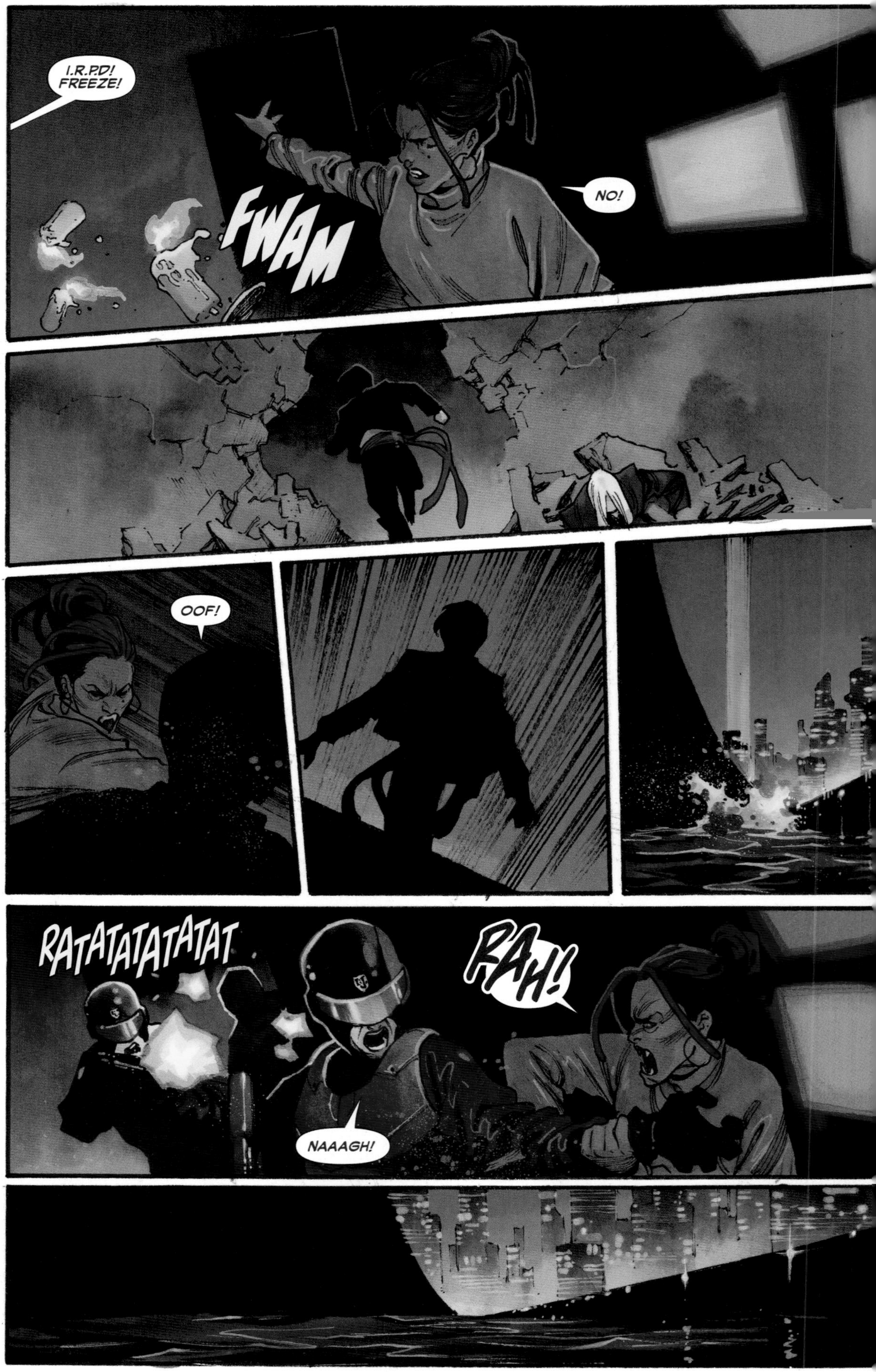
I.R.P.D! FREEZE!
FWAM
NO!
OOF!
RATATATATATAT
RAH!
NAAAGH!

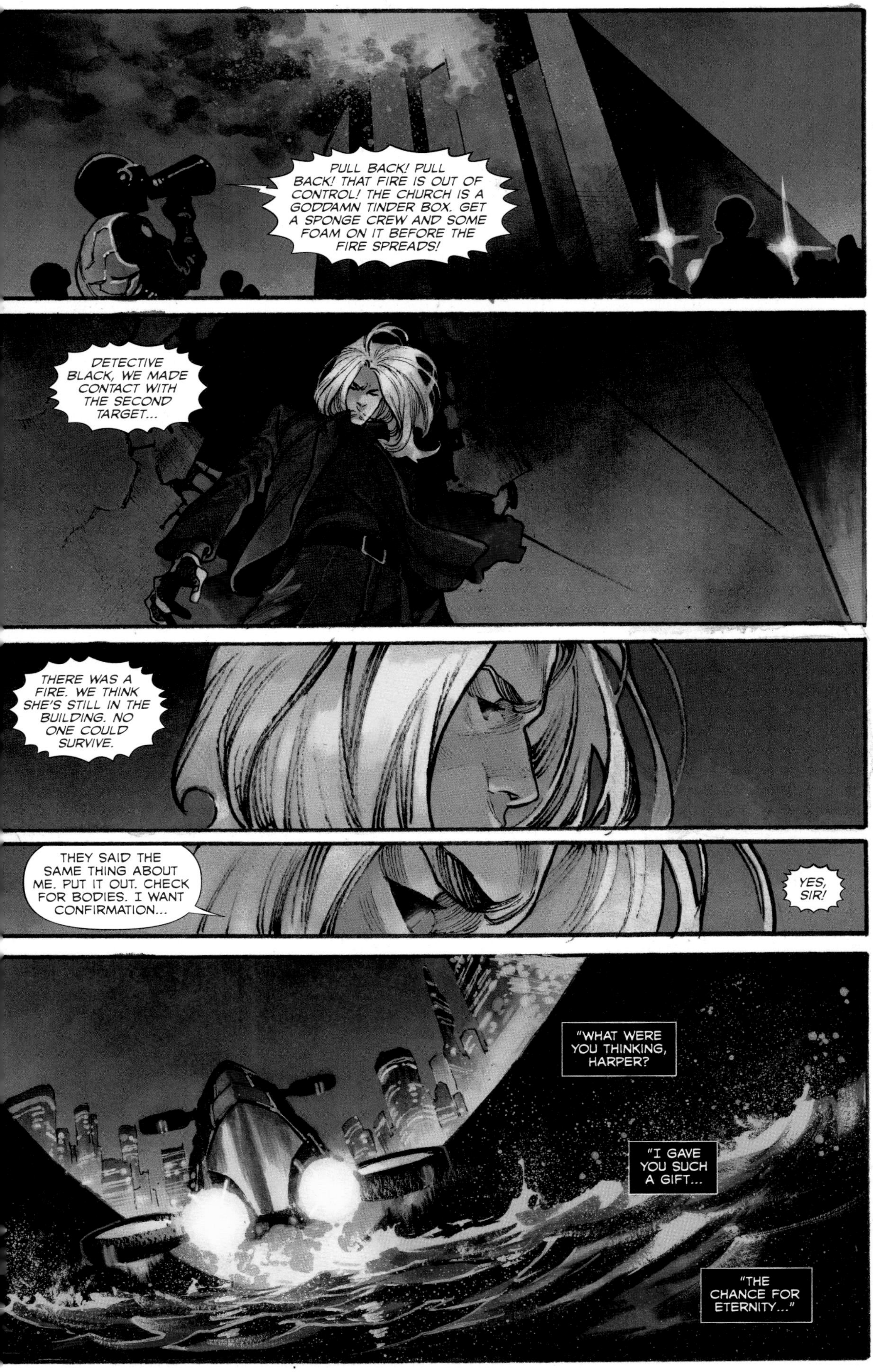
PULL BACK! PULL BACK! THAT FIRE IS OUT OF CONTROL! THE CHURCH IS A GODDAMN TINDER BOX. GET A SPONGE CREW AND SOME FOAM ON IT BEFORE THE FIRE SPREADS!
DETECTIVE BLACK, WE MADE CONTACT WITH THE SECOND TARGET...
THERE WAS A FIRE. WE THINK SHE'S STILL IN THE BUILDING. NO ONE COULD SURVIVE.
THEY SAID THE SAME THING ABOUT ME. PUT IT OUT. CHECK FOR BODIES. I WANT CONFIRMATION...
YES, SIR!
"WHAT WERE YOU THINKING, HARPER?
"I GAVE YOU SUCH A GIFT...
"THE CHANCE FOR ETERNITY..."

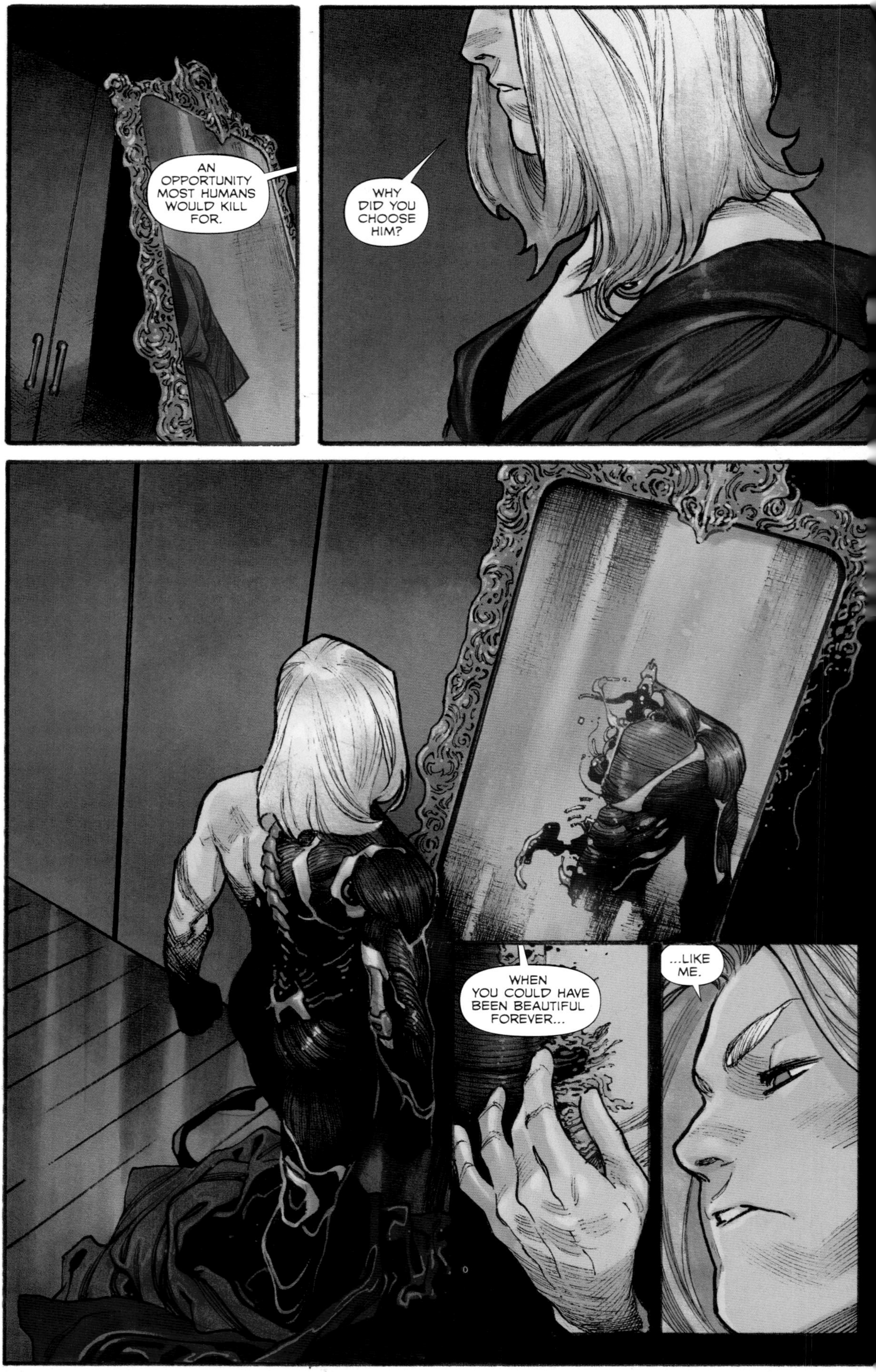
AN OPPORTUNITY MOST HUMANS WOULD KILL FOR.
WHY DID YOU CHOOSE HIM?
WHEN YOU COULD HAVE BEEN BEAUTIFUL FOREVER...
...LIKE ME.

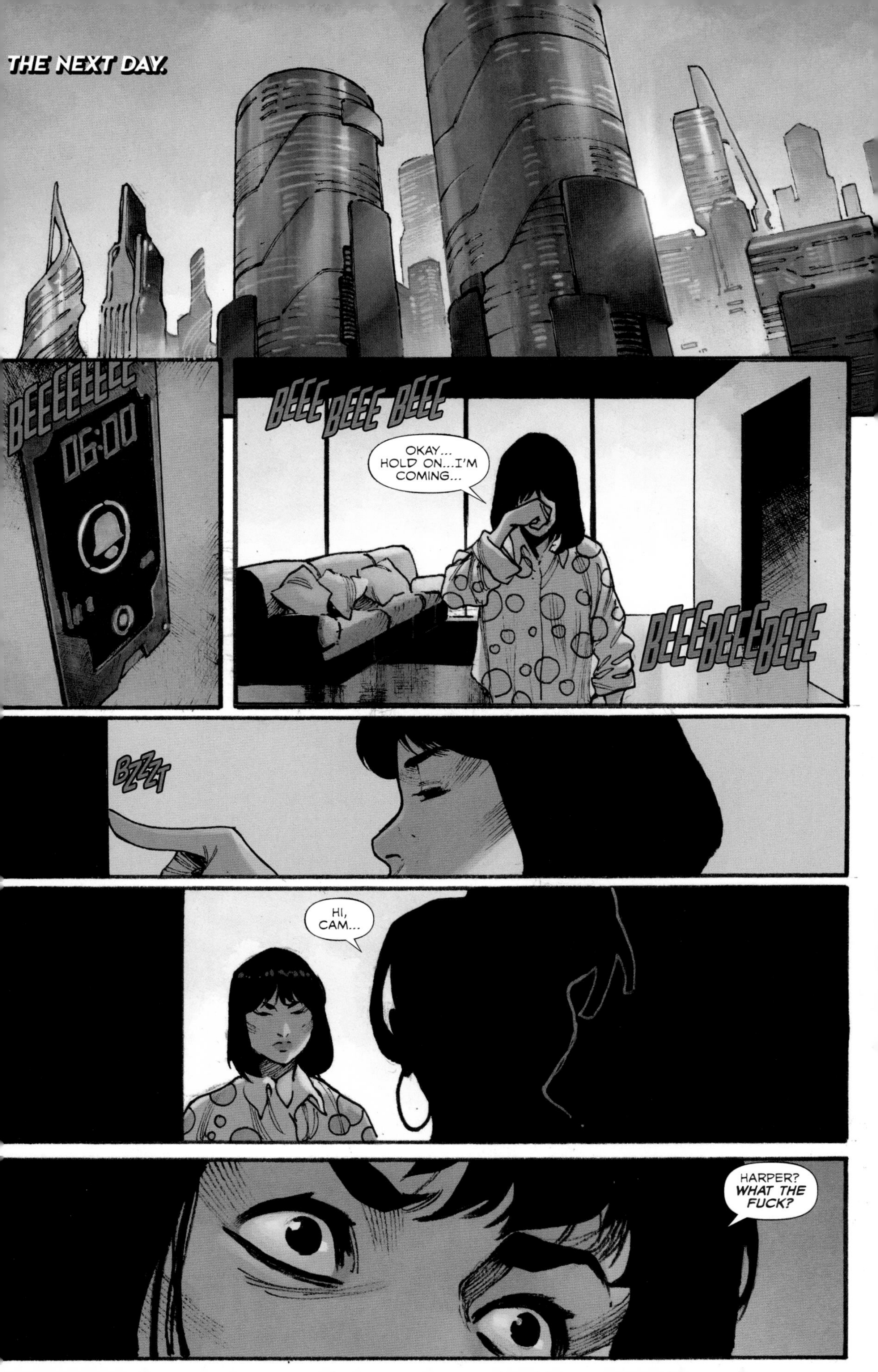
THE NEXT DAY.
BEEEEEEEEE
06:00
BEEE BEEE BEEE
OKAY... HOLD ON...I'M COMING...
BEEEBEEEBEEE
BZZZT
HI, CAM...
HARPER? WHAT THE FUCK?

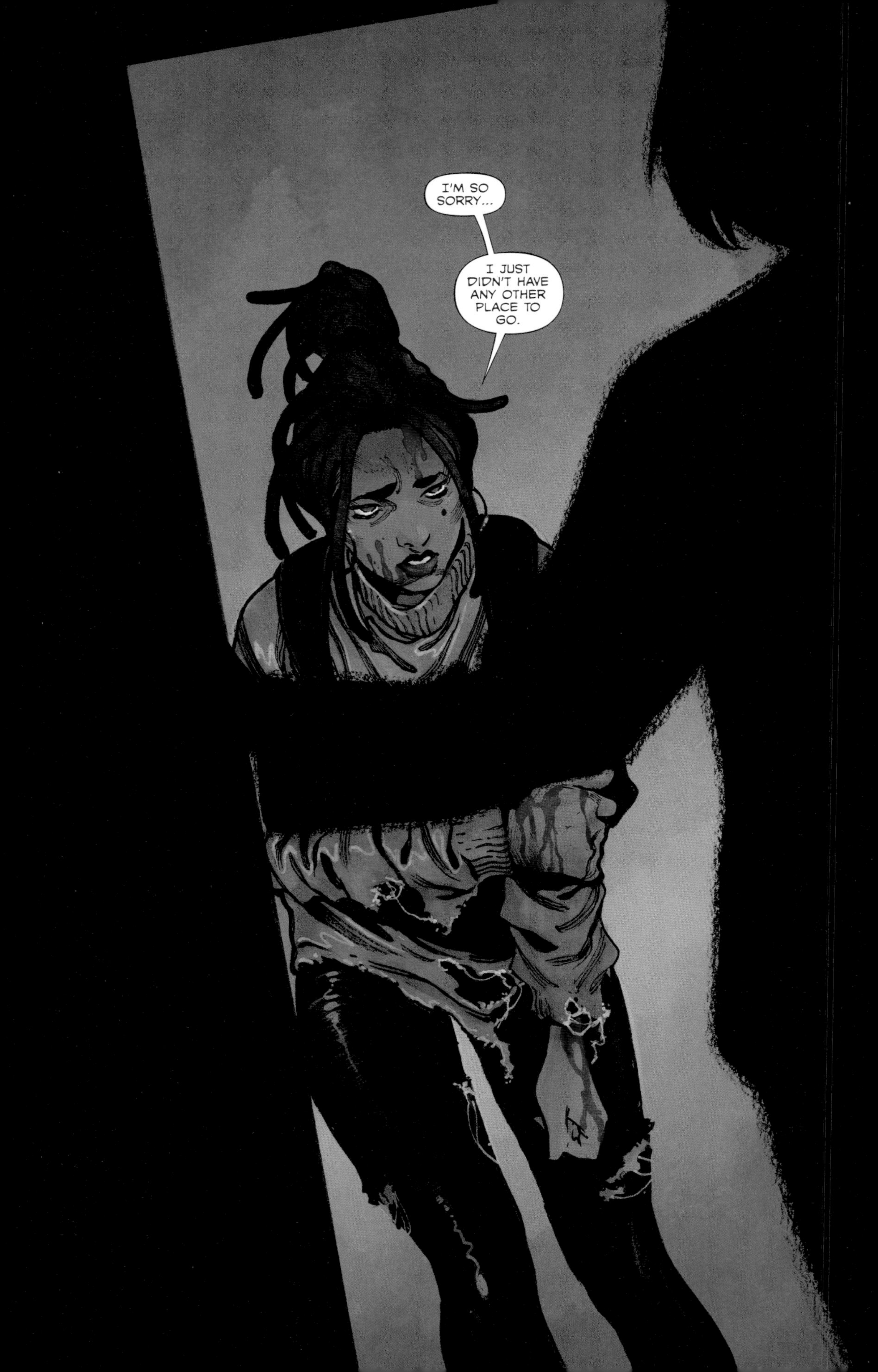
I'M SO SORRY...
I JUST DIDN'T HAVE ANY OTHER PLACE TO GO.

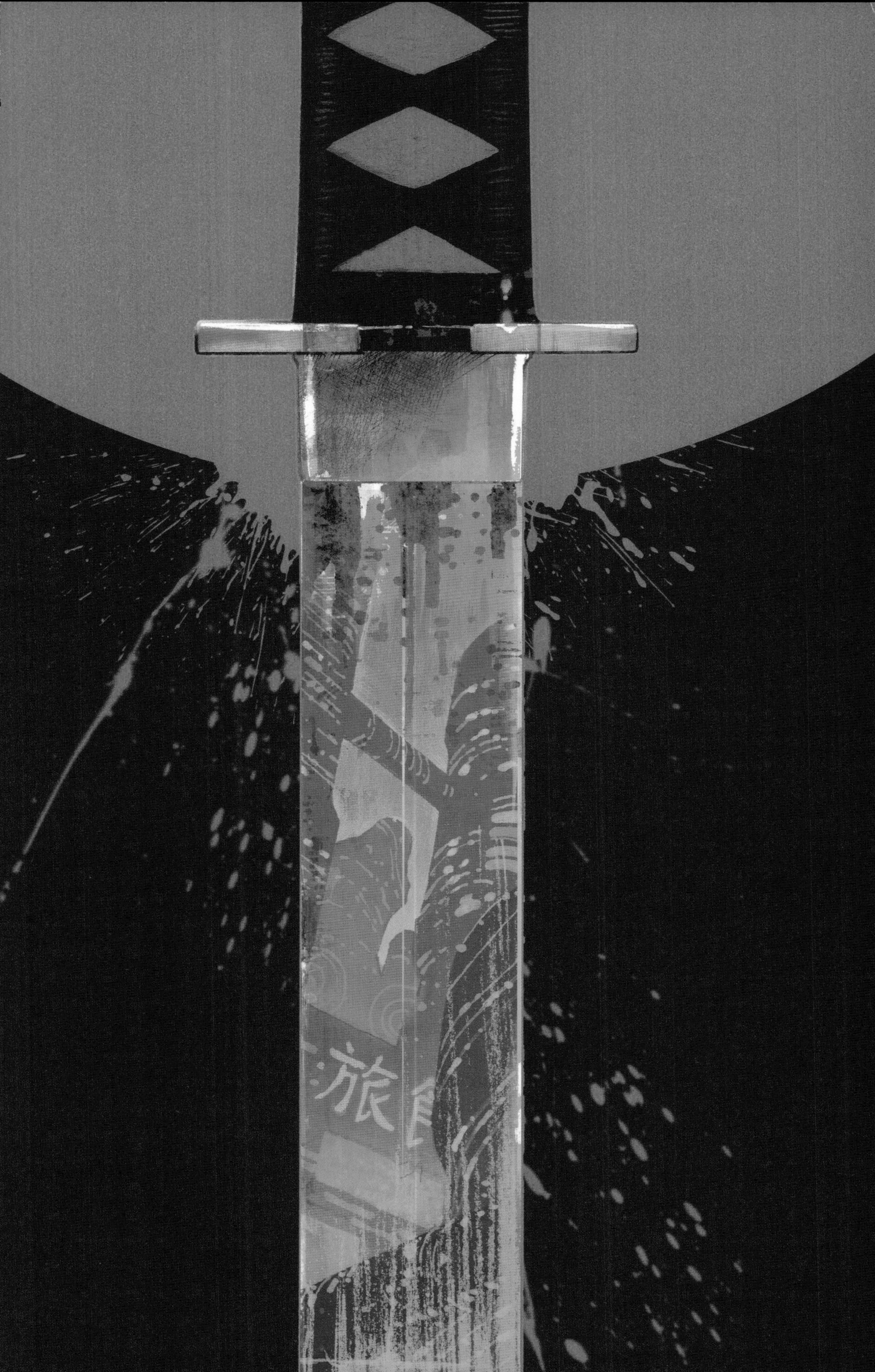
旅

FOUR

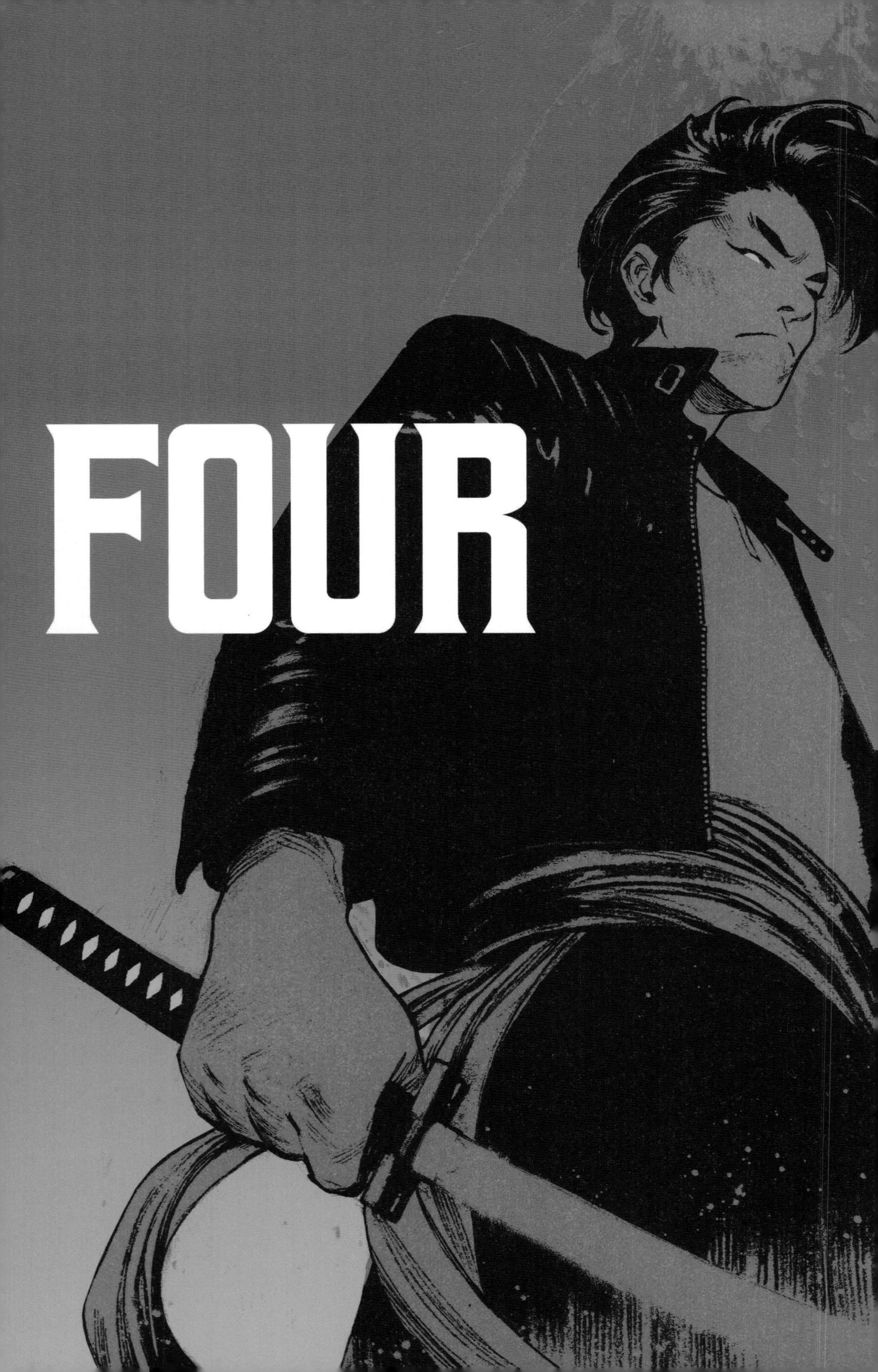

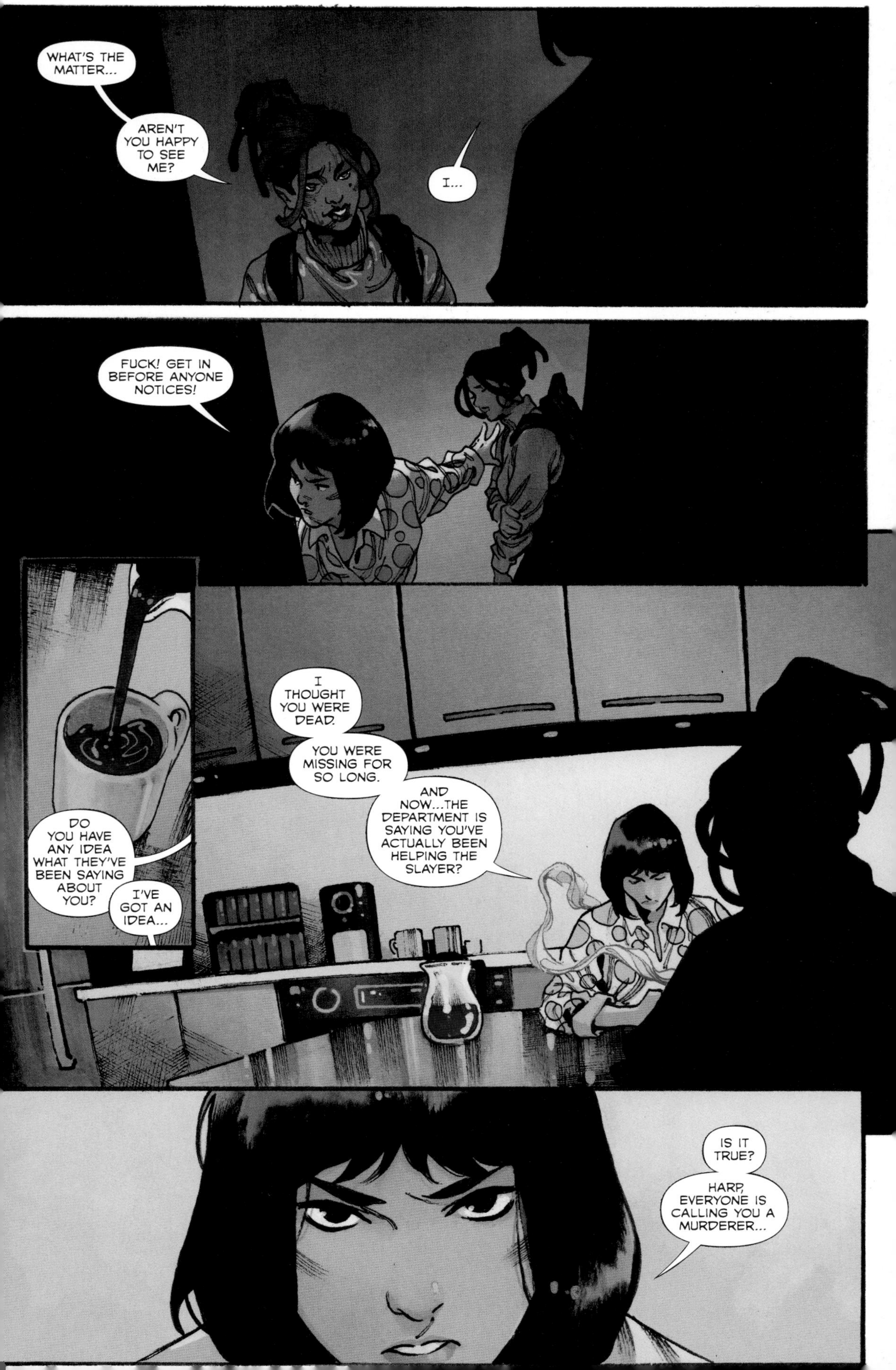
WHAT'S THE MATTER...
AREN'T YOU HAPPY TO SEE ME?
I...
FUCK! GET IN BEFORE ANYONE NOTICES!
DO YOU HAVE ANY IDEA WHAT THEY'VE BEEN SAYING ABOUT YOU?
I'VE GOT AN IDEA...
I THOUGHT YOU WERE DEAD.
YOU WERE MISSING FOR SO LONG.
AND NOW...THE DEPARTMENT IS SAYING YOU'VE ACTUALLY BEEN HELPING THE SLAYER?
IS IT TRUE?
HARP, EVERYONE IS CALLING YOU A MURDERER...

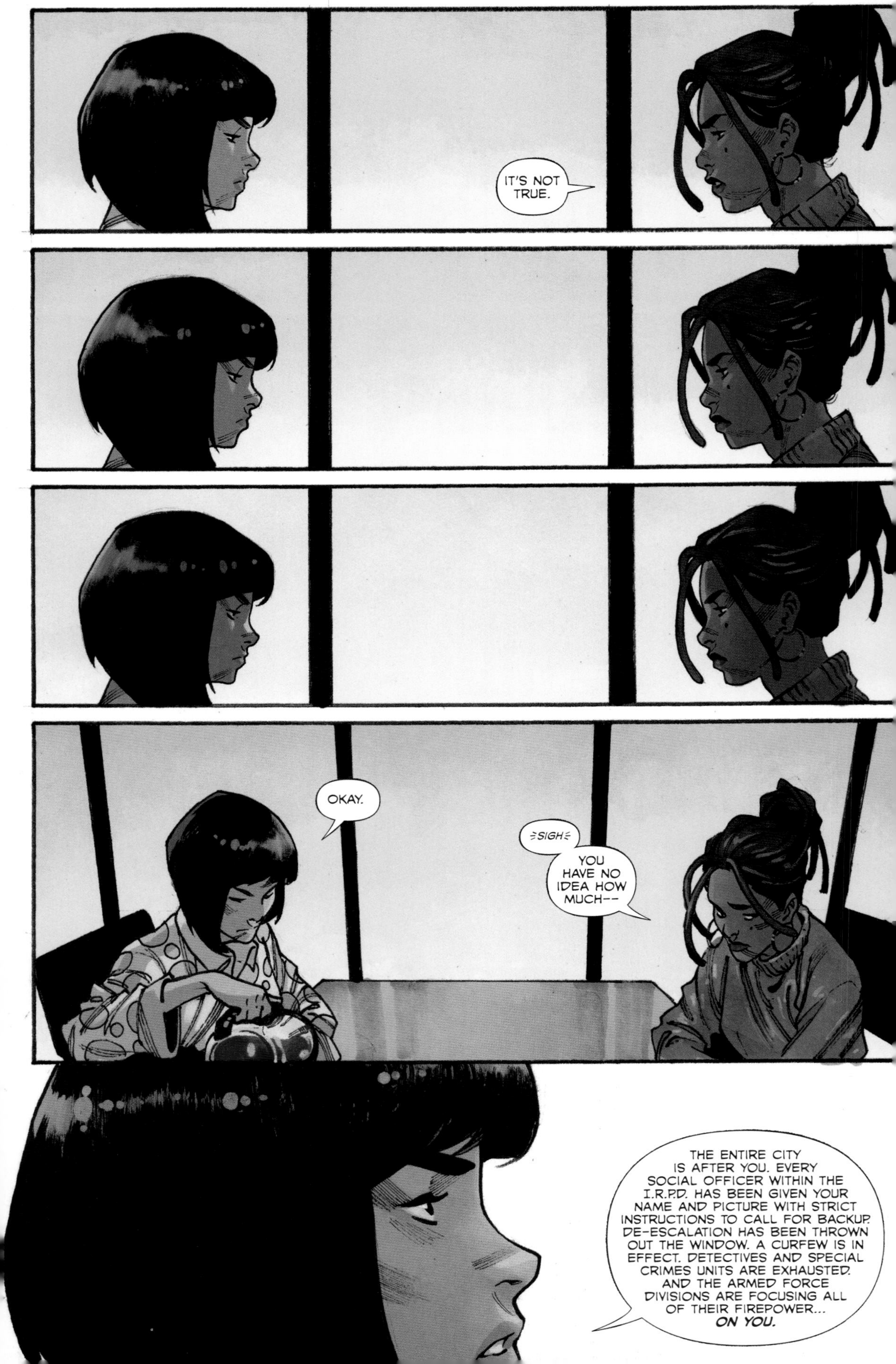
IT'S NOT TRUE.
OKAY.
≈SIGH≈
YOU HAVE NO IDEA HOW MUCH--
THE ENTIRE CITY IS AFTER YOU. EVERY SOCIAL OFFICER WITHIN THE I.R.P.D. HAS BEEN GIVEN YOUR NAME AND PICTURE WITH STRICT INSTRUCTIONS TO CALL FOR BACKUP. DE-ESCALATION HAS BEEN THROWN OUT THE WINDOW. A CURFEW IS IN EFFECT. DETECTIVES AND SPECIAL CRIMES UNITS ARE EXHAUSTED. AND THE ARMED FORCE DIVISIONS ARE FOCUSING ALL OF THEIR FIREPOWER... ***ON YOU.***

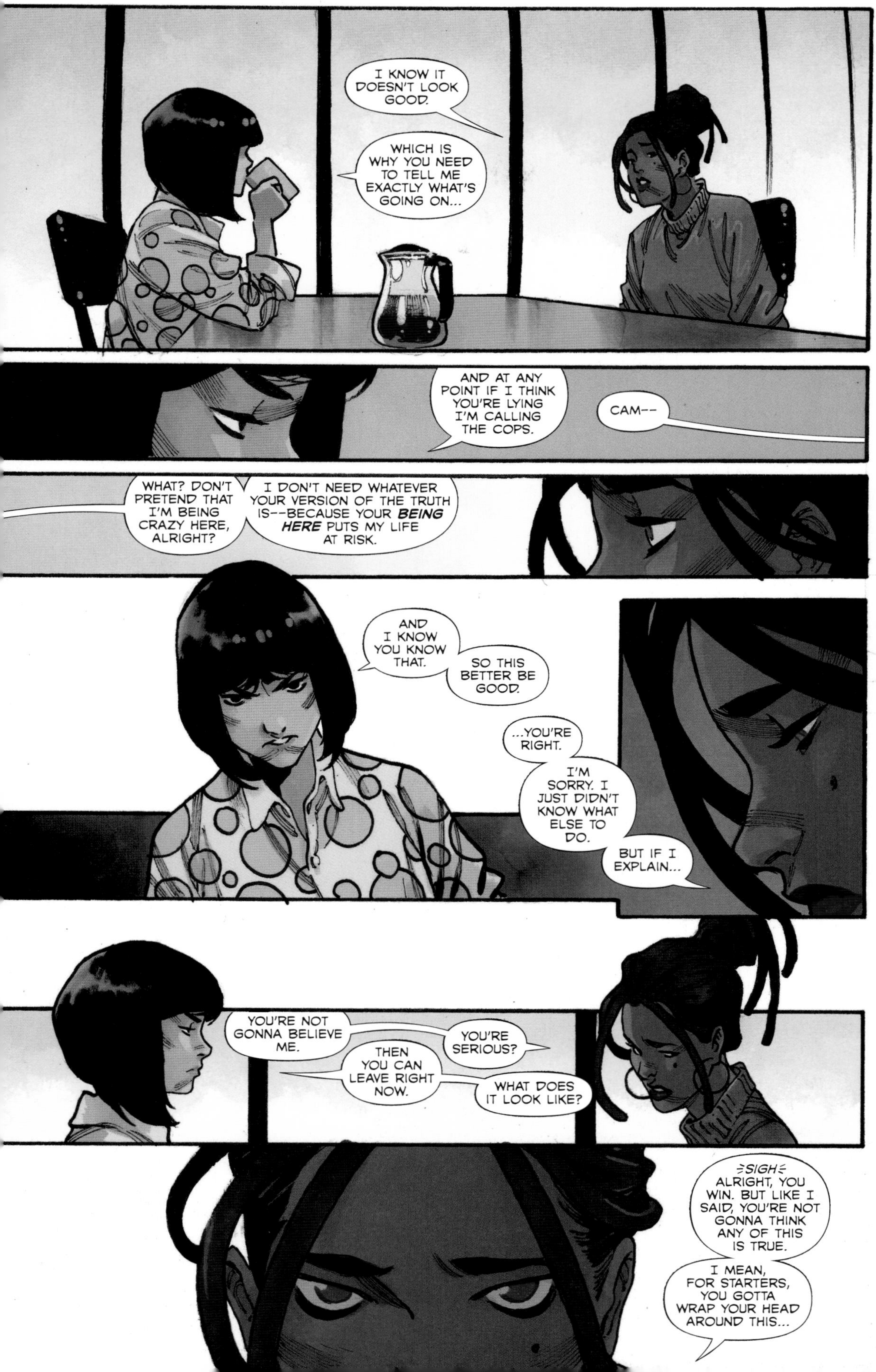
I KNOW IT DOESN'T LOOK GOOD.
WHICH IS WHY YOU NEED TO TELL ME EXACTLY WHAT'S GOING ON...
AND AT ANY POINT IF I THINK YOU'RE LYING I'M CALLING THE COPS.
CAM--
WHAT? DON'T PRETEND THAT I'M BEING CRAZY HERE, ALRIGHT?
I DON'T NEED WHATEVER YOUR VERSION OF THE TRUTH IS--BECAUSE YOUR ***BEING HERE*** PUTS MY LIFE AT RISK.
AND I KNOW YOU KNOW THAT.
SO THIS BETTER BE GOOD.
...YOU'RE RIGHT.
I'M SORRY. I JUST DIDN'T KNOW WHAT ELSE TO DO.
BUT IF I EXPLAIN...
YOU'RE NOT GONNA BELIEVE ME.
YOU'RE SERIOUS?
THEN YOU CAN LEAVE RIGHT NOW.
WHAT DOES IT LOOK LIKE?
SIGH ALRIGHT, YOU WIN. BUT LIKE I SAID, YOU'RE NOT GONNA THINK ANY OF THIS IS TRUE.
I MEAN, FOR STARTERS, YOU GOTTA WRAP YOUR HEAD AROUND THIS...

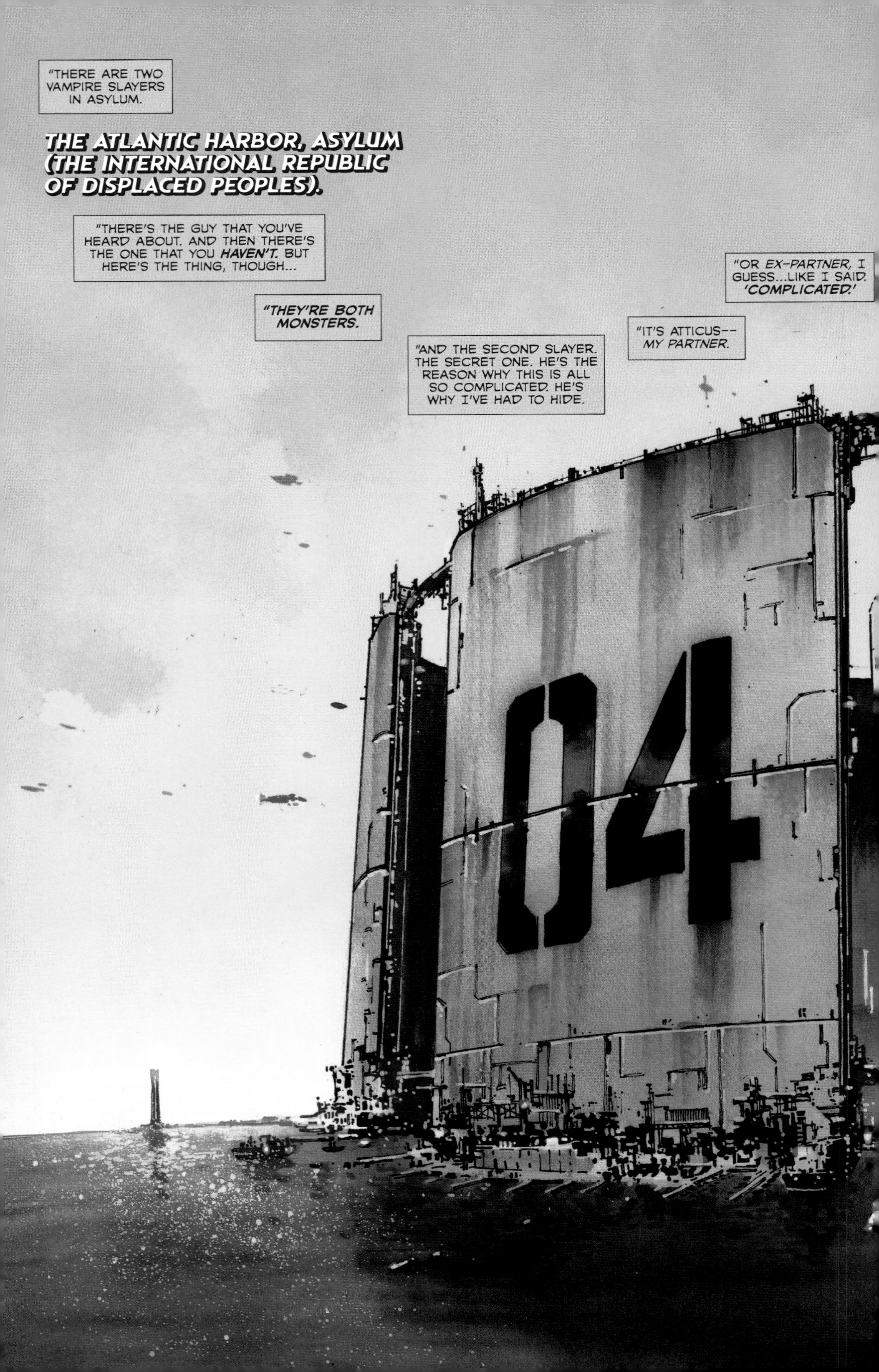
"THERE ARE TWO VAMPIRE SLAYERS IN ASYLUM.
THE ATLANTIC HARBOR, ASYLUM (THE INTERNATIONAL REPUBLIC OF DISPLACED PEOPLES).
"THERE'S THE GUY THAT YOU'VE HEARD ABOUT. AND THEN THERE'S THE ONE THAT YOU HAVEN'T. BUT HERE'S THE THING, THOUGH...
"THEY'RE BOTH MONSTERS.
"AND THE SECOND SLAYER. THE SECRET ONE. HE'S THE REASON WHY THIS IS ALL SO COMPLICATED. HE'S WHY I'VE HAD TO HIDE.
"IT'S ATTICUS-- MY PARTNER.
"OR EX-PARTNER, I GUESS...LIKE I SAID. 'COMPLICATED.'
04

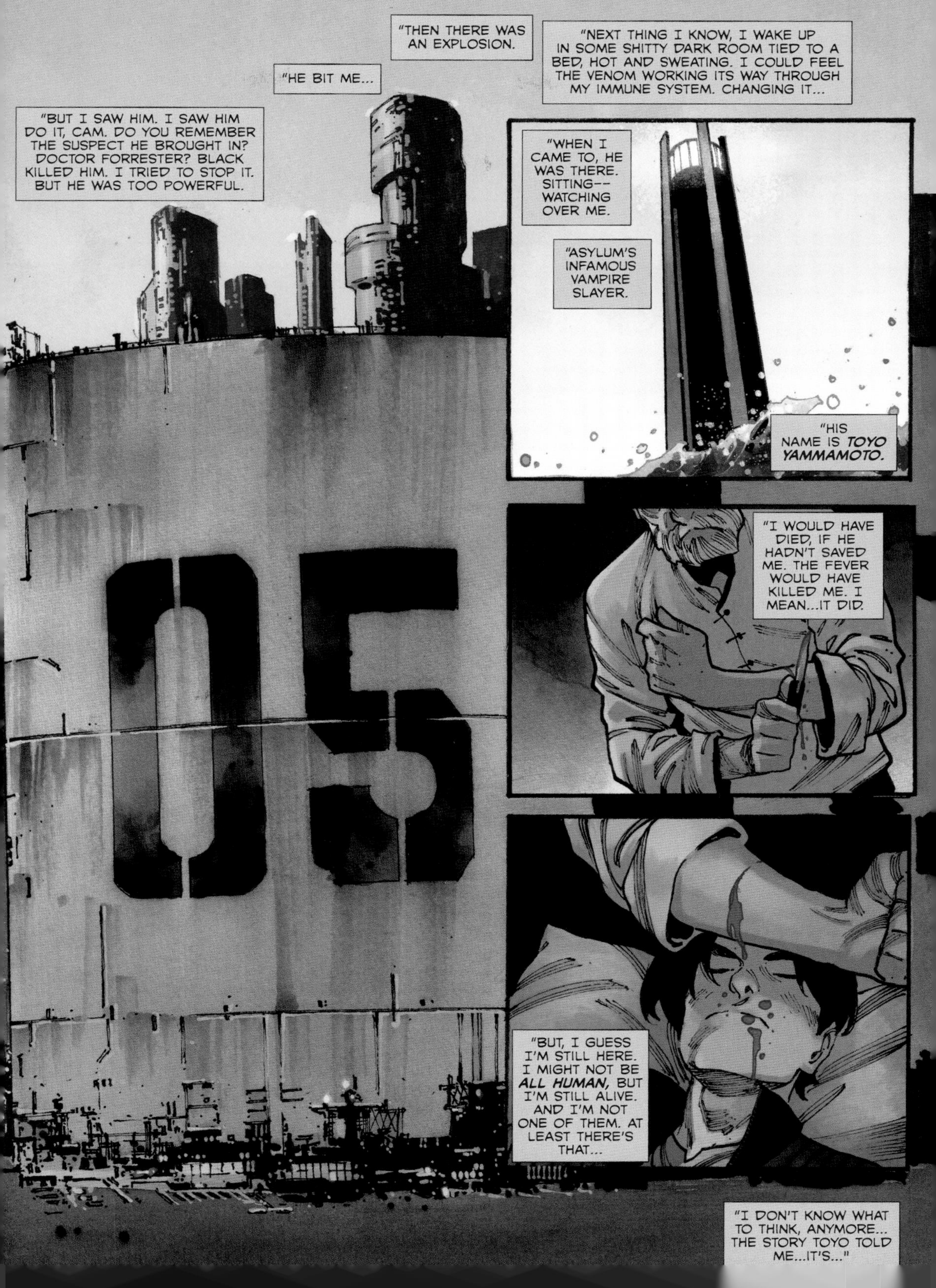
"BUT I SAW HIM. I SAW HIM DO IT, CAM. DO YOU REMEMBER THE SUSPECT HE BROUGHT IN? DOCTOR FORRESTER? BLACK KILLED HIM. I TRIED TO STOP IT. BUT HE WAS TOO POWERFUL.
"HE BIT ME...
"THEN THERE WAS AN EXPLOSION.
"NEXT THING I KNOW, I WAKE UP IN SOME SHITTY DARK ROOM TIED TO A BED, HOT AND SWEATING. I COULD FEEL THE VENOM WORKING ITS WAY THROUGH MY IMMUNE SYSTEM. CHANGING IT...
"WHEN I CAME TO, HE WAS THERE. SITTING--WATCHING OVER ME.
"ASYLUM'S INFAMOUS VAMPIRE SLAYER.
"HIS NAME IS *TOYO YAMMAMOTO.*
"I WOULD HAVE DIED, IF HE HADN'T SAVED ME. THE FEVER WOULD HAVE KILLED ME. I MEAN...IT DID.
"BUT, I GUESS I'M STILL HERE. I MIGHT NOT BE ***ALL HUMAN,*** BUT I'M STILL ALIVE. AND I'M NOT ONE OF THEM. AT LEAST THERE'S THAT...
05
"I DON'T KNOW WHAT TO THINK, ANYMORE... THE STORY TOYO TOLD ME...IT'S..."

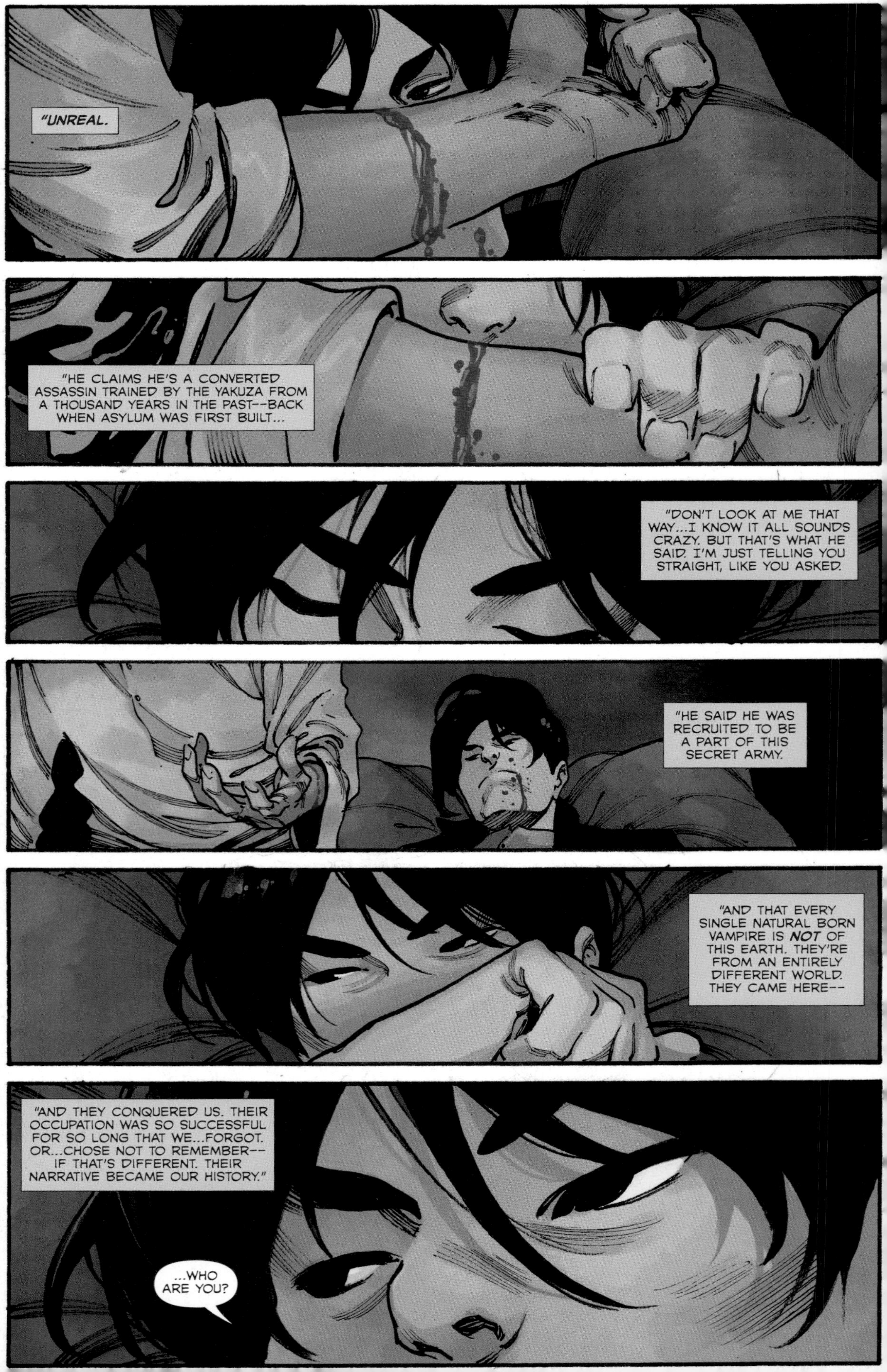
"UNREAL.
"HE CLAIMS HE'S A CONVERTED ASSASSIN TRAINED BY THE YAKUZA FROM A THOUSAND YEARS IN THE PAST--BACK WHEN ASYLUM WAS FIRST BUILT...
"DON'T LOOK AT ME THAT WAY...I KNOW IT ALL SOUNDS CRAZY. BUT THAT'S WHAT HE SAID. I'M JUST TELLING YOU STRAIGHT, LIKE YOU ASKED.
"HE SAID HE WAS RECRUITED TO BE A PART OF THIS SECRET ARMY.
"AND THAT EVERY SINGLE NATURAL BORN VAMPIRE IS ***NOT*** OF THIS EARTH. THEY'RE FROM AN ENTIRELY DIFFERENT WORLD. THEY CAME HERE--
"AND THEY CONQUERED US. THEIR OCCUPATION WAS SO SUCCESSFUL FOR SO LONG THAT WE...FORGOT. OR...CHOSE NOT TO REMEMBER--IF THAT'S DIFFERENT. THEIR NARRATIVE BECAME OUR HISTORY."
...WHO ARE YOU?

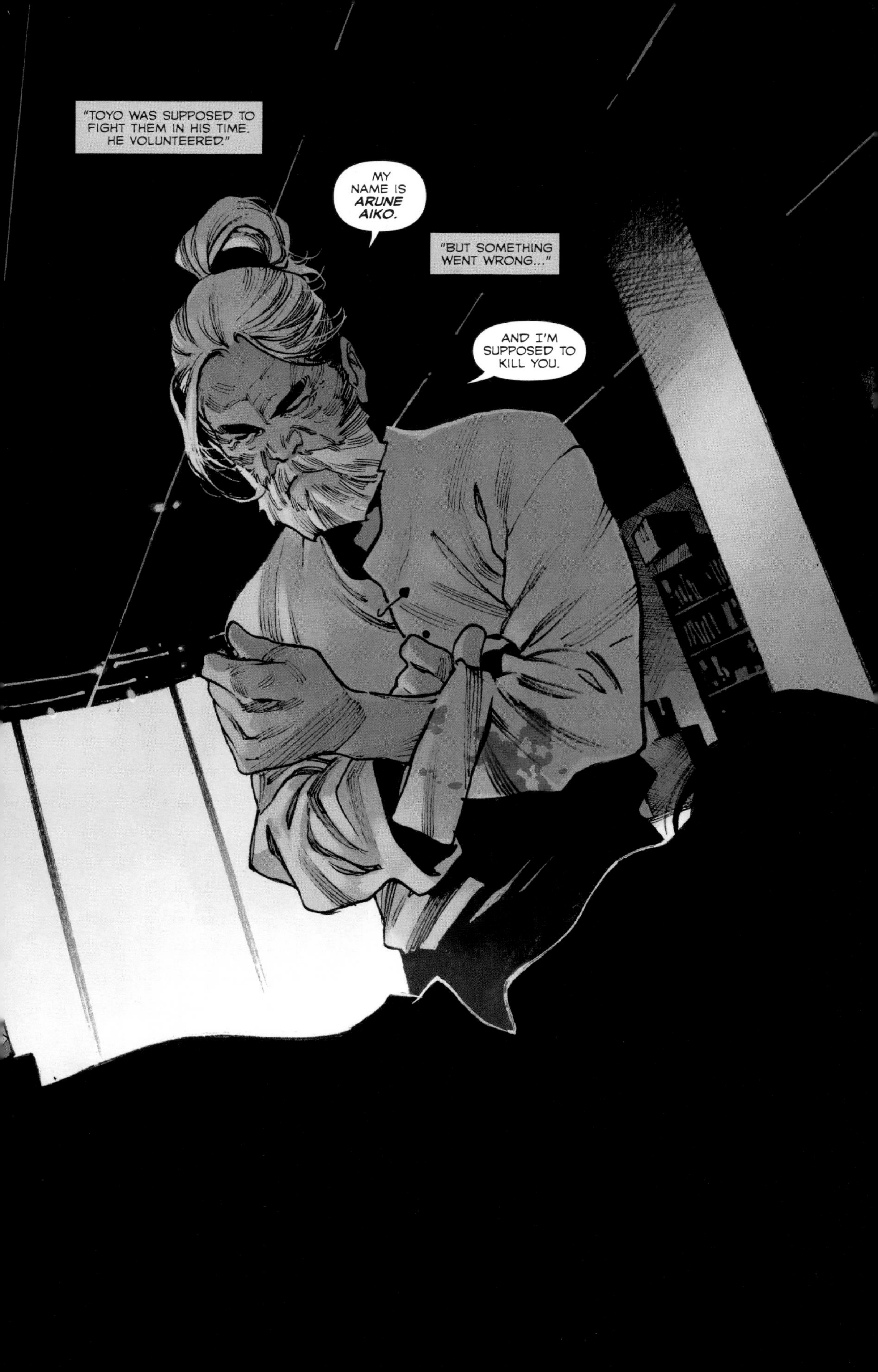
"TOYO WAS SUPPOSED TO FIGHT THEM IN HIS TIME. HE VOLUNTEERED."
MY NAME IS *ARUNE AIKO.*
"BUT SOMETHING WENT WRONG..."
AND I'M SUPPOSED TO KILL YOU.

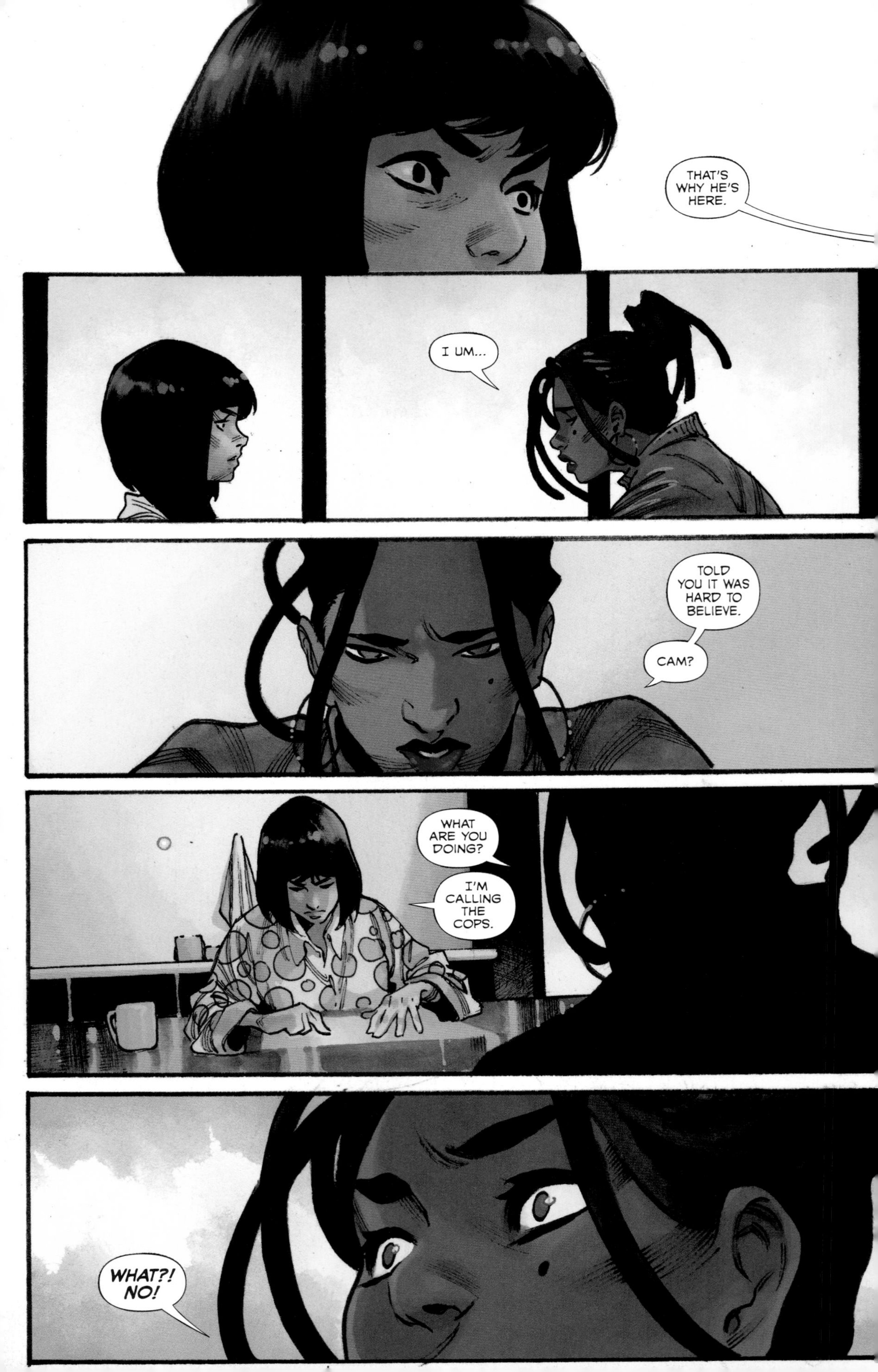
THAT'S WHY HE'S HERE.
I UM...
TOLD YOU IT WAS HARD TO BELIEVE.
CAM?
WHAT ARE YOU DOING?
I'M CALLING THE COPS.
WHAT?! NO!

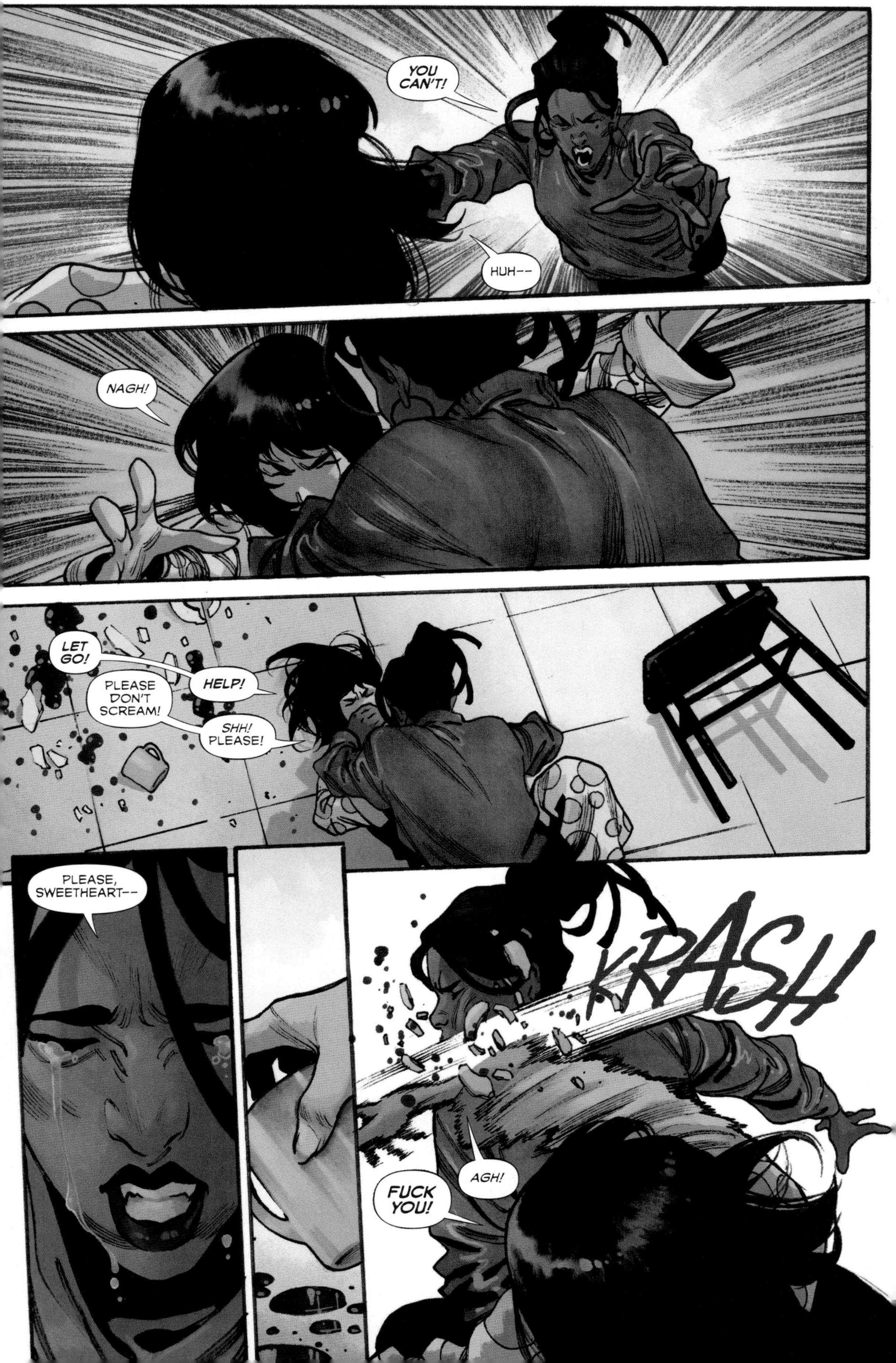
YOU CAN'T!
HUH--
NAGH!
LET GO!
HELP!
PLEASE DON'T SCREAM!
SHH! PLEASE!
PLEASE, SWEETHEART--
KRASH
AGH!
FUCK YOU!

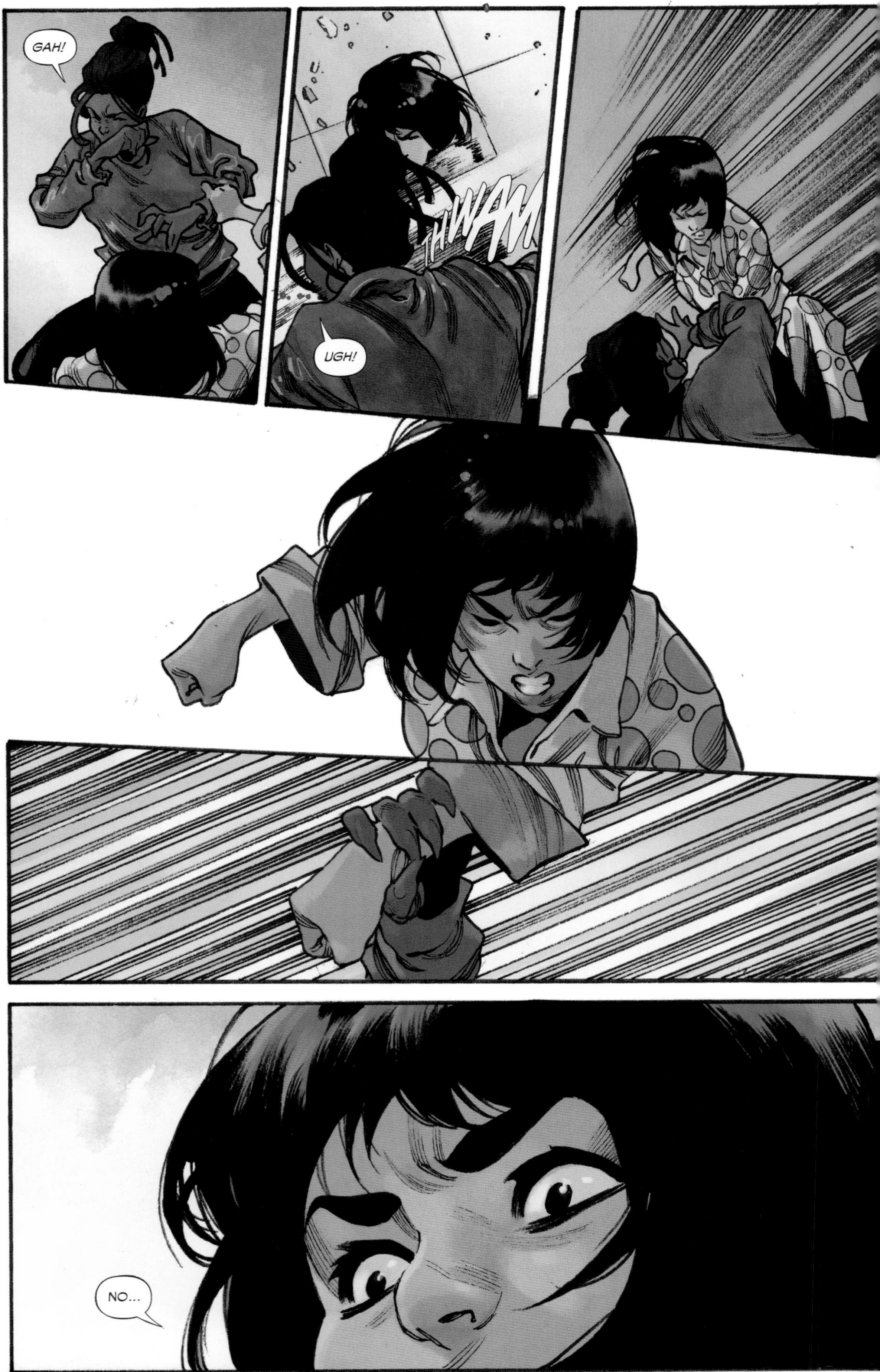
GAH!
THWAM
UGH!
NO...

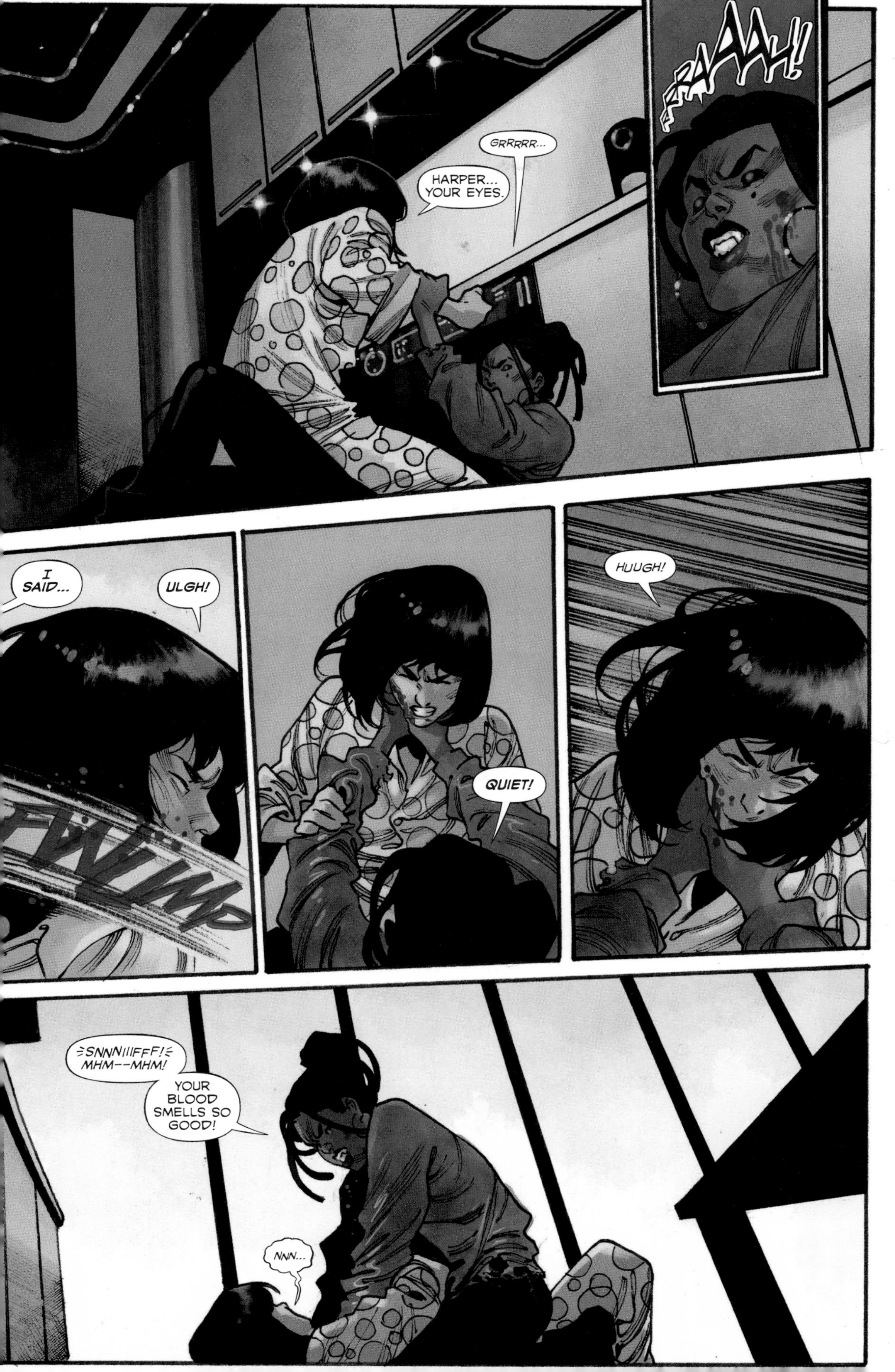
GRRRRR...
HARPER... YOUR EYES.
FRAAAH!
I SAID...
ULGH!
QUIET!
HUUGH!
SNNIIIFFF! MHM--MHM!
YOUR BLOOD SMELLS SO GOOD!
NNN...

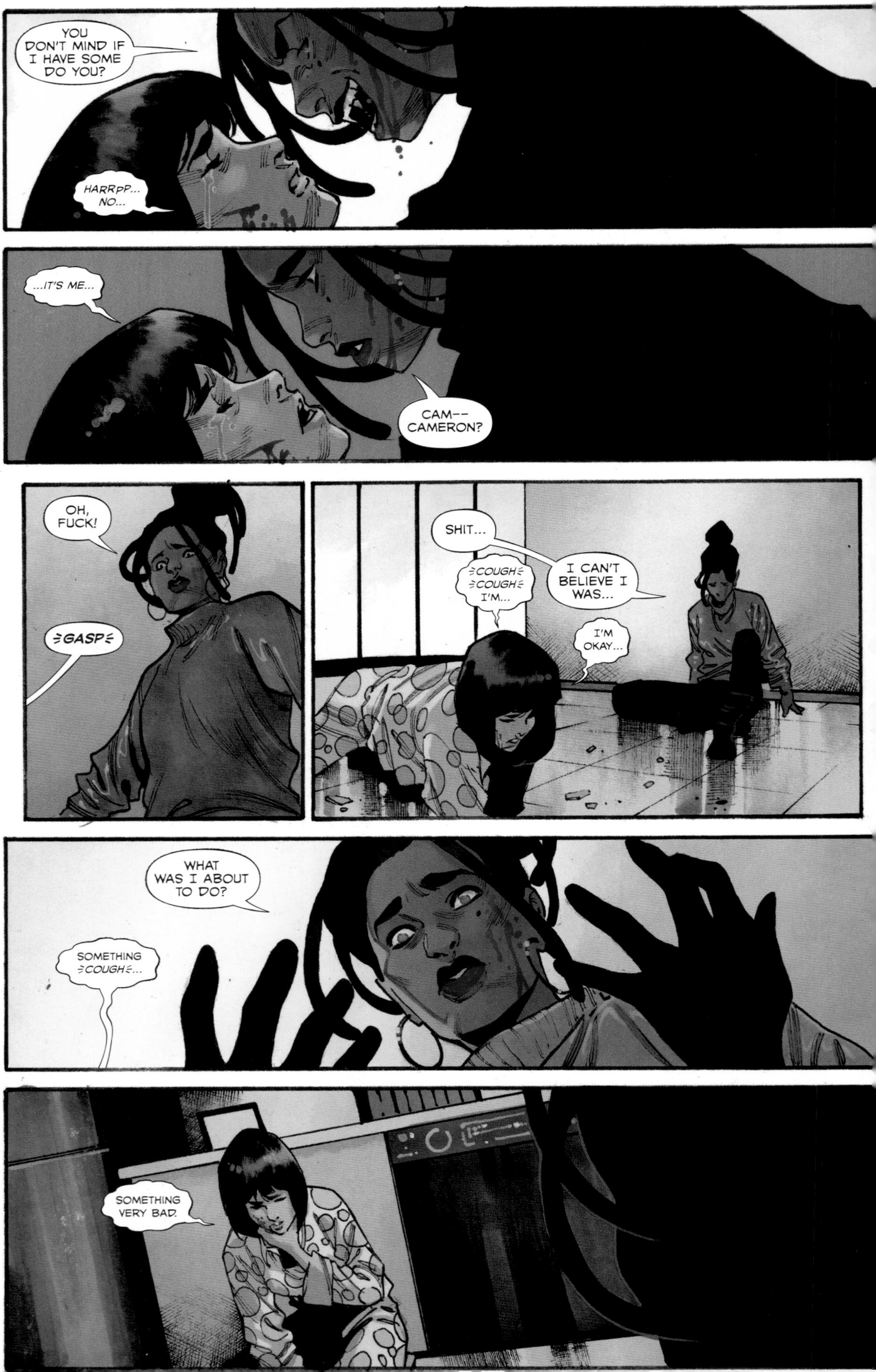

YOU DON'T MIND IF I HAVE SOME DO YOU?
HARRPP... NO...
...IT'S ME...
CAM-- CAMERON?
OH, FUCK!
GASP
SHIT...
COUGH COUGH I'M...
I CAN'T BELIEVE I WAS...
I'M OKAY...
WHAT WAS I ABOUT TO DO?
SOMETHING COUGH...
SOMETHING VERY BAD.

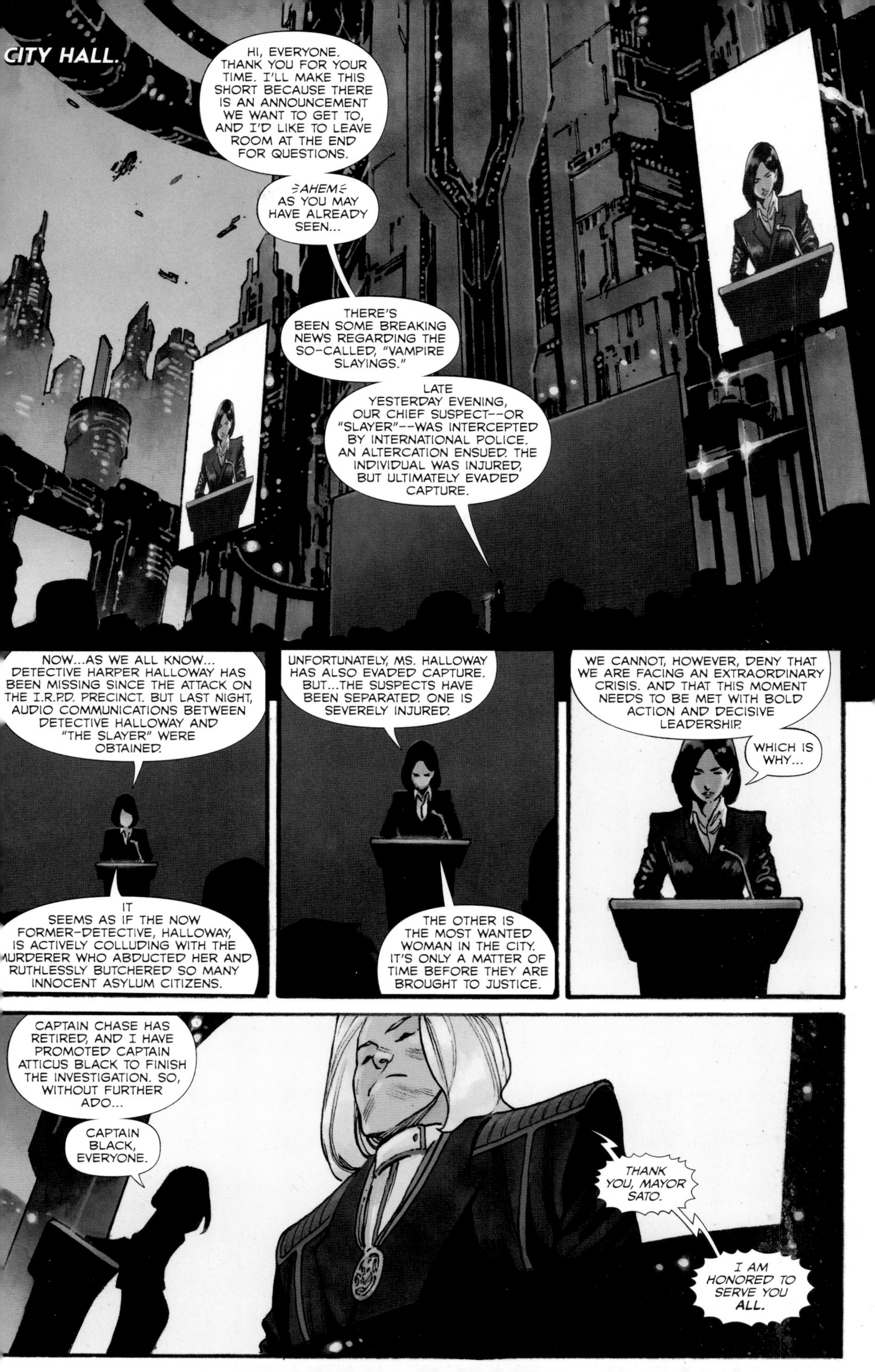
CITY HALL.
HI, EVERYONE. THANK YOU FOR YOUR TIME. I'LL MAKE THIS SHORT BECAUSE THERE IS AN ANNOUNCEMENT WE WANT TO GET TO, AND I'D LIKE TO LEAVE ROOM AT THE END FOR QUESTIONS.
AHEM AS YOU MAY HAVE ALREADY SEEN...
THERE'S BEEN SOME BREAKING NEWS REGARDING THE SO-CALLED, "VAMPIRE SLAYINGS."
LATE YESTERDAY EVENING, OUR CHIEF SUSPECT--OR "SLAYER"--WAS INTERCEPTED BY INTERNATIONAL POLICE. AN ALTERCATION ENSUED. THE INDIVIDUAL WAS INJURED, BUT ULTIMATELY EVADED CAPTURE.
NOW...AS WE ALL KNOW... DETECTIVE HARPER HALLOWAY HAS BEEN MISSING SINCE THE ATTACK ON THE I.R.P.D. PRECINCT. BUT LAST NIGHT, AUDIO COMMUNICATIONS BETWEEN DETECTIVE HALLOWAY AND "THE SLAYER" WERE OBTAINED.
IT SEEMS AS IF THE NOW FORMER-DETECTIVE, HALLOWAY, IS ACTIVELY COLLUDING WITH THE MURDERER WHO ABDUCTED HER AND RUTHLESSLY BUTCHERED SO MANY INNOCENT ASYLUM CITIZENS.
UNFORTUNATELY, MS. HALLOWAY HAS ALSO EVADED CAPTURE. BUT...THE SUSPECTS HAVE BEEN SEPARATED. ONE IS SEVERELY INJURED.
THE OTHER IS THE MOST WANTED WOMAN IN THE CITY. IT'S ONLY A MATTER OF TIME BEFORE THEY ARE BROUGHT TO JUSTICE.
WE CANNOT, HOWEVER, DENY THAT WE ARE FACING AN EXTRAORDINARY CRISIS. AND THAT THIS MOMENT NEEDS TO BE MET WITH BOLD ACTION AND DECISIVE LEADERSHIP.
WHICH IS WHY...
CAPTAIN CHASE HAS RETIRED, AND I HAVE PROMOTED CAPTAIN ATTICUS BLACK TO FINISH THE INVESTIGATION. SO, WITHOUT FURTHER ADO...
CAPTAIN BLACK, EVERYONE.
THANK YOU, MAYOR SATO.
I AM HONORED TO SERVE YOU ALL.

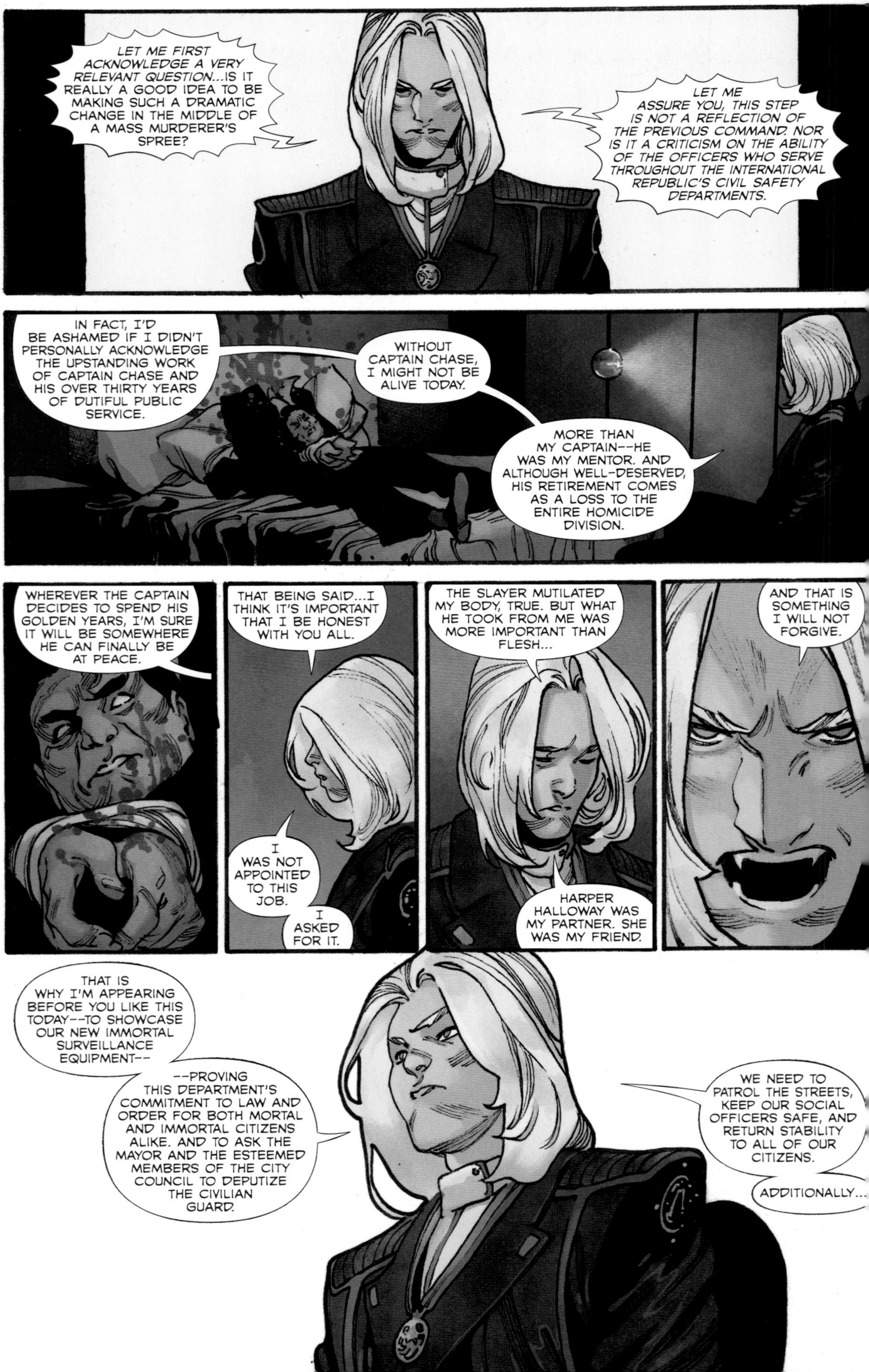
LET ME FIRST ACKNOWLEDGE A VERY RELEVANT QUESTION...IS IT REALLY A GOOD IDEA TO BE MAKING SUCH A DRAMATIC CHANGE IN THE MIDDLE OF A MASS MURDERER'S SPREE?
LET ME ASSURE YOU, THIS STEP IS NOT A REFLECTION OF THE PREVIOUS COMMAND. NOR IS IT A CRITICISM ON THE ABILITY OF THE OFFICERS WHO SERVE THROUGHOUT THE INTERNATIONAL REPUBLIC'S CIVIL SAFETY DEPARTMENTS.
IN FACT, I'D BE ASHAMED IF I DIDN'T PERSONALLY ACKNOWLEDGE THE UPSTANDING WORK OF CAPTAIN CHASE AND HIS OVER THIRTY YEARS OF DUTIFUL PUBLIC SERVICE.
WITHOUT CAPTAIN CHASE, I MIGHT NOT BE ALIVE TODAY.
MORE THAN MY CAPTAIN--HE WAS MY MENTOR. AND ALTHOUGH WELL-DESERVED, HIS RETIREMENT COMES AS A LOSS TO THE ENTIRE HOMICIDE DIVISION.
WHEREVER THE CAPTAIN DECIDES TO SPEND HIS GOLDEN YEARS, I'M SURE IT WILL BE SOMEWHERE HE CAN FINALLY BE AT PEACE.
THAT BEING SAID...I THINK IT'S IMPORTANT THAT I BE HONEST WITH YOU ALL.
I WAS NOT APPOINTED TO THIS JOB.
I ASKED FOR IT.
THE SLAYER MUTILATED MY BODY, TRUE. BUT WHAT HE TOOK FROM ME WAS MORE IMPORTANT THAN FLESH...
HARPER HALLOWAY WAS MY PARTNER. SHE WAS MY FRIEND.
AND THAT IS SOMETHING I WILL NOT FORGIVE.
THAT IS WHY I'M APPEARING BEFORE YOU LIKE THIS TODAY--TO SHOWCASE OUR NEW IMMORTAL SURVEILLANCE EQUIPMENT--
--PROVING THIS DEPARTMENT'S COMMITMENT TO LAW AND ORDER FOR BOTH MORTAL AND IMMORTAL CITIZENS ALIKE. AND TO ASK THE MAYOR AND THE ESTEEMED MEMBERS OF THE CITY COUNCIL TO DEPUTIZE THE CIVILIAN GUARD.
WE NEED TO PATROL THE STREETS, KEEP OUR SOCIAL OFFICERS SAFE, AND RETURN STABILITY TO ALL OF OUR CITIZENS.
ADDITIONALLY...

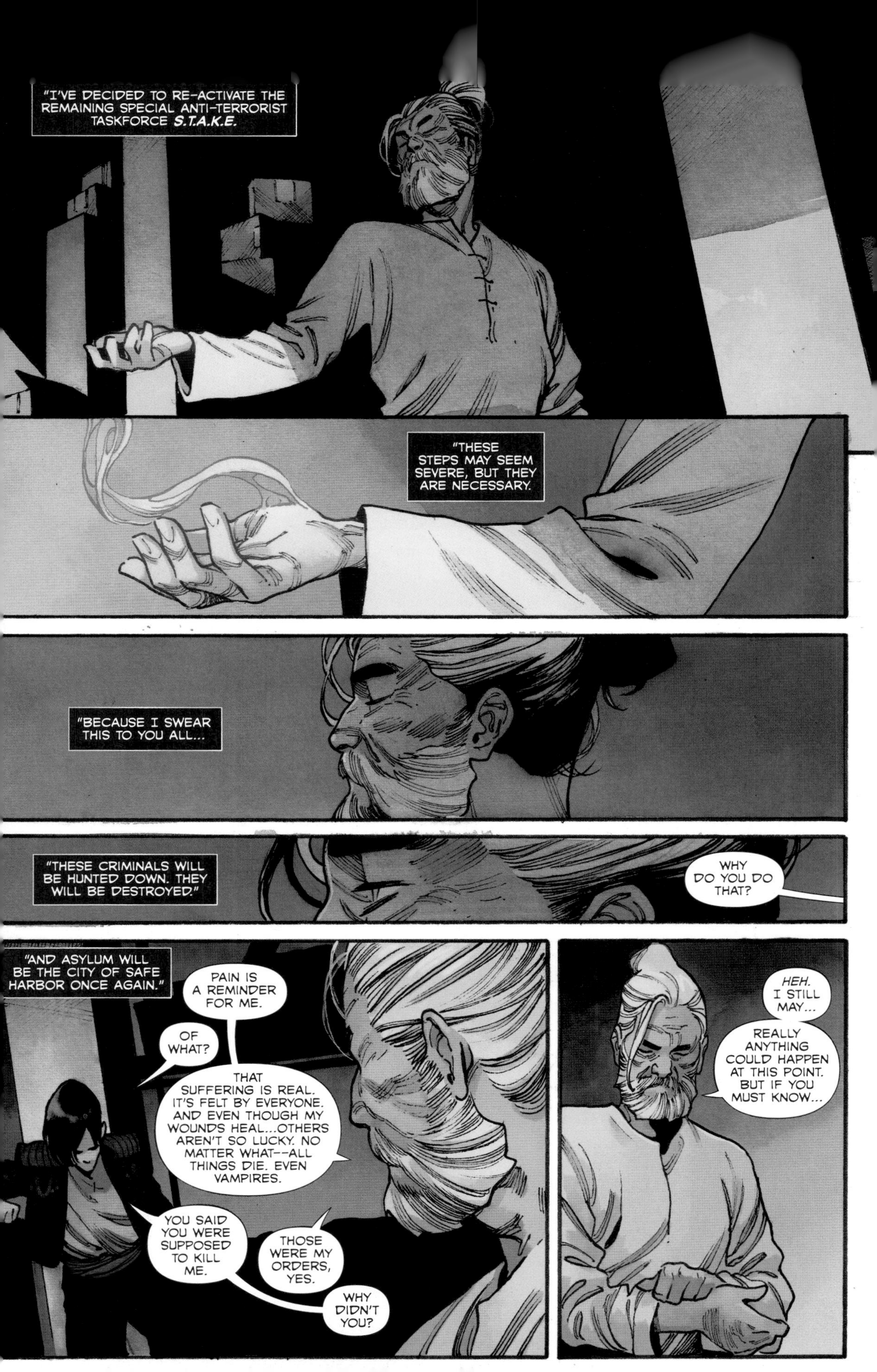
"I'VE DECIDED TO RE-ACTIVATE THE REMAINING SPECIAL ANTI-TERRORIST TASKFORCE *S.T.A.K.E.*
"THESE STEPS MAY SEEM SEVERE, BUT THEY ARE NECESSARY.
"BECAUSE I SWEAR THIS TO YOU ALL...
"THESE CRIMINALS WILL BE HUNTED DOWN. THEY WILL BE DESTROYED."
WHY DO YOU DO THAT?
"AND ASYLUM WILL BE THE CITY OF SAFE HARBOR ONCE AGAIN."
PAIN IS A REMINDER FOR ME.
OF WHAT?
THAT SUFFERING IS REAL. IT'S FELT BY EVERYONE. AND EVEN THOUGH MY WOUNDS HEAL...OTHERS AREN'T SO LUCKY. NO MATTER WHAT--ALL THINGS DIE. EVEN VAMPIRES.
YOU SAID YOU WERE SUPPOSED TO KILL ME.
THOSE WERE MY ORDERS, YES.
WHY DIDN'T YOU?
HEH. I STILL MAY...
REALLY ANYTHING COULD HAPPEN AT THIS POINT. BUT IF YOU MUST KNOW...

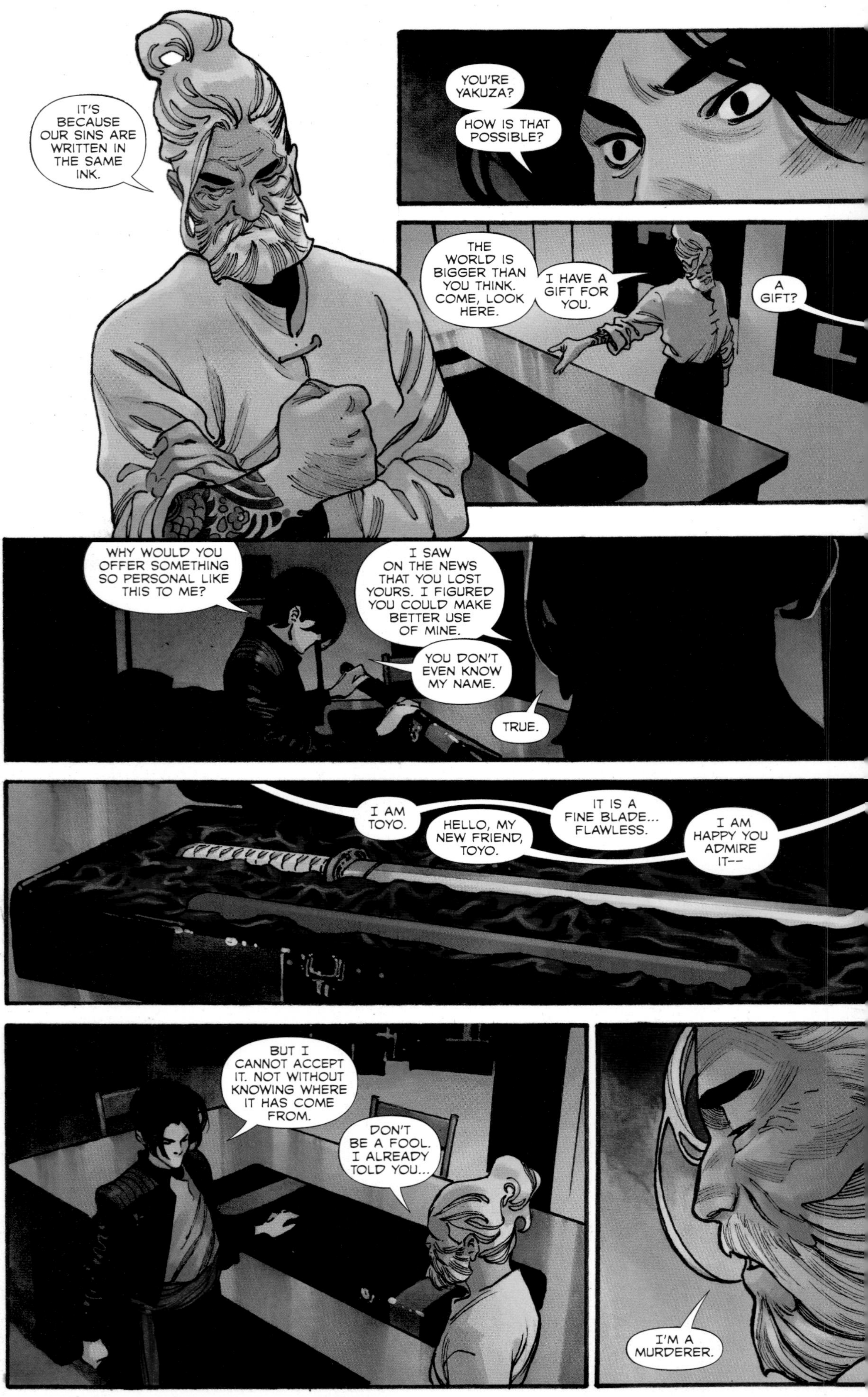
IT'S BECAUSE OUR SINS ARE WRITTEN IN THE SAME INK.
YOU'RE YAKUZA?
HOW IS THAT POSSIBLE?
THE WORLD IS BIGGER THAN YOU THINK. COME, LOOK HERE.
I HAVE A GIFT FOR YOU.
A GIFT?
WHY WOULD YOU OFFER SOMETHING SO PERSONAL LIKE THIS TO ME?
I SAW ON THE NEWS THAT YOU LOST YOURS. I FIGURED YOU COULD MAKE BETTER USE OF MINE.
YOU DON'T EVEN KNOW MY NAME.
TRUE.
I AM TOYO.
HELLO, MY NEW FRIEND, TOYO.
IT IS A FINE BLADE... FLAWLESS.
I AM HAPPY YOU ADMIRE IT--
BUT I CANNOT ACCEPT IT. NOT WITHOUT KNOWING WHERE IT HAS COME FROM.
DON'T BE A FOOL. I ALREADY TOLD YOU...
I'M A MURDERER.

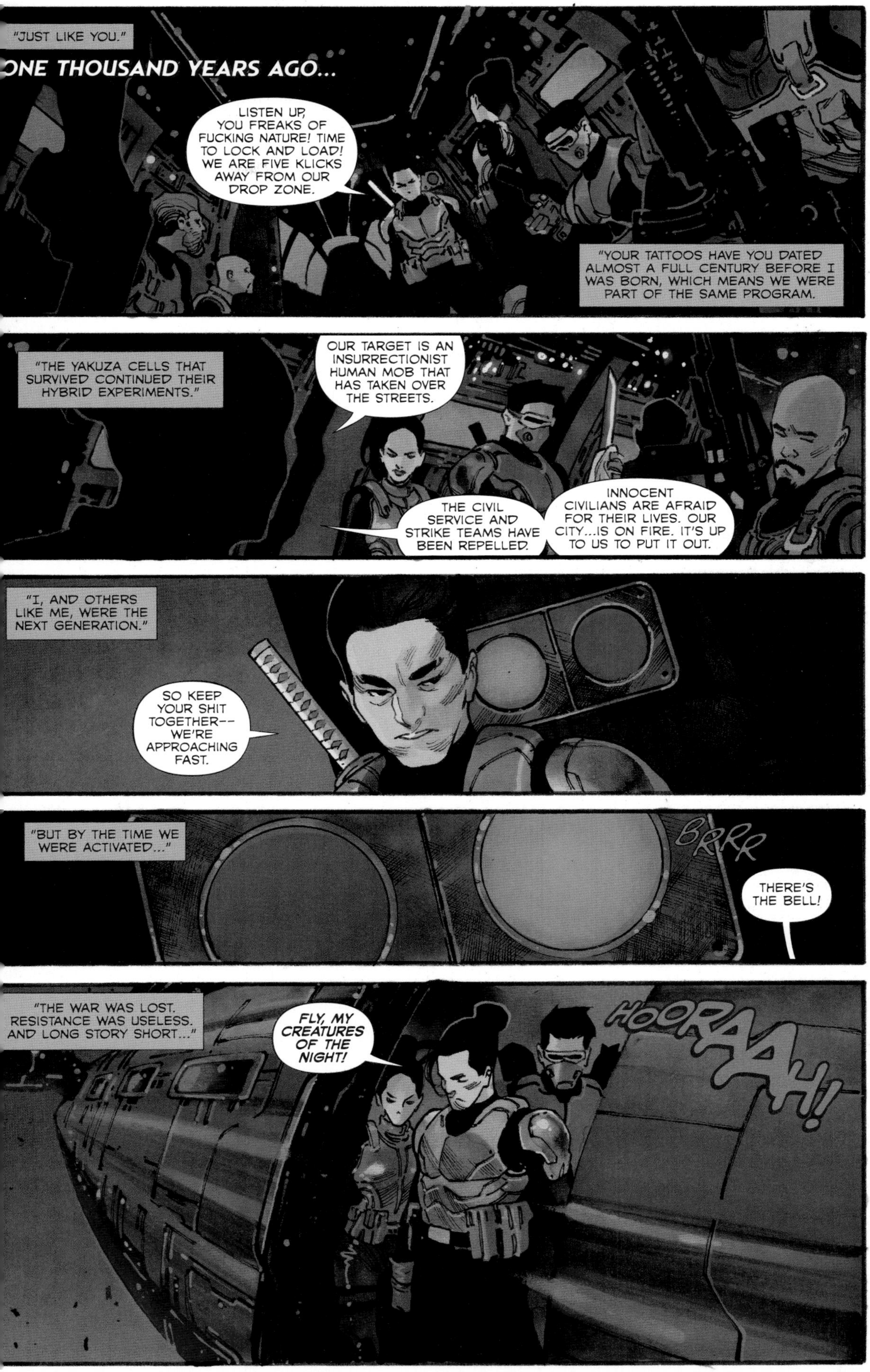

"JUST LIKE YOU."
ONE THOUSAND YEARS AGO...
LISTEN UP, YOU FREAKS OF FUCKING NATURE! TIME TO LOCK AND LOAD! WE ARE FIVE KLICKS AWAY FROM OUR DROP ZONE.
"YOUR TATTOOS HAVE YOU DATED ALMOST A FULL CENTURY BEFORE I WAS BORN, WHICH MEANS WE WERE PART OF THE SAME PROGRAM.
"THE YAKUZA CELLS THAT SURVIVED CONTINUED THEIR HYBRID EXPERIMENTS."
OUR TARGET IS AN INSURRECTIONIST HUMAN MOB THAT HAS TAKEN OVER THE STREETS.
THE CIVIL SERVICE AND STRIKE TEAMS HAVE BEEN REPELLED.
INNOCENT CIVILIANS ARE AFRAID FOR THEIR LIVES. OUR CITY...IS ON FIRE. IT'S UP TO US TO PUT IT OUT.
"I, AND OTHERS LIKE ME, WERE THE NEXT GENERATION."
SO KEEP YOUR SHIT TOGETHER-- WE'RE APPROACHING FAST.
"BUT BY THE TIME WE WERE ACTIVATED..."
BRRR
THERE'S THE BELL!
"THE WAR WAS LOST. RESISTANCE WAS USELESS. AND LONG STORY SHORT..."
FLY, MY CREATURES OF THE NIGHT!
HOORAAH!!

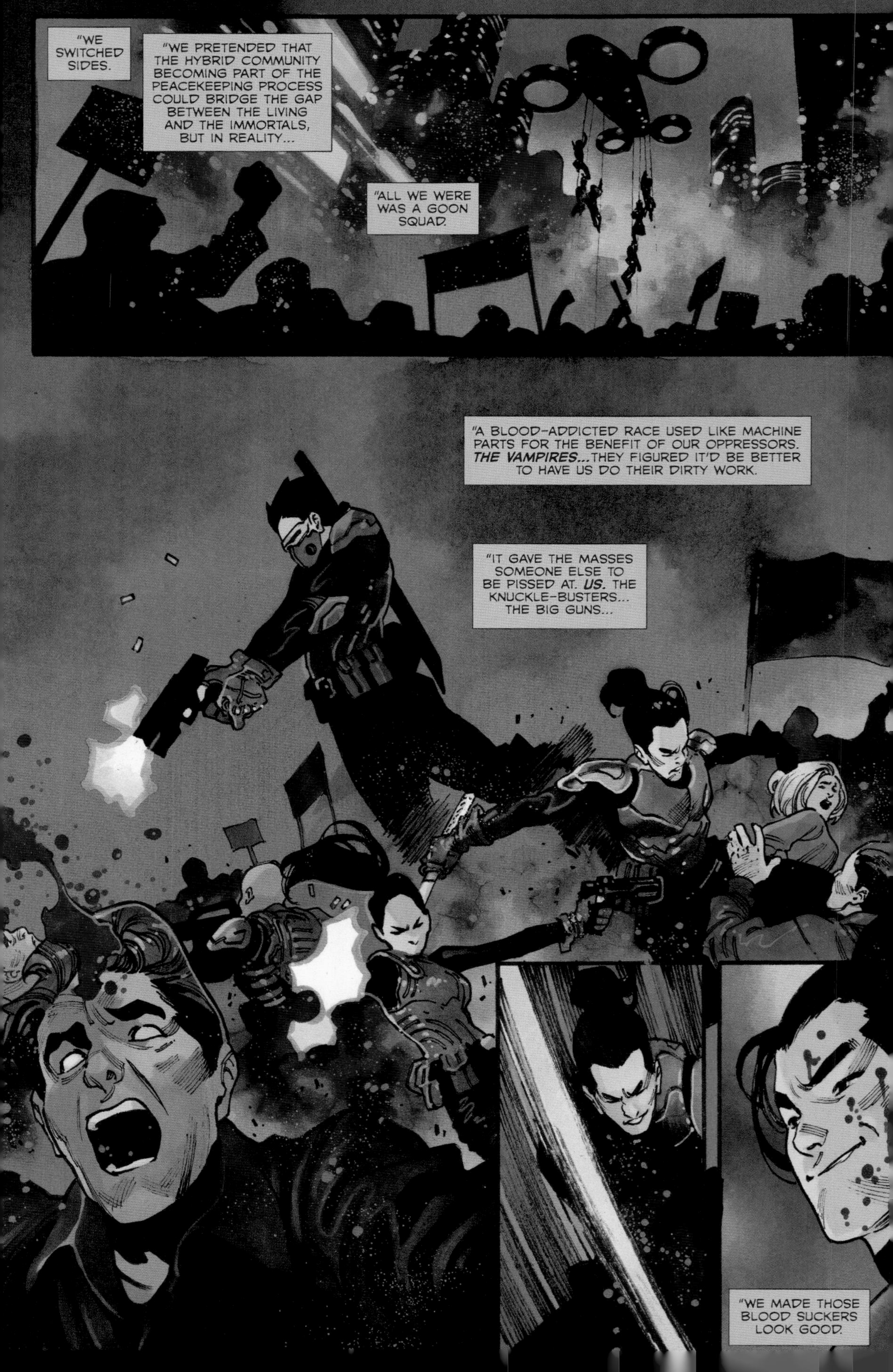
"WE SWITCHED SIDES.
"WE PRETENDED THAT THE HYBRID COMMUNITY BECOMING PART OF THE PEACEKEEPING PROCESS COULD BRIDGE THE GAP BETWEEN THE LIVING AND THE IMMORTALS, BUT IN REALITY...
"ALL WE WERE WAS A GOON SQUAD.
"A BLOOD-ADDICTED RACE USED LIKE MACHINE PARTS FOR THE BENEFIT OF OUR OPPRESSORS. *THE VAMPIRES...* THEY FIGURED IT'D BE BETTER TO HAVE US DO THEIR DIRTY WORK.
"IT GAVE THE MASSES SOMEONE ELSE TO BE PISSED AT. *US.* THE KNUCKLE-BUSTERS... THE BIG GUNS...
"WE MADE THOSE BLOOD SUCKERS LOOK GOOD.

THEY RETIRED S.T.A.K.E. HUNDREDS OF YEARS AGO. THERE WERE NO MORE TERRORISTS TO KILL. NO MORE SOCIAL STRIFE. THE IMMORTALS HAD WON. AND WORLD PEACE WAS ACHIEVED.

FOR CENTURIES I'VE WATCHED THIS CITY CHANGE.

I REMEMBER HOW IT ONLY TOOK ABOUT THREE GENERATIONS FOR US ALL TO FORGET.

WE ARE NOT THE SAME.

DON'T YOU GET IT? YOU AND I ARE THE SAME. I JUST...CAME LATER.

DO YOU REALLY THINK THIS IS WHAT I WANTED?

THEN HELP ME COMPLETE OUR MISSION. HELP ME--

NO.

I'VE HAD MY FILL OF BLOOD...

WHY DO YOU THINK I'M GIVING YOU MY SWORD?

YOU'RE RIGHT. AND I THANK YOU FOR IT.

BUT I WILL FAIL ALONE.

WHO WAS THAT WOMAN YOU WERE WORKING WITH?

HARPER?

YES. HER. LISTEN TO ME...

...I'VE BEEN FOLLOWING THE VAMPIRE SLAYINGS SINCE THEY BEGAN.

THE COPS COULDN'T SOLVE THE CASE BECAUSE THEY SAID THERE WAS NO PATTERN. BUT THAT'S BECAUSE THEY WERE ONLY LOOKING FOR ONE KILLER.

WHEN THERE ARE TWO...

EXACTLY. YOUR VICTIMS WERE ALL HIGH PROFILE. IMMORTALS WITH INFLUENCE. WHERE AS HIS...TOTALLY RANDOM.

THE SECOND SLAYER IS KEY.

MAYBE THERE'S STILL A CHANCE YOU CAN TURN THIS ALL AROUND.

PIN YOUR CRIMES ON THEM.

FIND A WAY OUT.

THANK YOU FOR YOUR KINDNESS, ARUNE.

HM...

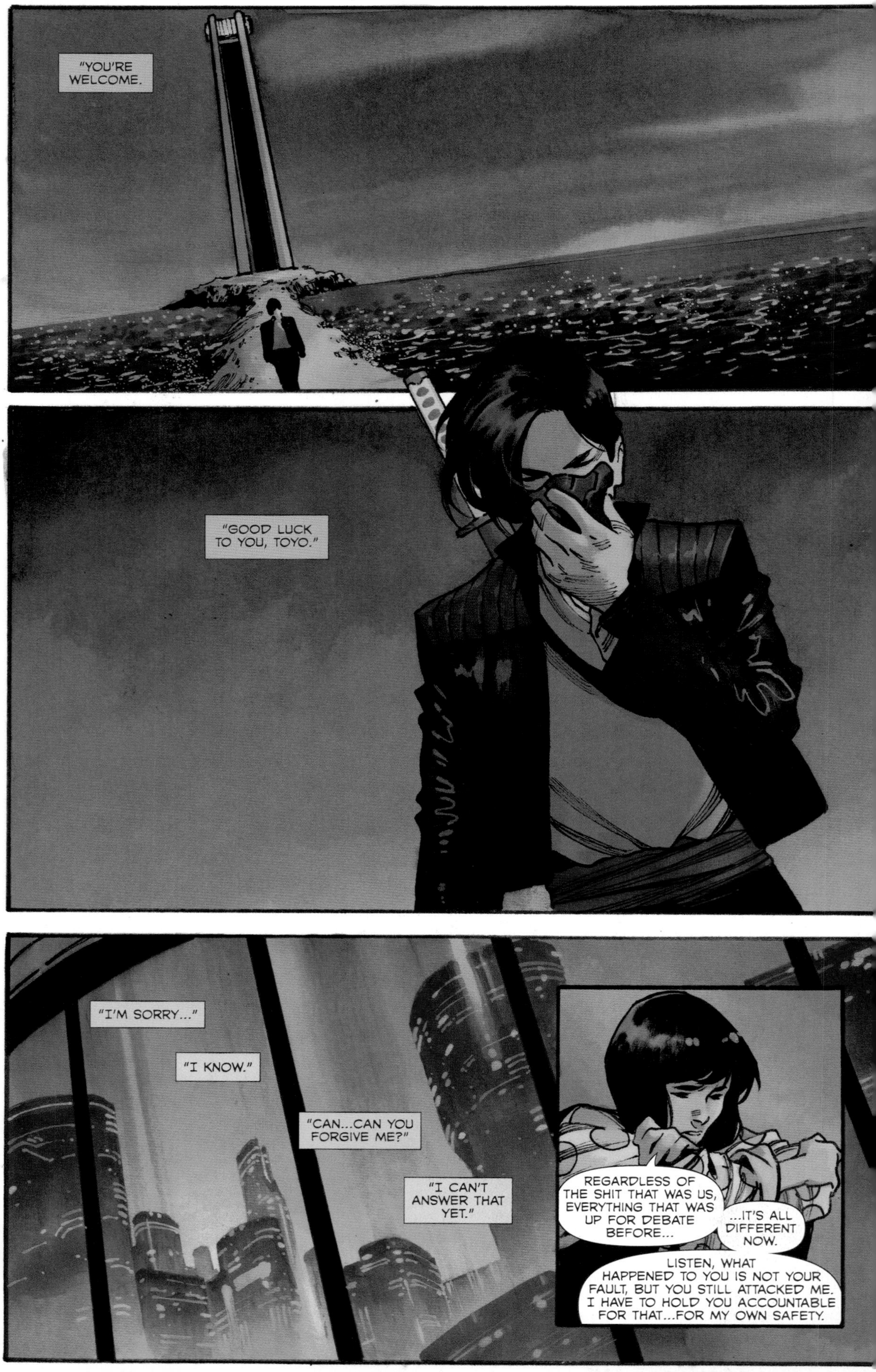
"YOU'RE WELCOME.
"GOOD LUCK TO YOU, TOYO."
"I'M SORRY..."
"I KNOW."
"CAN...CAN YOU FORGIVE ME?"
"I CAN'T ANSWER THAT YET."
REGARDLESS OF THE SHIT THAT WAS US, EVERYTHING THAT WAS UP FOR DEBATE BEFORE...
...IT'S ALL DIFFERENT NOW.
LISTEN, WHAT HAPPENED TO YOU IS NOT YOUR FAULT, BUT YOU STILL ATTACKED ME. I HAVE TO HOLD YOU ACCOUNTABLE FOR THAT...FOR MY OWN SAFETY.

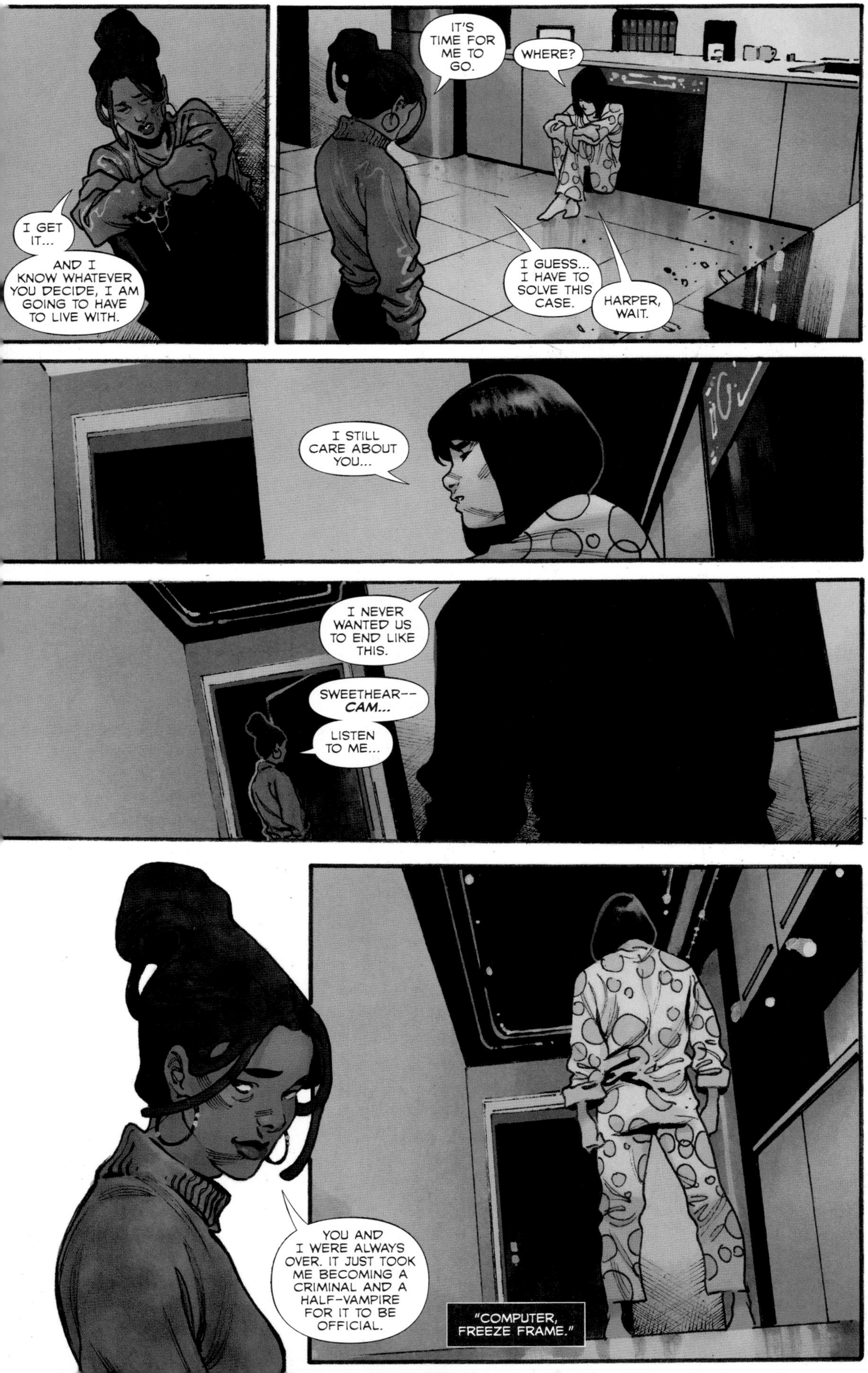
I GET IT...
AND I KNOW WHATEVER YOU DECIDE, I AM GOING TO HAVE TO LIVE WITH.
IT'S TIME FOR ME TO GO.
WHERE?
I GUESS... I HAVE TO SOLVE THIS CASE.
HARPER, WAIT.
I STILL CARE ABOUT YOU...
I NEVER WANTED US TO END LIKE THIS.
SWEETHEAR-- *CAM...*
LISTEN TO ME...
YOU AND I WERE ALWAYS OVER. IT JUST TOOK ME BECOMING A CRIMINAL AND A HALF-VAMPIRE FOR IT TO BE OFFICIAL.
"COMPUTER, FREEZE FRAME."

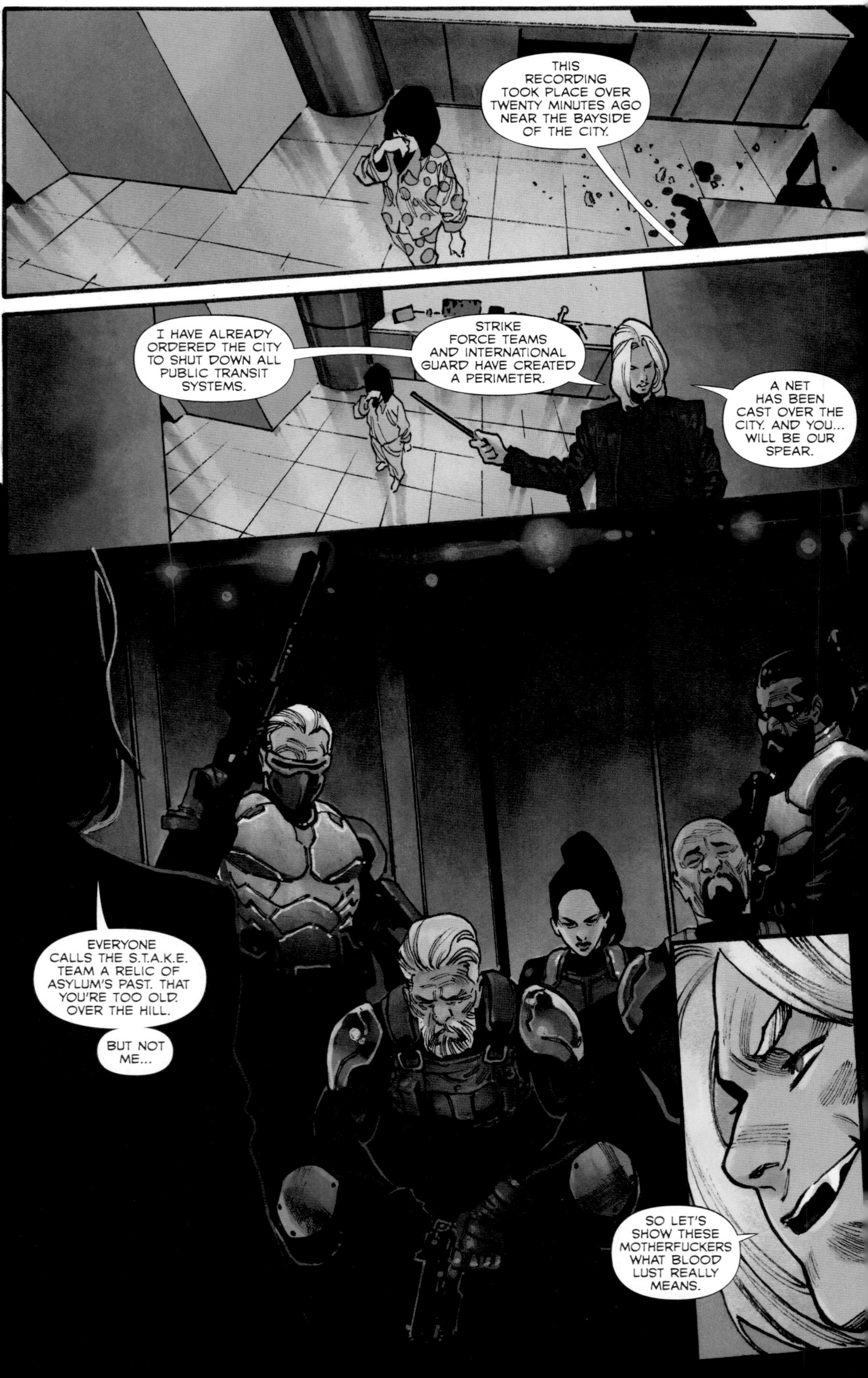
THIS RECORDING TOOK PLACE OVER TWENTY MINUTES AGO NEAR THE BAYSIDE OF THE CITY.
I HAVE ALREADY ORDERED THE CITY TO SHUT DOWN ALL PUBLIC TRANSIT SYSTEMS.
STRIKE FORCE TEAMS AND INTERNATIONAL GUARD HAVE CREATED A PERIMETER.
A NET HAS BEEN CAST OVER THE CITY. AND YOU... WILL BE OUR SPEAR.
EVERYONE CALLS THE S.T.A.K.E. TEAM A RELIC OF ASYLUM'S PAST. THAT YOU'RE TOO OLD. OVER THE HILL.
BUT NOT ME...
SO LET'S SHOW THESE MOTHERFUCKERS WHAT BLOOD LUST REALLY MEANS.

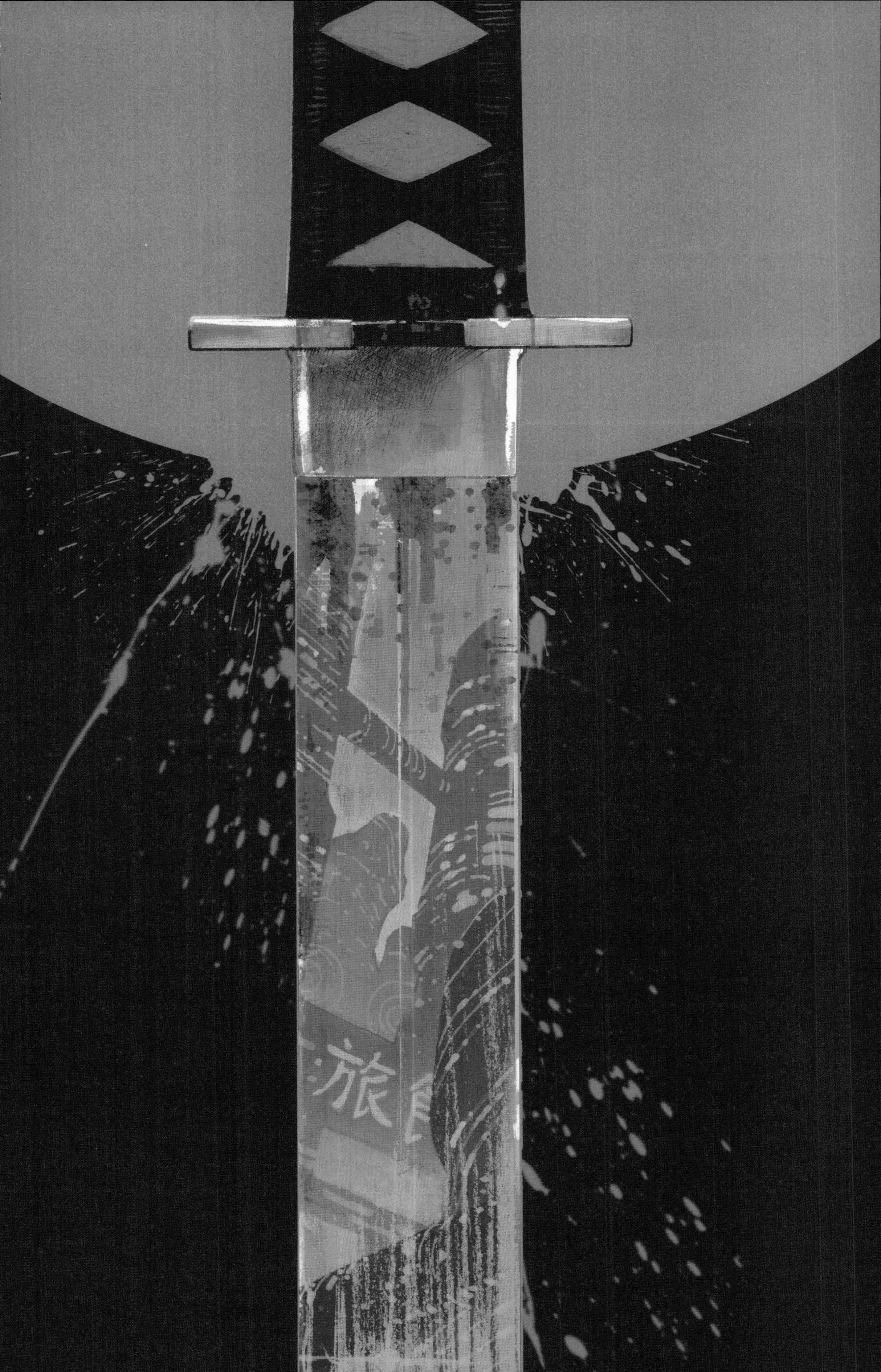
旅

FIVE

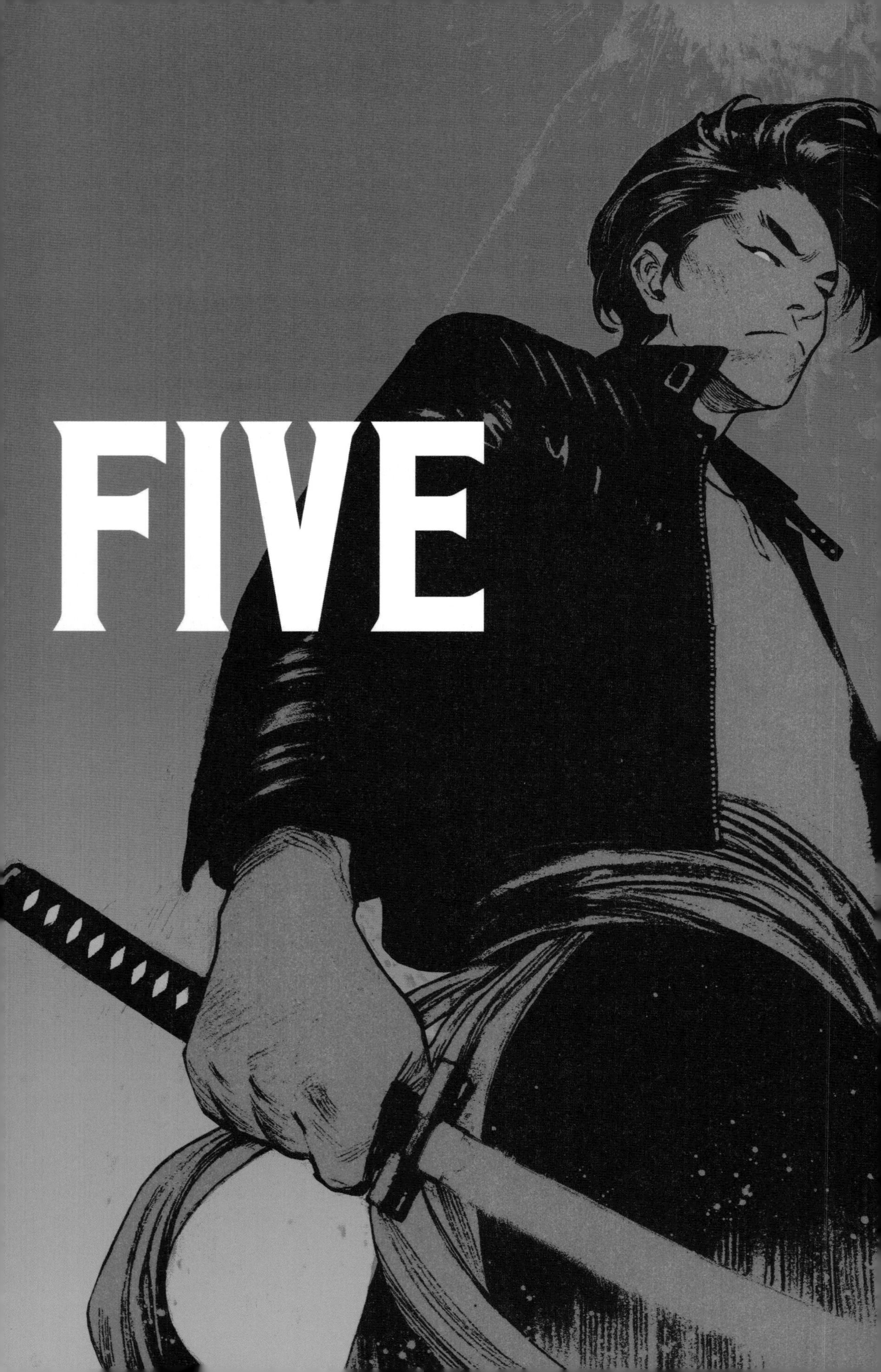

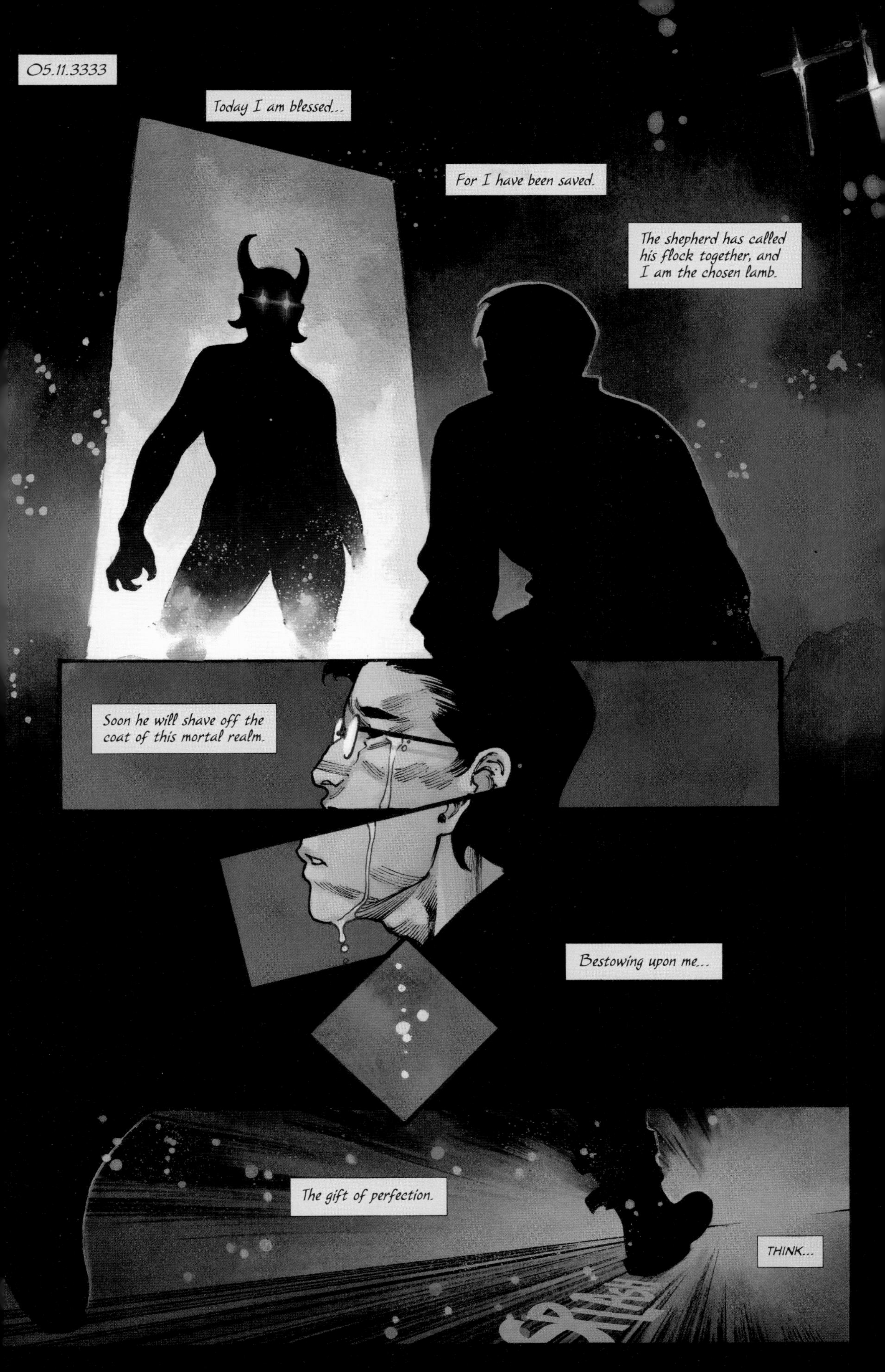
05.11.3333
Today I am blessed...
For I have been saved.
The shepherd has called his flock together, and I am the chosen lamb.
Soon he will shave off the coat of this mortal realm.
Bestowing upon me...
The gift of perfection.
THINK...

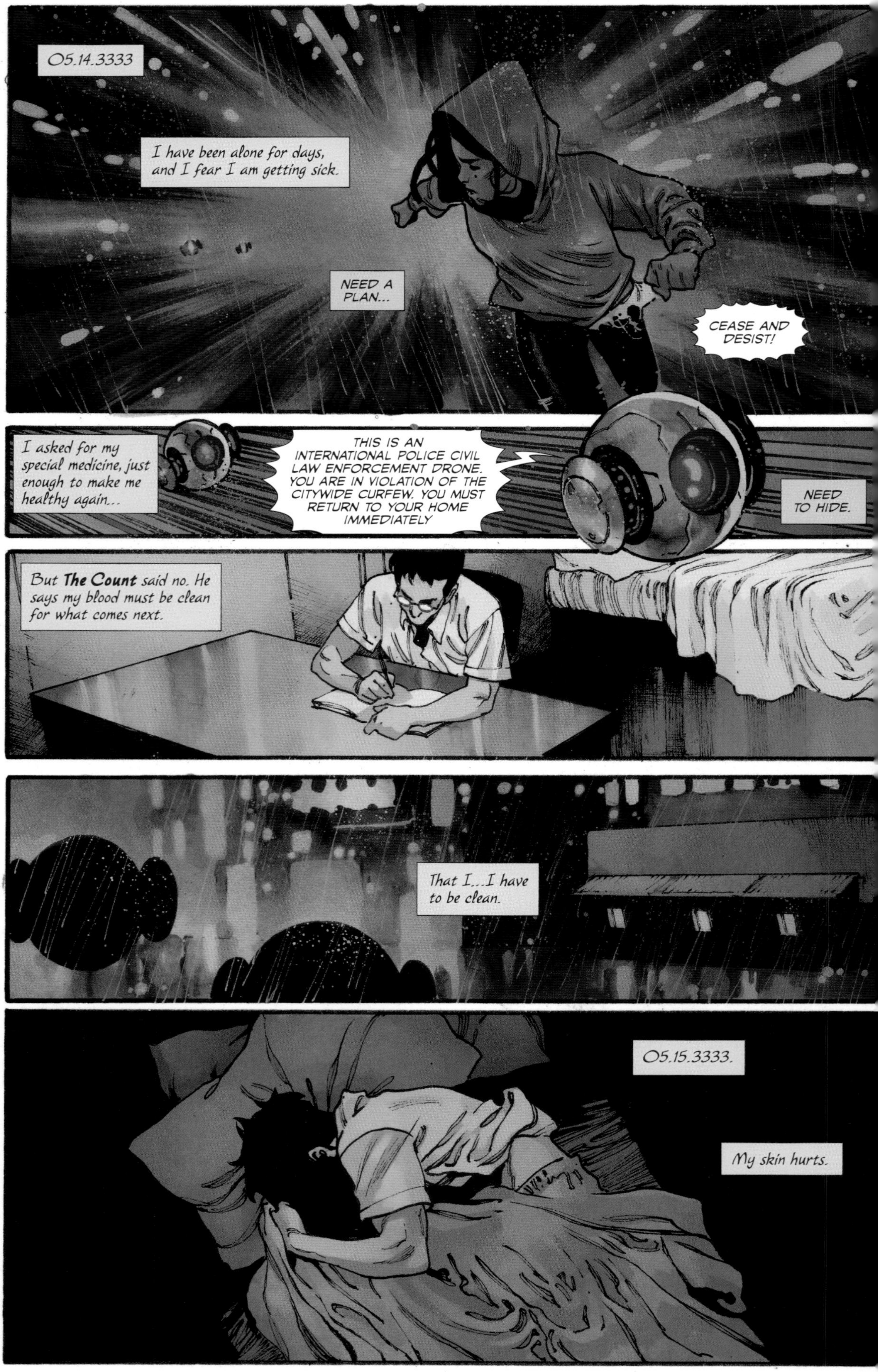
05.14.3333
I have been alone for days, and I fear I am getting sick.
NEED A PLAN...
CEASE AND DESIST!
I asked for my special medicine, just enough to make me healthy again...
THIS IS AN INTERNATIONAL POLICE CIVIL LAW ENFORCEMENT DRONE. YOU ARE IN VIOLATION OF THE CITYWIDE CURFEW. YOU MUST RETURN TO YOUR HOME IMMEDIATELY
NEED TO HIDE.
But The Count said no. He says my blood must be clean for what comes next.
That I...I have to be clean.
05.15.3333.
My skin hurts.

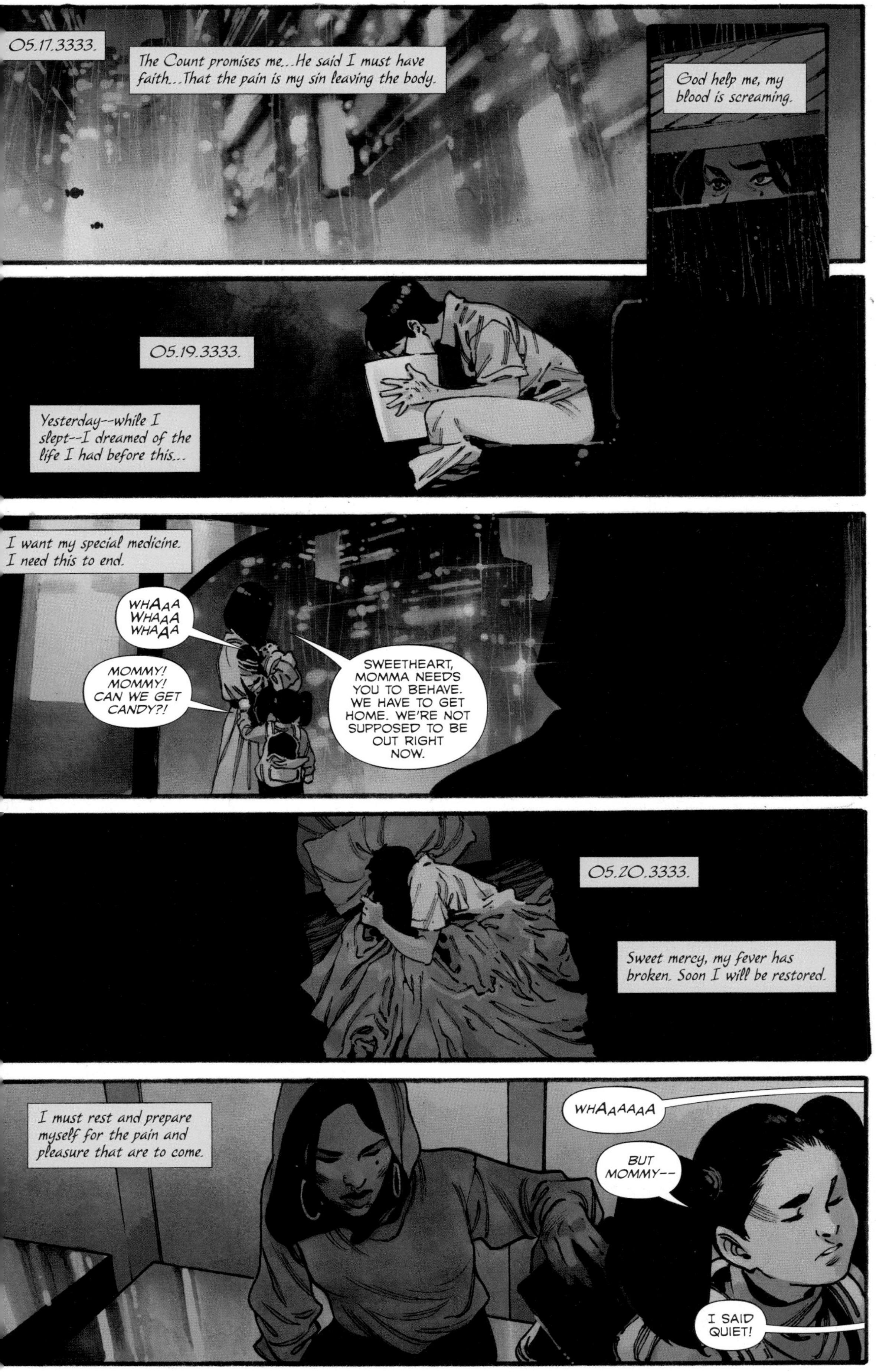

05.17.3333.
The Count promises me...He said I must have faith...That the pain is my sin leaving the body.
God help me, my blood is screaming.
05.19.3333.
Yesterday--while I slept--I dreamed of the life I had before this...
I want my special medicine. I need this to end.
WHAAA WHAAA WHAAA
MOMMY! MOMMY! CAN WE GET CANDY?!
SWEETHEART, MOMMA NEEDS YOU TO BEHAVE. WE HAVE TO GET HOME. WE'RE NOT SUPPOSED TO BE OUT RIGHT NOW.
05.20.3333.
Sweet mercy, my fever has broken. Soon I will be restored.
I must rest and prepare myself for the pain and pleasure that are to come.
WHAAAAAA
BUT MOMMY--
I SAID QUIET!

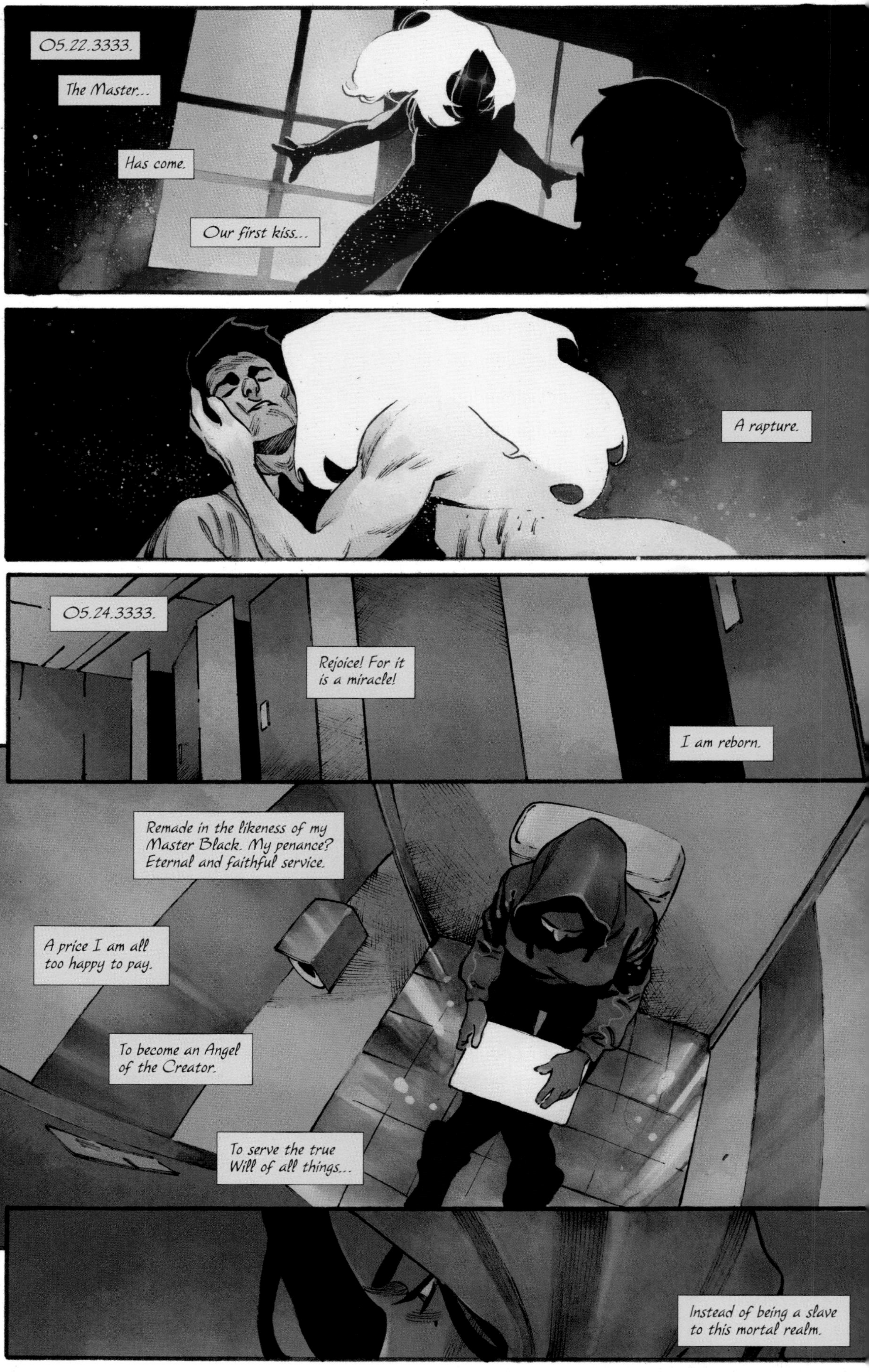
05.22.3333.
The Master...
Has come.
Our first kiss...
A rapture.
05.24.3333.
Rejoice! For it is a miracle!
I am reborn.
Remade in the likeness of my Master Black. My penance? Eternal and faithful service.
A price I am all too happy to pay.
To become an Angel of the Creator.
To serve the true Will of all things...
Instead of being a slave to this mortal realm.

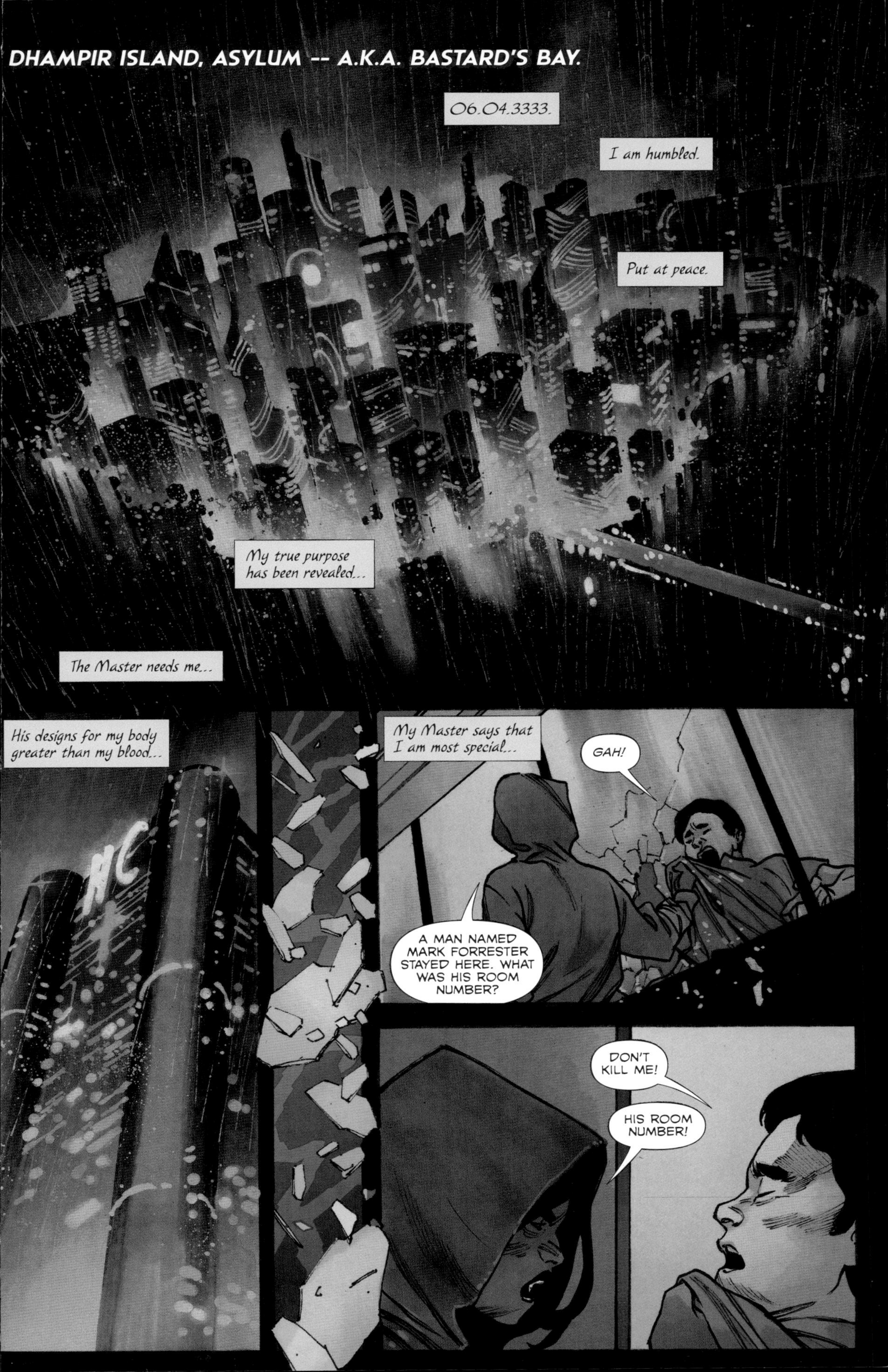
DHAMPIR ISLAND, ASYLUM -- A.K.A. BASTARD'S BAY.
06.04.3333.
I am humbled.
Put at peace.
My true purpose has been revealed...
The Master needs me...
His designs for my body greater than my blood...
My Master says that I am most special...
GAH!
A MAN NAMED MARK FORRESTER STAYED HERE. WHAT WAS HIS ROOM NUMBER?
DON'T KILL ME!
HIS ROOM NUMBER!

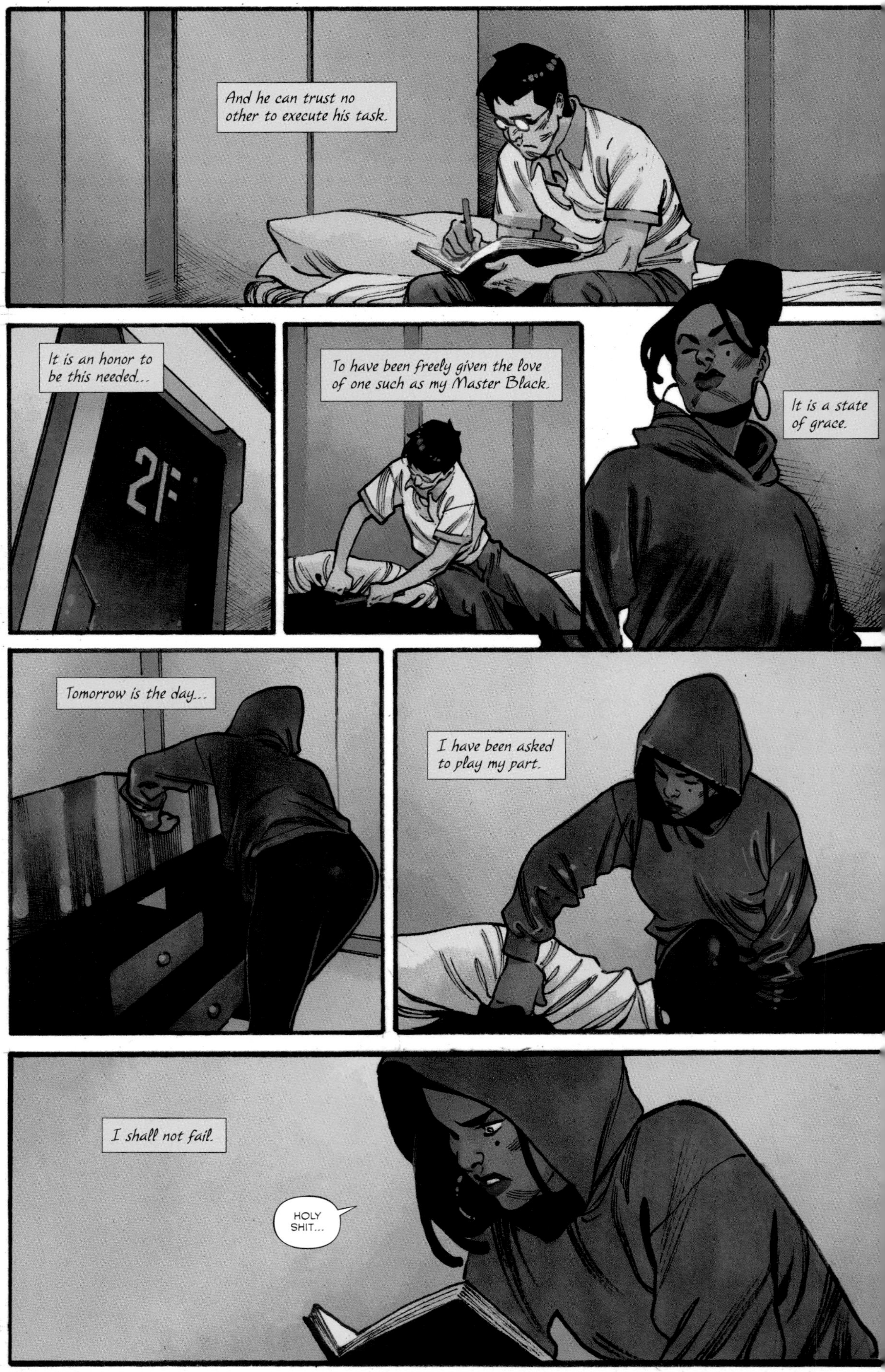
And he can trust no other to execute his task.
It is an honor to be this needed...
21F
To have been freely given the love of one such as my Master Black.
It is a state of grace.
Tomorrow is the day...
I have been asked to play my part.
I shall not fail.
HOLY SHIT...

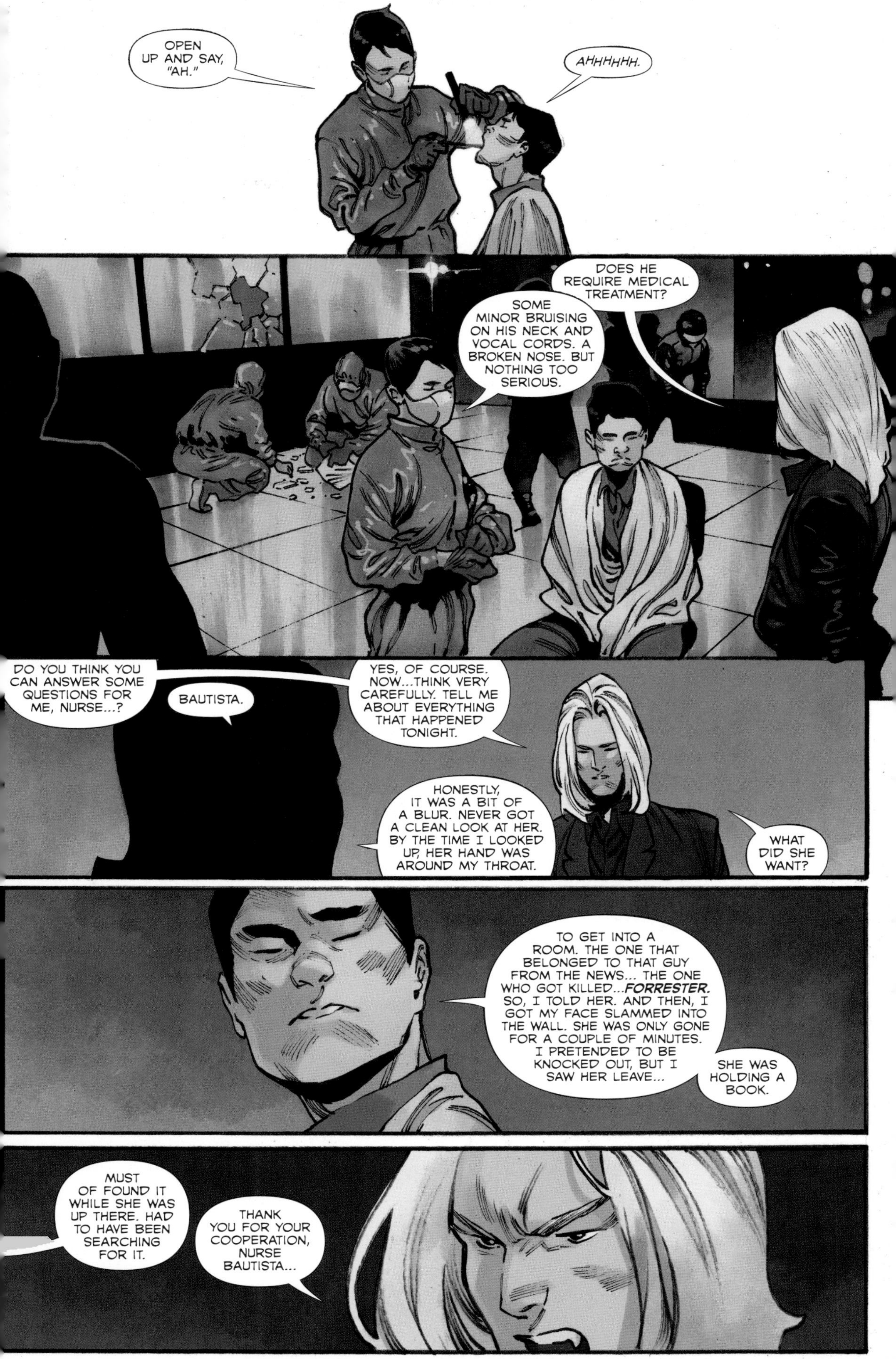
OPEN UP AND SAY, "AH."
AHHHHHH.
DOES HE REQUIRE MEDICAL TREATMENT?
SOME MINOR BRUISING ON HIS NECK AND VOCAL CORDS. A BROKEN NOSE. BUT NOTHING TOO SERIOUS.
DO YOU THINK YOU CAN ANSWER SOME QUESTIONS FOR ME, NURSE...?
BAUTISTA.
YES, OF COURSE. NOW...THINK VERY CAREFULLY. TELL ME ABOUT EVERYTHING THAT HAPPENED TONIGHT.
HONESTLY, IT WAS A BIT OF A BLUR. NEVER GOT A CLEAN LOOK AT HER. BY THE TIME I LOOKED UP, HER HAND WAS AROUND MY THROAT.
WHAT DID SHE WANT?
TO GET INTO A ROOM. THE ONE THAT BELONGED TO THAT GUY FROM THE NEWS... THE ONE WHO GOT KILLED...FORRESTER. SO, I TOLD HER. AND THEN, I GOT MY FACE SLAMMED INTO THE WALL. SHE WAS ONLY GONE FOR A COUPLE OF MINUTES. I PRETENDED TO BE KNOCKED OUT, BUT I SAW HER LEAVE...
SHE WAS HOLDING A BOOK.
MUST OF FOUND IT WHILE SHE WAS UP THERE. HAD TO HAVE BEEN SEARCHING FOR IT.
THANK YOU FOR YOUR COOPERATION, NURSE BAUTISTA...

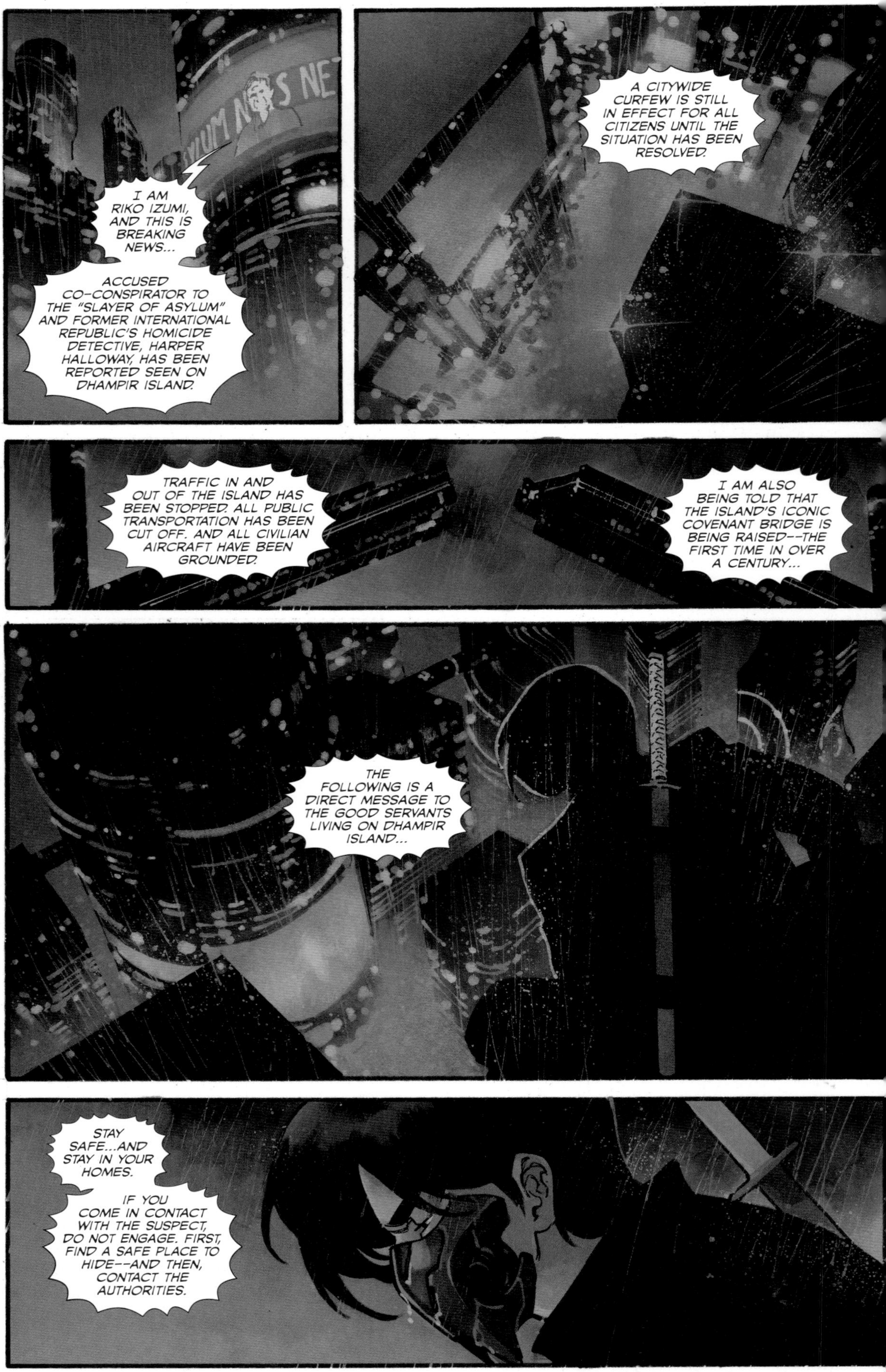
ASYLUM N S NE
I AM RIKO IZUMI, AND THIS IS BREAKING NEWS...
ACCUSED CO-CONSPIRATOR TO THE "SLAYER OF ASYLUM" AND FORMER INTERNATIONAL REPUBLIC'S HOMICIDE DETECTIVE, HARPER HALLOWAY, HAS BEEN REPORTED SEEN ON DHAMPIR ISLAND.
A CITYWIDE CURFEW IS STILL IN EFFECT FOR ALL CITIZENS UNTIL THE SITUATION HAS BEEN RESOLVED.
TRAFFIC IN AND OUT OF THE ISLAND HAS BEEN STOPPED. ALL PUBLIC TRANSPORTATION HAS BEEN CUT OFF. AND ALL CIVILIAN AIRCRAFT HAVE BEEN GROUNDED.
I AM ALSO BEING TOLD THAT THE ISLAND'S ICONIC COVENANT BRIDGE IS BEING RAISED--THE FIRST TIME IN OVER A CENTURY...
THE FOLLOWING IS A DIRECT MESSAGE TO THE GOOD SERVANTS LIVING ON DHAMPIR ISLAND...
STAY SAFE...AND STAY IN YOUR HOMES.
IF YOU COME IN CONTACT WITH THE SUSPECT, DO NOT ENGAGE. FIRST, FIND A SAFE PLACE TO HIDE--AND THEN, CONTACT THE AUTHORITIES.

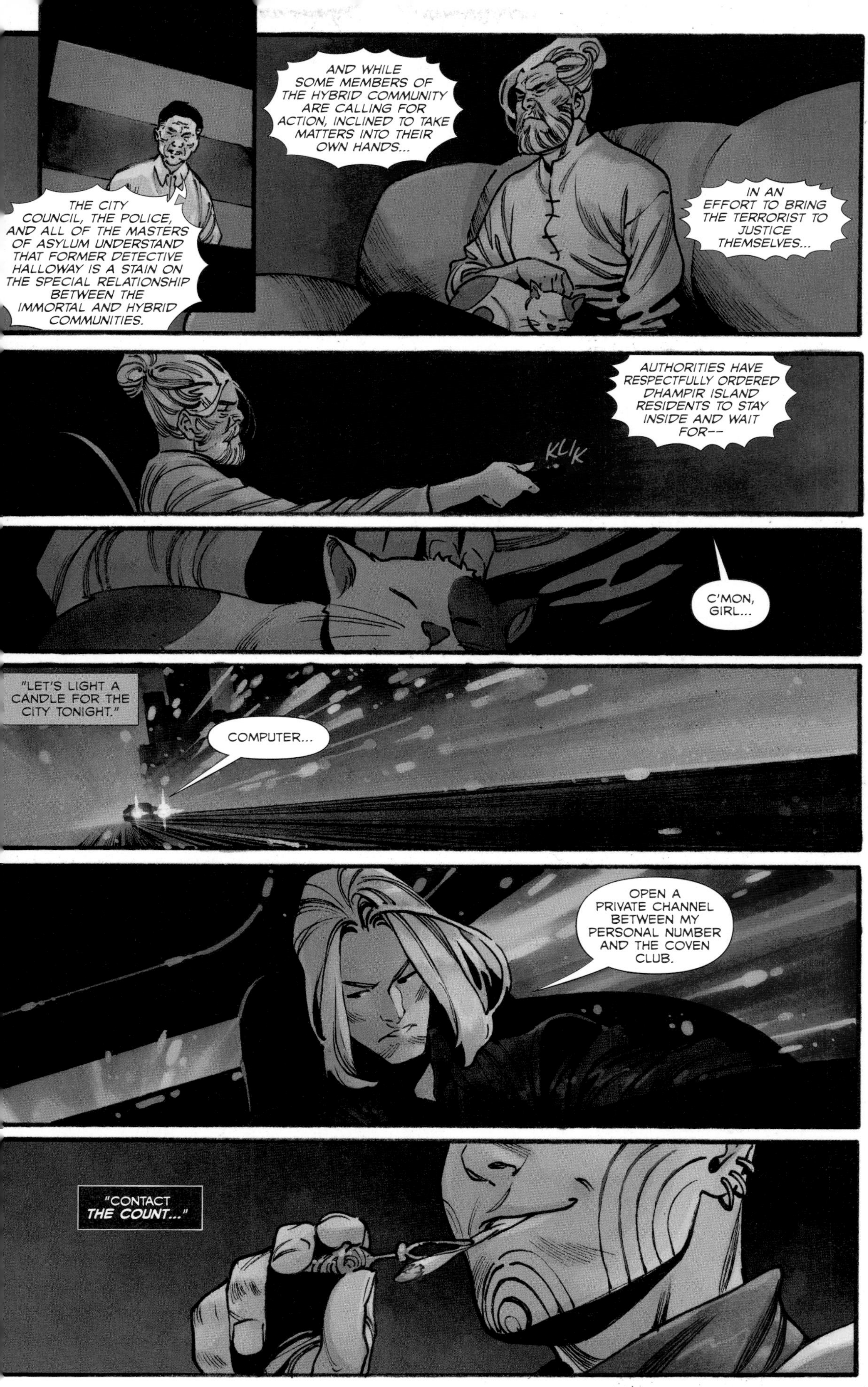
THE CITY COUNCIL, THE POLICE, AND ALL OF THE MASTERS OF ASYLUM UNDERSTAND THAT FORMER DETECTIVE HALLOWAY IS A STAIN ON THE SPECIAL RELATIONSHIP BETWEEN THE IMMORTAL AND HYBRID COMMUNITIES.
AND WHILE SOME MEMBERS OF THE HYBRID COMMUNITY ARE CALLING FOR ACTION, INCLINED TO TAKE MATTERS INTO THEIR OWN HANDS...
IN AN EFFORT TO BRING THE TERRORIST TO JUSTICE THEMSELVES...
AUTHORITIES HAVE RESPECTFULLY ORDERED DHAMPIR ISLAND RESIDENTS TO STAY INSIDE AND WAIT FOR--
KLIK
C'MON, GIRL...
"LET'S LIGHT A CANDLE FOR THE CITY TONIGHT."
COMPUTER...
OPEN A PRIVATE CHANNEL BETWEEN MY PERSONAL NUMBER AND THE COVEN CLUB.
"CONTACT THE COUNT..."

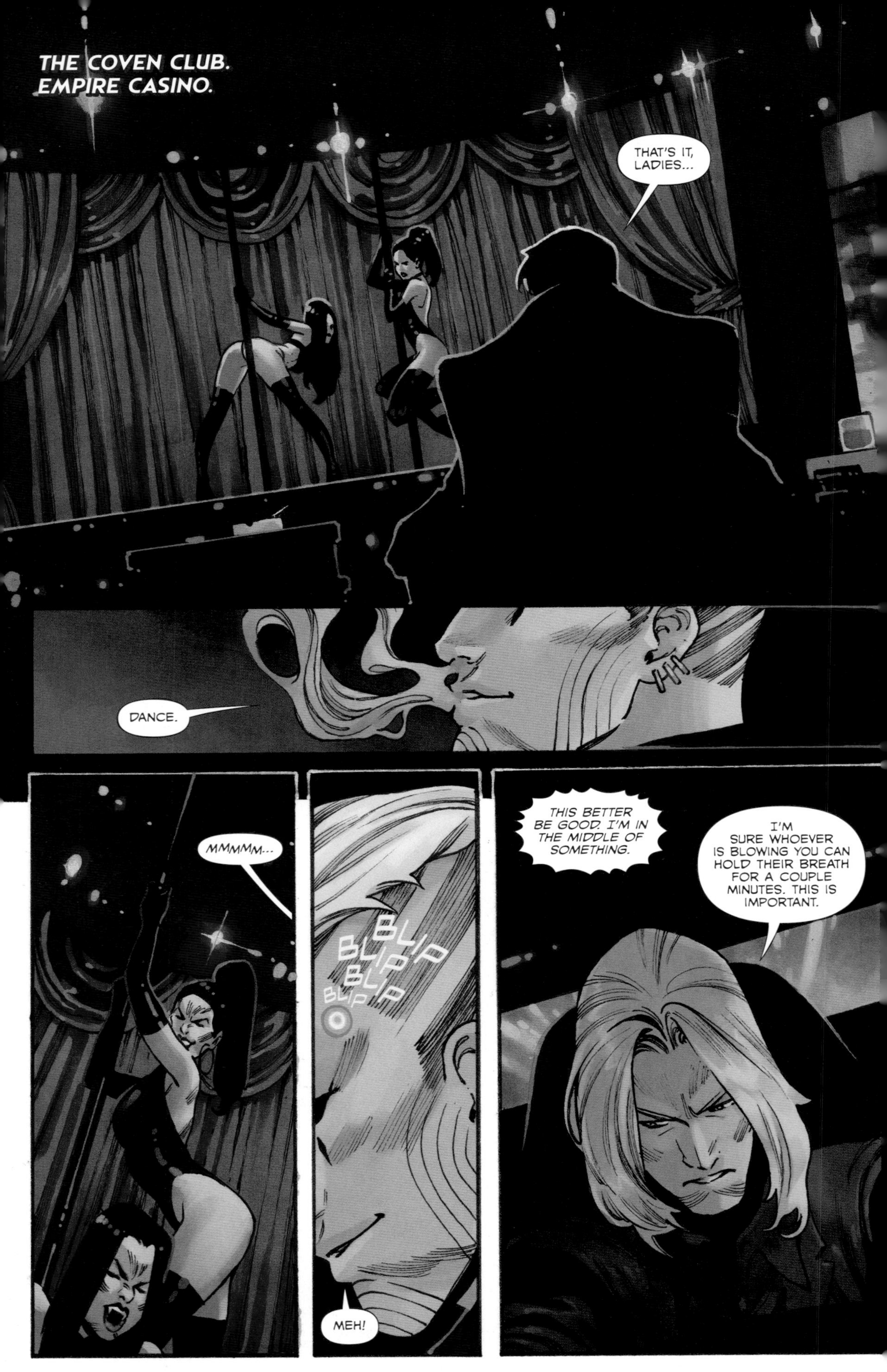
THE COVEN CLUB.
EMPIRE CASINO.
THAT'S IT, LADIES...
DANCE.
MMMMM...
BLIP BLIP BLIP BLIP
MEH!
THIS BETTER BE GOOD. I'M IN THE MIDDLE OF SOMETHING.
I'M SURE WHOEVER IS BLOWING YOU CAN HOLD THEIR BREATH FOR A COUPLE MINUTES. THIS IS IMPORTANT.

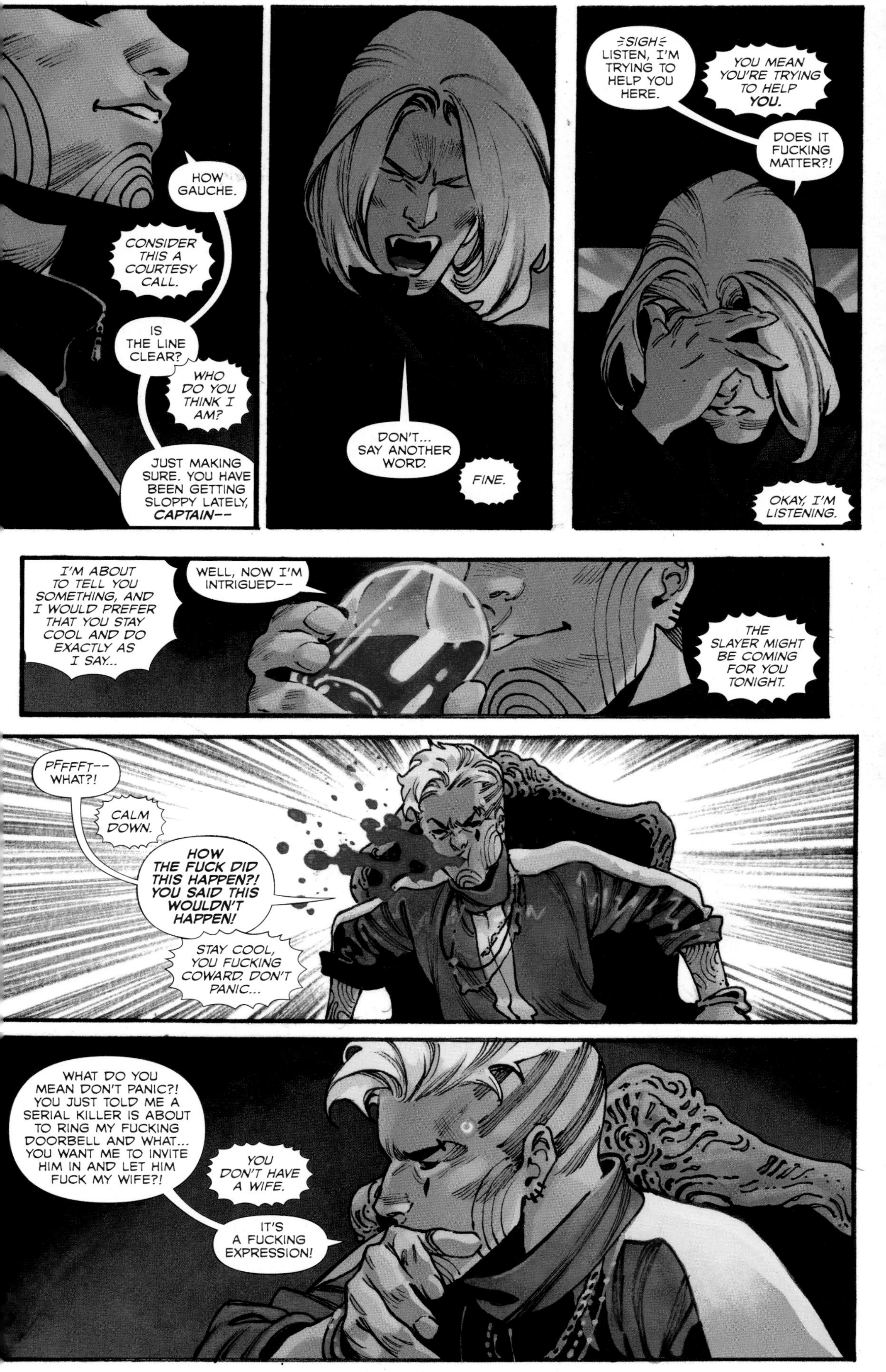
HOW GAUCHE.
CONSIDER THIS A COURTESY CALL.
IS THE LINE CLEAR?
WHO DO YOU THINK I AM?
JUST MAKING SURE. YOU HAVE BEEN GETTING SLOPPY LATELY, CAPTAIN--
DON'T... SAY ANOTHER WORD.
FINE.
≶SIGH≶ LISTEN, I'M TRYING TO HELP YOU HERE.
YOU MEAN YOU'RE TRYING TO HELP YOU.
DOES IT FUCKING MATTER?!
OKAY, I'M LISTENING.
I'M ABOUT TO TELL YOU SOMETHING, AND I WOULD PREFER THAT YOU STAY COOL AND DO EXACTLY AS I SAY...
WELL, NOW I'M INTRIGUED--
THE SLAYER MIGHT BE COMING FOR YOU TONIGHT.
PFFFFT-- WHAT?!
CALM DOWN.
HOW THE FUCK DID THIS HAPPEN?! YOU SAID THIS WOULDN'T HAPPEN!
STAY COOL, YOU FUCKING COWARD. DON'T PANIC...
WHAT DO YOU MEAN DON'T PANIC?! YOU JUST TOLD ME A SERIAL KILLER IS ABOUT TO RING MY FUCKING DOORBELL AND WHAT... YOU WANT ME TO INVITE HIM IN AND LET HIM FUCK MY WIFE?!
YOU DON'T HAVE A WIFE.
IT'S A FUCKING EXPRESSION!

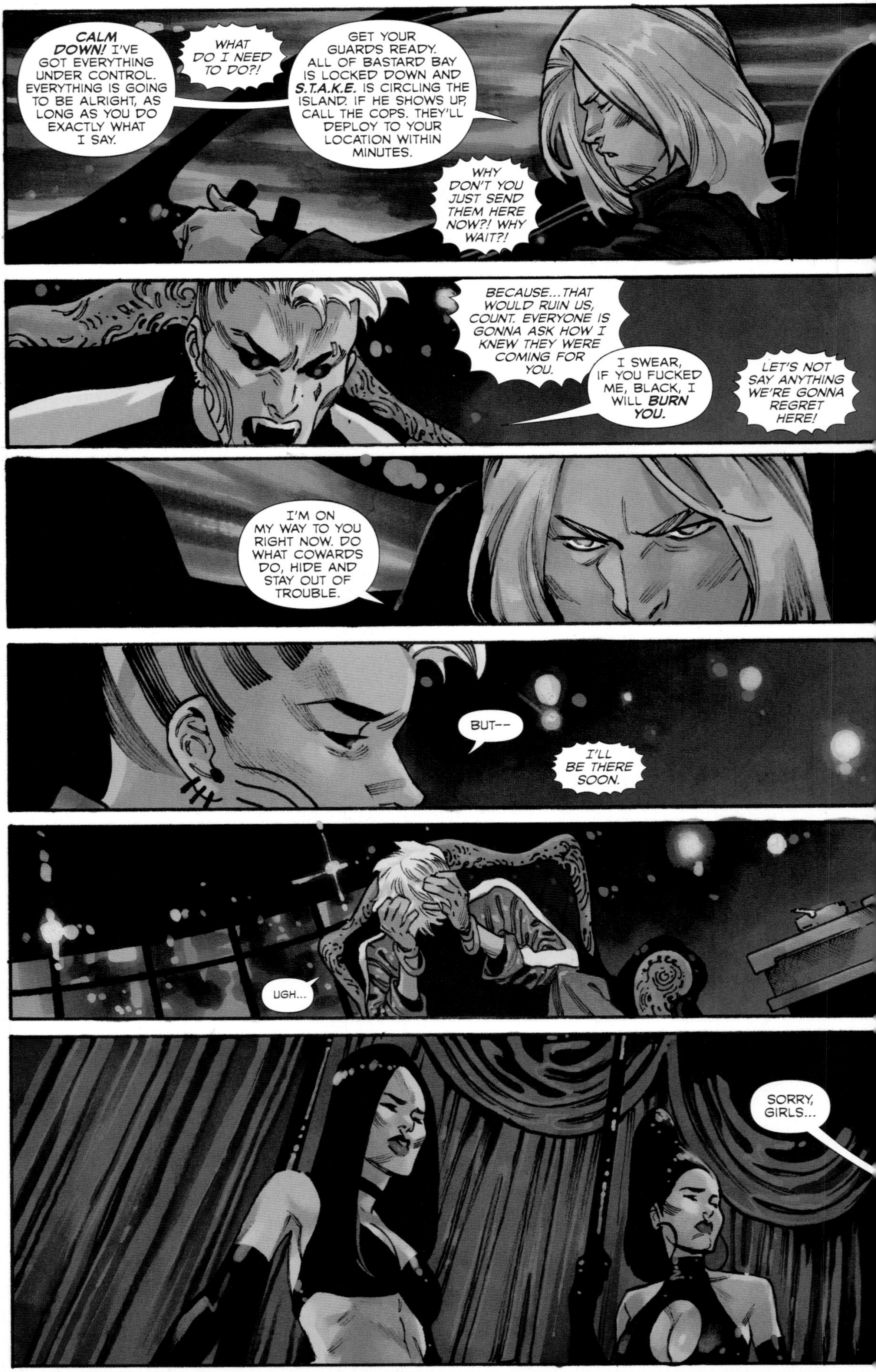
CALM DOWN! I'VE GOT EVERYTHING UNDER CONTROL. EVERYTHING IS GOING TO BE ALRIGHT, AS LONG AS YOU DO EXACTLY WHAT I SAY.
WHAT DO I NEED TO DO?!
GET YOUR GUARDS READY. ALL OF BASTARD BAY IS LOCKED DOWN AND S.T.A.K.E. IS CIRCLING THE ISLAND. IF HE SHOWS UP, CALL THE COPS. THEY'LL DEPLOY TO YOUR LOCATION WITHIN MINUTES.
WHY DON'T YOU JUST SEND THEM HERE NOW?! WHY WAIT?!
BECAUSE...THAT WOULD RUIN US, COUNT. EVERYONE IS GONNA ASK HOW I KNEW THEY WERE COMING FOR YOU.
I SWEAR, IF YOU FUCKED ME, BLACK, I WILL BURN YOU.
LET'S NOT SAY ANYTHING WE'RE GONNA REGRET HERE!
I'M ON MY WAY TO YOU RIGHT NOW. DO WHAT COWARDS DO, HIDE AND STAY OUT OF TROUBLE.
BUT--
I'LL BE THERE SOON.
UGH...
SORRY, GIRLS...

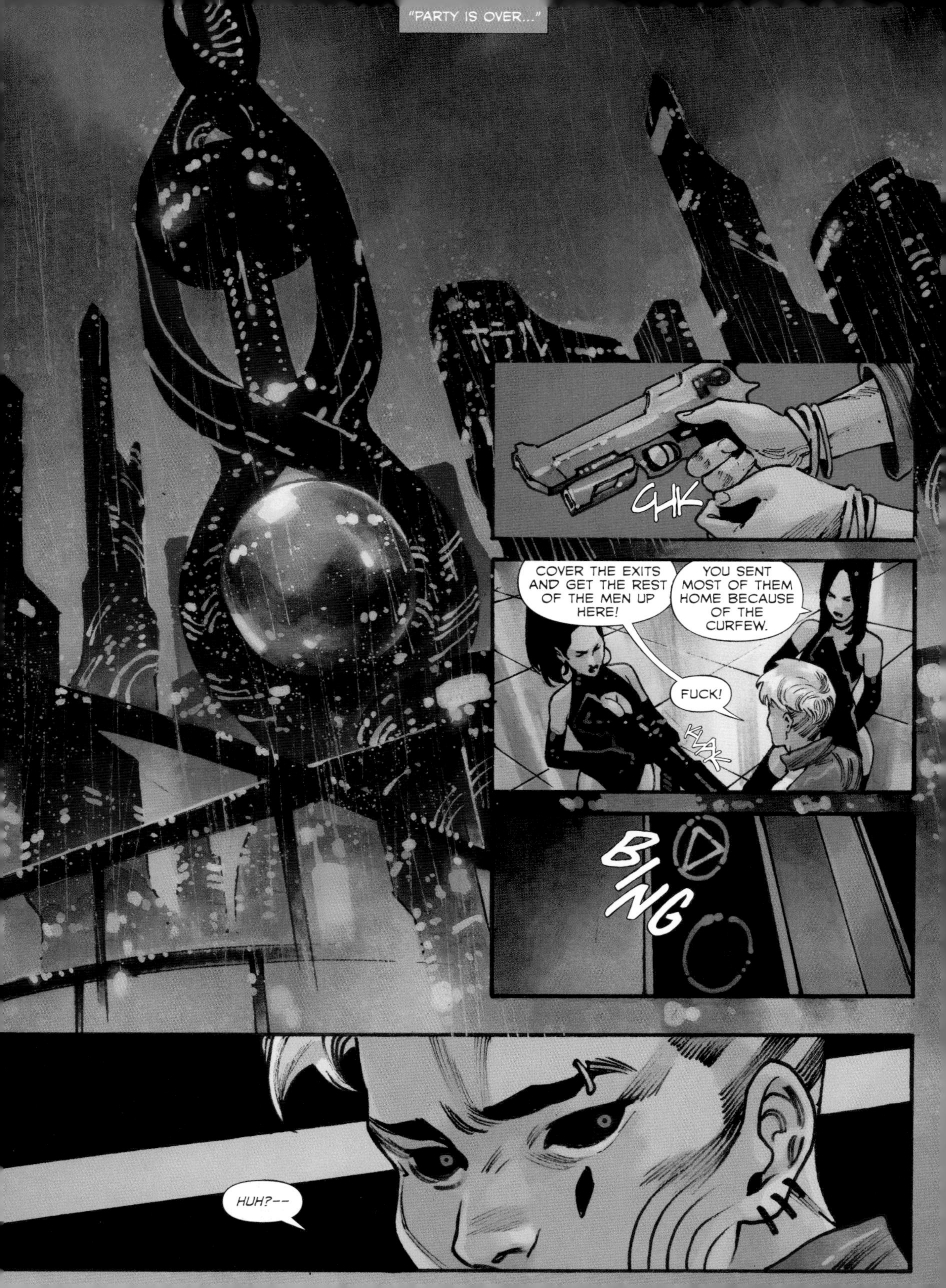
"PARTY IS OVER..."
CHK
COVER THE EXITS AND GET THE REST OF THE MEN UP HERE!
YOU SENT MOST OF THEM HOME BECAUSE OF THE CURFEW.
FUCK!
KLAK
BING
HUH?--

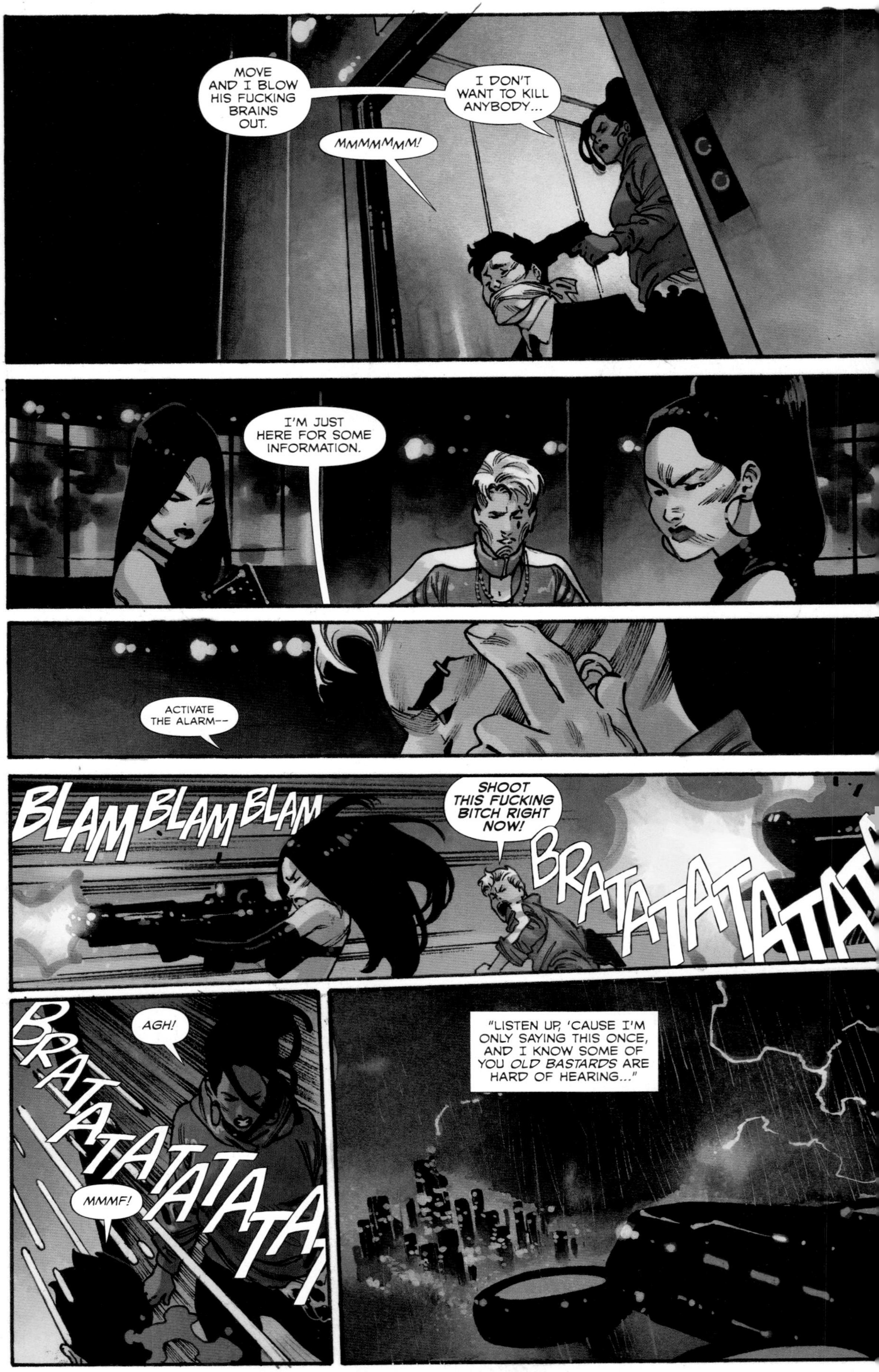
MOVE AND I BLOW HIS FUCKING BRAINS OUT.
I DON'T WANT TO KILL ANYBODY...
MMMMMMM!
I'M JUST HERE FOR SOME INFORMATION.
ACTIVATE THE ALARM--
BLAM BLAM BLAM
SHOOT THIS FUCKING BITCH RIGHT NOW!
BRATATATATAT
BRATATATATATAT
AGH!
MMMF!
"LISTEN UP, 'CAUSE I'M ONLY SAYING THIS ONCE, AND I KNOW SOME OF YOU *OLD BASTARDS* ARE HARD OF HEARING..."

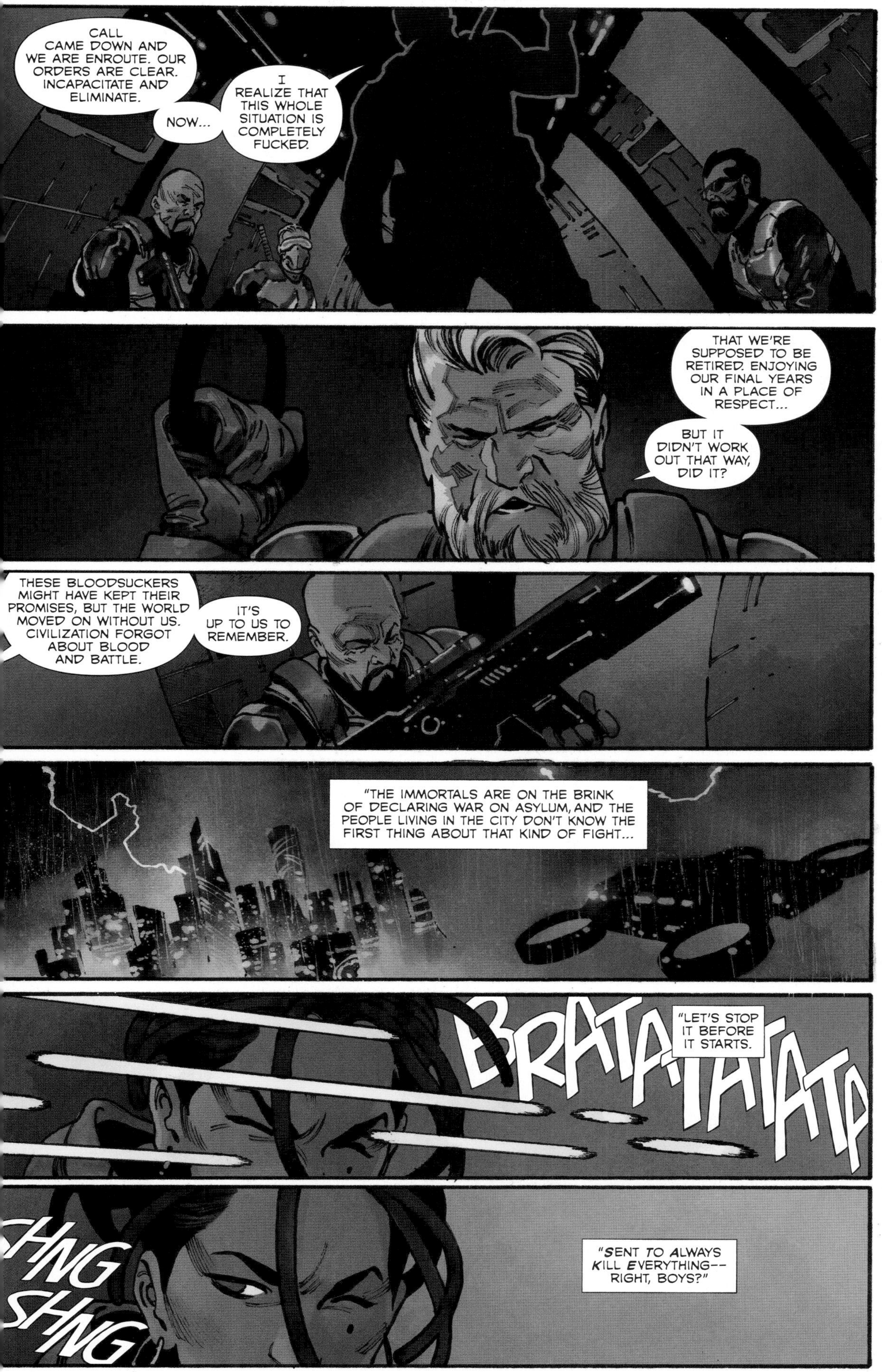
CALL CAME DOWN AND WE ARE ENROUTE. OUR ORDERS ARE CLEAR. INCAPACITATE AND ELIMINATE.
NOW...
I REALIZE THAT THIS WHOLE SITUATION IS COMPLETELY FUCKED.
THAT WE'RE SUPPOSED TO BE RETIRED. ENJOYING OUR FINAL YEARS IN A PLACE OF RESPECT...
BUT IT DIDN'T WORK OUT THAT WAY, DID IT?
THESE BLOODSUCKERS MIGHT HAVE KEPT THEIR PROMISES, BUT THE WORLD MOVED ON WITHOUT US. CIVILIZATION FORGOT ABOUT BLOOD AND BATTLE.
IT'S UP TO US TO REMEMBER.
"THE IMMORTALS ARE ON THE BRINK OF DECLARING WAR ON ASYLUM, AND THE PEOPLE LIVING IN THE CITY DON'T KNOW THE FIRST THING ABOUT THAT KIND OF FIGHT...
BRATATATATATA
"LET'S STOP IT BEFORE IT STARTS.
SHNG
SHNG
"SENT TO ALWAYS KILL EVERYTHING-- RIGHT, BOYS?"

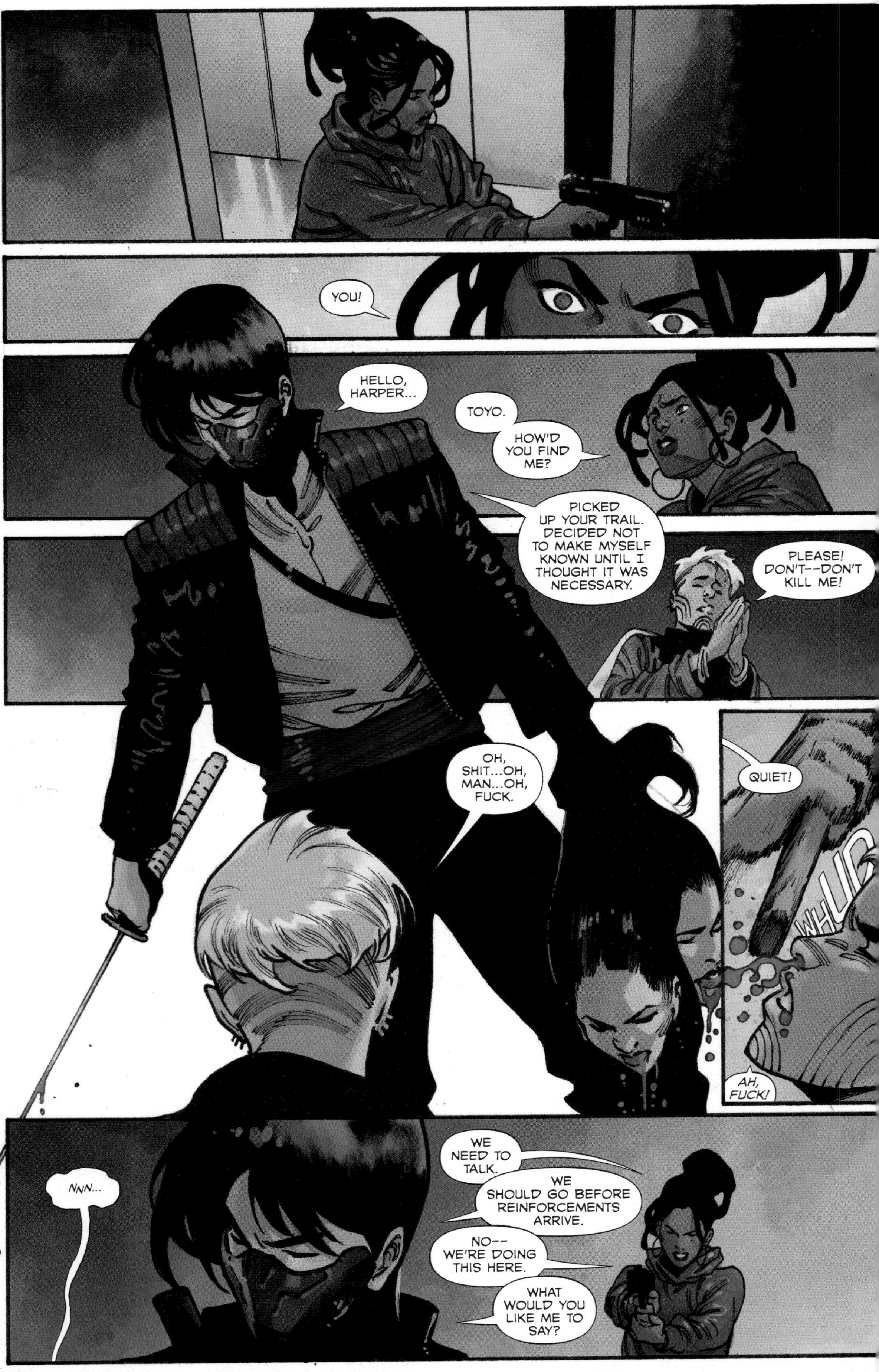
YOU!
HELLO, HARPER...
TOYO.
HOW'D YOU FIND ME?
PICKED UP YOUR TRAIL. DECIDED NOT TO MAKE MYSELF KNOWN UNTIL I THOUGHT IT WAS NECESSARY.
PLEASE! DON'T--DON'T KILL ME!
OH, SHIT...OH, MAN...OH, FUCK.
QUIET!
AH, FUCK!
NNN...
WE NEED TO TALK.
WE SHOULD GO BEFORE REINFORCEMENTS ARRIVE.
NO-- WE'RE DOING THIS HERE.
WHAT WOULD YOU LIKE ME TO SAY?

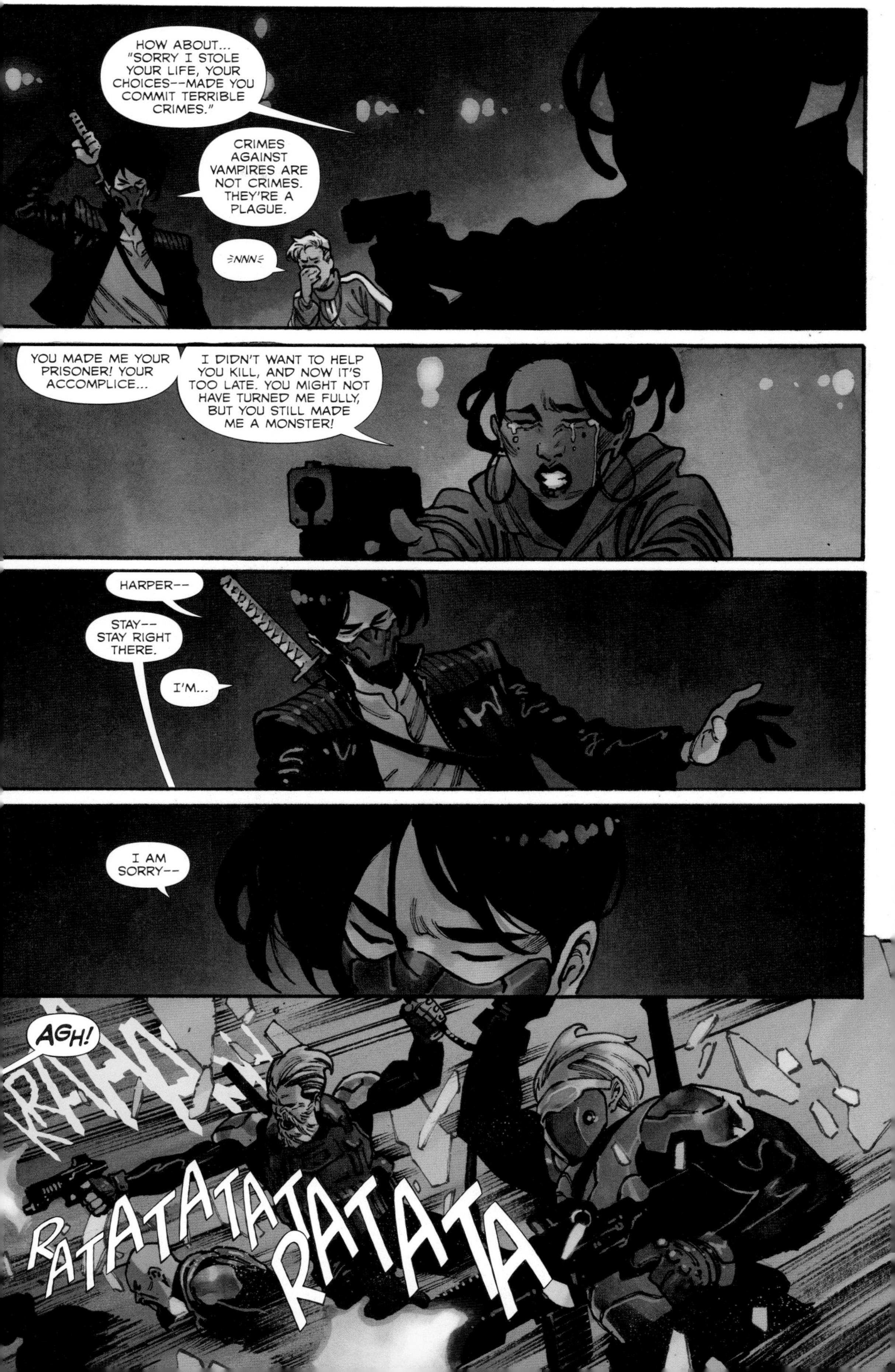
HOW ABOUT... "SORRY I STOLE YOUR LIFE, YOUR CHOICES--MADE YOU COMMIT TERRIBLE CRIMES."
CRIMES AGAINST VAMPIRES ARE NOT CRIMES. THEY'RE A PLAGUE.
NNN
YOU MADE ME YOUR PRISONER! YOUR ACCOMPLICE...
I DIDN'T WANT TO HELP YOU KILL, AND NOW IT'S TOO LATE. YOU MIGHT NOT HAVE TURNED ME FULLY, BUT YOU STILL MADE ME A MONSTER!
HARPER--
STAY-- STAY RIGHT THERE.
I'M...
I AM SORRY--
AGH!
RATATATATATA RATATA

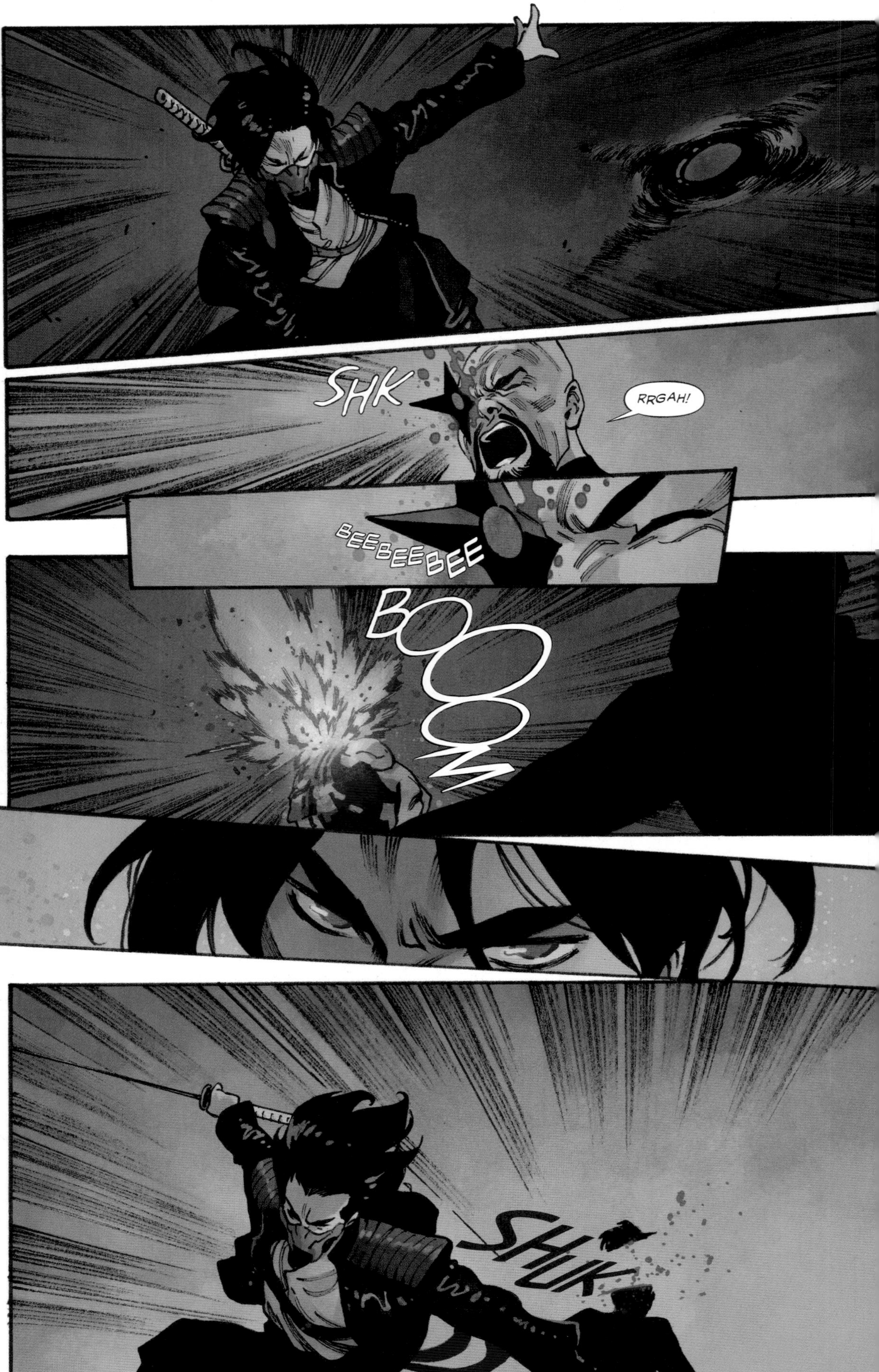
SHK
RRGAH!
BEEBEEBEE
BOOOM
SHUK

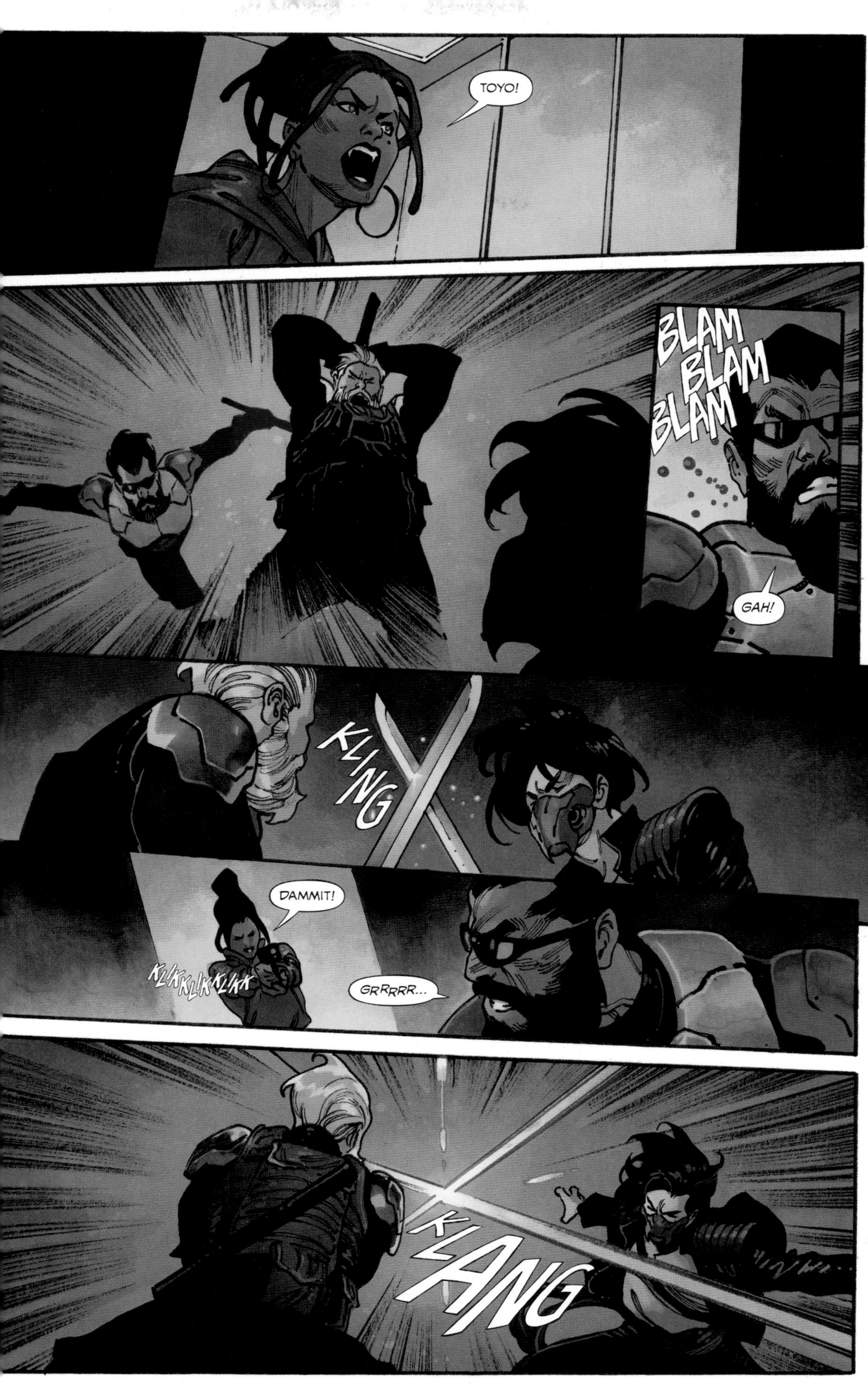
TOYO!
BLAM
BLAM
BLAM
GAH!
KLING
DAMMIT!
KLIKKLIKKLIKK
GRRRRR...
KLANG

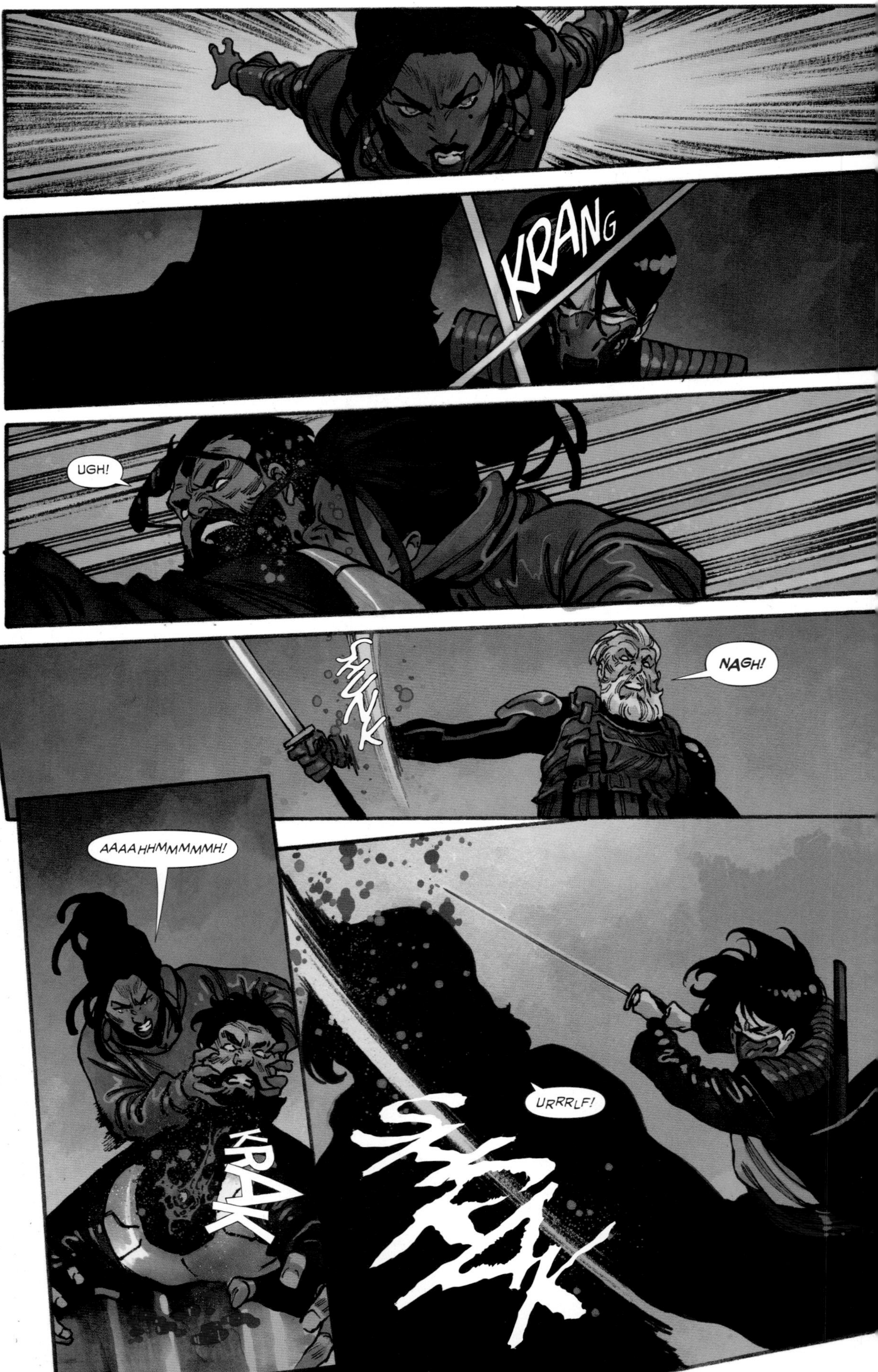
KRANG
UGH!
SHUNK
NAGH!
AAAAHHMMMMMH!
KRAK
URRRLF!

FUCK, MAN! SHIT...OH, PLEASE...

IT'S ALL OVER. YOU CAN COME OUT NOW.

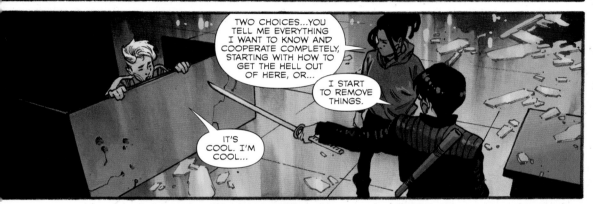

TWO CHOICES...YOU TELL ME EVERYTHING I WANT TO KNOW AND COOPERATE COMPLETELY, STARTING WITH HOW TO GET THE HELL OUT OF HERE, OR...

I START TO REMOVE THINGS.

IT'S COOL. I'M COOL...

I'VE GOT WHATEVER YOU NEED. I'LL SQUEAL ON WHOEVER THE FUCK WHENEVER THE FUCK. ASK AWAY.

I'VE GOT ANSWERS FOR DAYS. JUST PLEASE LET ME KEEP MY DICK AND BALLS-- I LOVE THEM SO MUCH.

WHO IS THIS...MAN, ANYWAY?

SOMEONE WITH DIRT ON BLACK. I'LL EXPLAIN WHEN WE FIND A WAY--

SHOOM

OH, SHIT!

WHAT WAS THAT?!

THIS IS THE INTERNATIONAL REPUBLIC OF DISPLACED PEOPLES POLICE DEPARTMENT!

WE HAVE THE BUILDING SURROUNDED! COME OUT WITH YOUR HANDS UP!

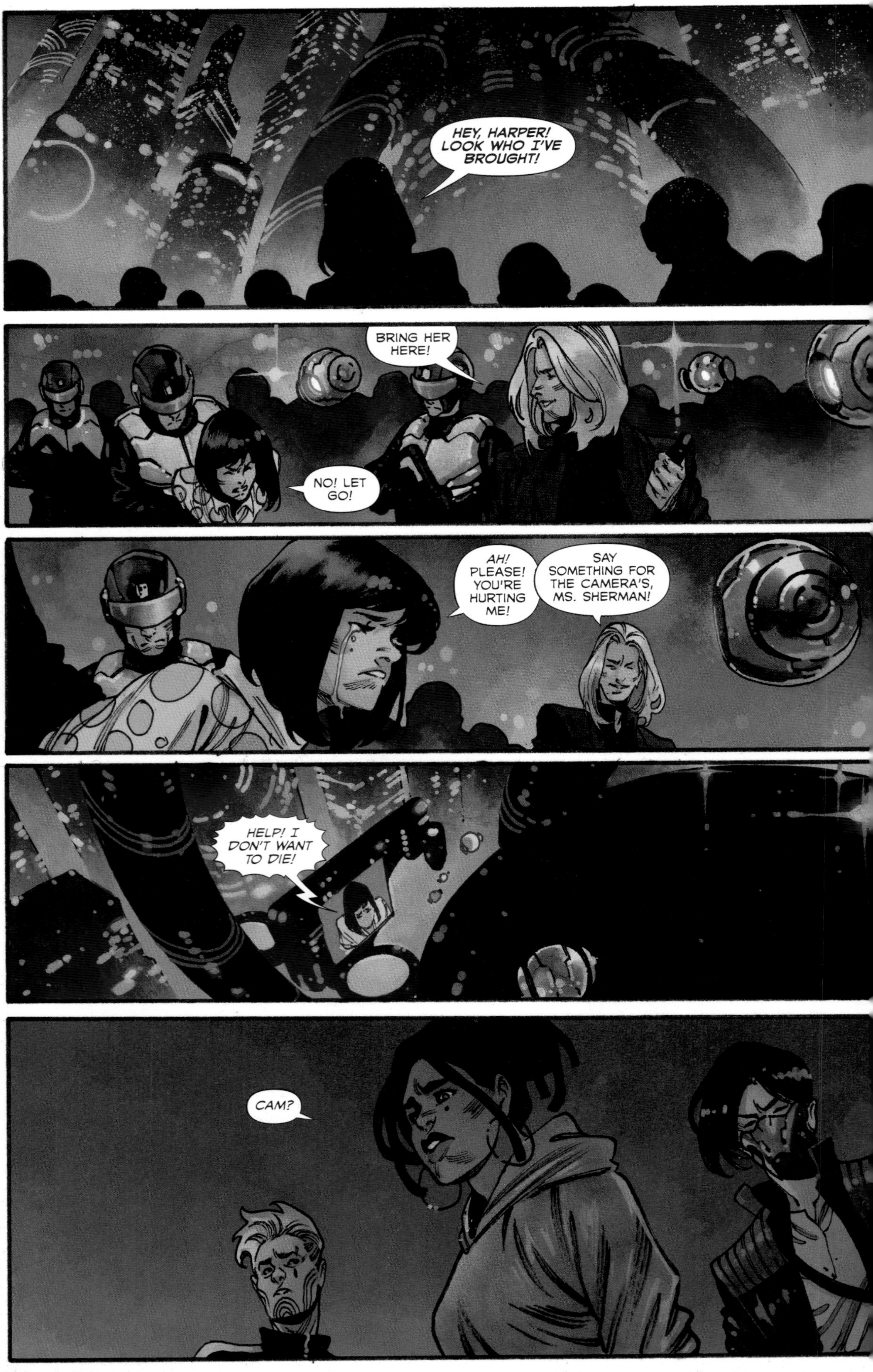
HEY, HARPER! LOOK WHO I'VE BROUGHT!
BRING HER HERE!
NO! LET GO!
AH! PLEASE! YOU'RE HURTING ME!
SAY SOMETHING FOR THE CAMERA'S, MS. SHERMAN!
HELP! I DON'T WANT TO DIE!
CAM?

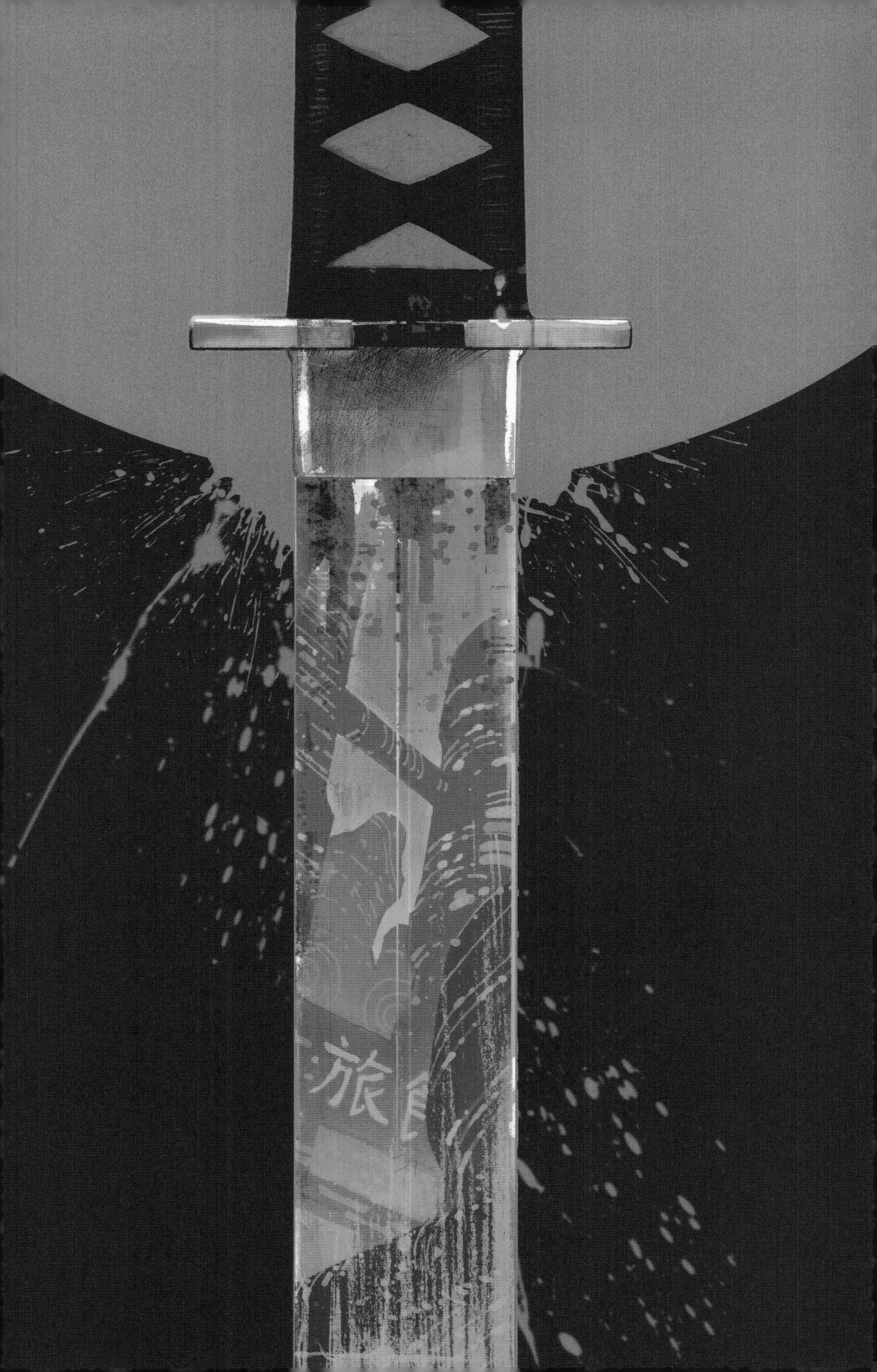
旅

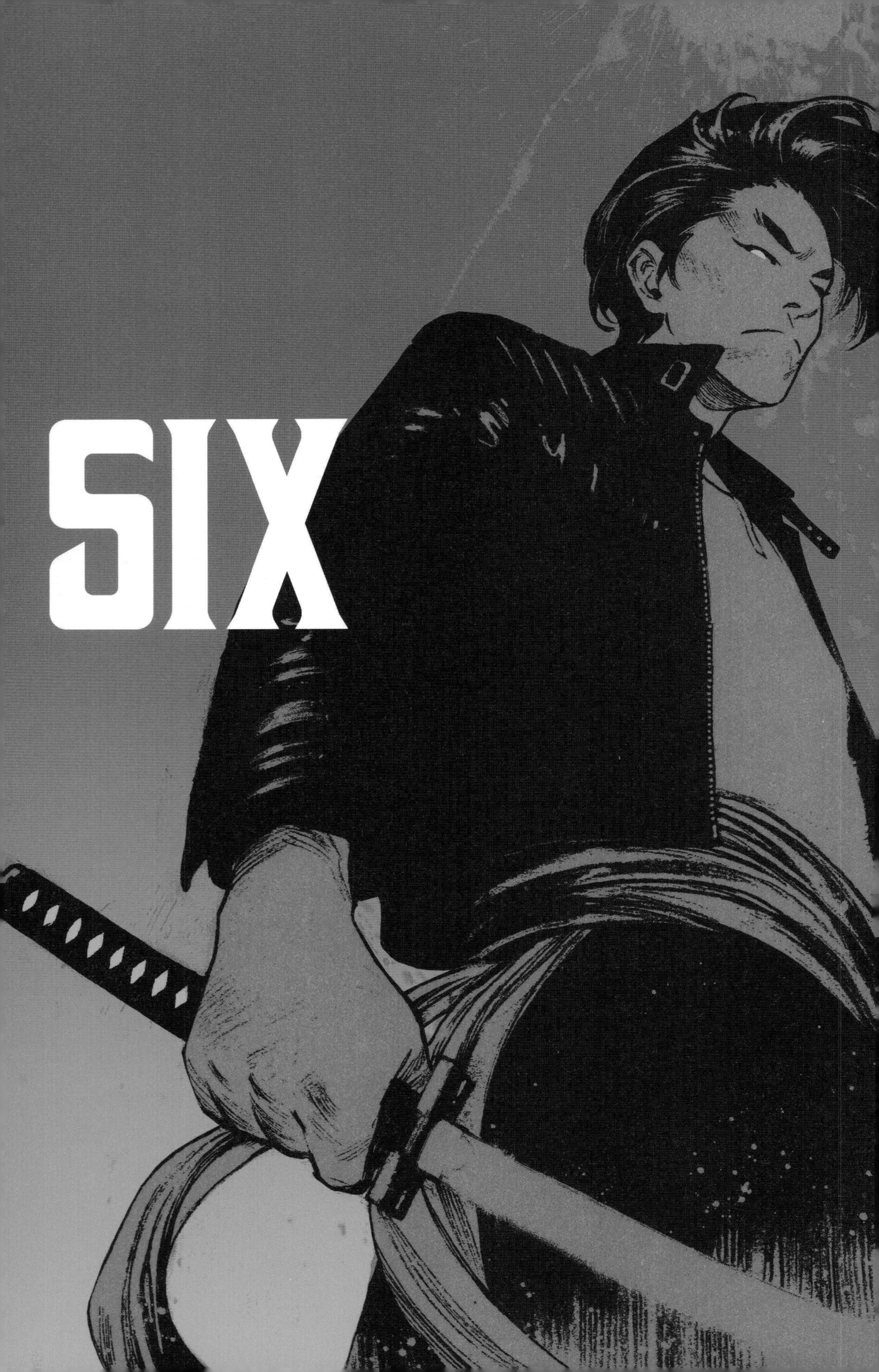
SIX

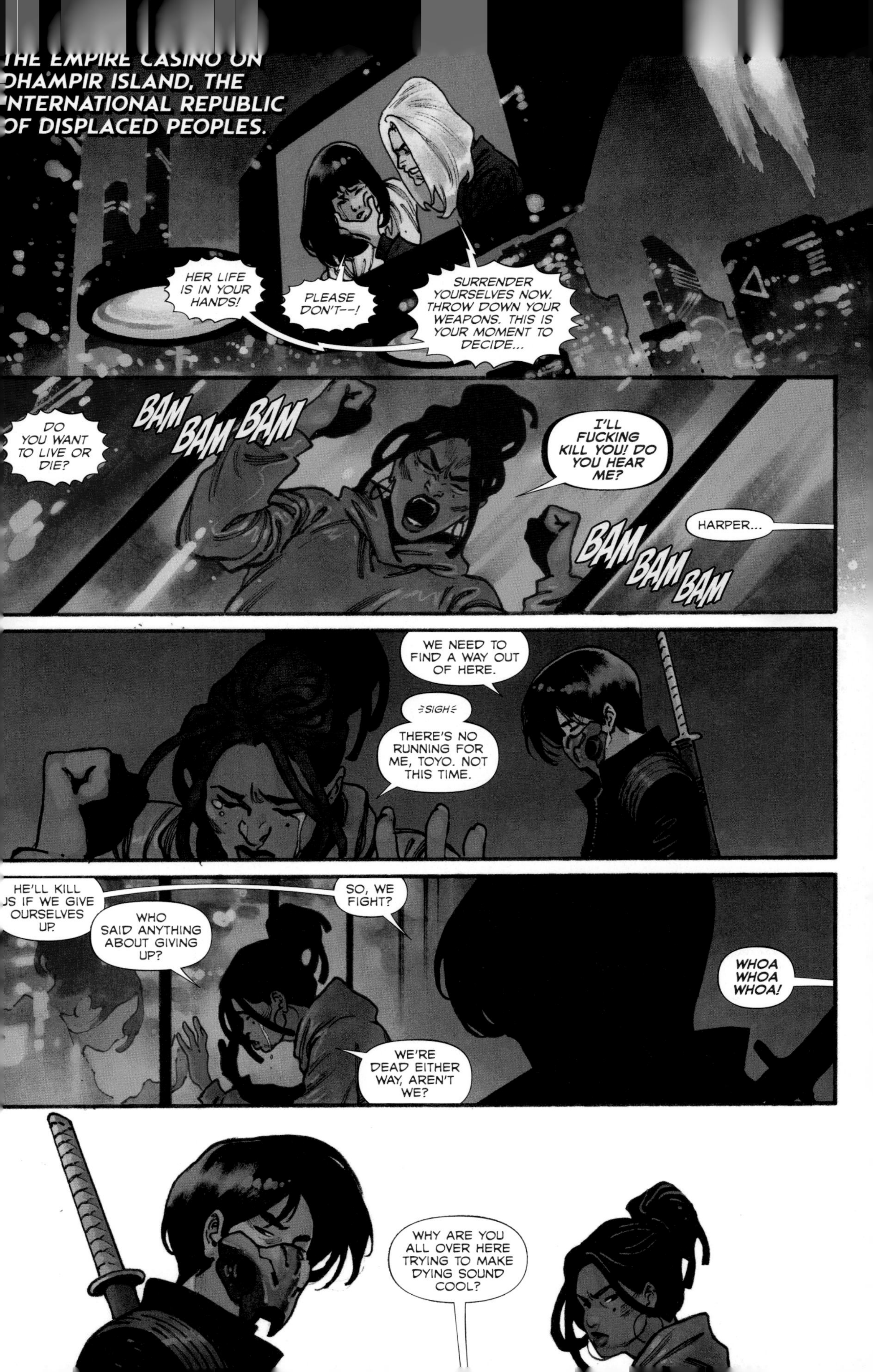
THE EMPIRE CASINO ON DHAMPIR ISLAND, THE INTERNATIONAL REPUBLIC OF DISPLACED PEOPLES.
HER LIFE IS IN YOUR HANDS!
PLEASE DON'T--!
SURRENDER YOURSELVES NOW. THROW DOWN YOUR WEAPONS. THIS IS YOUR MOMENT TO DECIDE...
DO YOU WANT TO LIVE OR DIE?
BAM BAM BAM
I'LL FUCKING KILL YOU! DO YOU HEAR ME?
HARPER...
BAM BAM BAM
WE NEED TO FIND A WAY OUT OF HERE.
SIGH
THERE'S NO RUNNING FOR ME, TOYO. NOT THIS TIME.
HE'LL KILL US IF WE GIVE OURSELVES UP.
SO, WE FIGHT?
WHO SAID ANYTHING ABOUT GIVING UP?
WHOA WHOA WHOA!
WE'RE DEAD EITHER WAY, AREN'T WE?
WHY ARE YOU ALL OVER HERE TRYING TO MAKE DYING SOUND COOL?

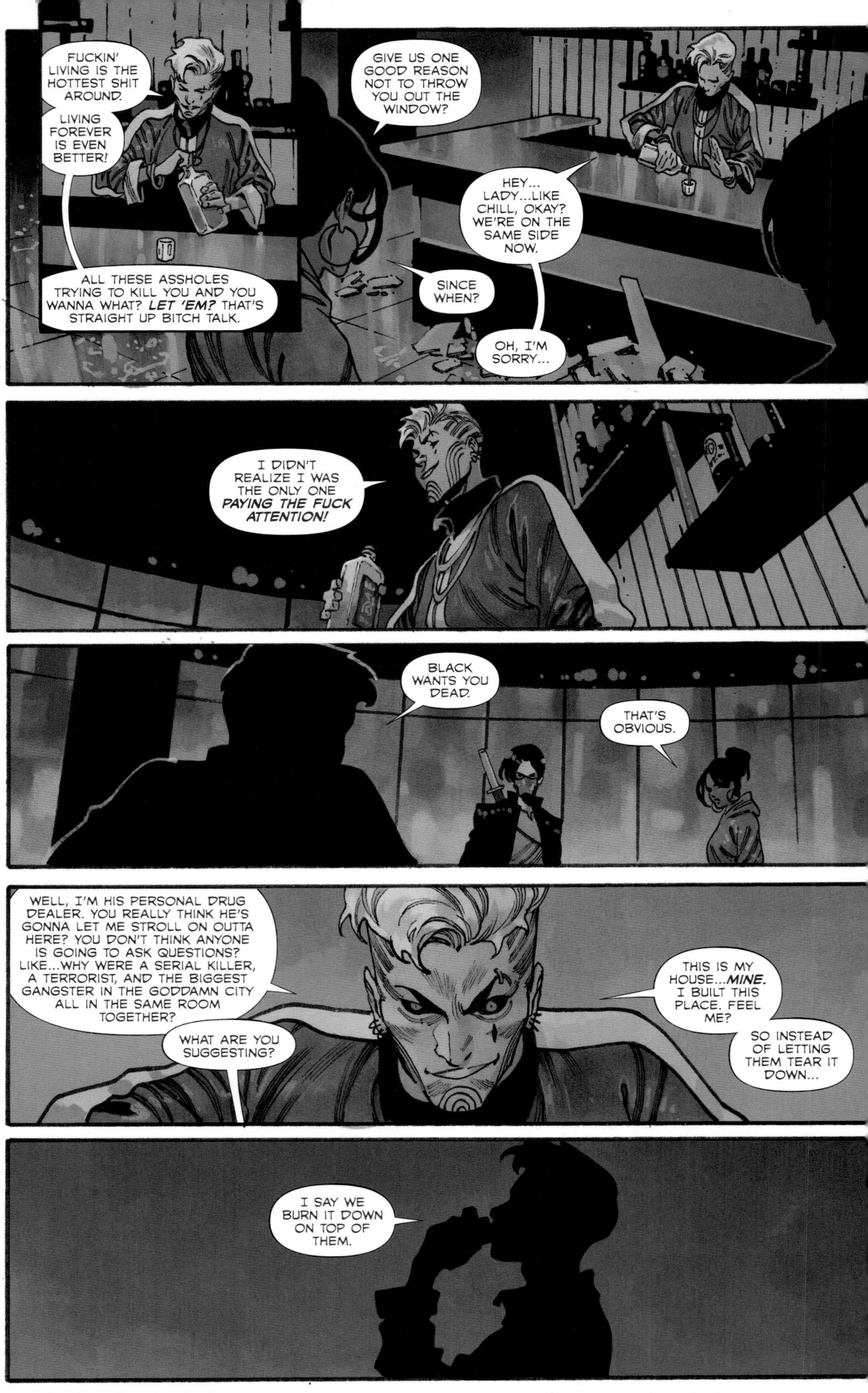
FUCKIN' LIVING IS THE HOTTEST SHIT AROUND.
LIVING FOREVER IS EVEN BETTER!
ALL THESE ASSHOLES TRYING TO KILL YOU AND YOU WANNA WHAT? ***LET 'EM?*** THAT'S STRAIGHT UP BITCH TALK.
GIVE US ONE GOOD REASON NOT TO THROW YOU OUT THE WINDOW?
SINCE WHEN?
HEY... LADY...LIKE CHILL, OKAY? WE'RE ON THE SAME SIDE NOW.
OH, I'M SORRY...
I DIDN'T REALIZE I WAS THE ONLY ONE ***PAYING THE FUCK ATTENTION!***
BLACK WANTS YOU DEAD.
THAT'S OBVIOUS.
WELL, I'M HIS PERSONAL DRUG DEALER. YOU REALLY THINK HE'S GONNA LET ME STROLL ON OUTTA HERE? YOU DON'T THINK ANYONE IS GOING TO ASK QUESTIONS? LIKE...WHY WERE A SERIAL KILLER, A TERRORIST, AND THE BIGGEST GANGSTER IN THE GODDAMN CITY ALL IN THE SAME ROOM TOGETHER?
WHAT ARE YOU SUGGESTING?
THIS IS MY HOUSE...***MINE.*** I BUILT THIS PLACE. FEEL ME?
SO INSTEAD OF LETTING THEM TEAR IT DOWN...
I SAY WE BURN IT DOWN ON TOP OF THEM.

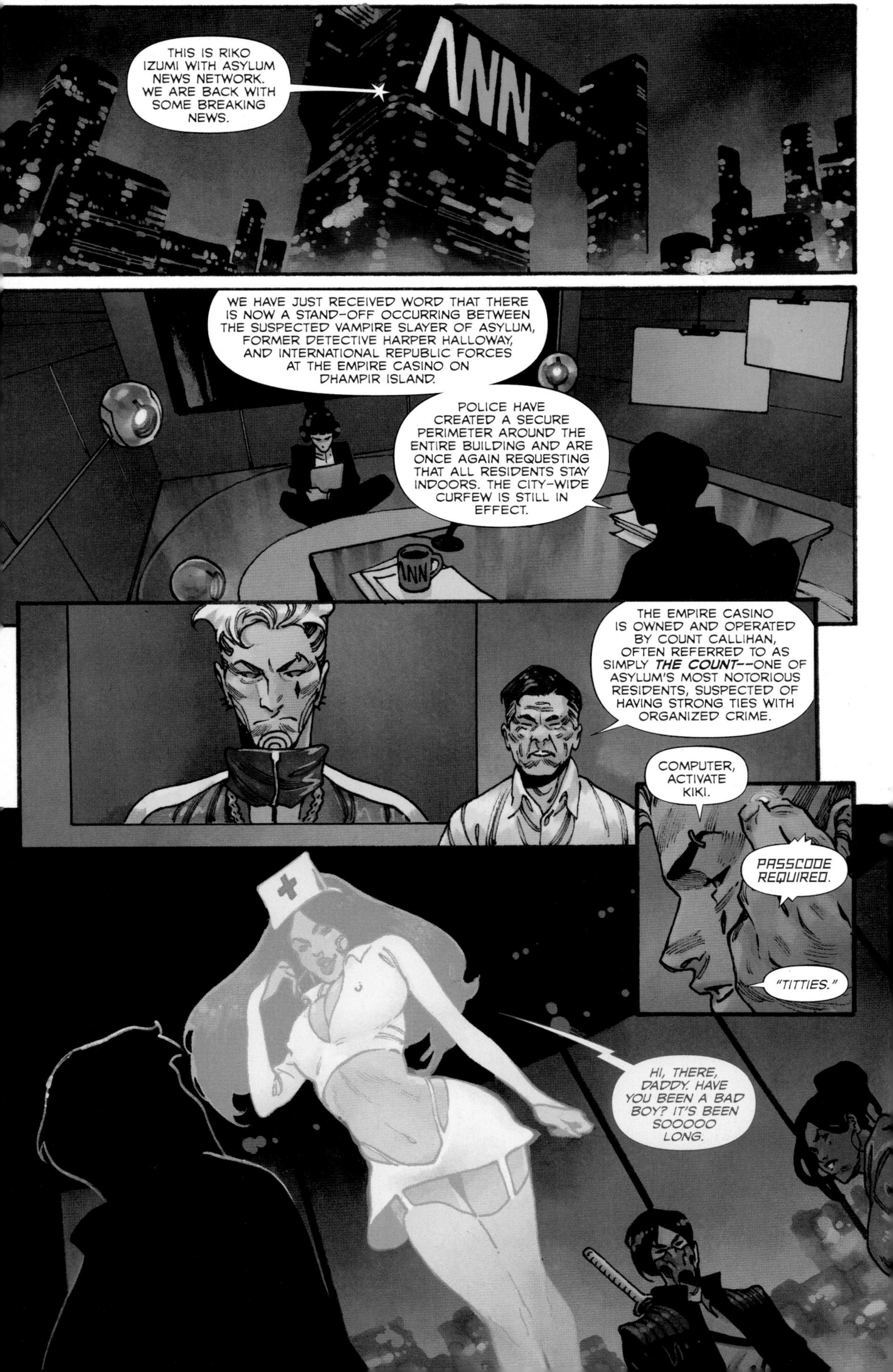

THIS IS RIKO IZUMI WITH ASYLUM NEWS NETWORK. WE ARE BACK WITH SOME BREAKING NEWS.
ANN
WE HAVE JUST RECEIVED WORD THAT THERE IS NOW A STAND-OFF OCCURRING BETWEEN THE SUSPECTED VAMPIRE SLAYER OF ASYLUM, FORMER DETECTIVE HARPER HALLOWAY, AND INTERNATIONAL REPUBLIC FORCES AT THE EMPIRE CASINO ON DHAMPIR ISLAND.
POLICE HAVE CREATED A SECURE PERIMETER AROUND THE ENTIRE BUILDING AND ARE ONCE AGAIN REQUESTING THAT ALL RESIDENTS STAY INDOORS. THE CITY-WIDE CURFEW IS STILL IN EFFECT.
ANN
THE EMPIRE CASINO IS OWNED AND OPERATED BY COUNT CALLIHAN, OFTEN REFERRED TO AS SIMPLY ***THE COUNT***--ONE OF ASYLUM'S MOST NOTORIOUS RESIDENTS, SUSPECTED OF HAVING STRONG TIES WITH ORGANIZED CRIME.
COMPUTER, ACTIVATE KIKI.
PASSCODE REQUIRED.
"TITTIES."
HI, THERE, DADDY. HAVE YOU BEEN A BAD BOY? IT'S BEEN SOOOOO LONG.

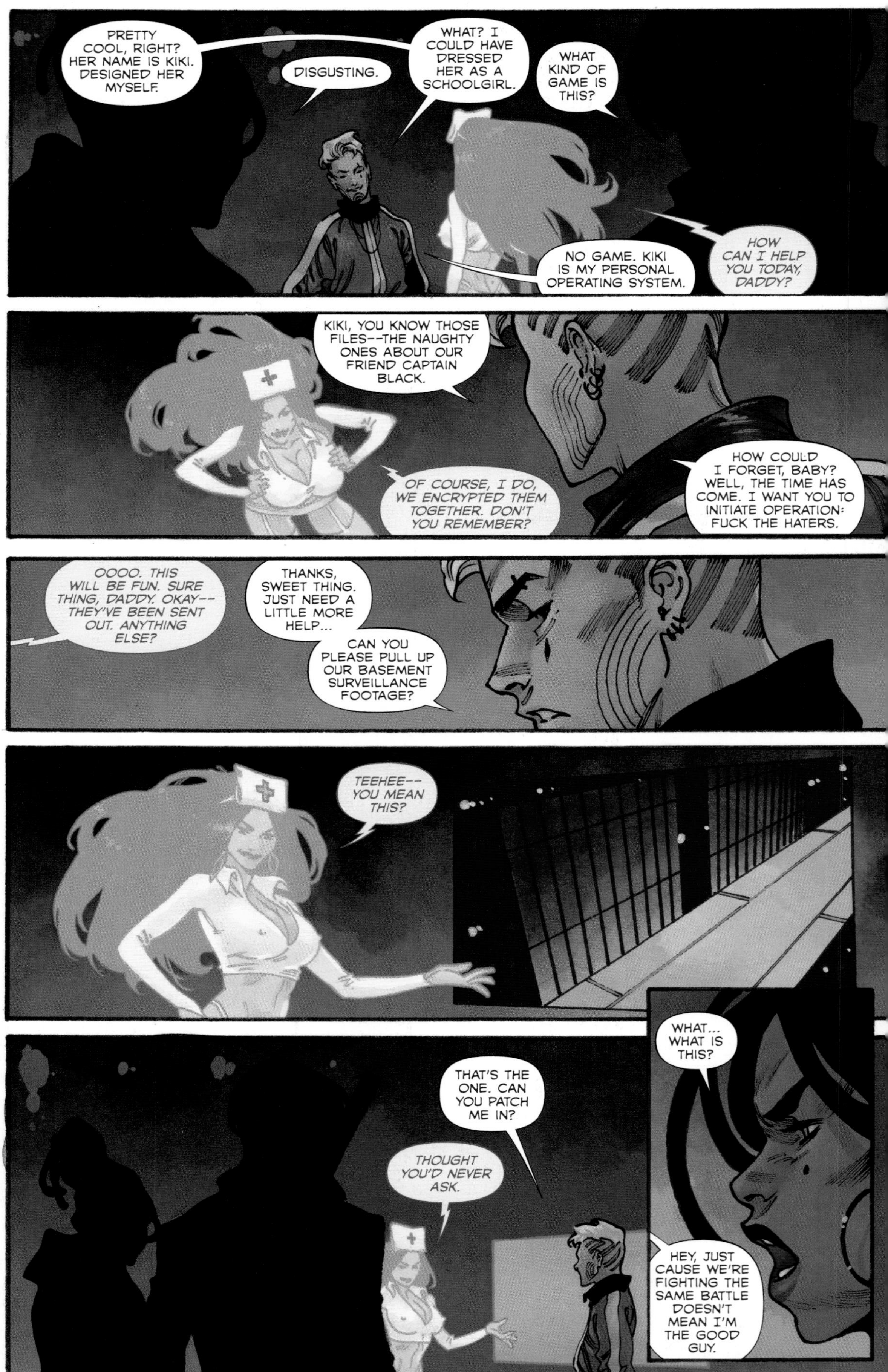
PRETTY COOL, RIGHT? HER NAME IS KIKI. DESIGNED HER MYSELF.
DISGUSTING.
WHAT? I COULD HAVE DRESSED HER AS A SCHOOLGIRL.
WHAT KIND OF GAME IS THIS?
NO GAME. KIKI IS MY PERSONAL OPERATING SYSTEM.
HOW CAN I HELP YOU TODAY, DADDY?
KIKI, YOU KNOW THOSE FILES--THE NAUGHTY ONES ABOUT OUR FRIEND CAPTAIN BLACK.
OF COURSE, I DO, WE ENCRYPTED THEM TOGETHER. DON'T YOU REMEMBER?
HOW COULD I FORGET, BABY? WELL, THE TIME HAS COME. I WANT YOU TO INITIATE OPERATION: FUCK THE HATERS.
OOOO. THIS WILL BE FUN. SURE THING, DADDY. OKAY--THEY'VE BEEN SENT OUT. ANYTHING ELSE?
THANKS, SWEET THING. JUST NEED A LITTLE MORE HELP...
CAN YOU PLEASE PULL UP OUR BASEMENT SURVEILLANCE FOOTAGE?
TEEHEE--YOU MEAN THIS?
THAT'S THE ONE. CAN YOU PATCH ME IN?
THOUGHT YOU'D NEVER ASK.
WHAT... WHAT IS THIS?
HEY, JUST CAUSE WE'RE FIGHTING THE SAME BATTLE DOESN'T MEAN I'M THE GOOD GUY.

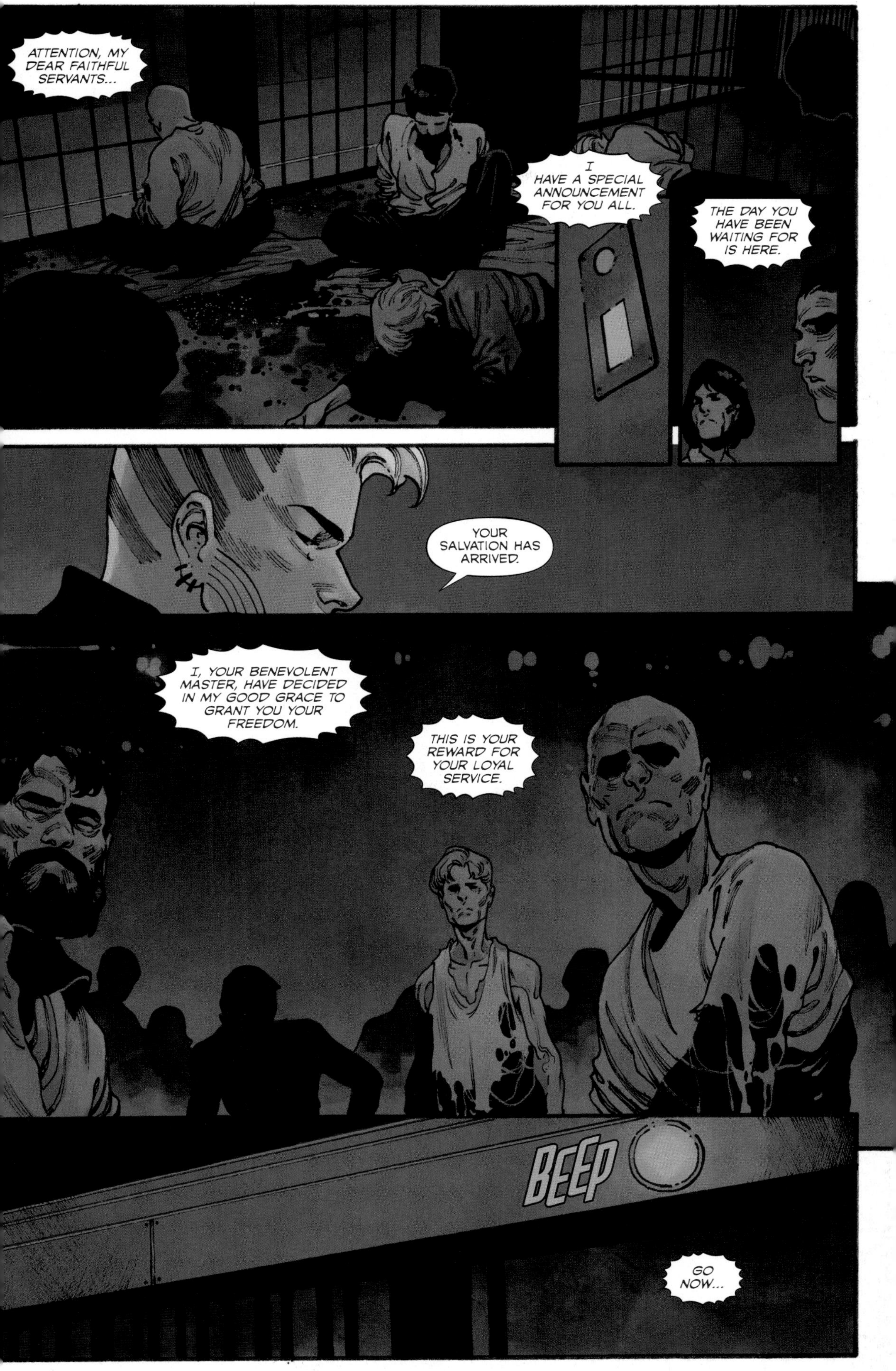
ATTENTION, MY DEAR FAITHFUL SERVANTS...
I HAVE A SPECIAL ANNOUNCEMENT FOR YOU ALL.
THE DAY YOU HAVE BEEN WAITING FOR IS HERE.
YOUR SALVATION HAS ARRIVED.
I, YOUR BENEVOLENT MASTER, HAVE DECIDED IN MY GOOD GRACE TO GRANT YOU YOUR FREEDOM.
THIS IS YOUR REWARD FOR YOUR LOYAL SERVICE.
BEEP
GO NOW...

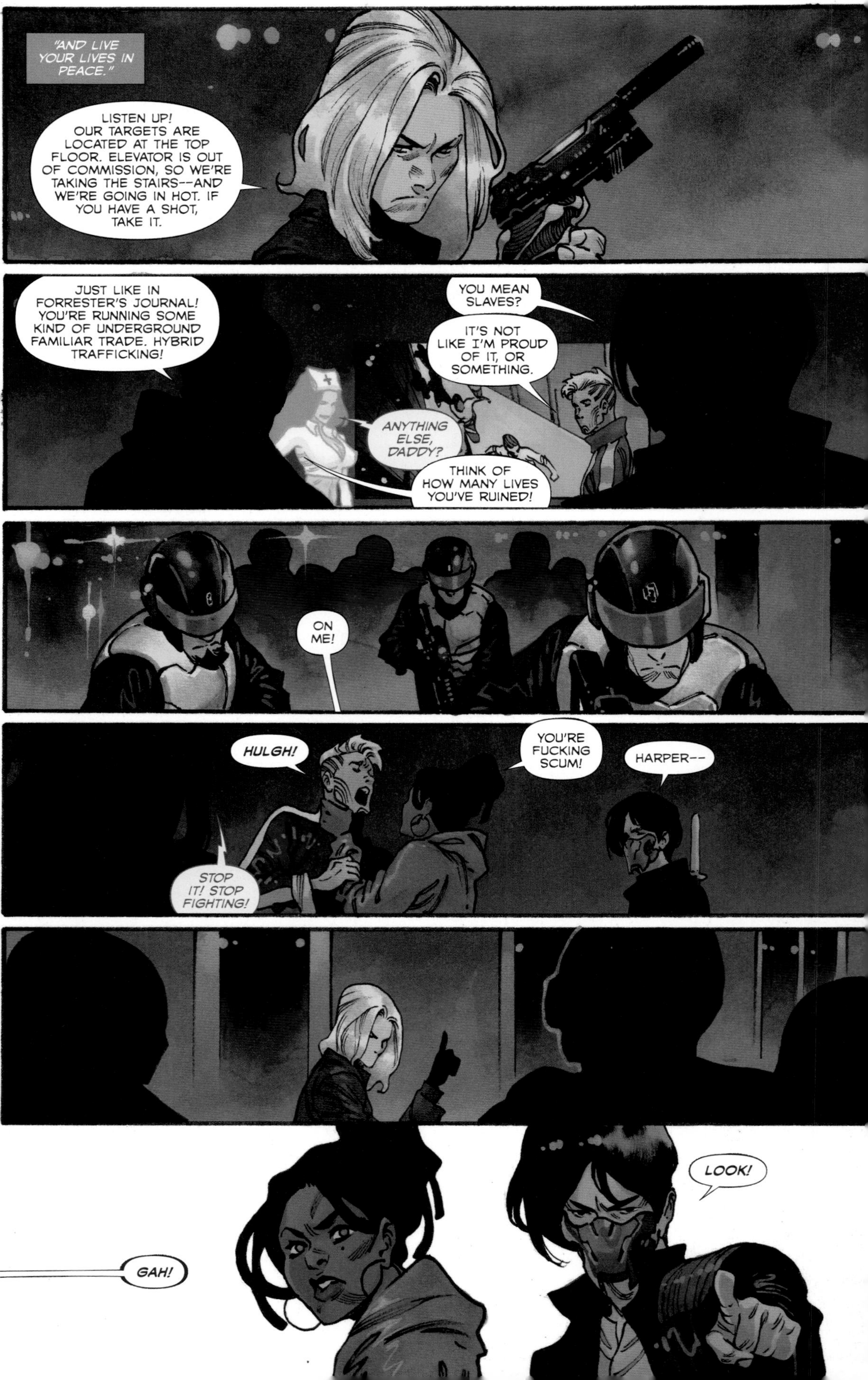
"AND LIVE YOUR LIVES IN PEACE."
LISTEN UP! OUR TARGETS ARE LOCATED AT THE TOP FLOOR. ELEVATOR IS OUT OF COMMISSION, SO WE'RE TAKING THE STAIRS--AND WE'RE GOING IN HOT. IF YOU HAVE A SHOT, TAKE IT.
JUST LIKE IN FORRESTER'S JOURNAL! YOU'RE RUNNING SOME KIND OF UNDERGROUND FAMILIAR TRADE. HYBRID TRAFFICKING!
YOU MEAN SLAVES?
IT'S NOT LIKE I'M PROUD OF IT, OR SOMETHING.
ANYTHING ELSE, DADDY?
THINK OF HOW MANY LIVES YOU'VE RUINED!
ON ME!
HULGH!
YOU'RE FUCKING SCUM!
HARPER--
STOP IT! STOP FIGHTING!
LOOK!
GAH!

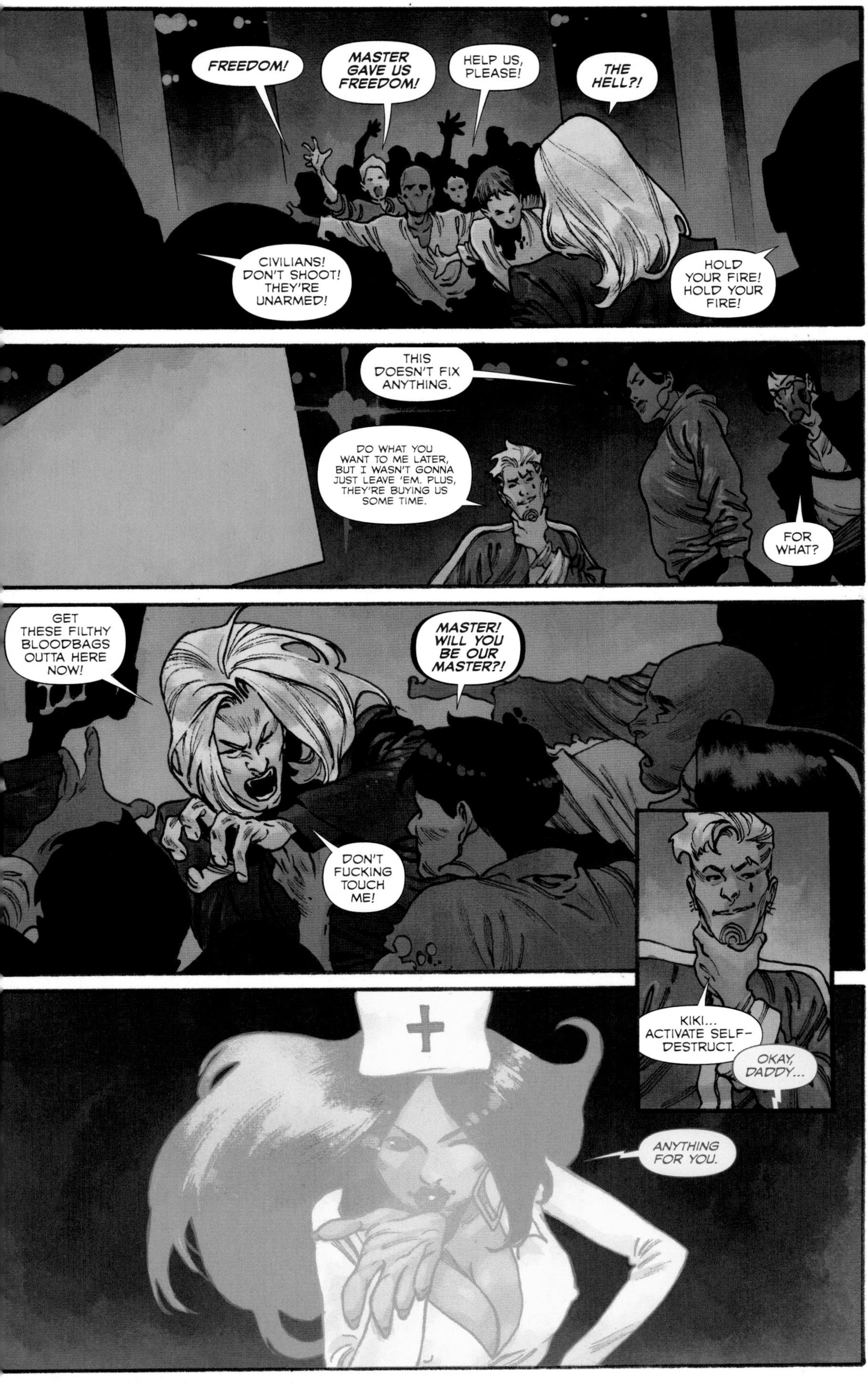
FREEDOM!
MASTER GAVE US FREEDOM!
HELP US, PLEASE!
THE HELL?!
CIVILIANS! DON'T SHOOT! THEY'RE UNARMED!
HOLD YOUR FIRE! HOLD YOUR FIRE!
THIS DOESN'T FIX ANYTHING.
DO WHAT YOU WANT TO ME LATER, BUT I WASN'T GONNA JUST LEAVE 'EM. PLUS, THEY'RE BUYING US SOME TIME.
FOR WHAT?
GET THESE FILTHY BLOODBAGS OUTTA HERE NOW!
MASTER! WILL YOU BE OUR MASTER?!
DON'T FUCKING TOUCH ME!
KIKI... ACTIVATE SELF-DESTRUCT.
OKAY, DADDY...
ANYTHING FOR YOU.

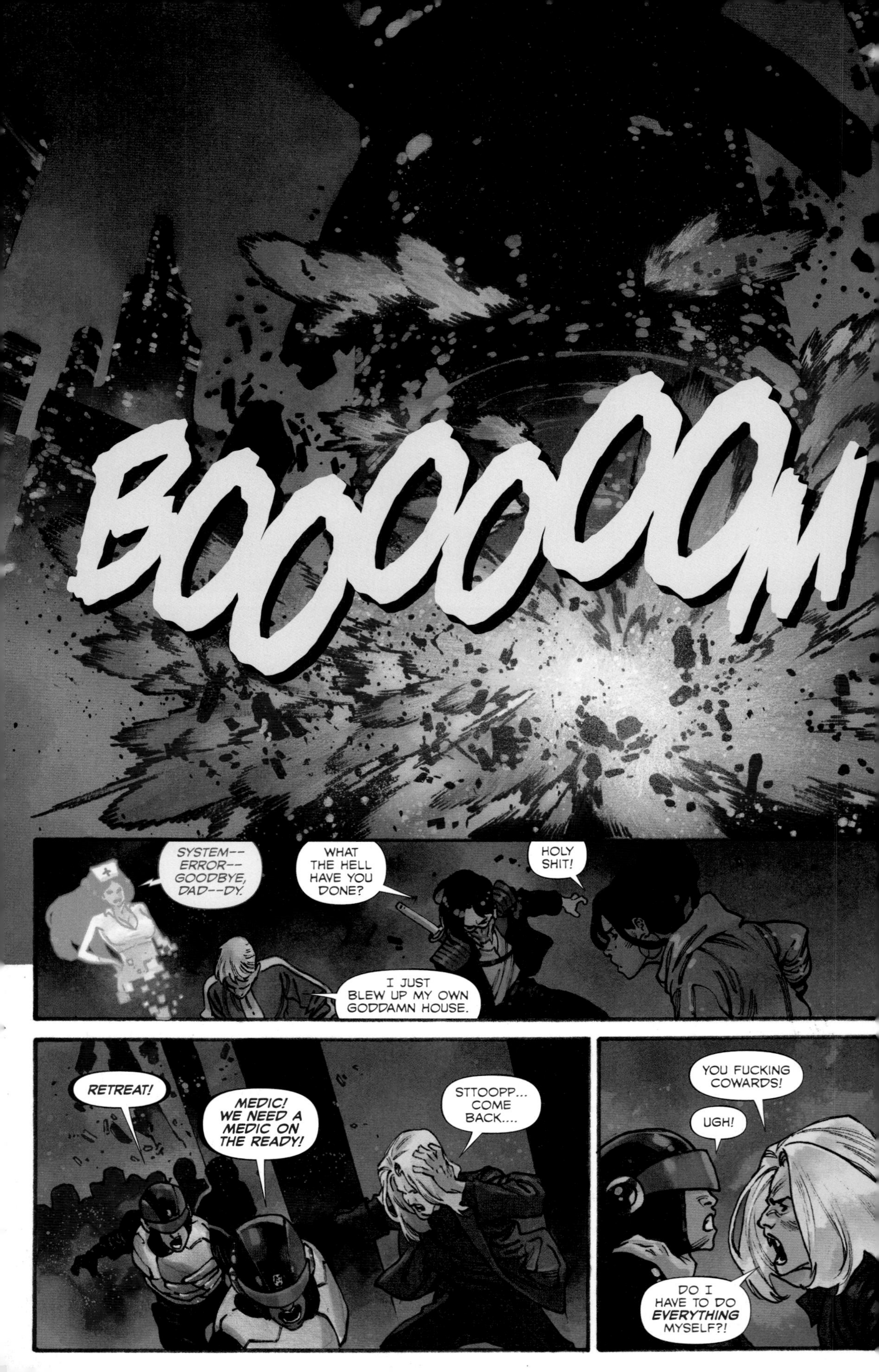
BOOOOOOM
SYSTEM-- ERROR-- GOODBYE, DAD--DY.
WHAT THE HELL HAVE YOU DONE?
HOLY SHIT!
I JUST BLEW UP MY OWN GODDAMN HOUSE.
RETREAT!
MEDIC! WE NEED A MEDIC ON THE READY!
STTOOPP... COME BACK....
YOU FUCKING COWARDS!
UGH!
DO I HAVE TO DO EVERYTHING MYSELF?!

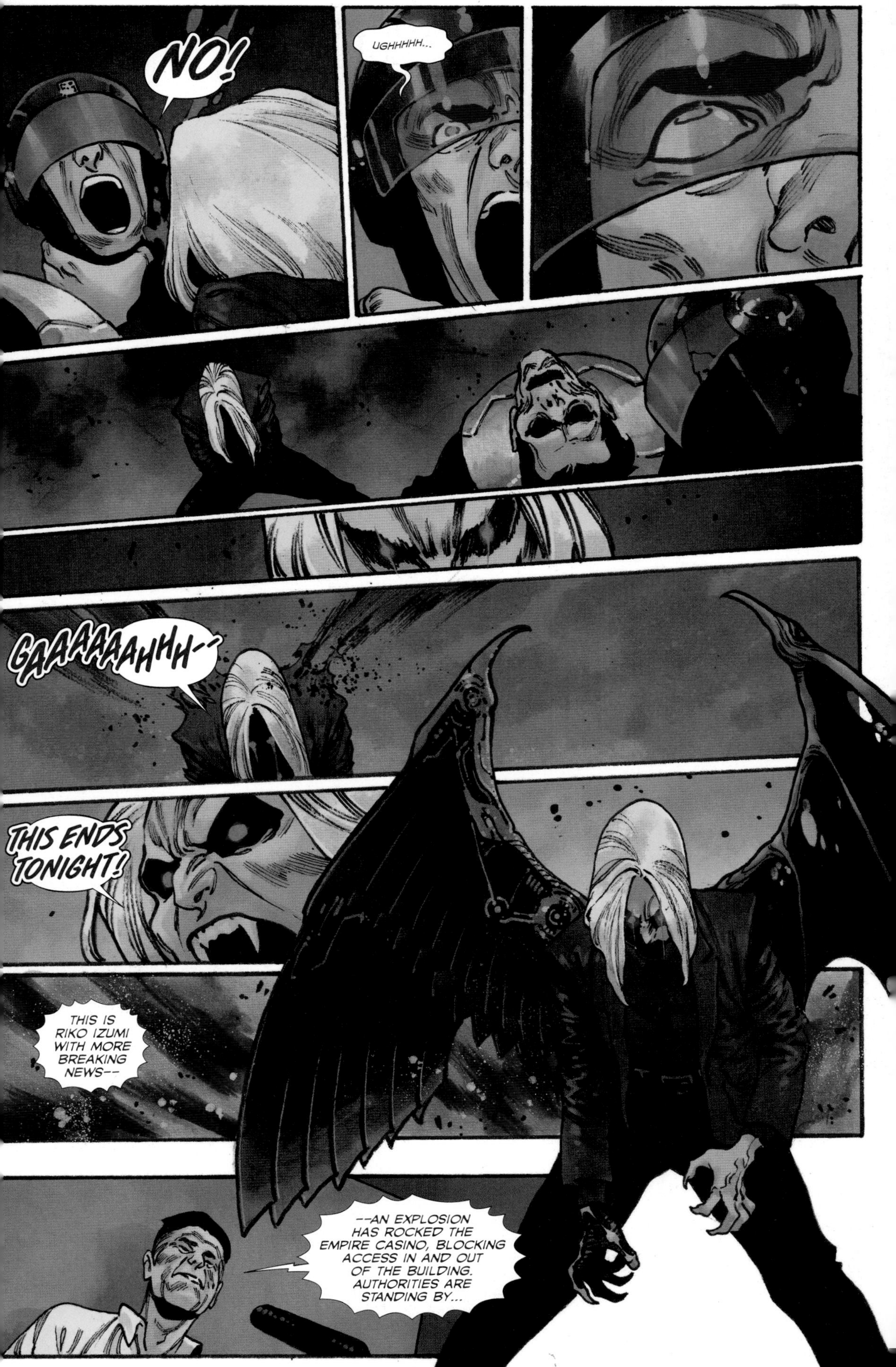
NO!
UGHHHHH...
GAAAAAAHHH--!
THIS ENDS TONIGHT!
THIS IS RIKO IZUMI WITH MORE BREAKING NEWS--
--AN EXPLOSION HAS ROCKED THE EMPIRE CASINO, BLOCKING ACCESS IN AND OUT OF THE BUILDING. AUTHORITIES ARE STANDING BY...

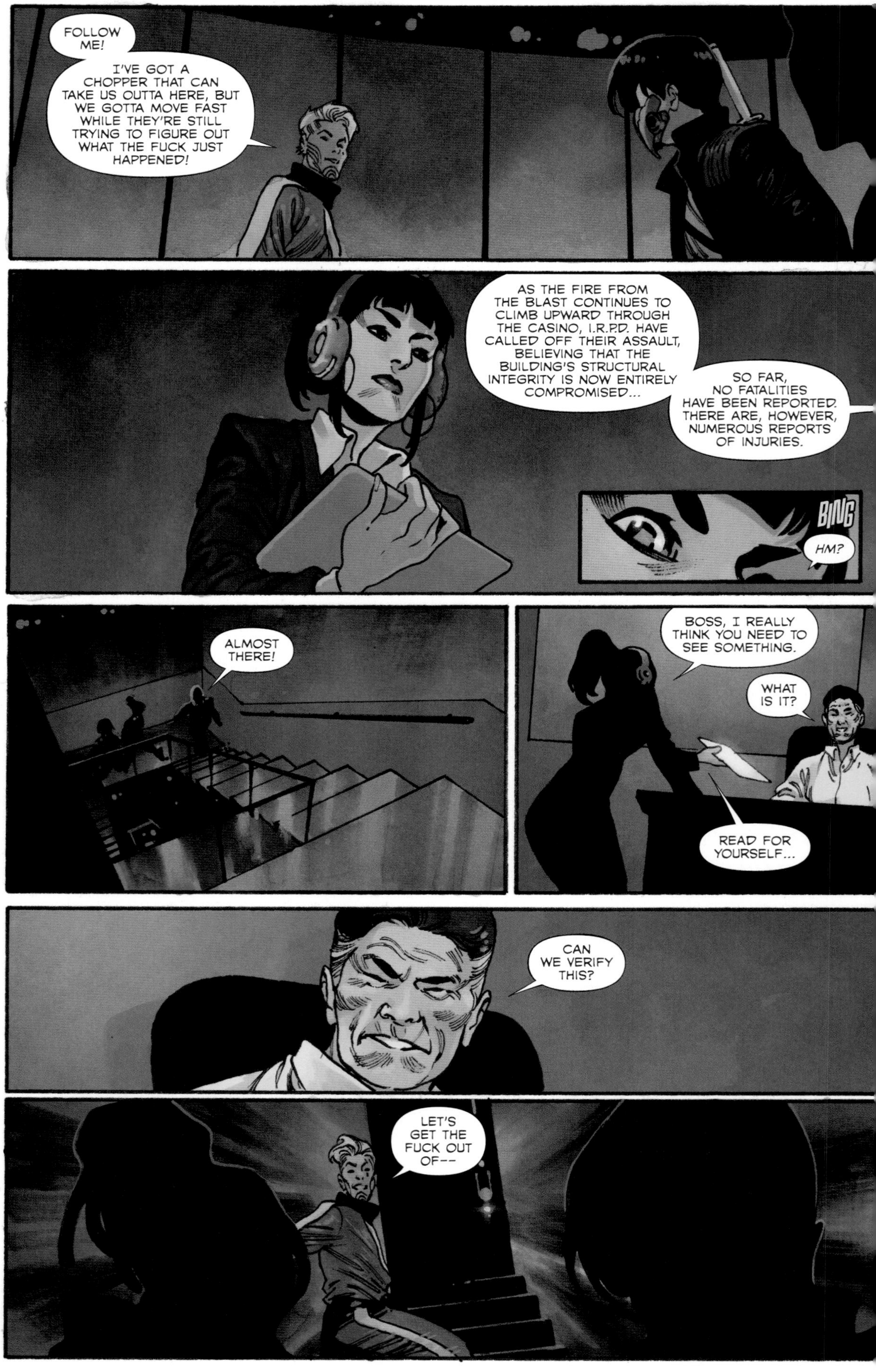
FOLLOW ME!
I'VE GOT A CHOPPER THAT CAN TAKE US OUTTA HERE, BUT WE GOTTA MOVE FAST WHILE THEY'RE STILL TRYING TO FIGURE OUT WHAT THE FUCK JUST HAPPENED!
AS THE FIRE FROM THE BLAST CONTINUES TO CLIMB UPWARD THROUGH THE CASINO, I.R.P.D. HAVE CALLED OFF THEIR ASSAULT, BELIEVING THAT THE BUILDING'S STRUCTURAL INTEGRITY IS NOW ENTIRELY COMPROMISED...
SO FAR, NO FATALITIES HAVE BEEN REPORTED. THERE ARE, HOWEVER, NUMEROUS REPORTS OF INJURIES.
BING
HM?
ALMOST THERE!
BOSS, I REALLY THINK YOU NEED TO SEE SOMETHING.
WHAT IS IT?
READ FOR YOURSELF...
CAN WE VERIFY THIS?
LET'S GET THE FUCK OUT OF--

SHRRRP

...HERE?

OH... DAMN.

PETULANT VERMIN...

UM...SINCE WHEN COULD HE FLY?

HOW DARE YOU?! DISGUSTING COW...

HAVE YOU LEARNED NOTHING? YOU ARE NOT LIKE ME. YOU ARE NOT *PURE.*

I COME FROM THE PLACE WHERE YOUR NIGHTMARES ARE BORN.

SHK

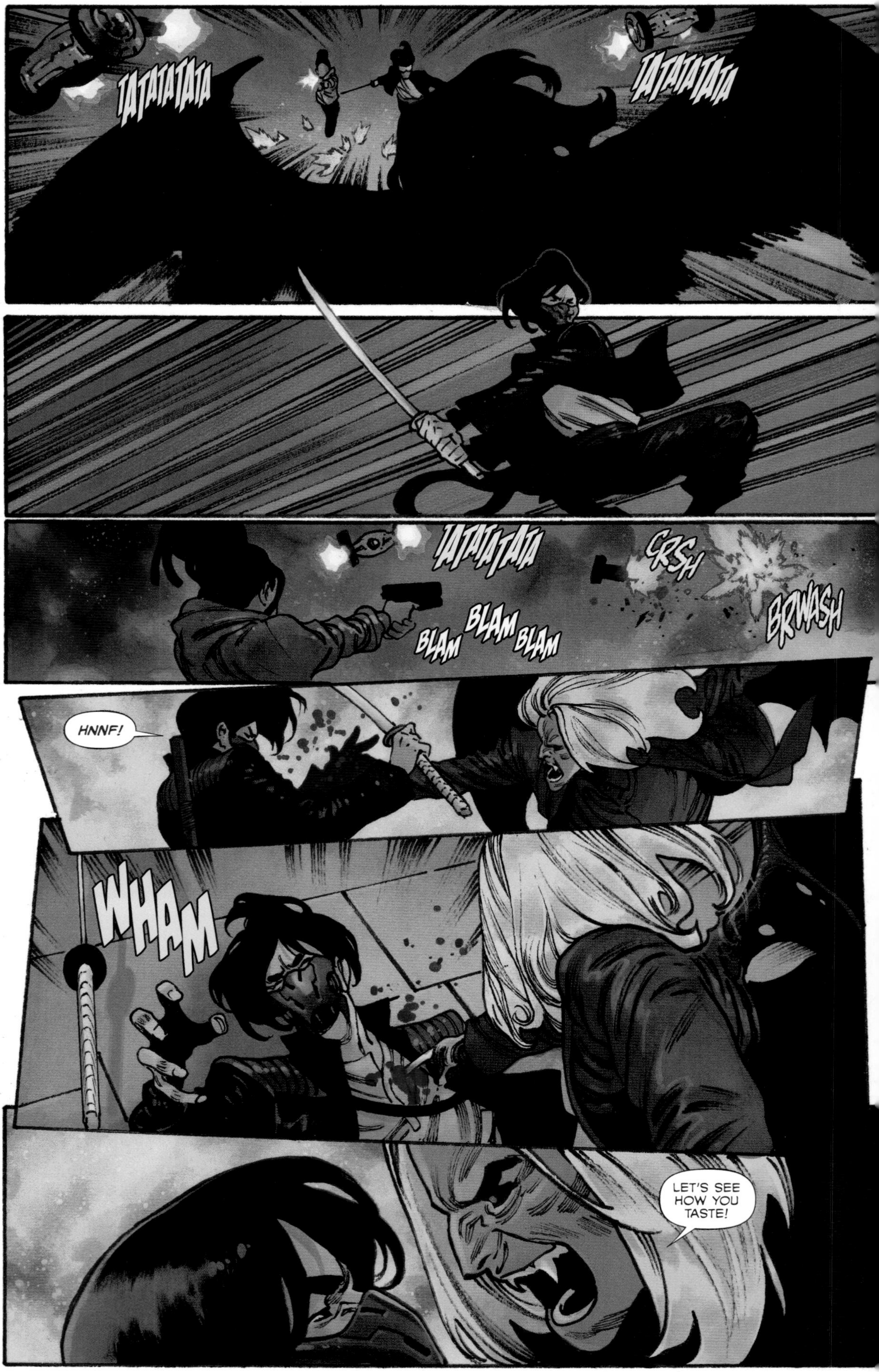
TATATATATA
TATATATATA
TATATATATA
BLAM
BLAM
BLAM
CRSH
BRWASH
HNNF!
WHAM
LET'S SEE HOW YOU TASTE!

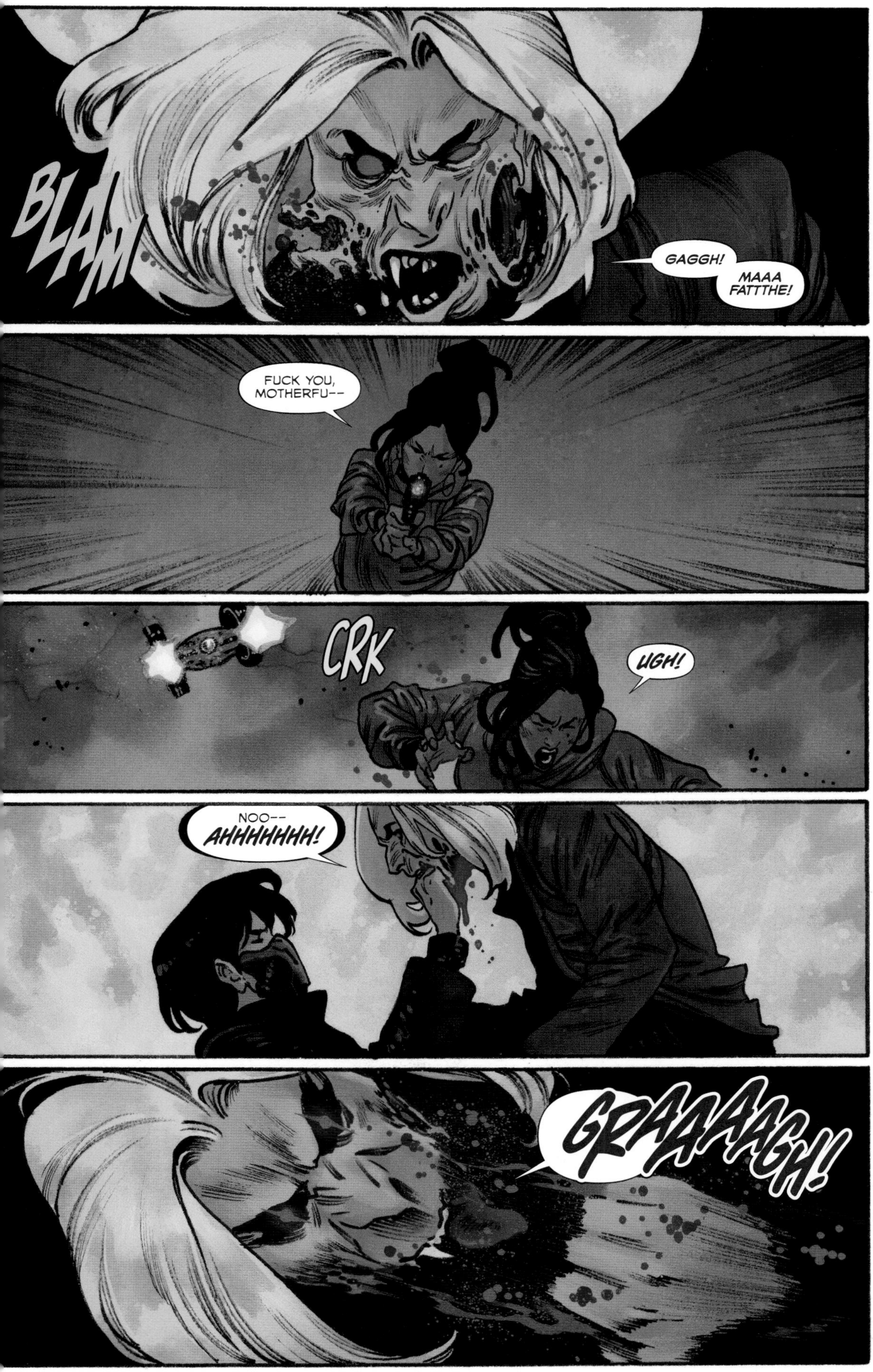
BLAM
GAGGH!
MAAA FATTTHE!
FUCK YOU, MOTHERFU--
CRK
UGH!
NOO-- AHHHHHHH!
GRAAAAAGH!

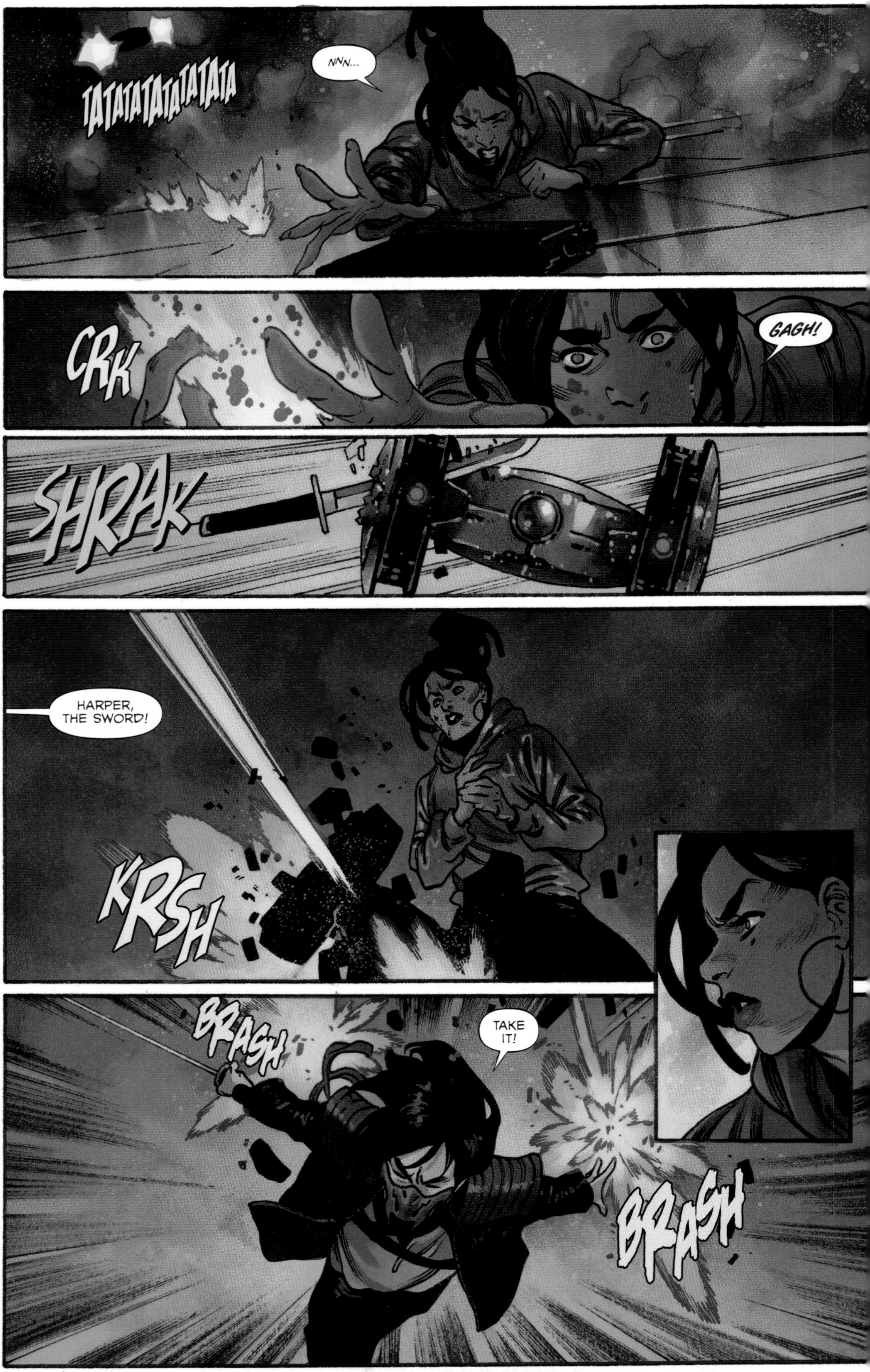
TATATATATATATA
NNN...
CRK
GAGH!
SHRAK
HARPER, THE SWORD!
KRSH
BRASH
TAKE IT!
BRASH

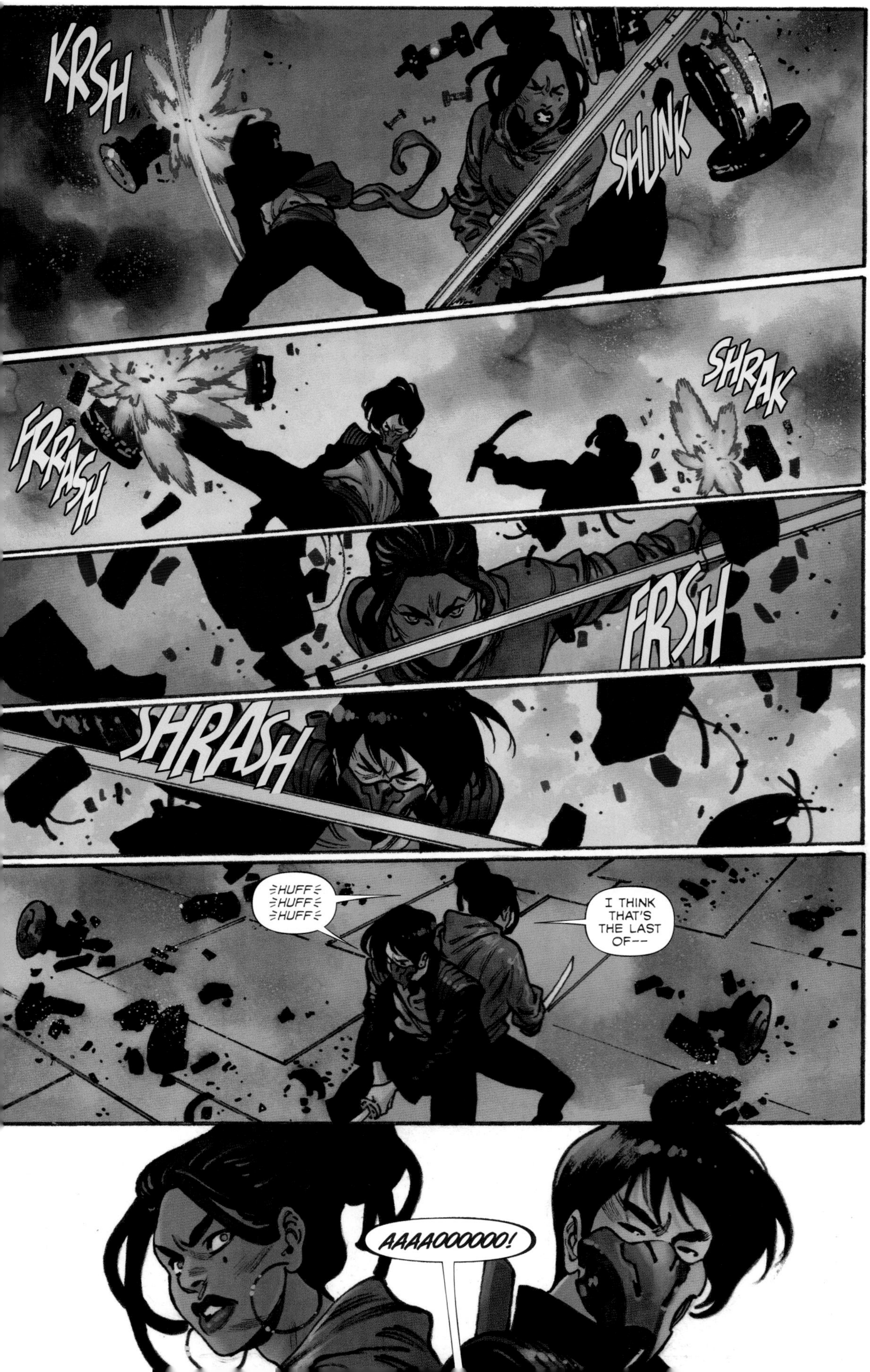
KRSH
SHUNK
FRRASH
SHRAK
FRSH
SHRASH
HUFF HUFF HUFF
I THINK THAT'S THE LAST OF--
AAAAOOOOOO!

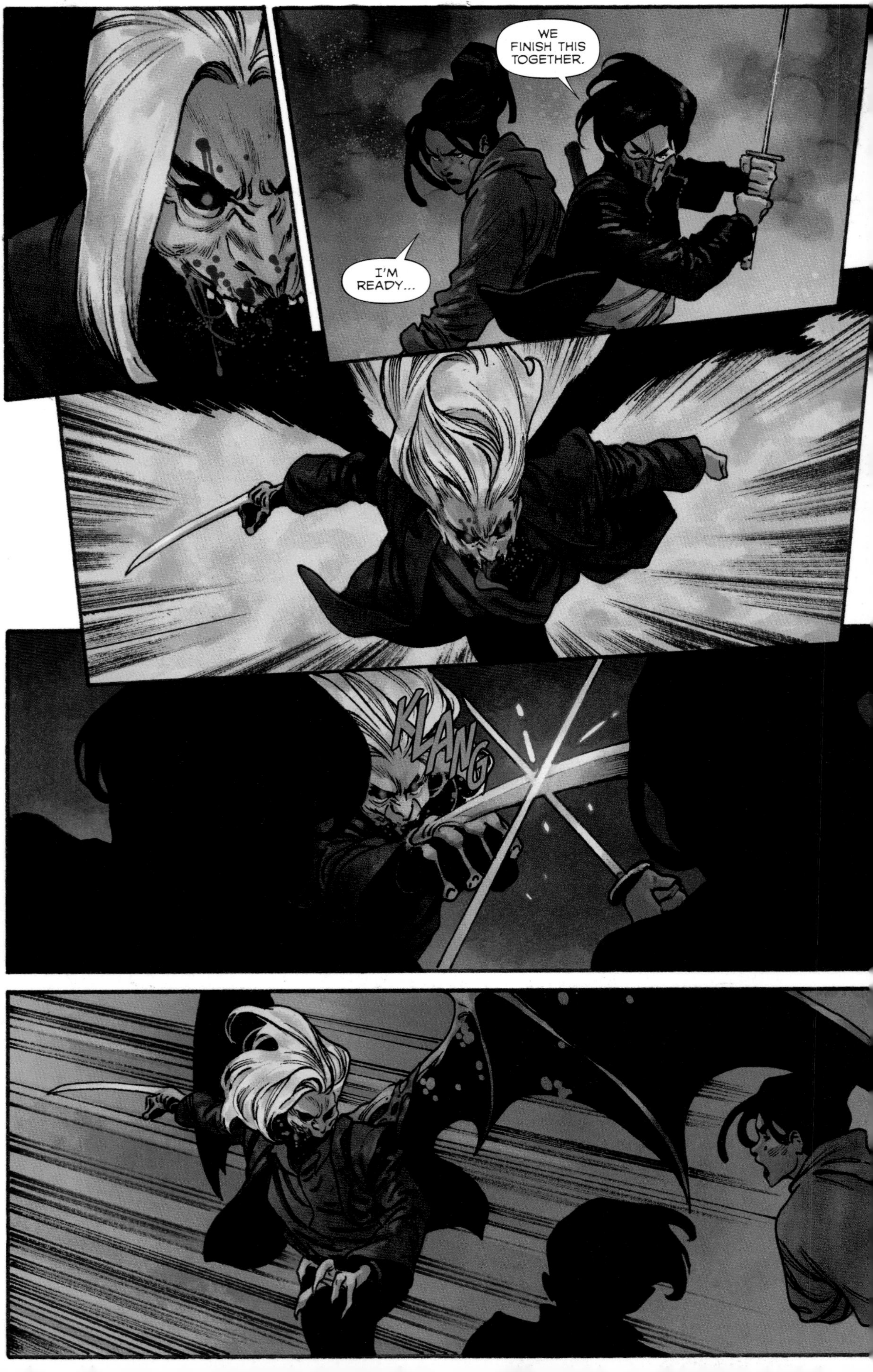
WE FINISH THIS TOGETHER.
I'M READY...
KLANG

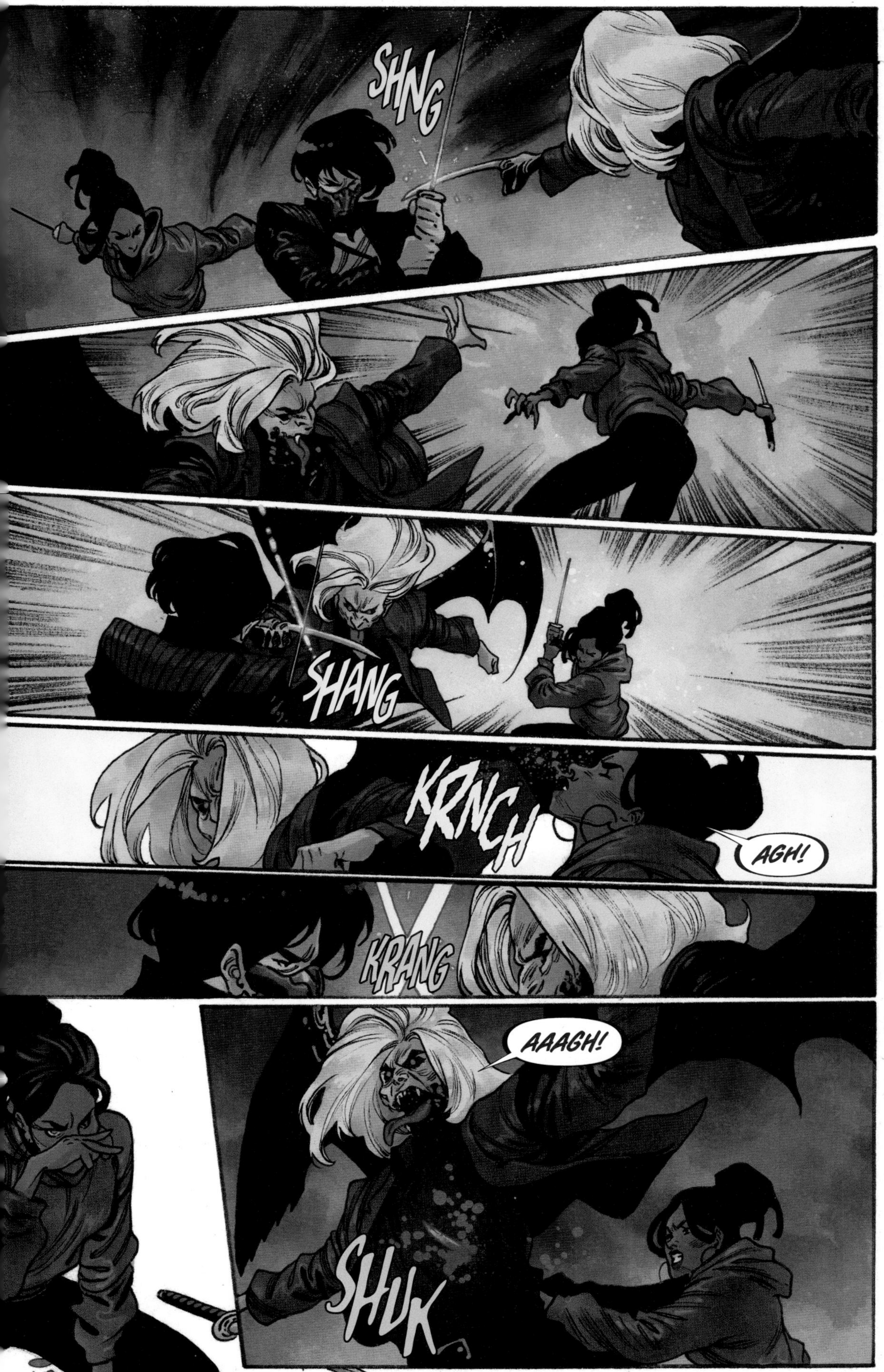
SHNG
SHANG
KRNCH
AGH!
KRANG
AAAGH!
SHUK

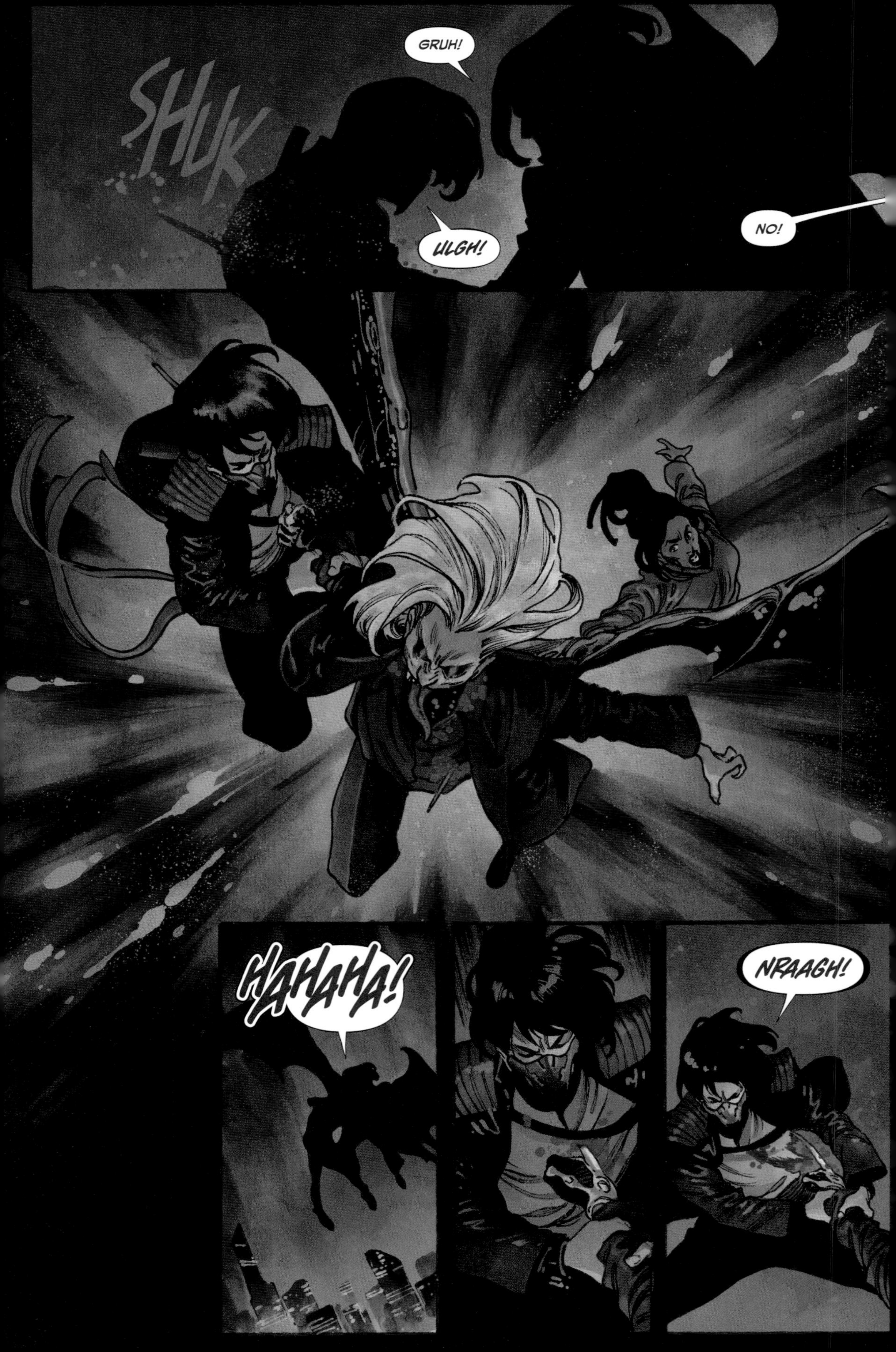
SHUK
GRUH!
ULGH!
NO!
HAHAHA!
NRAAGH!

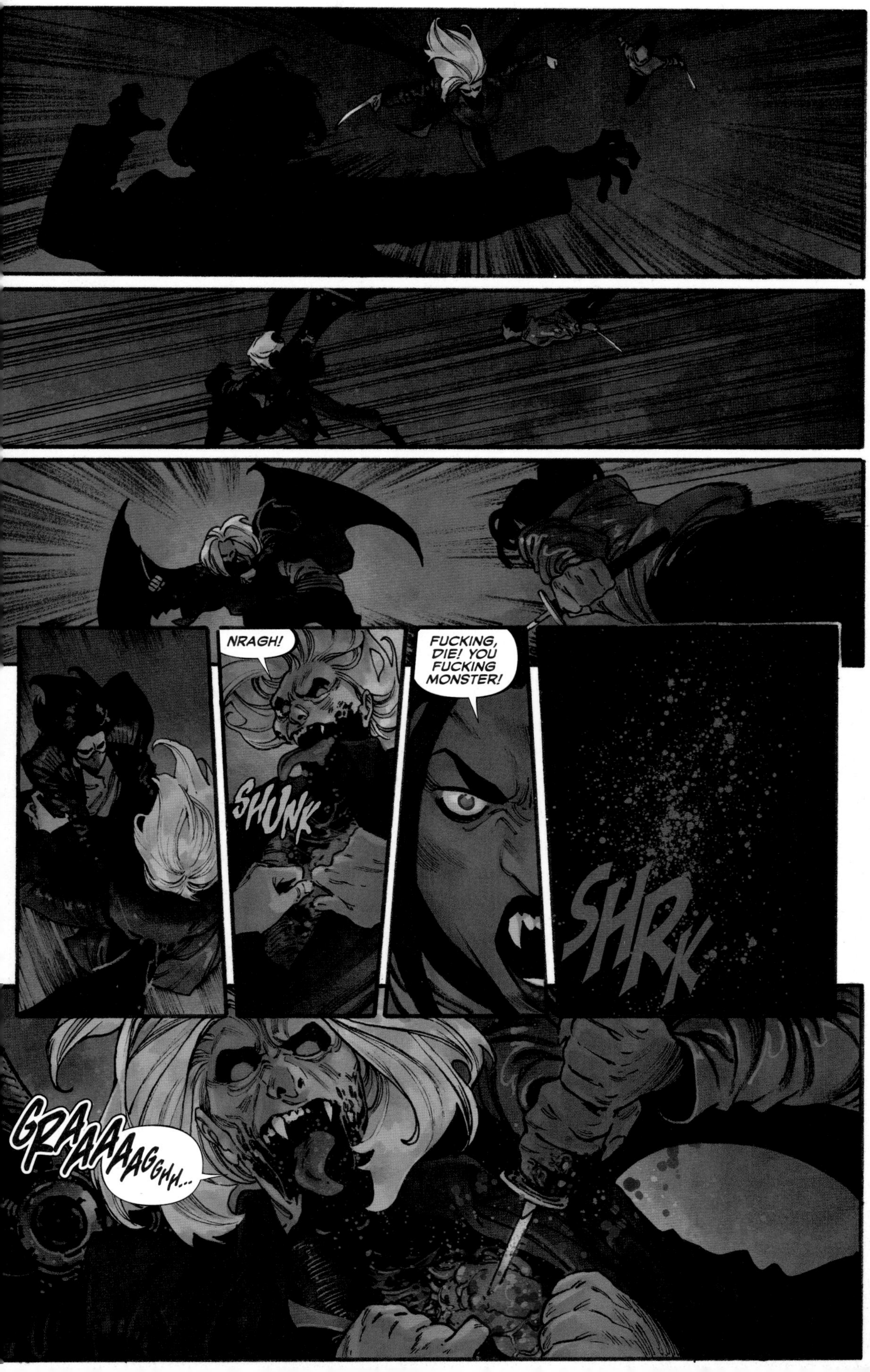
NRAGH!
SHUNK
FUCKING, DIE! YOU FUCKING MONSTER!
SHRK
GRAAAAAGGHH...

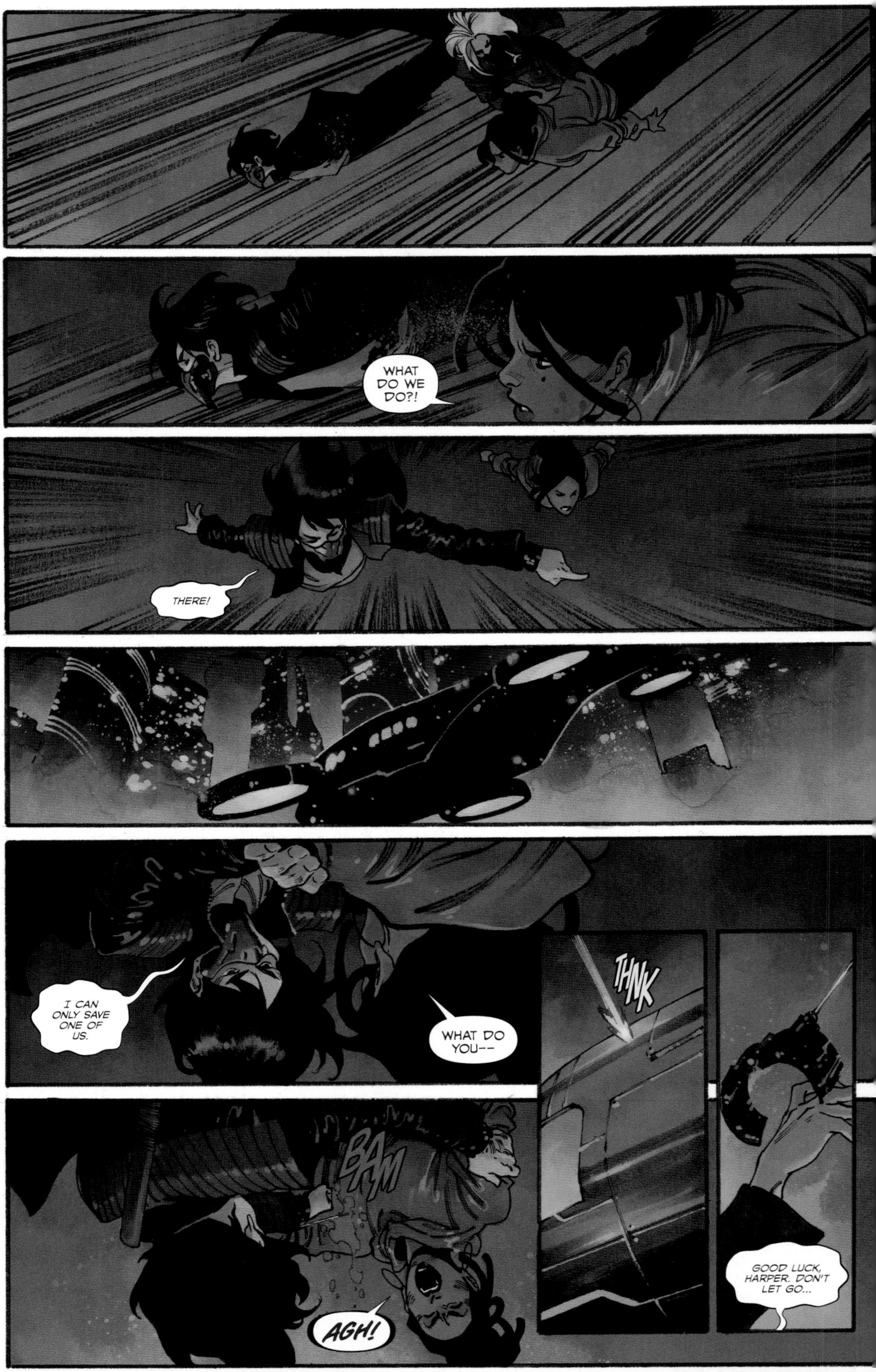
WHAT DO WE DO?!
THERE!
I CAN ONLY SAVE ONE OF US.
WHAT DO YOU--
BAM
AGH!
THNK
GOOD LUCK, HARPER. DON'T LET GO...

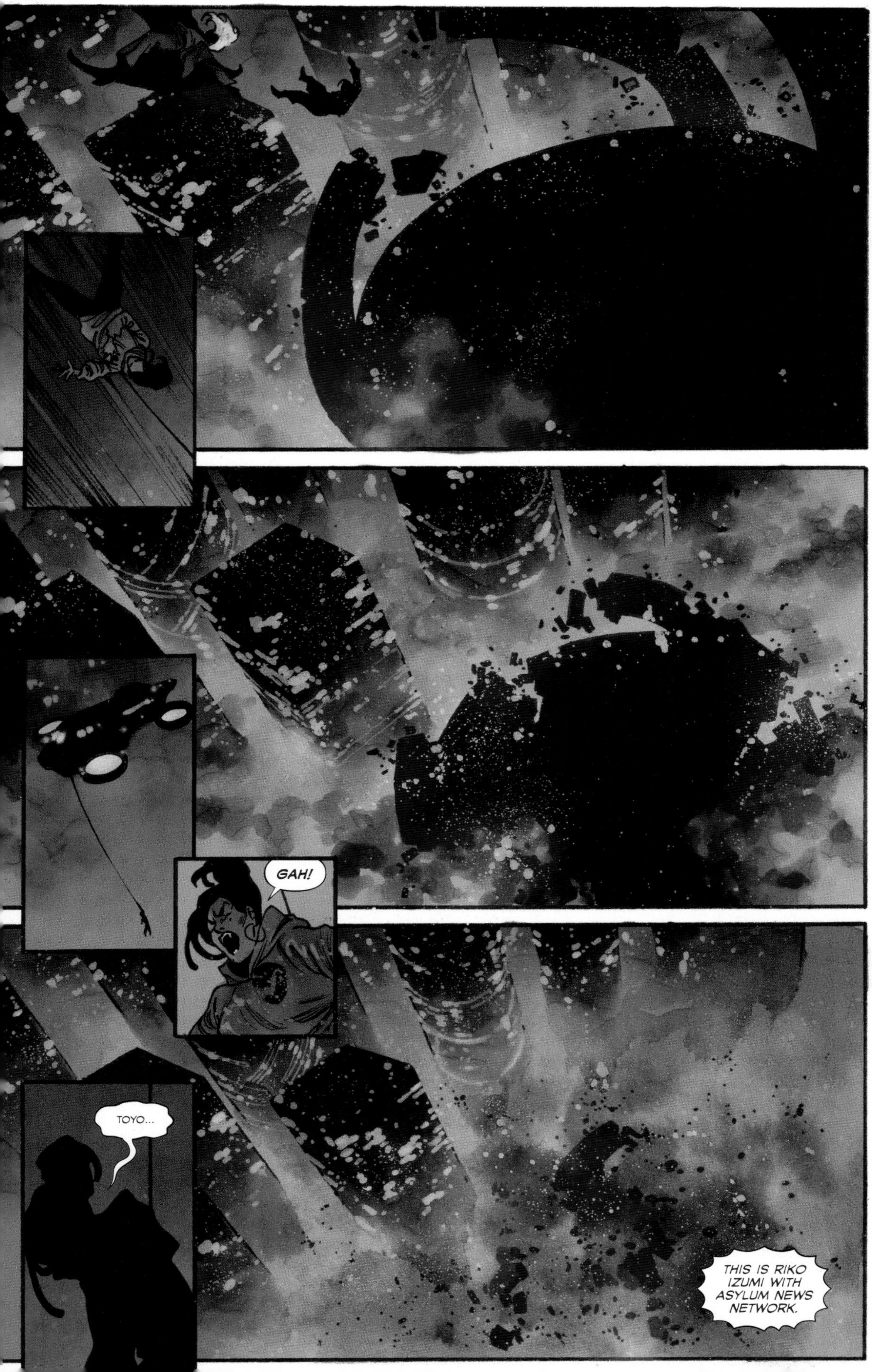
GAH!
TOYO...
THIS IS RIKO IZUMI WITH ASYLUM NEWS NETWORK.

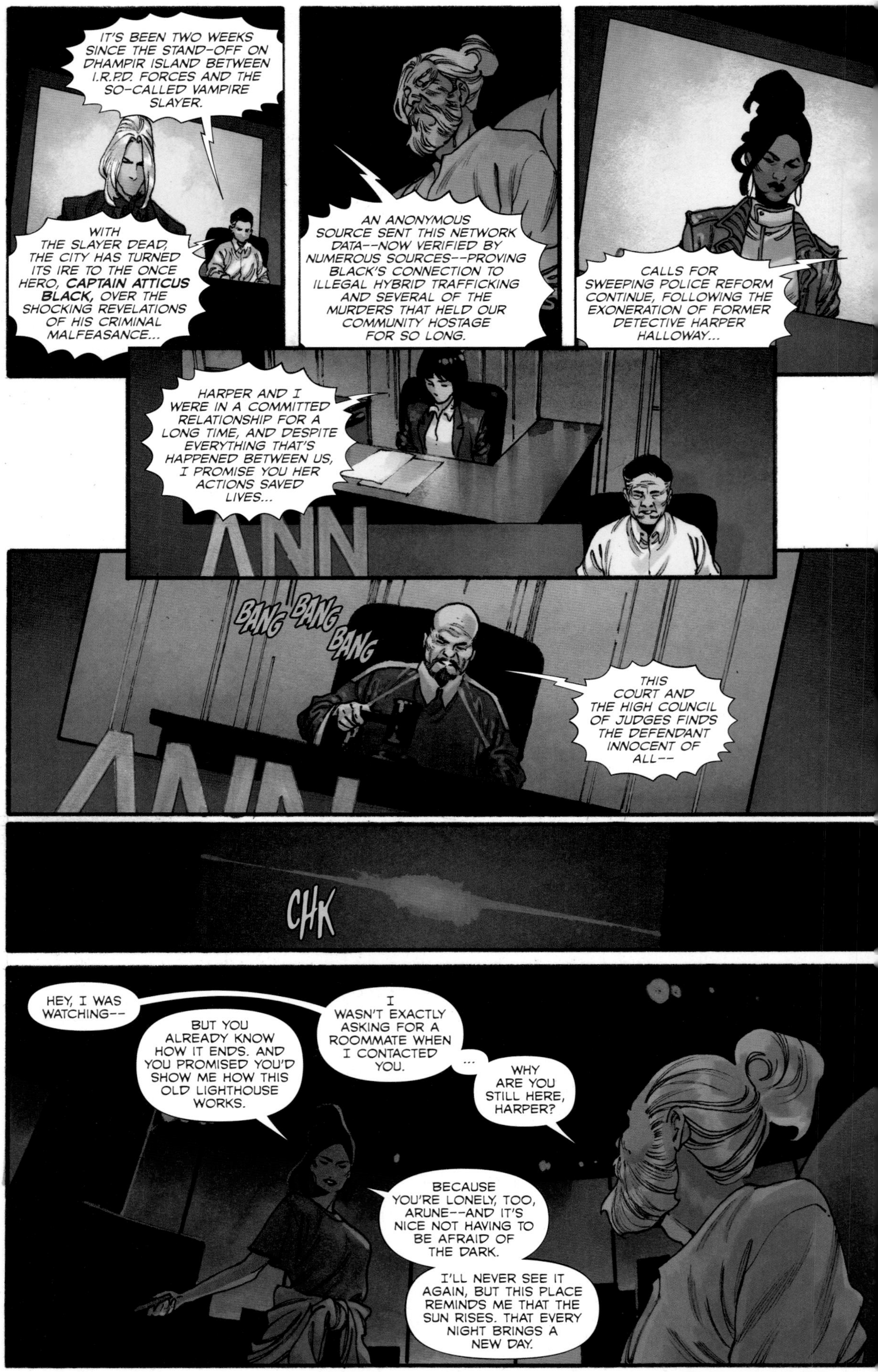

IT'S BEEN TWO WEEKS SINCE THE STAND-OFF ON DHAMPIR ISLAND BETWEEN I.R.P.D. FORCES AND THE SO-CALLED VAMPIRE SLAYER.
WITH THE SLAYER DEAD, THE CITY HAS TURNED ITS IRE TO THE ONCE HERO, **CAPTAIN ATTICUS BLACK,** OVER THE SHOCKING REVELATIONS OF HIS CRIMINAL MALFEASANCE...
AN ANONYMOUS SOURCE SENT THIS NETWORK DATA--NOW VERIFIED BY NUMEROUS SOURCES--PROVING BLACK'S CONNECTION TO ILLEGAL HYBRID TRAFFICKING AND SEVERAL OF THE MURDERS THAT HELD OUR COMMUNITY HOSTAGE FOR SO LONG.
CALLS FOR SWEEPING POLICE REFORM CONTINUE, FOLLOWING THE EXONERATION OF FORMER DETECTIVE HARPER HALLOWAY...
HARPER AND I WERE IN A COMMITTED RELATIONSHIP FOR A LONG TIME, AND DESPITE EVERYTHING THAT'S HAPPENED BETWEEN US, I PROMISE YOU HER ACTIONS SAVED LIVES...
BANG BANG BANG
THIS COURT AND THE HIGH COUNCIL OF JUDGES FINDS THE DEFENDANT INNOCENT OF ALL--
CHK
HEY, I WAS WATCHING--
BUT YOU ALREADY KNOW HOW IT ENDS. AND YOU PROMISED YOU'D SHOW ME HOW THIS OLD LIGHTHOUSE WORKS.
I WASN'T EXACTLY ASKING FOR A ROOMMATE WHEN I CONTACTED YOU.
...
WHY ARE YOU STILL HERE, HARPER?
BECAUSE YOU'RE LONELY, TOO, ARUNE--AND IT'S NICE NOT HAVING TO BE AFRAID OF THE DARK.
I'LL NEVER SEE IT AGAIN, BUT THIS PLACE REMINDS ME THAT THE SUN RISES. THAT EVERY NIGHT BRINGS A NEW DAY.

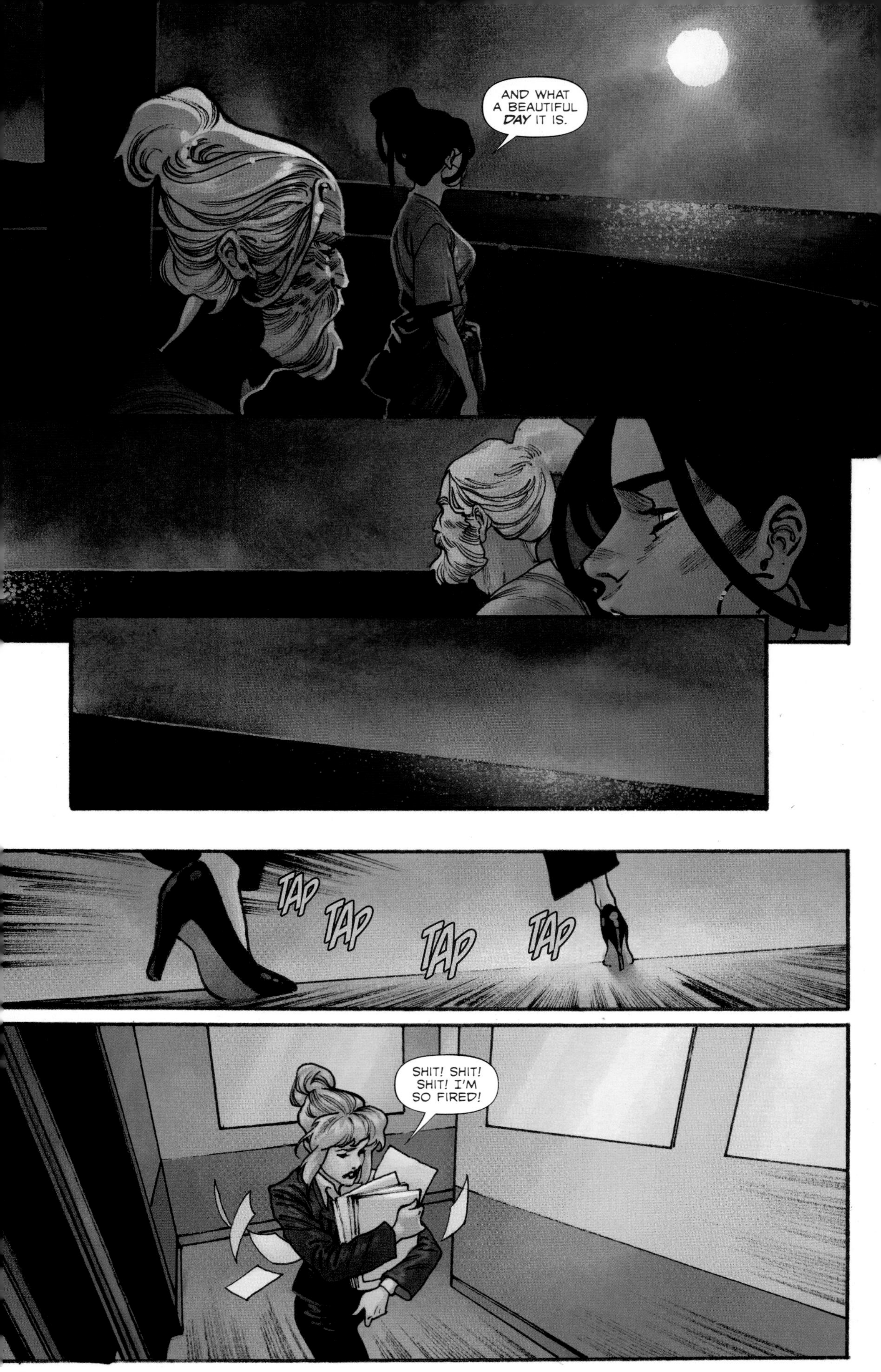
AND WHAT A BEAUTIFUL DAY IT IS.
TAP TAP TAP TAP
SHIT! SHIT! SHIT! I'M SO FIRED!

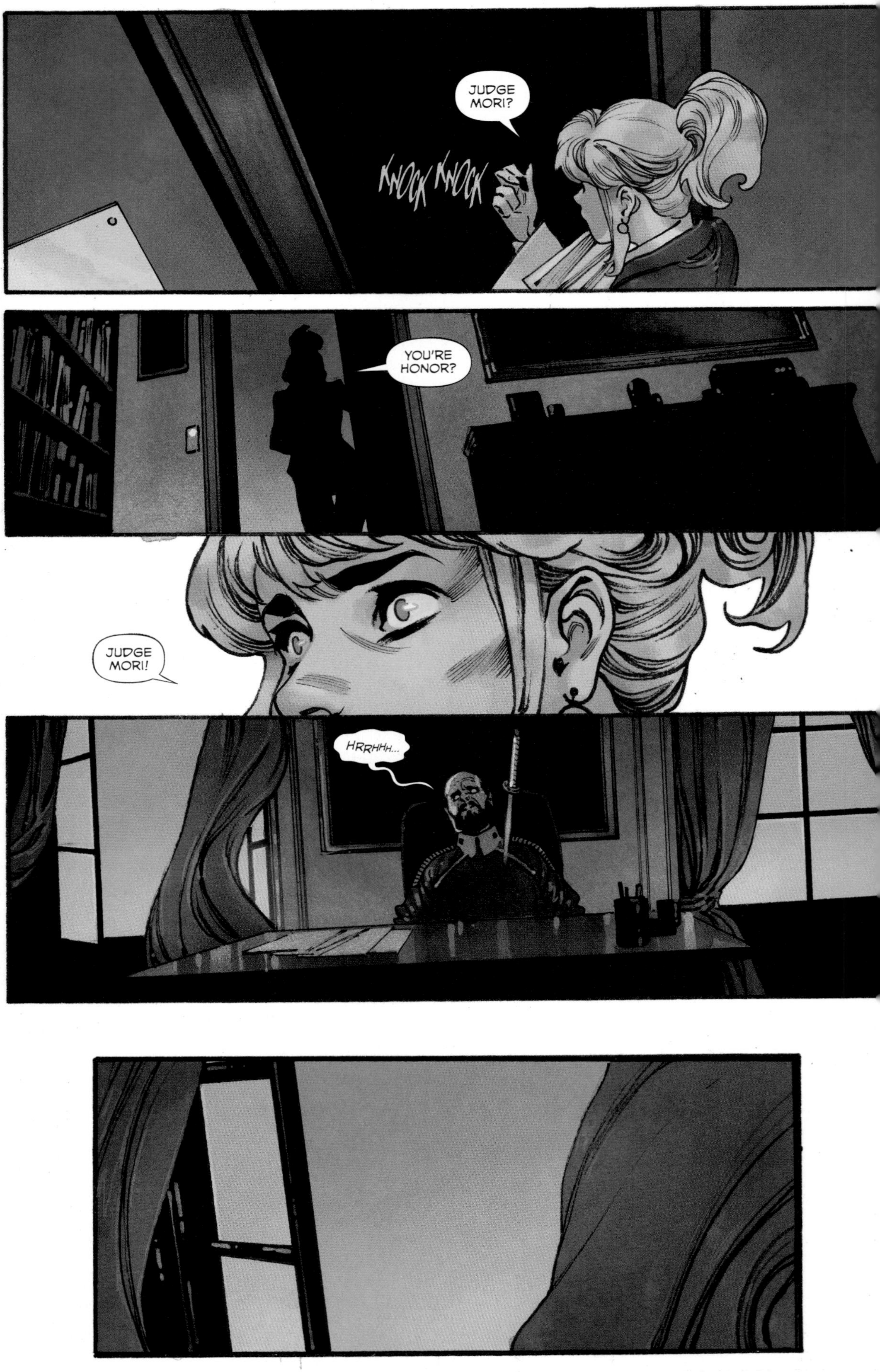
JUDGE MORI?
KNOCK KNOCK
YOU'RE HONOR?
JUDGE MORI!
HRRHHH...

COVER 1 - RUAN

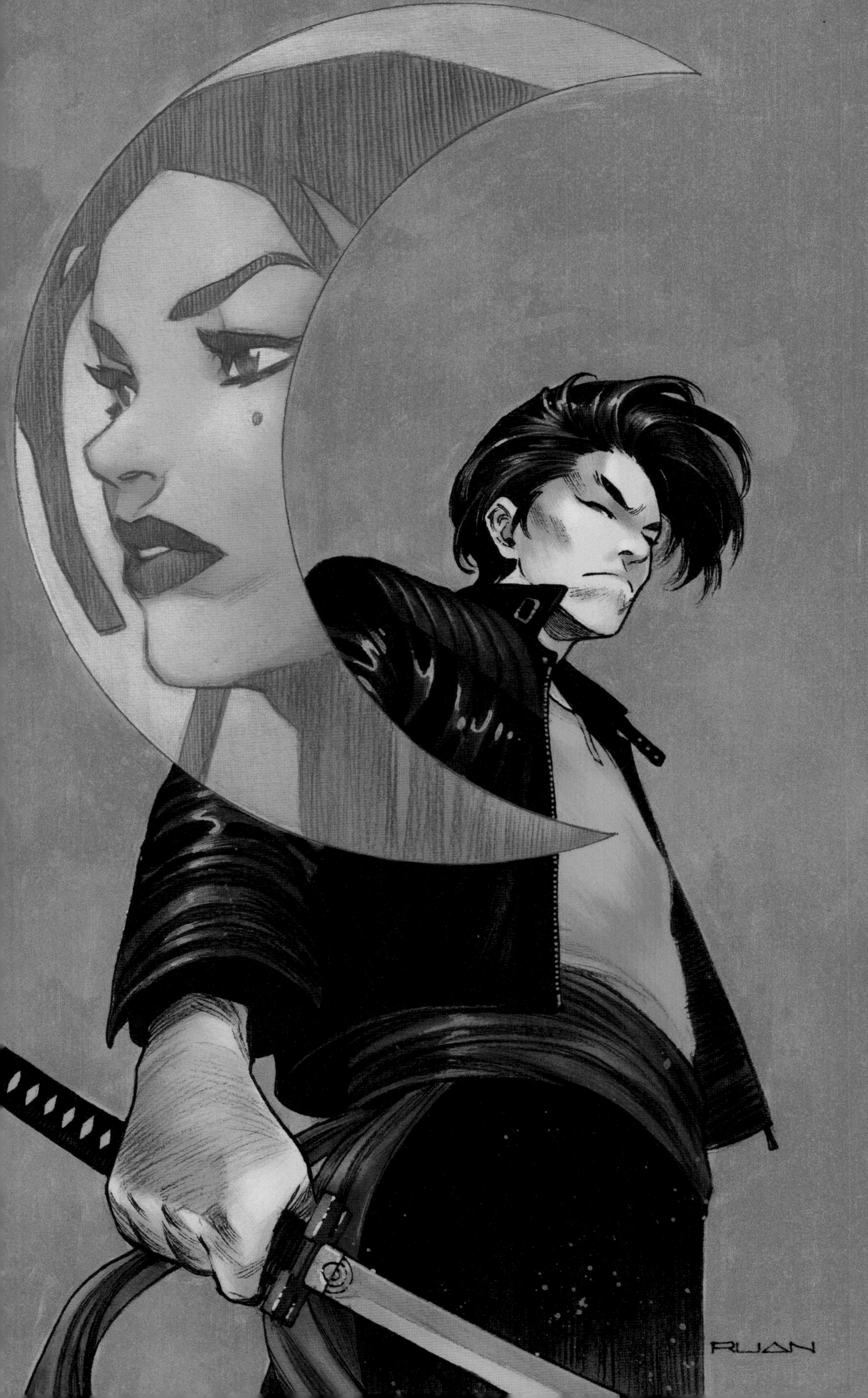
RUAN

COVER 2 - RUAN

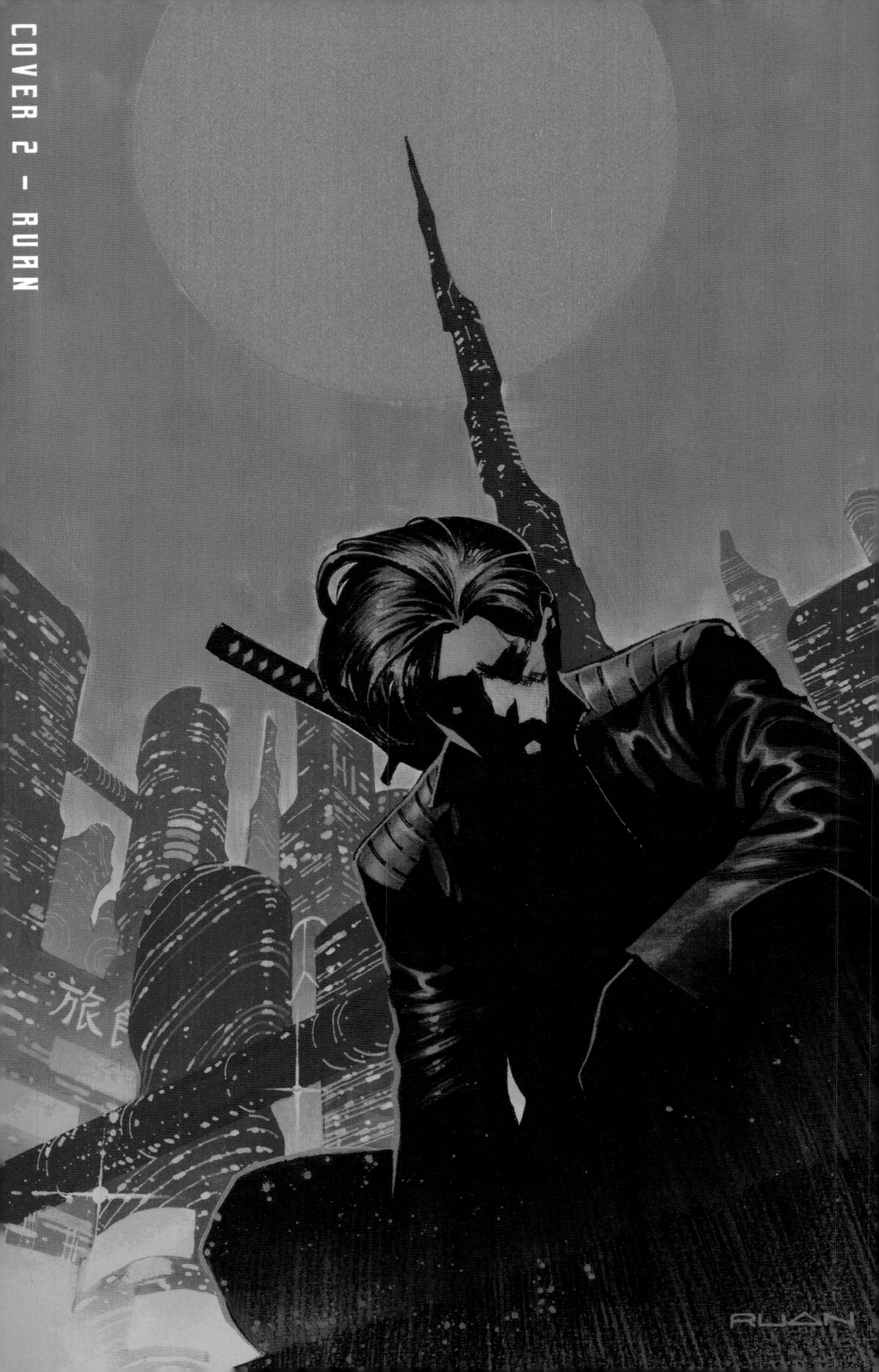

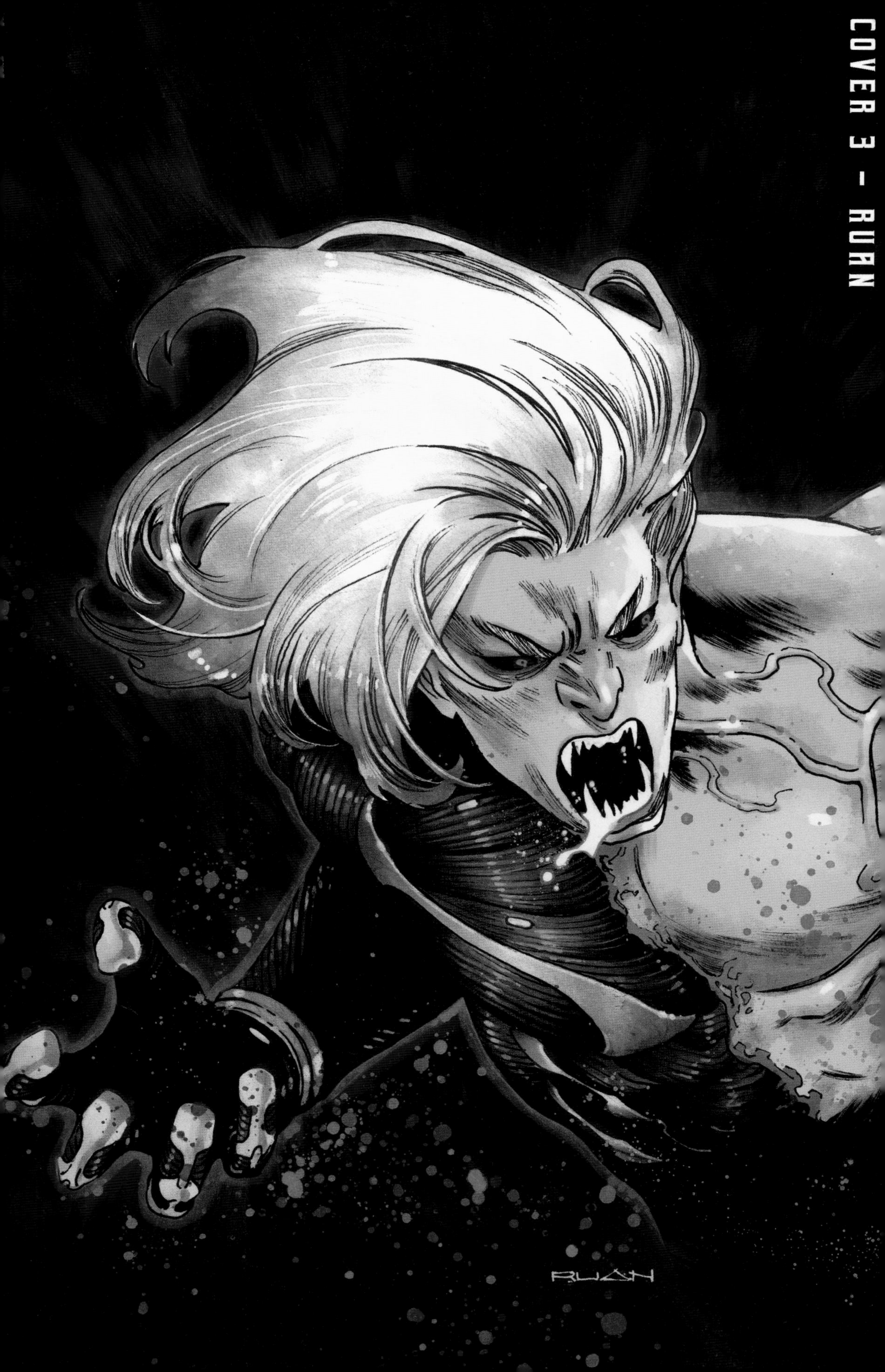
RUAN

COVER 3 - RUAN

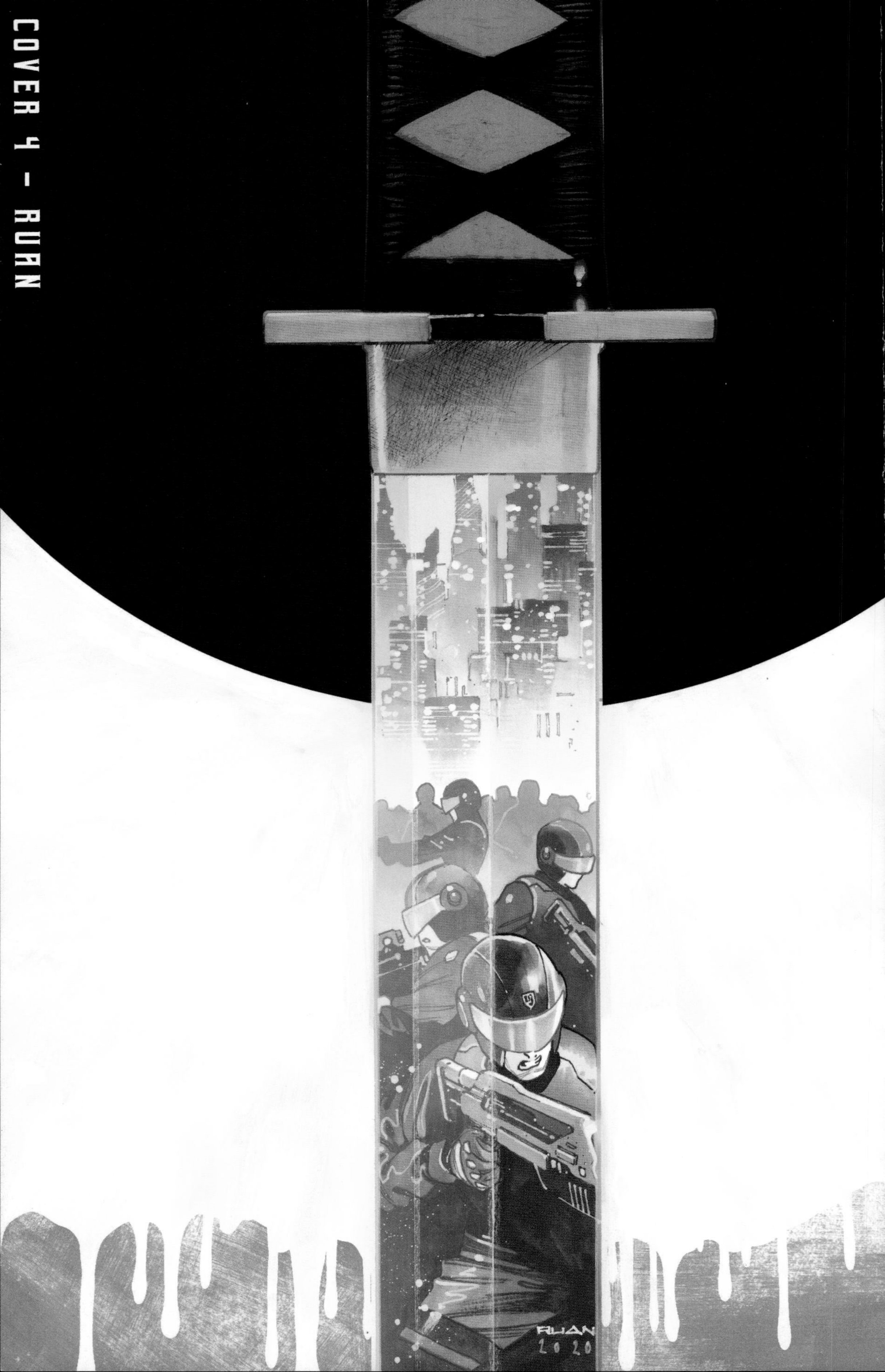
COVER 4 - RUAN
RUAN
2020

COVER 5 – RUAN

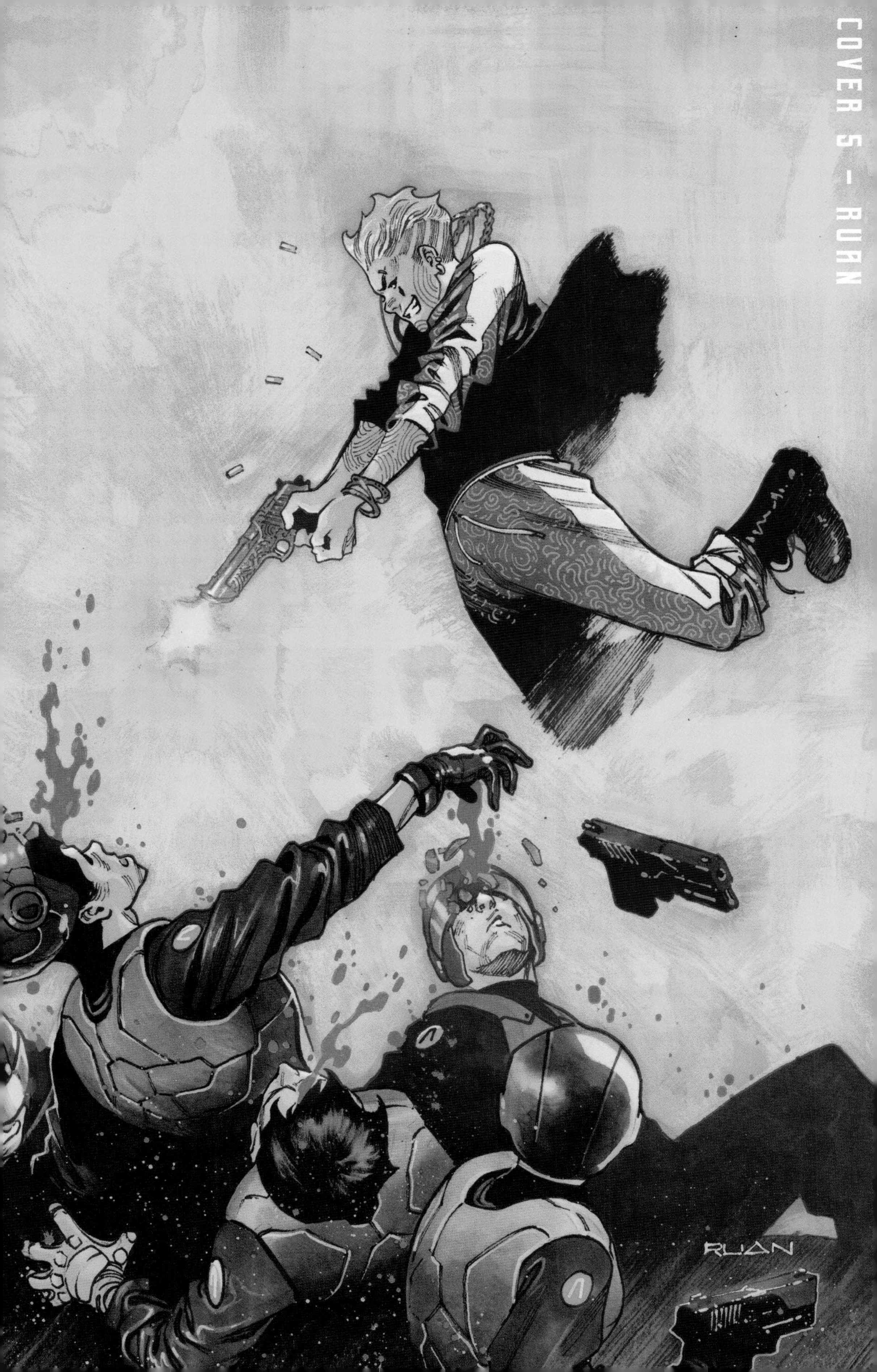
RUAN

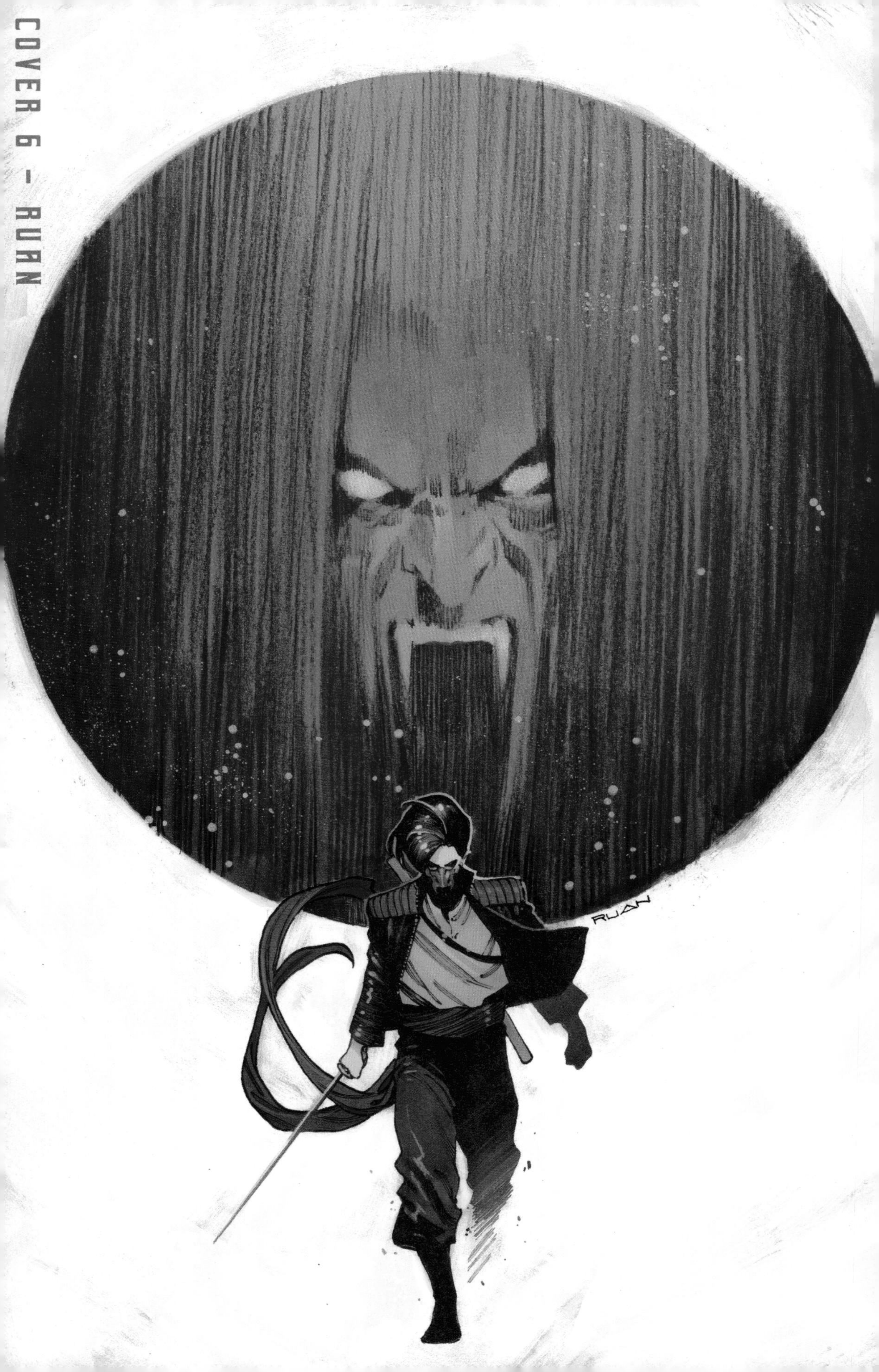
COVER 6 – RUAN
RUAN

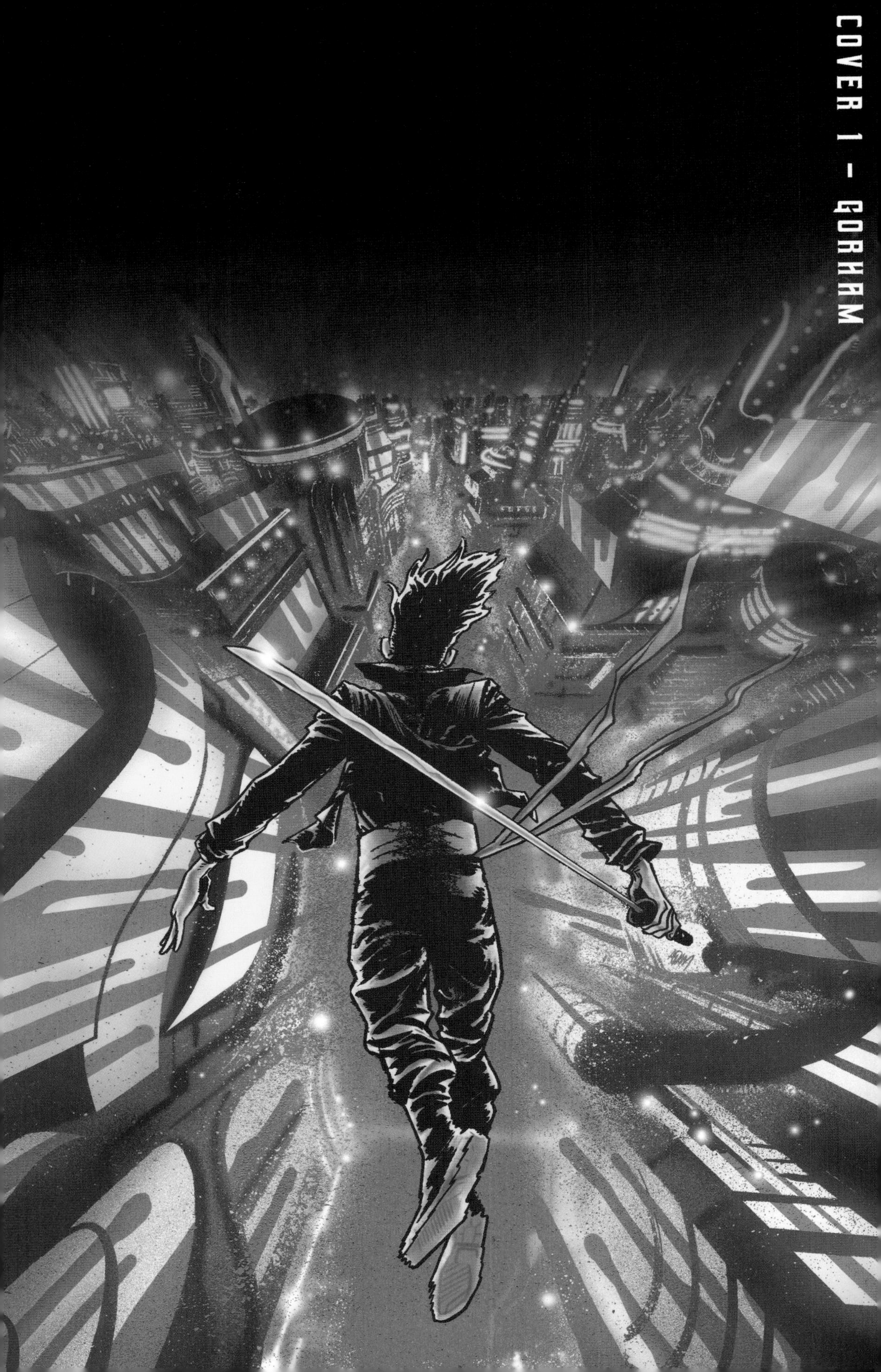

COVER 1 - GORHAM

COVER 2 – GORHAM

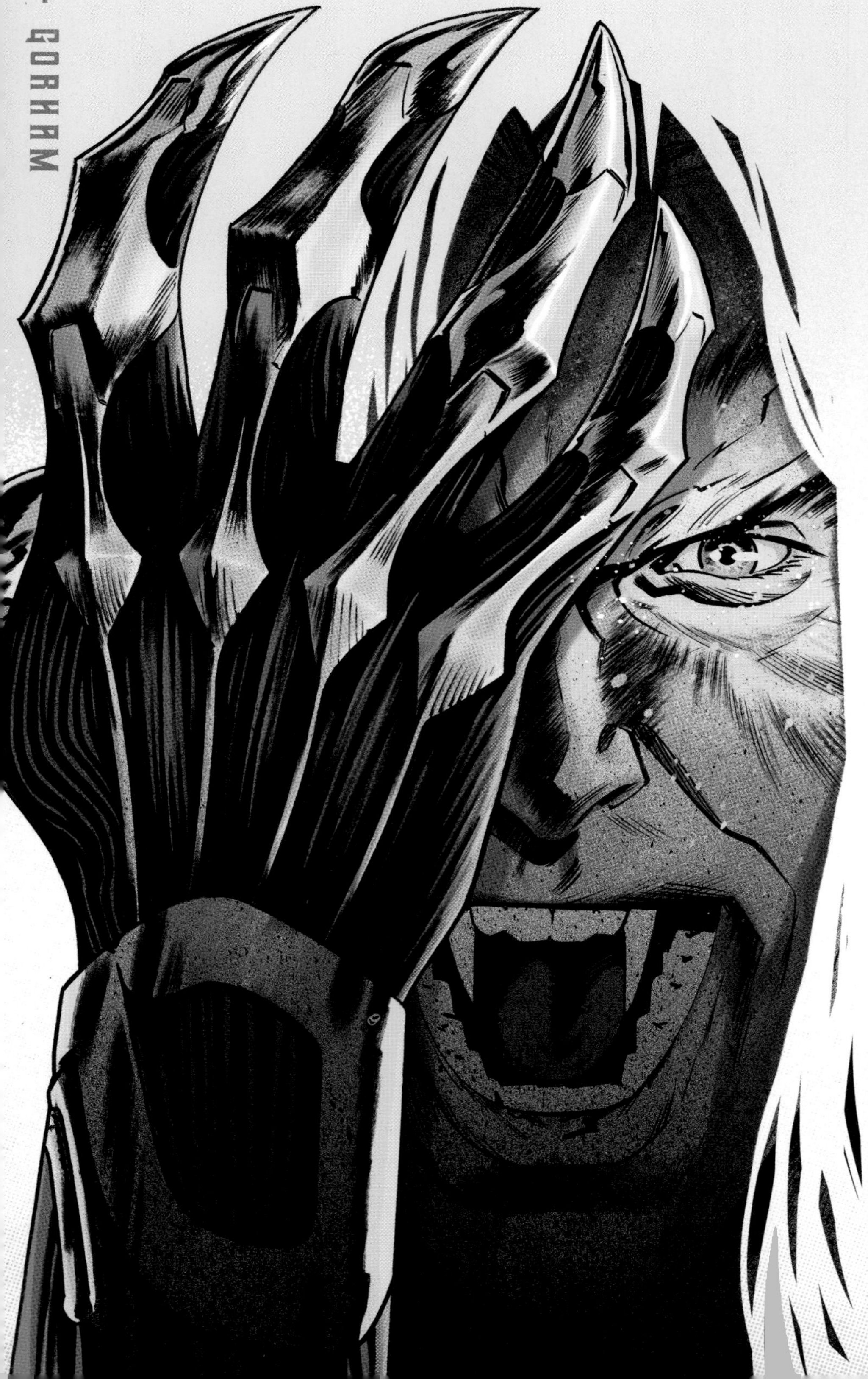

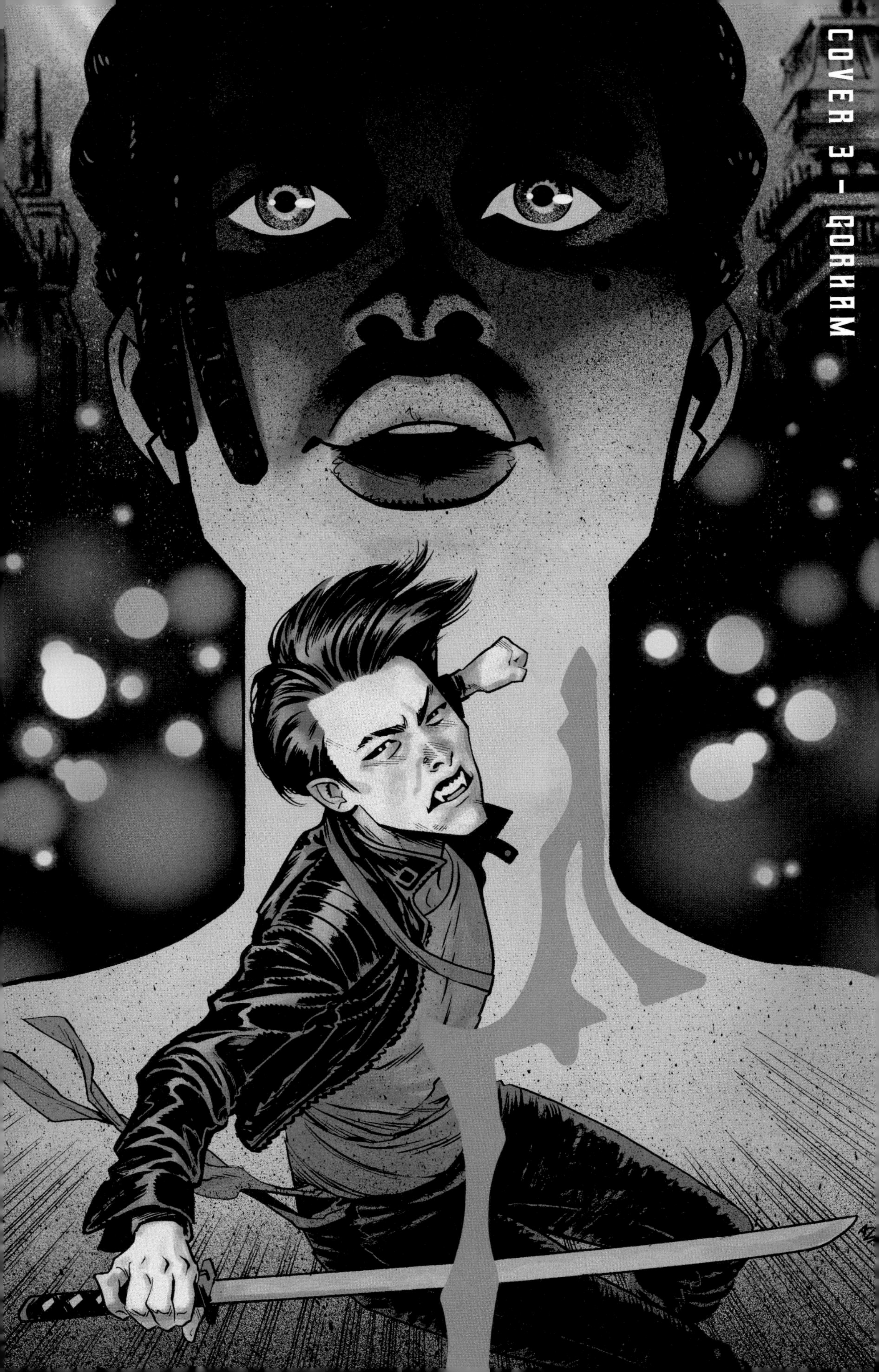
COVER 3 – GORHAM

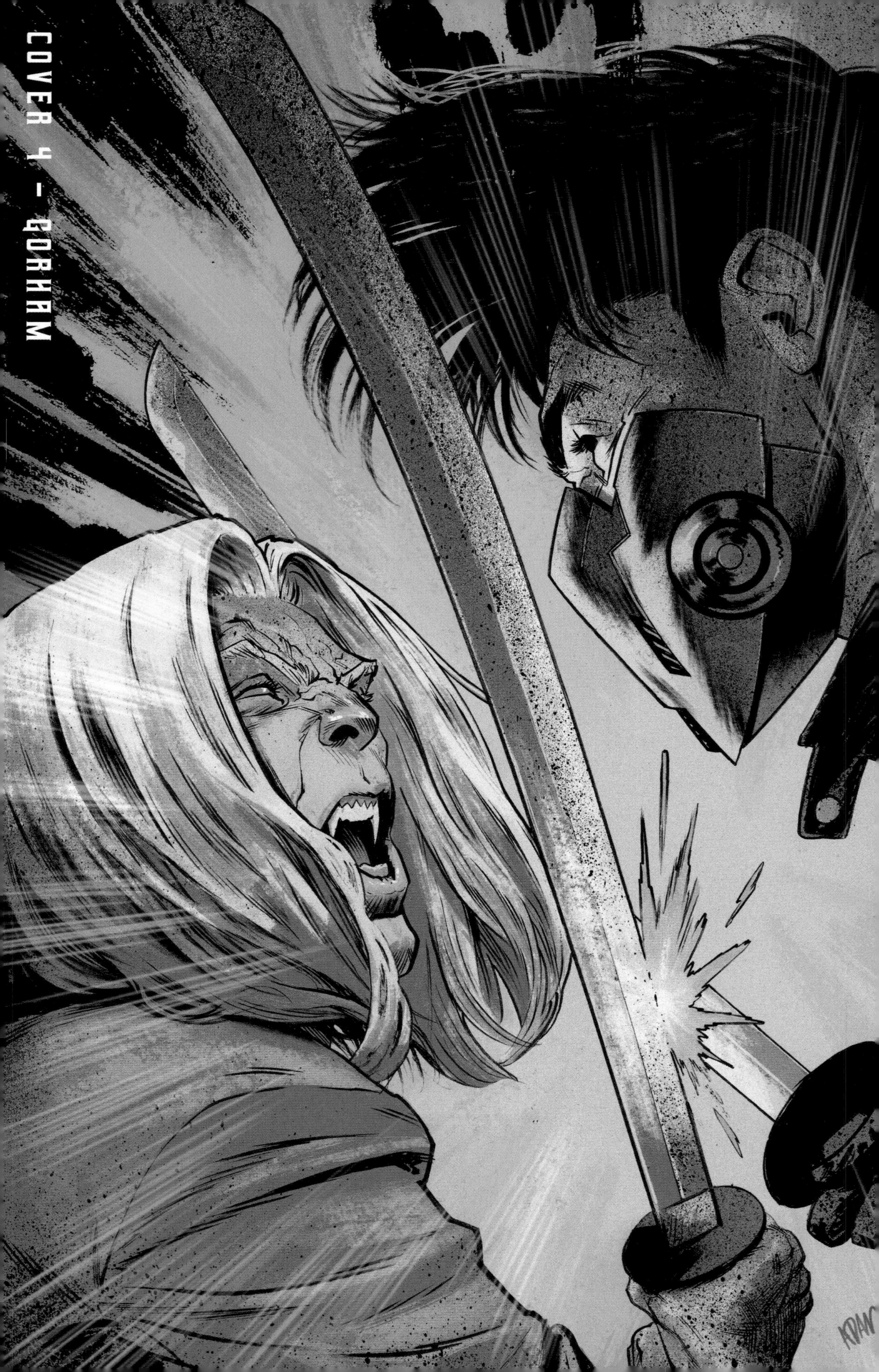

COVER 4 - GORHAM

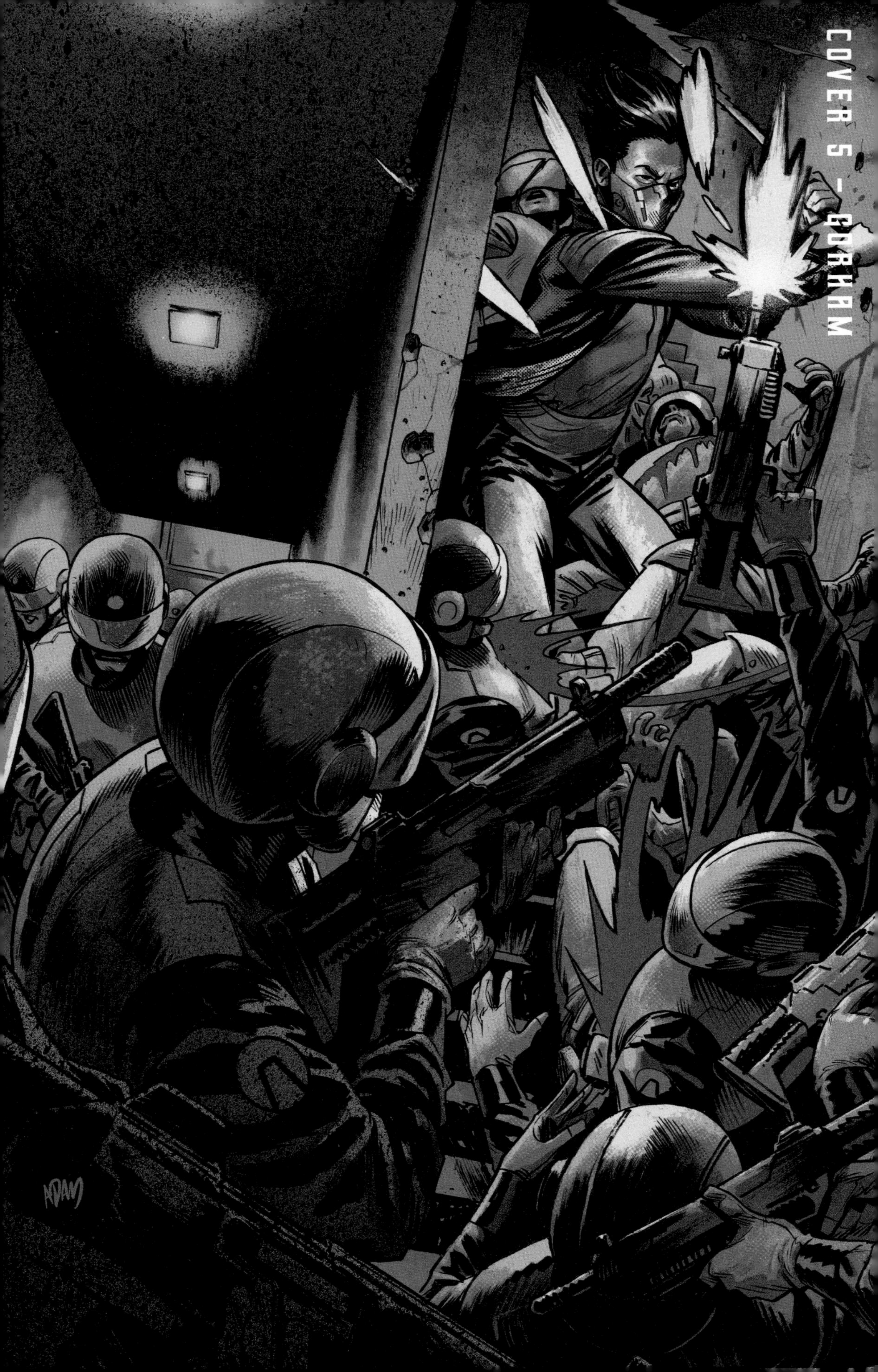
COVER 5 - GORHAM
ADAM

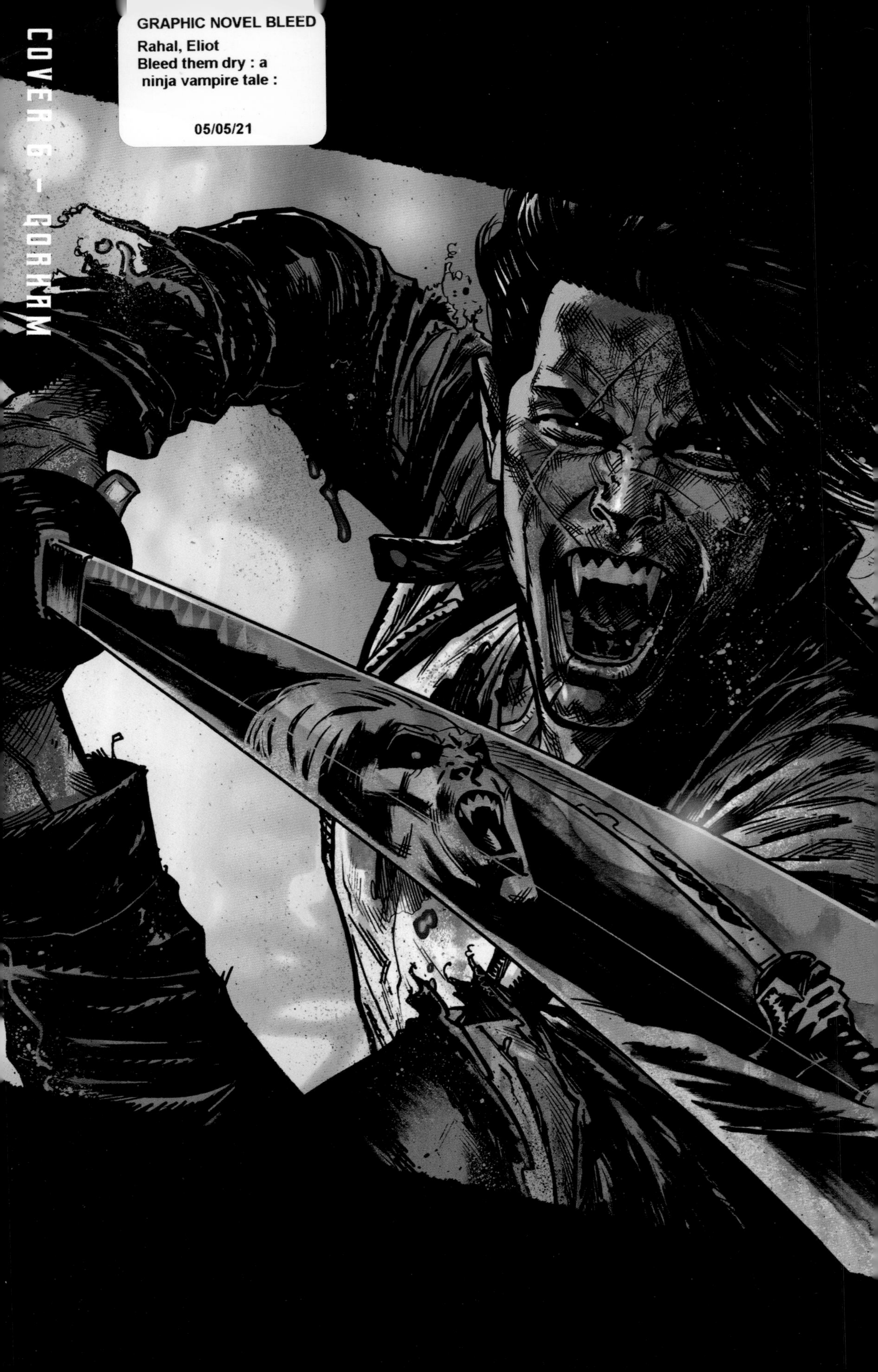
COVER B - GORHAM